In the Grip of the Law

In the Grip of the Law

Trials, Prisons and the Space Between

Edited by Monika Fludernik
and Greta Olson

PETER LANG
Frankfurt am Main · Berlin · Bern · Bruxelles · New York · Oxford · Wien

Bibliographic Information published by Die Deutsche Bibliothek
Die Deutsche Bibliothek lists this publication in the Deutsche Nationalbibliografie; detailed bibliographic data is available in the internet at <http://dnb.ddb.de>.

Cover illustration:
„Great News“

Published by courtesy of
Stu's Views, San Diego, CA, USA

ISBN 3-631-52455-2
US-ISBN 0-8204-6592-5

www.peterlang.de

For Paul K. Goetsch on his 70th Birthday

Acknowledgements

This volume goes back to a workshop entitled "Law and Literature: Representations of Trial and Imprisonment," which Jacqeline Berben-Masi and Monika Fludernik organized at the Sixth ESSE Conference in Strasbourg in August/September 2002. The two sessions were conceived of as a forum for open discussion rather than a panel. Each of the participants had read the others' papers, and the discussion then revolved around key issues addressed in several contributions. The first session, chaired by Jacqueline Berben-Masi, explored the 'Law and Literature' underpinnings of the topics of trial and prison. We started with the analysis of the term *equity* in Martin Kayman's paper (Kayman 2002) and from there went on to look at trials as part of the legal system. Of the papers published in this volume, Hesse, Kayman, and Olson contributed to this first session. In the second session, chaired by Monika Fludernik and devoted to the topic of imprisonment, the discussion revolved around the social significance of imprisonment (Lauterbach's paper) and the literary depiction of the prison experience (Alber, Berben, Fludernik, Macpherson). Moreover, in connection with Heidi Macpherson's paper, the relevance of the Benthamite prison model to literary representations of imprisonment was debated at some length.

The present volume includes six essays that have been significantly revised from their original form at the Strasbourg symposium. In addition, we sent out a call for supplementary papers on the trial and imprisonment themes, and thus arrived at the final fourteen papers of the collection.

In this place we would like to thank Jacqueline Berben-Masi for her initiative in organizing the workshop at Strasbourg. We are grateful to Jan Alber, Thomas Lederer, and Kerstin Fest for helping with the proof-reading of the essays throughout the summer of 2003. Our thanks moreover go to Susanne Nagel for helping with the typing and to Thomas Lederer for the formatting of the volume.

This book is dedicated to our mentor and colleague Paul Goetsch on the occasion of his seventieth birthday on March 11, 2004.

Reference

Kayman, Martin A. (2002) "Law-and-Literature: Questions of Jurisdiction." *REAL Yearbook of Research in English and American Literature 18: Law and Literature*. 1-20.

CONTENTS

"It's nice to see the police toughening up on juvenile crime"

Introduction

Monika Fludernik and Greta Olson

1. In the Grip of the Law: The Prisonization of American Society

Trials and Prisons, indeed the whole machinery of law and punishment, are obviously part of our everyday experience, if only – to the lucky ones – *ex negativo*. The ordinary citizen, alerted by non-stop exposure to TV crime series, is made continuously aware of what not to do to avoid incurring the wrath of the law. Besides this general relevance of the theme to everyday experience, the subject under discussion has recently attained a topicality, significance, and even notoriety that are in excess of previous levels of public awareness. When Jacqueline Berben-Masi and Monika Fludernik planned the session at the ESSE VI conference in Strasbourg which gave rise to this volume (see Acknowledgements, above), their main reference point had been the increasingly punitive atmosphere in domestic politics both in Europe and the United States, with its policies of 'no tolerance' law enforcement, rising conviction rates and surging figures of incarceration. At the same time Berben-Masi and Fludernik, who have both worked on the African-American novel and on postcolonial literature, were referencing the situation in the United States, where rates of imprisonment including jails and juvenile facilities hit the 2 million mark in 1998 and are now up at 2,100,146[1] out of a population of 281.4 million (US Census Bureau 2001),[2] i.e. at roughly just under one per cent of the population at large. At the end of 2001, one in every 112 men and one in every 1,724 women were sentenced prisoners under the jurisdiction of State or Federal authorities. Or, put differently, at the end of 2001, 686 US citizens out of every 100,000 were in Federal or State prisons.[3] In 2000,

---

1 The latest figures from the US Department of Justice "Bureau of Justice Statistics Bulletin," downloaded 10 September 2003 from <www.ojp.gov/bjs/pub/pdf/p01.pdf>.

2 This is based upon the 2000 Census at Population and Housing. See <http://factfinder.census.gov>.

3 According to the statistics of the US Department of Justice, there has been a markedly slower growth in the prison population since the end of 2000. See Figure 1 on p. 2 of <www.ojp.gov/bjs/pub/pdf/p01.pdf>, last accessed 24 October 2003.

the United States housed a quarter (25 %) of the world's prison population.[4] Among the inmate population a spectacularly large percentage are non-whites or other minorities.[5] As Ward Churchill (1992: 12) predicted, statistically every second African-American male in the United States had acquired first-hand prison experience by the year 2000 (quoted Grossheim 3).[6]

This disconcerting situation in the United States constituted the background that motivated Berben-Masi and Fludernik to organize the session at Strasbourg, underlined by the fact that in the United States themselves the topic of imprisonment had become a major academic issue. Thus, the 1999 MLA Convention in San Francisco offered no less than eight different sessions on the question of prisons and prison literature. However, none of this could compete with the aftermath of 9/11 which, by the time of writing (September 2003), has triggered a series of developments in the legal and correctional systems of the US and the UK that even further, and much more dramatically, highlight the current topicality of the issues discussed in this volume.

The most radical consequence of the attacks on the World Trade Center and the Pentagon has been the reintroduction to American society of the category of the political prisoner – somebody targeted by the state for his (or her) ideas, political affiliations, and presumed plans for terrorist activities. Although human rights

---

4 See Campbell (2000) as quoted in Grossheim (2001: 1).

5 46 % overall of State and Federal inmates are African Americans and 16 % Hispanics (2001 figures). It is therefore now statistically the case that 10 % of black males between the ages of 25 and 29 are in prison and only slightly fewer between the ages of 30 and 34 (see table 15 of <www.ojp.gov/bjs/pub/pdf/p01.pdf>).

6 The figures from the official statistics of the US Department of Justice do not completely correspond with figures currently available in the press and in other publications. Thus, Colin Kidd in a recent essay in the *London Review of Books* gives a much higher figure: "America has more than six million citizens in jail, on probation or on parole, with an incarceration rate, Morone notes, five times higher than other industrialised democracies." On this figure little less than "3 per cent of the adult population" have been absorbed into the US' "criminal justice system" (all Kidd 2003: 12).

As for the percentage of the non-white prison population, this has risen steadily during recent decades. Tonry cites an increase of black prisoners from 40 % of the prison population in 1971 to 50 % in the early 1990s (Tonry 1998: 10), and the 1998 report by Amnesty International on the USA for the year 1997 gives a stunning figure of over 60 % for all non-white prisoners (1998: 99). According to the 2000 census, 12.3 % of Americans consider themselves to be African Americans, 3.6 % Asians, and 12.5 % Hispanics.

The rise in figures of imprisonment in the second half of the twentieth century has been particularly steep in relation to female inmates. Between 1971 and 1980, the female prison population doubled (Tonry 1998:10); in fact, as Heger demonstrates, the number of imprisoned women trebled between 1986 and 1999 (a rise in 220 % as against an increase of 130 % for men). Currently, 6.6 % of prisoners are women, but the rate is 11.2 % in jails (imprisonment under one year). Between 1990 and 1999 alone, the number of sentenced women prisoners rose by 106 %. As Heger goes on to show, non-white women are imprisoned on a ratio of 8 to 1 in relation to white women. This drastic increase in female incarceration rates is due to mandatory sentencing laws (see below in the introduction) and to the rise in drug-related convictions. As Heger shows, the conviction rates for women in drug-related sentencing rose by 908 % between 1986 and 1998. (All references to Heger 2001: 1.)

activists have argued that even after the Civil Rights Movement the political imprisonment of suspect groups (like the MOVE activists) and individuals connected with various ethnic liberation movements (Leonard Pelletier) continued in the US (see esp. Churchill/Vander Wall 1992), the aftermath of 9/11 with its abolishment of *habeas corpus* for suspected terrorists clearly established a new level of politicial criminalization and normalized the suspension of the basic legal rights of defendants. Of the 650 terrorist suspects currently held at Camp Delta by the US military without access to legal council, a large number still have not been officially charged. The institution of military tribunals before which prisoners are to be judged and the restrictions on the right to a lawyer of choice and on client/lawyer confidentiality, as well as the lower standards of evidence in this court and the lack of right of appeal have caused great international concern. Even more controversially, the conditions of incarceration of prisoners made in conjunction with the war in Afghanistan have given rise to international outcries and repeated interventions by Amnesty International, Human Rights Watch, and other humanitarian groups.[7] Even though a few of the detainees held at Guantánamo Bay have meanwhile been released and the administration is finally planning to charge a dozen or so detainees before special tribunals, hundreds of "illegal fighters" (but, really, prisoners of war) continue to be held captive without any prospect of release. Given the dehumanizing conditions of imprisonment equivalent to those of Federal maximum security prisons like Marion Prison in Illinois, it is not surprising to hear of thirty or more attempts at suicide on the part of the detainees. The plight of prisoners – at all times worth remembering – is thus given topical reference by the US treatment of its Afghan prisoners of war. In fact, the international public – in the wake of Guantánamo Bay – is only now starting to learn what goes on in American penal institutions of the maximum security type.

These developments in the US are paralleled by recent British anti-terrorism legislation (though partly incapacitated by the House of Lords) in the 9/11 aftermath.[8] Current plans by Tony Blair to deprive defendants of the legal right to a jury trial plus the additional lopping off of several safeguards of defendants are marketed as a policy to make trials shorter and more efficient.[9] These developments in Britain and the US demonstrate with uncanny force how the legal guarantees of the innocent accused may be swept aside in times of public hysteria. They moreover illustrate the latent danger of a politicization of the legal apparatus in response to current concerns, popular policies, and opportunistic vote-catching. As a consequence of such political manipulations of the law, trials, which are meant to guarantee due legal process, suddenly turn into shows at which the foredoomed outcome is scripted in advance

7 See, for instance, <www.amnestyusa.org/news/2003/uk07182003.html>, a press release by the UK office of Amnesty International, which also notes that "Amnesty International has repeatedly requested access to Camp X-Ray and Camp Delta at Guantánamo Bay, but has been denied this access."

8 In fact, the Blair government brought out a first Terrorism Act in 2000 even before 9/11 and topped this by passing the Anti-Terrorism, Crime and Security Act (ATCSA) in 2001. See <www.homeoffice.gov.uk/terrorism/govprotect/legislation/index.html>.

9 See Upton (2003).

much as during Elizabethan treason trials. It is surely telling that the recent American Nobel prize winner, Peter Agre, announced that he would use part of his prize money to finance legal revision of the American anti-terrorism laws. Agre cited the example of a colleague who was "arrested and taken away in chains" after he reported having lost some lab samples.[10]

Although the events of 9/11 have demonstrated the sad relevance of the issues of trial and imprisonment to be discussed in this volume, they merely highlight the general power of the legal and penal network in its potentially frightening, manipulative, and dangerous aspects. As we noted earlier, the topical relevance of criminal justice issues reaches back into the decades since the Civil Rights Movement and the general prisonization[11] of American society. These developments have increasingly started to serve as a model that politicians in Europe are emulating as part of a general "no-tolerance" movement in Western industrialized democracies. This is not the place to provide a history of recent calls for rougher justice in Europe and the United States.[12] However, four aspects of the American penal system should be discussed here briefly in order to highlight issues that will be relevant to some of the papers in the volume.

The first of these aspects concerns the continuity between American slavery and the penitentiary system in the late nineteenth century. In the American South, imprisonment replaced slavery in terms of cheap labor, particularly in the institutions of the lease system and the chain gangs (Lupa 2001). In addition, the high percentage of African Americans among the prisoner population underlines a perceived continuity of black prison labor as a different type of slave labor. These associations are further underlined by the widespread social inequality that, despite the existence of a black middle class, has left African Americans as a whole at the lower end of the social scale.

The second major aspect of recent developments in the American prison archipelago has been the privatization of correctional facilities and their advance to a prominent industrial factor in rural areas. Thus, crime has become "big business" (Hallinan 2001: xiv) for many communities hit by unemployment. Prisons provide jobs for prison personnel and they sponsor a host of incidental business (medical support, food supplies, clothing industry). As Hallinan puts it,

> [...] after the end of the Cold War, the military-industrial complex has given way to a prison-industrial complex. Like military bases, prisoners provide jobs while simultaneously providing a sense of security – in their case not from communists but from criminals. (xii)

---

10 See *The Daily Telegraph* (9 October 2003) "Nobel Prize Winner to Fight US Terror Rules," by Roger Highfield, Science Editor 09/10/2003.

11 Prisonization: "The process of being socialized into the culture and social life of prison society to the extent that adjusting to the outside society becomes difficult" <www.ola.bc.ca/ou/sociglossary/prisonization.html>, 19 October 2003.

12 See, among others, Christie (1993), Tonry (1998), Shichor/Sechrest (1996), Garland (2000, 2001), Pratt (2000).

The privatization of crime management (currently 5.8 % of Federal prisoners are housed in private facilities)[13] has given rise to the profit-related running of correctional facilities in which low pay for guards and the minimization of costs for prisoners' upkeep conspire to render prison conditions particularly harsh and dangerous (Lupa 2001: 5-6). In terms of these frame conditions, the rise in the American prison population has not merely political and moral roots (the emphasis on punishment rather than reform) but constitutes a major economic factor which leaves little hope for rapid improvements. Although tough measures against crime have been pushed through by Republican legislation on a moral platform of retribution, no tolerance, and the war on drugs, the economic advantages of cheap labor and new jobs in deprived rural areas hint at a submerged agenda for the institution of mandatory sentencing laws or 'Three Strikes and You're Out' legislation.[14] Mandatory sentencing laws, in particular, are related to the war on drugs and ironically were instituted precisely when drug-related charges started to decrease (Tonry 1998). Judges lost part of their discretionary powers, and the law gave rise to a number of hair-raising injustices such as sentencing 80-year old grandmothers to life imprisonment for the drugs their grandsons had dumped on them. As Heger notes, federal sentencing laws include a minimum five-year mandatory sentence for being caught with one gram of LSD or five ounces of crack, even for first offenders, and New York has instituted an obligatory fifteen years to life sentence for the possession of four ounces of drugs (Heger 2001: 2; quoting from an Amnesty International report on women).

Parallel to these truly draconian sentencing patterns, a third major aspect of the present-day American prison system concerns its widely noted human rights abuses which include not only the treatment of prisoners in maximum security facilities (where inmates are locked up for 23 hours a day and refused all occupation including reading and work [Hallinan 2001: xv; Amnesty International 1998: 122-28]), but also especially cruel measures of disciplining and restraint (Amnesty International 1998: 120-22; 111-18) and the undignified and disproportionally cruel treatment of women, especially pregnant women (Amnesty International 1998: 118-22; Heger 2001). In addition, minimal standards for health care, food quality, and exercise are frequently not met, with prisoners risking serious physical and mental injuries as a consequence.

Perhaps the most obvious way in which the United States is out of step with democracies around the world concerns its recent reinstitution of the death penalty. Although this volume is concerned with trials and imprisonment to the exclusion of the death penalty as such, the historical essays nevertheless deal with scenarios in which a verdict of guilty might indeed result in the death penalty (see esp. Giovanopoulos and Lederer). The topical concerns that led to the planning of this volume therefore clearly included an awareness of the US-American capital punishment record and its recent questioning in the wake of DNA analyses that

---

13 Figures of 31 December 2001. See Bureau of Department of Justice Statistics, <www.ojp.gov/bjs/pub/pdf/p01.pdf>, 24 October 2003.

14 On the Californian three-strikes legislation see Shichor/Sechrest (1996). On the regulation of the workforce through prison labor, see the classic study by Melossi/Pavarini (1972).

proved the innocence of a substantial number of death-row inmates.[15] Likewise, the high number of African Americans on death row in comparison with the general conviction rate of murderers additionally demonstrates the bias of the system.[16] In fact, the vagaries of the American judicial system nowhere show up more clearly than with respect to capital punishment; those who face most risk of ending up on death row frequently cannot afford an expensive criminal lawyer and have to make do with ill-paid and ill-qualified public defenders.

Following our remarks on the current relevance of the subjects of trial and imprisonment and their political and ideological framing, let us now turn to the reflection of courts and prisons, the legal machinery, and its punitive performance in literature. As Jan Alber observes in his paper, most prison movies focus on an innocent convict or generally on a victim figure. The same is true of many – though by no means all – depictions of the prison experience in novels. Literary texts and films seem to deliberately attempt a kind of imaginary compensation for society's strategies of stigmatization of the criminal. Many of the following essays also address the negotiation of power and fair process in the material which they analyze, probing the risks of falling into the legal and penal 'net' of the Law-and-Punishment complex. In particular, these essays illustrate the circumscribed parameters of resistance and self-preservation available to defendants and prisoners, their victimization or shrewd 'playing' of the system to their own advantage (see esp. Lederer and Kayman). In addition, some texts manage to critically engage with the injustices, imbalances, and slantedness of the legal-penal system, providing incisive analyses and critiques of the current state of affairs.

Literature, in this volume, is, however, not merely a reflection of, or on, the realities of prisons and the law. Not only does literature imaginatively rework human experience and provide virtual scenarios of alternative perspectives, courses of actions or evaluations; literature moreover transports images of crime and punishment, guilt and innocence, identity and alterity which are constitutive of our ideas of criminality. In this way, too, the essays are topical to present-day concerns since they analyze in historical contexts how the concept of criminality is constructed, institutionally and linguistically grounded, and then functionalized in a variety of ways, by means of a proliferation of discourses of which literature is only one, but a very important, genre.

Having traced the relevance of our topic and having related it to the 'real world' – even if indirectly so – we would also like to point out that our concern in this collection is not exclusively with the literary text as source, symbol, or symptom; indeed, it is the peculiarly *literary* qualities of the texts that the essays are analyzing that will be emphasized, including the aesthetic, generic, and linguistic aspects of the source material. Precisely because literary texts are fictions, they have been put together with specifically literary and aesthetic purposes in mind. Paramount among such purposes are the texts' narrative impact, their attempt at closure and tellability. Even though the narrative structure of some of our example texts (including the dramatic works) are centrally engaged with the aim of apologetic self-presentation,

15 See Armstrong/Mills (1999a, 1999b, 1999c, 1999d, 1999e).

16 For an excellent discussion, see Laqueur (2000).

this factor does not by any means exhaust their narrative qualities. Ironically, both trials and experiences of imprisonment are subject matters inherently unsuited to narrativization. Trials really consist in argument in dialogue form (though with a strong suspense moment and a definite point of closure); prison plots, on the other hand, suffer from a lack of exciting events, since the prison routine consists of either no 'real' events or of a deadening repetition of the same events. It is therefore particularly worthwhile to probe the ingenious narrative strategies used to present such intractable material in so manifestly entrancing ways.

2. Literary Perspectives on Trials

For the twenty-first century reader, court trials may be familiar in one or more of three ways. We write "court" trials to distinguish judicial tribunals from those other tests of conscience and the heart often called trials in order to characterize life's many challenges. Readers may have experienced trials firsthand as plaintiffs in divorce proceedings or as defendants in traffic hearings or, for citizens of the UK and the US, by being called on to serve jury duty. On the other hand, more spectacular trials are familiar to us through the media and historical narratives. These include Stalin's show trials in the 1930s and the Nuremberg War Crimes Trials from 1945-1949; in the United States one may think of the 1925 Scopes "Monkey" Trial about the right to teach evolutionary theory in school or the impeachment proceedings against Presidents Nixon and Clinton, or – lest anyone be tempted to forget – the criminal trial against O. J. Simpson for double murder in 1995. Moreover, the current debate about US participation in the International Criminal Court has raised interest in this tribunal as well as fueled fires about what many critics perceive to be the United States' unilateral and misguided foreign policy under President George W. Bush. Finally, trials are familiar though literary accounts of them, and we understand literature in this context to include any variety of text types.

Literature may be particularly well-suited for depicting trials as a number of commentators have pointed out.[17] As Richard Posner puts it,

> Whether historically the trial is modeled on the theater and offers the litigants and society (the audience) the type of catharsis that the theater does, or vice versa, or whether both the trial and the drama have a common origin in religious rituals, few social practices are so readily transferable to a literary setting and so well suited to the literary depiction of conflict as the trial. (1998: 22)

Drama is inherent in the Anglo-American courtroom contest between oppositional viewpoints that are presented in front of a judge and a jury as spectators. Thus the courtroom has been a favorite topic of prose and drama since the early modern period, and images of legal tribunals continue to figure widely in novels, TV series, and movies today. Victor Turner has argued that trials, like religious rituals, are "social

17 Cf. Watt on the novel (1957: 31); Kornstein on literature in general (1994: 12-13); and Dolin on representations of injustice in fictional trials (1999: 19-20).

dramas" in which crises are addressed and dealt with in a ritualized process of reflection that occurs in a space set off from other forms of interaction (1986: 75-94). Hence it comes as no surprise that the cultural performances enacted by trials should be a frequent literary motif and should serve both symbolic as well as socially critical purposes.

Images of trials mark some of the seminal texts of Anglo-American culture and even world literature. Each of the Gospels tells the story of Jesus' trial before religious authorities, then before Pontius Pilate, and, finally, the people of Jerusalem. Whether Mark, Matthew, Luke, or John relates the events, important elements remain the following: Jesus' arrest, his insistence that his disciples do not hurt (cut off the ear of) one of the arresting parties, his examination by the priests, his torture, and crucifixion. One of the elements that will come up continually in literary depictions of trials is the figure of the innocent accused, who eloquently defends him- or herself but does not stand a chance of being acquitted due to the bias of the legal apparatus.[18] When the trial occurs as a spectacle, sympathy is elicited for the defendant who alone must face the power of impersonal legal authority. Taken together, these elements direct the reader's sympathy to the figure of the accused and heighten critical awareness of the legal system as a whole. The processual quality of trials, their chronologically ordered series of parts, and the figure of the outsider as defendant are all present in the trial accounts of Jesus. Christ is figured by the Gospel writers not only as a religious hero, but also as a social rebel. His non-aggression, eloquence, and suffering render his plight all the more compelling.

An equally powerful pre-modern narrative is that of Antigone, eponymous heroine in Sophocles' play (ca. 441 BC), in which her trial for civil disobedience (burying her brother against the State's injunctions to the contrary) becomes a public tribunal for discussing the merits of the law of kinship versus the law of state. Again the accused is a highly articulate as well as sympathetic figure, whose persuasive arguments show up weaknesses in the prevailing legal system. George Steiner has read the play to find that it showcases all of the fundamental human conflicts, including that between age and youth, woman and man, society and the individual, the gods versus humankind (1984: 231). Whether or not Steiner is correct in his assessment of which fundamental conflicts determine human existence, Antigone's trial like that of Jesus demonstrates that tribunals and their representations often serve as vehicles for discussions of larger social issues rather than as rehashings of judicial procedure. The inherent drama of Antigone's trial, the equivocal position of her judge and sentencer (Creon), and the confrontation of a rebellious individual with the legal norms of a society all mark this play as a prototype of law in action.

We suspect that one reason that literary perspectives on the courtroom focus so often on the innocent accused is a historical one: until the later part of the eighteenth

---

18 To gain an impression of the symbolic power of the figure of the innocent accused and its widespread use in literature across the centuries, see Lederer's analysis of Elizabethan hagiographies, Colatrella's examination of nineteenth-century American and English prose works, Hesse's exploration of twentieth-century British courtroom dramas, as well as Alber's discussion of prison movies, all in this volume.

century, defendants had no right to counsel and were forced to speak in their own defense; rules against hearsay evidence were absent (the admission of statements made about the case that occurred outside of court) as were clear guidelines about the admissibility of evidence; furthermore, judges could punish juries for verdicts they did not agree with (Langbein 1978, 2002). The inequity of the power relationship between the defendant and the prosecution was then enormous. Stephen Hedley describes the intended consequences of the old style of trial as follows: "It was directed to establishing, by largely unjust means, the guilt of the accused as a prelude to brutal punishment or, occasionally, ostentatious clemency" (2003: 15). Thus many literary representations of trials taking place before the advent of what we know as the modern criminal trial focus on the accused person's relative powerlessness before a legal system that controlled the jury, evidence, and the discourse in the courtroom. This plight of the defendant is explored in this volume in Thomas Lederer's essay on trials of religious dissidents, in Greta Olson's article on Shakespearean trials, and in Anna-Christina Giovanopoulos's review of the trials of William Kidd. Besides being a powerful symbolic figure, the isolated defendant is also part of our cultural memory.

Leaping into England of the late fifteenth and early sixteenth centuries, we find an enormous interest in trials and legal procedure as reflected in the plays of William Shakespeare and John Webster, among others. Webster's *The White Devil* (first performed in 1612) sets "The Arraignment of Vittoria" at the heart of the play, Act III, scene ii, and provides a forum in which to discuss issues of retribution for crime, here adultery and murder, as well as to query the correctness of trial procedure. Defending herself, the articulate Vittoria manages to effect a procedural change. She objects to the lawyer who charges her with whoredom speaking in Latin. Importantly, it is not that she is unable to understand the language of those men who accuse her and are invested with legal and religious power. Rather she wishes for everyone who witnesses the trial to be able to understand its proceedings (III. ii. 17-19). Webster's central trial scene profiles another consistent literary motif – the woman accused of sexually transgressive behavior.[19] Shakespeare makes trials, both symbolic and actual procedural ones, the centerpiece of many of his plays (Kornstein xii, Olson in this volume). Such scenes may either demonstrate the power of monarchs to use courtrooms to further their own ends as in *Henry VIII* (1612-13) or, conversely, show how a clever individual may control the legal system when he or she has a thorough grasp of the law and a mastery of rhetoric; the image of Portia disguised as a doctor of law in the trial scene from *The Merchant of Venice* (1596-97) comes immediately to mind. Some commentators have even suggested that Shakespeare's presentation of royal spectacle, including trials presided over by monarchs, contributed to the English eventually taking their own king to court (Karsten 1986: 460-61). Doubtlessly, the frequency of trial scenes in Renaissance drama highlights contemporary interest in the law as dramatic spectacle as well as suggesting the specificity of legal knowledge that authors like Webster and Shakespeare expected to find in their audiences.

Let us now take another historical leap. The end of the seventeenth and the eighteenth century were marked by a well-documented fascination with criminality,

19 Cf. Shaw's and Macpherson's essays in this volume as well as Olson on *Measure for Measure*.

criminals, and all things legal, including trials, imprisonment, and executions (Bell 1991, Faller 1996, Richetti 1992). Trial accounts are frequent in eighteenth-century novels, which very often feature criminality; in their more popular versions, such as the *Bloody Register* or the *Select Trials*, they also provided reading fodder for an audience wider than contemporary novel readers (Gladfelder 1997: 24-34). Singling out the story of one designated criminal, Anna-Christina Giovanopoulos illustrates how popular contemporary accounts of Captain Kidd's crimes and trials in the *General History of the Pirates* (1728) and in the *Bloody Register* (1764) mixed fact and fiction: the adventure story pleased the public and also served prevailing political interests. In a limited sampling, we find a selection of the best-known novelists of the age. Daniel Defoe's *Moll Flanders* (1722) includes a scene in which the criminal protagonist describes the trial against her with the accuracy and vocabulary of a lawyer. Henry Fielding used his knowledge as a magistrate to critique judicial abuses in many of his novels. In *Joseph Andrews* (1742), for instance, the justice who tries Adams and Fanny for theft regards this event as a sporting adventure; he is drunk, ignorant of procedure, and susceptible to being influenced by rank. In *Clarissa* (1747-48) Samuel Richardson portrays how the rapist Lovelace notes with satisfaction that he would win any trial that was brought against him. He recognizes that his family's aristocratic reputation would influence the tribunal. Furthermore, Lovelace pictures how he would utilize his personal attractiveness to make a crew of young virgins plead for him from the sidelines of the court (1833: 190). William Godwin's *Caleb Williams* (1794) took issue with court procedure as well as reactionary politics at the end of the century. As Martin Kayman points out in the essay included in this collection, Godwin's novel also documents the changing nature of evidentiary rules in the courtroom.

Recently Jonathan Grossmann has argued that the shift from an interest in the genre of criminal biography to that of the novel at the beginning of the nineteenth century mirrored a change in people's conceptualizations of the judicial paradigm. Whereas this paradigm had been concentrated on the gallows, it now came to be focused on the courtroom (2002: 36). In analogy to John Bender's thesis that the evolution of the eighteenth-century novel anticipated the development and institutionalization of the penitentiary versus the old-style prison (1987), Grossman argues that the development of the novel in the first half of the nineteenth century took its cue from structures of the legal trial. As society lost its belief in the existence of an ultimate tribunal before God, individuals increasingly perceived the need to tell and have their stories corroborated as effectively as possible in the here and now (Grossman 2002: 173). They modeled their story telling on the courtroom. The turning point from criminal biography to trial-inspired novel came with *Caleb Williams*, in which the narrative corresponds first to the former and then to the latter generic form.[20]

20 See in this volume both Kayman's analysis of the novel in conjunction with generic paradigms and Houswitschka's reading of it in the context of the legal culture that surrounded the High Treason Trials of 1794.

Caleb Williams also marks the beginning of an era in which novels increasingly came to document abuses in the judicial process and sometimes even initiated judicial reform. The depiction of law in Charles Dickens's *Bleak House* (1852-53) is most often cited for the novel's damning representation of the Court of Chancery, where the excessive duration of time in which civil law cases are handled destroys people's lives and whole families' fortunes. Yet for many readers the highhanded treatment of the impoverished street sweeper Joe at an inquest remains in mind as the novel's most powerful image of legal abuse. The inquest is intended to determine the circumstances of a mysterious man's death. While reading Dickens's account of it, readers are also made witness to the systematic neglect of justice in institutionalized trial law. Before Joe may testify about his knowledge of the man named Nemo he must be questioned himself:

> Name, Jo. Nothing else that he knows on. Don't know that everybody has two names. Never heerd of sich a think. Don't know that Jo is short for a longer name. Thinks it long enough for *him* – *he* don't find no fault with it. Spell it? No, *he* can't spell it. No father, no mother, no friends. Never been to school. What's home? Knows a broom's a broom, and knows it's wicked to tell a lie. Don't recollect who told him about the broom, or about the lie, but knows both. Can't exactly say what'll be done to him arter he's dead if he tells a lie to the gentlemen here, but believes it'll be something wery bad to punish him, and serve him right – and so he'll tell the truth.
>
> "This won't do, gentlemen!" says the Coroner, with a melancholy shake of the head.
>
> "Don't you think you can receive his evidence, sir?" asks an attentive Juryman.
>
> "Out of the question," says the Coroner. "You have heard the boy. 'Can't exactly say' won't do, you know. We can't take *that*, in a Court of Justice, gentlemen. It's terrible depravity. Put the boy aside."
>
> Boy put aside; to the great edification of the audience; – especially of Little Swills, the Comic Vocalist. [...] While the coroner buttons his great coat, Mr Tulkinghorn and he give private audience to the rejected witness in a corner. (162)

The bitter irony of this scene is that while the knowledge that Joe has to impart will not do for the Court of Justice, it will indeed suffice to further the purposes of the malicious lawyer Tulkinghorn who questions the boy after the inquest.

Accounts of trials like the above in which the verdict is predetermined and other instances of the miscarriage of justice abound in English-language literatures of the twentieth century. In Britain, John Galsworthy exposed the two-tier system of justice that lets a rich man go free and a poor man go to jail for theft in *The Silver Box* (1906). In *Justice* (1910), Galsworthy uses the trial scene to indict a legal system that refuses to look at causes or mitigating circumstances. Frome, a young and idealistic lawyer, pleads with the jury not to turn the defendant into a criminal by convicting him: "Gentleman, men like the prisoner are destroyed daily under our law for want of that human insight which sees them as they are, patients and not guilty" (49). Beatrix Hesse shows in her essay on courtroom dramas that during the twentieth century the genre became increasingly critical of the system it portrayed.

As in *Justice*, trial scenes are also used to highlight wider social inequities. Prominent among these texts is E. M. Forster's novel *A Passage to India* (1924) in which the trial of Dr. Aziz for rape of a young English woman is fair, but the machinations of the British before and during the proceedings expose their racist and imperialist attitudes. In a symbolic rendition of a trial scene, Susan Glaspell's short story "A Jury of Her Peers" (1917) demonstrates a number of inequities between men and women. Based on Glaspell's play "Trifles," which was first performed in 1916, the story demonstrates how two women judge another woman's killing of her husband as a form of self-defense against his emotional cruelty rather than as murder. Henry Miller's play *The Crucible* from 1953 depicts a historical episode in Salem, Massachusetts, where in 1692 group hysteria led to the conviction and execution of a number of innocent men and women in witchcraft trials. At the same time the play indicts the public hysteria that was incited by the House Committee of Un-American Activities and Joseph McCarthy's 'witch hunt' investigations into the lives of alleged communist sympathizers during the early 1950s. Similarly, Harper Lee's novel *To Kill a Mockingbird* (1960) reminds its audience of the injustice wrought by racist legal practices, practices which continue, it may be argued, into the present. Portraying the conviction of Tom Robinson for the rape of a white woman which he did not commit, the novel's trial scene, with its balcony full of tensely waiting black spectators, recalls the injustice of Jim Crow laws in the American South. Robinson's wrongful conviction also makes reference to the hysterical fear of miscegenation that led to the frequent lynching of black men suspected of consorting with white women. The depiction of Atticus, the attorney who defends Robinson, by Gregory Peck in the film version of *To Kill a Mockingbird* (1964) established the figure of the lawyer as hero and social critic that has informed television series such as *Perry Mason*.

While the trial scene in twentieth-century literature has often been used as a forum for discussing general social problems, it is also a favorite vehicle for melodrama and escapism. The end of the twentieth century and the beginning of the twenty-first century have witnessed the depiction of sexy, many would argue fetishized, women lawyers in figures such as television's Ally McBeal or Elle Wood in the *Legally Blonde* movies (2001, 2003). Furthermore, lawyers also now take on the role of the Everyman in both novels and films. They are presented as fallible and troubled by personal problems such as alcoholism or marital strife. Yet in more attractive portrayals, these figures become valiant defenders of the innocent accused, whether this innocent is a child, as in John Grisham's novel *The Client* (1993), or the victim of medical malpractice, as in the film *The Verdict* (1998).[21]

No single narrative strand can be singled out in the variety of contemporary texts about trials, because trials in literature, as it became clear in the last century, serve many different purposes: to entertain, to titillate, to voice social criticism. It appears that courtrooms will continue to figure in English-language literatures due to their symbolic weight as social practices, their inherent drama, and the possibilities they offer for highlighting institutionalized injustice.

21 For an overview of images of lawyers in film and television, see Denvir (2000).

3. Literary Prison Worlds – Images of Incarceration

Literary texts teem with prison settings and prison metaphors just as they are filled with issues relating to crime and the legal process (Fludernik 2003a). In some centuries, the topic of imprisonment is more prominent than in others, and sometimes one genre rather than another proves to be most taken with the theme. Thus, as regards the English novel, the eighteenth- and nineteenth-century canon has abundant examples of prison settings and prison metaphors, whereas in the twentieth century, the popularity of the theme dropped dramatically in fiction (until recently, when it has come back with a vengeance) but rose to prominence in both the early twentieth-century and post-World War II writing for the British stage. Twentieth-century poetry, on the other hand, to our knowledge, has largely eschewed prison settings and prison metaphors. However, there existed a thriving medieval and Renaissance tradition of love poetry using the prison metaphor (*la prison amoureuse*), and Romantic poetry, like Gothic fiction, indulged in the use of both prison settings and prison metaphors. As Monika Fludernik has outlined elsewhere (1999), the most traditional prison metaphor is that of the world (and the body) as prison, a religious trope of prominence from Plato to St. Thomas More and beyond, and it is a metaphor that occurs in philosophical, theological, as well as literary texts.

Given this pervasiveness of the prison as setting, theme, and metaphor in literature – and, owing to our disciplinary groundings, we here refer mainly to texts from literatures in English –, the question arises why there is this preoccupation with the institution of the prison on the one hand and the experience or conditions of imprisonment on the other. Clearly, imprisonment and the prison must have some peculiar relevance to readers and writers.

Although the distinction between the penal institution and the situation of those affected by it are, in practice, difficult to distinguish, in theory at least they betoken entirely different areas of experience and almost opposite social concerns. Whereas the *institution* correlates with issues of law and order, the whole legal apparatus and the ramifications of crime-and-punishment, the *depiction of imprisonment* in literature, by contrast, is frequently made to resonate with moral questions, with issues of social (in)justice, the prisoner's suffering, the psychological effects of imprisonment, and prisoners' corporeal abjection. Literary discussions of imprisonment in fact often serve to complement the external view of society on those it has relegated to the domains of the carceral; they provide an internal perspective, allowing the reader to sympathize with the marginalized and the condemned. One primary function of the carceral theme in literature, one could argue, is therefore the echoing of real-world attitudes and feelings about penal institutions and the experience of imprisonment, an echoing that reflects many perspectives and enriches readers' insight into the social processes of justice, penal exclusion, and the carceral condition.

Why Prisons? The Functions of the Prison in Literature

Prisons are, first and foremost, a social fact of society. It is, therefore, quite natural that literature should include references to carceral institutions alongside references to factories, hotels, schools, parliaments, or town halls. On the other hand, prisons belong to those marginal spaces and taboo subjects which do not relate to most people's first-hand experience. This, incidentally, is a consequence of the invention of the penitentiary model. In the 'old' prison type, the prison was a place open to the public, one which a high percentage of citizens knew from first-hand experience as incarcerated debtors or as visitors. It therefore did not involve the secrecy and the connotations of shameful moral turpitude which are so characteristic of nineteenth-century penitentiaries and present-day so-called 'correctional facilities.' As a consequence of the marginalization of the prison experience after the abolishment of imprisonment for debt, the topic of imprisonment has receded from general social prominence and, at least in the mainstream novel, until recently all but disappeared.

In the last decade, this trend has been significantly reversed in response to a sensational rise of imprisonment rates in the United States and the UK as well as most European countries. (Rates dropped dramatically in Russia and elsewhere during the same period.) Moreover, the pervasiveness of world-wide imprisonment for political reasons – including the detention, incarceration, and torture of both terrorists and prisoners of conscience – has additionally helped to bring the subject of imprisonment back into the limelight. (See section 1 above.) The topic has meanwhile been revived in popular literature, as for instance in the work of Stephen King and in the HBO series *All Things Oz* on American television or the German RTL series *Hinter Gittern – der Frauenknast*. After a long period in which prisons were no longer important facets of contemporary reality, the theme is now again painfully relevant, in real life and therefore also in literature. From the 'margins' of the colonial novel the topic is beginning to move back into prominence even in mainstream serious fiction.

Over and above the simple fact that literature in one way or another reflects contemporary reality, literature moreover has a tendency to symbolically infuse, generalize, and emotionally heighten the real-world settings and experiences that it fictionalizes and projects. Books that deal with the subject of imprisonment imply that their choice of the topic is not haphazard, that the experience of imprisonment does not merely concern the writer and reader exclusively in terms of a very specific personal life story. On the contrary, the very choice of the subject seems to imply some kind of general relevance. Readers and critics frequently interpret fictional prison scenarios as implying that the prison is a metaphor for our lives, for our society, for our times. In this reading, the prison becomes *like* our world and, conversely, our world turns into a kind of prison. This topos of the 'prison as world/world as prison'[22] is not restricted to contemporary experience. In the English Renaissance and until the eighteenth century, it was quite common to point out that prisons, like society, were hierarchically structured, with the rich receiving much better treatment than the poor. (Since prisoners had to pay for their board and lodging,

---

22 On the 'prison as world/world as prison' topos see Fludernik (2003b).

the replication of societal inequalities was inevitable.) It was also argued, most famously in *The Beggar's Opera* (1728), that the morality of criminals inside prison was not so very different from that of supposedly respectable folk outside, successful crooks who had simply been too shrewd to be caught at their tricks. This homology between penal institutions and society at large has clearly great relevance for many societies ruled by authoritarian governments. Thus, for people criticizing the apartheid state in pre-1991 South Africa, the country's prisons symbolized the iniquity of a dehumanizing social reality. Similarly, African Americans even today see American prisons as epitomes of the continuing enslavement of their race – a view that does not appear far-fetched if one looks at current incarceration rates.

Literary Semiotics: Symbolizations, Topoi, and Metaphors

As the last two examples demonstrate, implying that prisons are homologous with the structure of society is not always a neutral statement of fact. Whereas Michel Foucault's theses about the disciplinary society can, but need not, be taken as descriptive of modern society, the example from South Africa clearly shows that the equation of prison and society goes hand in hand with manifest political struggle and the indictment of that society for social injustice. Comparisons between the prison reality and society at large therefore allege that society displays negative features and qualities that are usually reserved for its marginal sites of punishment. Besides the most glaring feature of injustice, other qualities of the prison-and-society homology have been proposed at various times. Total control is one of these alternative grounds of the metaphor, for instance in Orwell's *1984* (1949), where society operates like a prison of total surveillance. Another aspect that has often been associated with prisons since the institutionalization of the penitentiary is the carceral dehumanization of its inmates, usually aligned with the pervasive anonymity and routinization prevalent in penal institutions. The modern prison strategy of warehousing inmates, and, generally, the prison mentality of rules and regulations enforced with no consideration for human, much less personal needs – these features of modern prison life are clearly extreme variants of the types of constraint and the quality of anonymity pervasive generally in modern life. The 'carceral iciness' (*le froid pénitentiaire*) described by Buffard (1973) in her study of metaphors of imprisonment can therefore be regarded as an analogue of conveyor-belt production, cubicle-like housing in ugly concrete skyscrapers, or of urban loneliness and anonymity. Norman Mailer even compares expensive housing in safe concierged residential units to imprisonment with wall-to-wall carpeting, thereby ironically suggesting that security overkill results in a general conversion of society into a luxury prison (Mailer 1982: xiii-iv).

Whereas the above utilizations of the prison metaphor to characterize society as a whole have concentrated on a homology, even a continuity, between the world of the prison and the 'real' world outside, thereby paradoxically inverting the marginality of the prison scenario, many literary (and non-literary) texts deploy the prison setting to create a counter-world in which everything is structurally the same but morally and experientially the opposite of our familiar world outside. These projections echo the theological topos of hell. Hell is a site of punishment (opposed to heaven as a place of reward), and in hell social stratification is mirrored by penal stratification (one need only think of Dante's *Inferno*). The comparison of prison with hell is of medieval origin and factually 'motivated' (in the linguistic sense) by old type prison conditions (underground vaults, darkness, shackling, etc.). Characterizing prison as hell emphasizes the negative aspects of imprisonment; prison is a place of suffering. The metaphor can, however, be inverted to yield a positive reading of prison as paradise, a place of refuge, meditation, and creativity. Romantic literature, in particular, often presents places of confinement as happy prisons in which the incarcerated are able to write, to think, and to grow spiritually. Victor Brombert (1978) is the critic who has analyzed this most extensively. Indeed, the concept of the penitentiary itself relied on Romantic images of the convent and tried to place inmates in an environment conducive to self-analysis and repentance. Convicts were supposed to become minor saints, experiencing spiritual transcendence.

Most basically, however, the penitentiary has become the site of social or societal *otherness*, the locus of criminality, monstrosity, and dangerous deviancy. The alterity of the prison is conceived of as spatial otherness – corresponding to the contemporary practice of hiding away correctional institutions – and this spatial otherness is then enriched by the alleged moral and qualitative alterity of the criminal subjects. The prison in this reading is less a hell than a jungle or a zoo for dangerous beasts of prey. The prison and its inmates in fact come to represent that which society ejects and rejects: in Kristevan terms, they come to symbolize the abject, the human as animal. Or, as Frank Lauterbach has ingeniously proposed (Lauterbach, forthcoming), the prison serves as a locus of social discrimination. Society assures itself of its own respectability by differentiating itself from its others, men and women considered to be beyond the moral or human pale, whether criminals, revolutionaries, or those refusing to conform. The ease with which former Palestinian freedom fighters have recently been converted into mere terrorists uncannily illustrates these processes of the strategic attribution of otherness for the purpose of social or political disciplining. The prison and the inmate are "other" spatially and socially, but this otherness (like the similarity in the 'prison as world/world as prison' topos) rarely remains neutral. When society is said to be 'like prison' or that a prisoner 'properly belongs there,' these locutions clearly indicate that the normality of society is at stake and that the prisoner has been evicted from societal membership. What is particularly interesting in this connection is the way in which the *fact* of marginalization becomes symbolically loaded and leads to evaluative (negative) characterization and metaphoric deployment. Spatial dislocation automatically entails moral judgment and condemnation.

Prisons, as we have seen, are important locations in literature. They can either be represented realistically or charged symbolically. Except perhaps in the sensationalism of the Gothic novel, their very presence in literary texts is never innocuous; it usually serves the function of social criticism or attempts to gain the reader's sympathy for victims of oppression and the sufferings of confinement. Only rarely do literary texts gloat over the merited suffering of a criminal (Wordsworth's "Sonnets upon the Punishment of Death" [1839] are deservedly infamous for their reactionary views), even though literature does frequently manipulate the plot to effect poetic justice – the virtuous are rewarded by money and marriage, the villains die (in battle, suicide, natural disaster) or are otherwise punished. If retribution occurs, it is often seen as divine punishment – villains are rarely subjected to the rigors of the law, at least before the advent of the Realist novel.

As we have seen above, literary texts moreover deploy different types of imagery which are perhaps more important for their effect on the reader than the mere choice of the prison as subject or setting. Similes as in the 'prison as world/world as prison' topoi ('the prison is *like* the world at large'; 'the world is *like* a prison') are among several recurring tropes that proliferate in literature. Another typical use of imagery concerns the deployment of prison as the vehicle of a metaphor, usually by means of a set of metonyms of confinement and dungeon scenarios (shackles, chains, grates, bars, walls). Thus, when David in Chapter 14 of *David Copperfield* (1849-50) introduces the reader to Miss Murdstone, his evil step-aunt, he characterizes her ferocity metonymically by describing her purse:

> When she paid the coachman she took her money out of a hard steel purse, and she kept the purse in a very jail of a bag which hung upon her arm by heavy chains, and shut up like a bite. I had never, at that time, seen such a metallic lady altogether as Miss Murdstone was. (Dickens 1997: 45)

Miss Murdstone's bag is a "jail" that "bites" at intruders, "shut[s] up" the coins and is secured by "chains." Although the passage seems to simply present the child's perspective of fright – converting the closing of a harmless purse into imprisonment in an institution of forced confinement – the ultimate meaning of the metaphor lies in its metonymic reference to the "metallic lady." After all, as we come to learn presently, Miss Murdstone will 'imprison' David and terrorize him (biting and chaining him metaphorically).

The metaphoric characterization of imprisonment therefore interconnects with metonymy at several levels besides engaging a set of equivalent carceral spaces that underline the prison as a heterotopia, counterworld, or place of suffering. Especially in Elizabethan prison autobiographies and in Dekker's contributions to Sir Thomas Overbury's character sketches, the prison figures as hell, as a ship, as a hospital, and even a university (Fludernik 2003b: 153-56), and sometimes as a zoo or wilderness when jailors are figured as tigers.

In the following essays, descriptive and metaphoric representations of prisons and imprisonment come in a whole variety of shapes which posit the question of their aesthetic, cultural, and ideological functions in literary and non-literary texts. Labels attributed to prison spaces, to the situation of confinement, and to criminals, as well as metaphors applying carceral descriptors and analogues to what are perceived to be equally restrictive or deadening predicaments outside the penal complex – they all invoke a cultural imaginary that figures captivity and penal confinement in culture-specific ways. An analysis of how language represents carcerality therefore allows one to tap the cultural subconscious of desires, fears, and unacknowledged cathectic drives. As Martha Grace Duncan demonstrates in *Romantic Outlaws, Beloved Prison* (1996), our fascination with great criminals partakes both of our unlawful urges towards violence and crime and of our disgust at our own animalistic instincts figured in the abject of the criminal other. This fascination with criminal spaces and criminal subjects clearly carries over into the carceral imaginary, which is figured as a place of abjection and suffering but also of seclusion, transcendence, and glorification. Ultimately, imprisonment is always at least partly metaphorical since the very act of shutting somebody up or away participates in the concept of the container (IN/OUT) as extensively described in recent metaphor theory (Lakoff/Johnson 1980: 29-30; Lakoff 1987: 272-73, 383-89). And this, on an even more basic level, raises the question of the ideological roots of the prison as institution and as a practice of safekeeping, containment, or disciplining. Such practices are the concern of more than merely criminology; they correlate with the "uncreated conscience" of society "forge[d] in the smithy" of the human subconscious.[23]

4. Law *and* Literature versus Law *as* Literature: Dissenting Opinions

This introduction is preceded by a cartoon which represents figures readers will know so well that they require no introduction. Yet the familiar fairy tale image has been given a twist. We do not see the expected image of Goldilocks escaping from punishment for having trespassed into the family home and damaged the property of the law-abiding bears. Instead, we see her being handcuffed while she is pressed face down to the ground by a policeman in a bullet-proof vest, while another policeman aims his gun at her; the bears look on at her treatment silently, except for Little Bear, who comments: "It's nice to see the police toughening up on juvenile crime." A helicopter hovers overhead, another policeman is positioned with a long-range rifle on the roof of the Bear family home, an armed car stands in readiness in the background: all are indications that the delinquent Goldilocks has been being pursued in a large-scale operation. In this cartoon a fictional narrative has been turned into a form of political commentary which may lead its viewers to critically examine current penal practices concerning the treatment of juveniles. That a fairy tale can be given a new interpretation in order to critique a socio-political phenomenon is an instance of Law and Literature at work.[24]

What, then, is Law and Literature? With its focus on literary and historical experiences of trial and imprisonment, this volume belongs to the growing body of interdisciplinary scholarship now known as Law and Literature. In this section of the introduction we aim to give a brief overview of literature-and-law studies. Since the 1970s[25] interest in the nexus of literature and law has rapidly increased as is evidenced by the two interdisciplinary journals that are now devoted to the subject (the *Yale Journal of Law and the Humanities* and *Cardozo Studies in Law and Literature)*.

---

23 Compare Joyce (1974: 253).

24 Law and Literature is capitalized in the following when we are referring to the Law and Literature movement. When we refer to the relationship between literature and law, we do not capitalize the terms. In the following we also alternate the order of "literature" and "law" in their adjectival usage to avoid any suggestion of a hierarchal relationship between the two.

25 Rockwood cites the widespread notice of James Boyd White's *The Legal Imagination* (1973) as the beginning of the movement (1998: 1)

Currently more law schools offer courses on this subject than do not (Ward 1995: 206, fn 3). Yet unambiguously defining law-and-literature scholarship is no straightforward task. To begin with, whether one should call studies of the kind performed in this volume "law *and* literature" or "law *as* literature" (or critical legal studies) is a contested point of debate, one that relates to the dissenting opinions about what this discipline is and what its aims ought to be.

Overviews of literature-and-law studies often describe it as a battleground where competing theories about the relationship between literature and law are fought out:[26]

> Legal scholarship has been marked by ambivalence about what benefits literature promises the study of law. The two opposing views essentially reflect an ancient struggle within the legal profession between law as humanism and law as science. To one faction, which believes in the synergy of law and literature, law is romantic in ideology, more like poetry, an act of persuasion, a cultural practice of justification using language, ritual, drama, and legitimating ideology. The other group, which assumes that nothing could be more remote from law's theory and practice than poetry and literature, sees law as a science of reason and analysis, of coercive and imperative commands (expressed as clearly as possible), or organized coercion, a system operated by lawyers who, at best, resemble scientists and engineers. (Kornstein 1994: 5).

The battle to define literature's significance to law may reflect the adversarial nature of Anglo-American law itself. As Martin Kayman points out in his essay on *Caleb Williams* in this volume, English and American trial procedure admits only one narrative truth about the issue at hand which is determined with the verdict at the end of the trial: it is either the prosecutor's or the defendant's version of what happened that becomes fixed with the verdict as the one and only truth. However, what wins in the courtroom is often not the truth but the story that was told best, using persuasive rhetoric. This is the lesson that Caleb learns from Mr. Forester as does anyone who witnesses the sometimes blatantly partial machinations of the legal system close at hand.[27]

In what follows we would like to play a discursive game in which counter-arguments will be presented in the manner of the courtroom. Let us ask readers to take on the role of jury members. We request that they decide on the conundrum of how to name (and how to understand) the studies on literature and law undertaken in this volume within a larger context. The prosecutor will argue that studying Law and Literature has only an additive value: the disciplines in themselves remain discrete. The counsel for the defense, by contrast, will attest that literature and law are fundamentally interactive disciplines that cannot be pursued in isolation from one another. You Ladies and Gentlemen of the jury will have to determine which of our two attorneys presents a more compelling theory about the case at hand.

---

26 Cf. Dolin (1999: 2-10), Grey (1991: 1-9), Rockwood (1998: 1-6), Ward (1995: 4-27), Thomas (1991: 524-31), and Weisberg (1992: x-xiv).

27 For an extended analysis of how juries arrive at verdicts based on their trying out competing narratives and choosing the one that 'fits' best, see Cotterill's linguistic analysis of the O. J. Simpson trial (2003: 221-26.).

Two oppositional parties approach the bar in this hypothetical trial. A leading proponent of the law-*and*-literature movement, Professor and Judge Richard A. Posner takes on the prosecutor's role. A political conservative, Posner in his opening statement will argue that the separation between the disciplines of law and literature, which became solidified in the eighteenth and nineteenth centuries, must remain intact. Whereas law effects difficult, potentially painful decisions, literature reflects on law only metaphorically. In this case, law "*and* Literature" gives a title to the type of scholarship pursued in Posner's bestselling book on the subject (1998 [1988]).[28] "And" is meant in the sense of literature's being ancillary to the serious and often tricky business of law and litigation; literature supplements law in the pre-Derridean sense.

Given the virulence with which Posner describes his opponents' poor thinking, any number of scholars – not few of them lawyers themselves – might apply for the job of defending literature's integral relation to law.[29] Counsel for the defense in our imaginary courtroom is Richard Weisberg, who will argue for a law *as* literature interpretation of the Law and Literature movement. Weisberg holds advanced degrees in both law and literature studies and was responsible for founding Cardozo's interdisciplinary journal. He is therefore eminently qualified for the job of defending the view that law is inherently integrated with literature. Weisberg's *Poethics and Other Strategies of Law and Literature* (1992) presents a "guidebook to Law and Literature theory and practice" (x) that is directly intended to contradict the dismissive attitude towards literature propounded by Posner and others. Indeed, *Poethics* concludes with the statement: "law and literature, for all their disparities, are one" (1992: 252).

When a trial begins, counsels must argue their version of the events which will be decided on during the course of the tribunal. Milner Ball has described this process as a form of competitive storytelling (1999: 216). The stories Posner and Weisberg will tell the jury about literature and law might well begin with their differing evaluations of an essay from 1925 by the Supreme Court Justice Benjamin N. Cardozo. In "Law and Literature" Cardozo classifies and evaluates six styles of legal argument, lauds the merit of selection in the presentation of evidence, and distinguishes, on the one hand, between the stylistics of dissenting and majority opinions, and, on the other, between arguments that are directed to the bar versus those aimed at the trial audience, the jury. These careful differentiations are intended as advice to "[y]oung men as they approach admission to the bar" (1947: 355) and are subsumed under Cardozo's general argument that substance and form are "fused into a unity" in legal prose (340). Showing his indebtedness to one of the founding fathers of literary theory, Cardozo cites master of style Henry James as his source for his belief in this unity.

---

28 As evidence for his argument, Posner reports that his *Law and Literature* (1998) is the most frequently assigned or recommended book of nonfiction in courses on law and literature in law schools (vii).

29 For instance, Robin West might volunteer to lead the counsel for the defense. Posner characterizes this scholar's work as a deluded example of the legal academic left; her readings of Kafka are, according to him, notable for their "peculiarity" (1998: 193) and "perversity" (188). Posner also throws many brickbats against the supposed didacticism of James Boyd White, whose work will be summarized below.

Posner interprets Cardozo quite critically. Subscribing to a theory of law called the law and economics movement (1998: 301), which asserts the values of efficacy and "cost-benefit" (182) and employs mathematical equations to understand how law works, Posner evaluates Cardozo's judicial and nonjudicial "literary" style as rhetorically successful but at the same time a patent threat to the workings of the hard reasoning of law.[30] Cardozo's affection for metaphor has, according to Posner, a dangerous tendency to "muddy" and confuse legal reasoning (279), which he thinks ought to strive to be as scientific as possible. The division between legal and literary text and language is reified by Posner's argument. By contrast, Weisberg lauds Cardozo for recognizing early on that literature is the primary teacher of legal argument. Reacting to the traditional opinion that words are a "holding" place or vessel for substance, Cardozo postulates the inseparability of words and their meanings (Weisberg 1992: 6-7): hence writing judicial decisions is a creative act that relies on, and cannot be separated from, questions of form and persuasion. From the basis of this premise, Weisberg moves on to an argument about what literature may teach us about law: by giving the disempowered a voice, literature shows – in a way that other discourses cannot – how the law often stigmatizes those who are perceived as different by a specific society, whether they are citizens of color, women, or homosexuals. Taking a position often argued in critical legal studies, Weisberg asserts that law and lawyers take their pay from institutions that, while perceiving themselves as impartial, work to uphold power structures that put those considered different at a disadvantage (41).

The term critical legal studies (or CLS) has been introduced to the courtroom, and we now need to pause in our trial proceedings to explain it. Arising during the late seventies, CLS was intended to challenge acceptance of the power relationships that inform the practice of law in society. With its roots in Vietnam anti-war protest and the Civil Rights Movement, CLS has gone on to spawn feminist legal theory and critical race theory and maintains a clearly political and critical agenda.[31] CLS argues, for example, that the outcome of legal contests does not derive from impartial laws but is the result of a process of interpretation which is influenced by prejudicial social practices. A typical example of the politics of this movement is Harvard Law Professor Duncan Kennedy's monograph from 1983 *Legal Education and the Reproduction of Hierarchy: A Polemic Against the System*, which argues that legal

30 For two critiques of Posner's economics-inspired understanding of law with its quantifiable notion of justice, see Dimock (1996: 140-45) and Nussbaum, particularly in her reading of the character Gradgrind from Dickens's *Hard Times* (1995)

31 Thomas characterizes the movement as follows: "Interested in the social implications of the law, many members of the critical legal-studies movement recognize the limitations of a reflection theory, which explains the law as a mirror of society's existing power structure. [...] Although the law's ability to maintain order by peacefully resolving conflict is often seen as its most positive function, the critical legal-studies movement reminds us of the extent to which the rhetoric of the law helps to maintain order at the price of disguising or denying the conflicts produced by the existing order, thereby helping to legitimate that order" (1987: 4). For a history of the development of CLS in Europe and an examination of its focused politics of resistance, see the introduction to Douzinas et al. (1994: 1-3); as well as Goodrich (1990).

education has ideological foundations and that law schools acculturate lawyers-to-be into practices of subordination.[32] CLS' dual emphasis on hierarchical power relations and the indeterminacy of legal interpretation has given rise to several kinds of scholarship. Applying critical theory to legal texts, Alan Hyde, for instance, explores how bodies are constructed by law and legal discourse as "property" or "different," as raced, sexed or disabled, and shows how these constructions have social consequences (1997: 261). In critical race theory, law professor Patricia Williams has used the autobiographical mode to make visible the continued oppression of African Americans (1991). Derrick Bell is also credited with using story-telling techniques to make underlying issues of race oppression apparent to his law school students. Most notably, Bell's story "The Space Traders' Solution" from *Faces at the Bottom of the Well* (1992) introduces an allegory about the United States selling all African Americans to space travelers as a counter-narrative to the hypothetical case work students do in law school.[33] Williams and Bell, among others, have also contributed to a new field called narrative legal studies.

Such examples provide an initial overview of some of the ways CLS can be undertaken:

1. CLS may examine legal texts to determine how they underpin social hierarchies (Hyde);
2. CLS may develop or analyze alternative texts to those traditionally considered part of the canon of legal studies; such texts may include autobiography and allegory (Williams, Bell);
3. CLS may contrast 'legal' and 'literary' texts to show their overlaps and contradictions (Hyde).

One will note that all of these enterprises are, first of all, text oriented. Text is here understood to include any variety of human productions and actions: hence alternative types of text may be juxtaposed with legal cases and their interpretations. To the extent that CLS theorizes the manner in which narratives underlie both legal and literary texts, it shows that issues of interpretation, ambiguity, and social formation are crucial factors in Law and Literature. Second, CLS points out that the practice of law is influenced by political and economic interests. Thus notions of justice which are grounded in abstract principles are found to be suspect and can be shown to have ideological underpinnings. Third, by pointing out how legal procedures work as

---

32 "Law schools are intensely political places. The trade-school mentality, the endless attention to trees at the expense of forests, the alternating grimness and chumminess of focus on the limited task at hand – all these are only a part of what is going on. The other part is the ideological training for willing service in the hierarchies of the corporate, welfare state" (Kennedy 1983). See also the introduction to the British *Critical Lawyers' Handbook* Vol. 1: "In short, law generally acts to consolidate and maintain an extensive system of class, gender and racial oppression. Critical lawyers seek a theory and practice that makes the overcoming of such oppression a central political task" (1992).

33 Cf. Bell's "The Power of Narrative" for a reprint of the story and an analysis of the impact of his work on critical race theory (1999).

normative cultural practices and by introducing alternative non-canonical texts into the classroom, critical legal theorists aim to bring about reform in law school and the way law is practiced.

We now return to our hypothetical courtroom to hear the opposing counsels' closing statements. Posner might argue that the validity of his approach has been demonstrated by the popularity of his book, now in the second printing of its second edition. After all, Posner judges the value of literature on the basis of its "universality" (1998: 7, 18, 21) – shades of T. S. Eliot – and its capacity to withstand time, or, to borrow Posner's preferred vocabulary, its consistently high market value. Furthermore, Posner would argue that the various ways of performing law-*and*-literature scholarship that he outlines and evaluates in his book have in fact been realized. According to Posner, law-*and*-literature studies

1. primarily treats literary texts that – to use a loaded word for those who see literature as culturally productive – "reflect" on the law, mostly metaphorically rather than in terms of actual procedure: literary treatments of law muse about the "antinomies" inherent in judicial practice, such as the difference between law and equity; they do not add insight to legal argument or practice;
2. secondarily, law-*and*-literature reads legal texts using the methods of literature studies, a project whose value Posner describes as only slight (1998: viii).[34]

Posner also notes and dismisses what he characterizes as the third branch of the law-*and*-literature movement. This is the untoward desire by some scholars

3. "to bring works of imaginative literature into the legal classroom in order to present vivid pictures of the despised, the overlooked, and the downtrodden, and by fostering empathy for them to encourage legal reform along egalitarian or even revolutionary lines" (6). Posner's criticism of what he sees as the rigid didacticism of these projects and their efforts to influence moral attitudes follows in the third part of his book;
4. finally, law-*and*-literature studies concerns itself with how literature is controlled by legal practices. This includes questions of who owns the text and how it may be used, and involves questions of defamation, copyright, and censorship.

In summary, Posner's typology marginalizes literature and the methods of critical literary studies from the 'hard' practice of the law. Posner concedes that lawyers and judges may refer to 'great' literature to hone their rhetorical skills. Yet in his opinion the digressive arguments of deconstructive and post-structuralist theory and practitioners of narrative legal studies should not be allowed to interfere with the

34 For an interesting interpretation of the fictional qualities of one of Posner's opinions regarding a case on sexual harassment, see Ranney (1999).

serious business of making legal decisions. Literature is only of minimal usefulness for actual legal debate. Given this understanding of literature, Posner's views lead to the following implications for law-and-literature scholarship. He argues that:

> [...] the movement will make a greater contribution to illuminating jurisprudential issues than to improving law at the operating level, that it will contribute little to statutory or constitutional interpretation, and that it will not guide legal scholars, judges, and other members of the legal profession to a resolution of the burning issues that confront American law today. [...] Law is a system of social control as well as a body of texts, and its operation is illuminated by the social sciences and judged by ethical criteria. Literature is an art, and the best methods of interpreting and evaluating it are aesthetic. (1998: 7)

Posner's last two sentences, definitional and normative in tone, reject the idea that law might rely in any manner on literature or literary method. Literature is marginalized as belonging to the realm of the aesthetic, whose judgments are evaluations and criticism without a firm base in positive truth. It remains radically separate from "the burning issues that confront" legal practice. Yet by seeing law as framed by the trinity of social control, textuality, and morality, Posner in fact opens the way to much more extensive applications of the literary method. Since the law is partly a textual matter, the philological expertise of literary studies is entirely appropriate for analyzing legal discourse; at the same time, morality and social control do not necessarily fit the image of rationality and empirical objectivity that Posner is at pains to establish. Instead, they suggest that social power structures and the constitution of social norms (and normality) lie at the heart of the law. Such a view of law as social figuration then comes very close to literary studies' analysis of political and cultural norms and discursivities. Significantly, Posner's discursive formation excludes the notion of truth or justice. Indirectly, Posner admits the possibility that legal decision making and interpretation is contingent (and political), an insight from critical legal studies.

In contrast to Posner, Weisberg might argue in his closing remarks to the jury that, given the difficult questions and complex issues that face us in legal practice and debate, we cannot look to some abstracted notion of law as an economic science but need to turn to literature:

> We must be open to learn and apply, not to memorize and apply. We must seek to implement, at every point on our professional spectrum, a reflected sense of human experiences, our own and indeed those described in imaginative literature. Literature teaches us what social science cannot, because literature is the best source (outside of ourselves) of sense and sensibility. (1988: 110)

Weisberg postulates a theory of literature as teaching ethics and the intricacies of human experience in a manner that the social sciences cannot do. Left to themselves, lawyers, whether interpreting the US constitution or racial policy in Vichy France, will avoid examining the effects of their actions by referring to the rules of their profession (145). Lawyers, Weisberg argues, "need textual standards of conduct and cannot rely on the practices of their profession alone to avoid future catastrophes" (ibid.)

For those members of the reading jury who are still unable to decide on what to name literature-and-law studies and how to understand this practice, it may be important to note that Weisberg and Posner articulate extreme positions in the debate. This may result in part from the rhetorical necessity of their defining their standpoints in contradistinction to one another. Two other law-and-literature theorists take on more circumspect positions with respect to the question of how integrally literature and law relate. These are Ian Ward and Brook Thomas.

In his introduction to the subject, Ward sidesteps the conundrum of choosing between law *and* literature versus law *as* literature by emphasizing the value of both (*Law and Literature: Possibilities and Perspectives*, 1995). He suggests that literature-and-law studies work on the basis of two premises. Either they see "law *in* literature," which is roughly equivalent to Posner's first category, or they read "law *as* literature" by employing methods of literary studies to read legal texts for their linguistic, metaphorical, and creative qualities (Ward 1995: 20). Ward suggests that both approaches have validity and are by no means mutually exclusive. Nonetheless, he sees the future of law-in/as-literature scholarship in its ability to suggest alternative ways of thinking. Law and Literature should be used to teach about the slippery, undecipherable quality of the language that creates laws, judicial opinions, and meaning in general. This would help lawyers in training to avoid the trap of thinking of the law as an objective and stable reality (26). Furthermore, unlike much law school work, studying literature, as Weisberg pointed out in his essay from 1988, is fun. With his eye trained steadily on the pedagogical relevance of law-and-literature study, Ward argues that most people form their notions of law and morality early on by reading children's literature and later by discussing texts like William Golding's *The Lord of the Flies* (1954) in classrooms.

As noted above, the second standpoint on literature and law's relation to each other is provided by Brook Thomas, who begins his overview of literature-and-law studies with a review of the movement towards scientificity within legal thought ("Reflections on the Law and Literature Revival"). This synopsis is intended to supply some context to Posner's denunciation of the supposed merits of literary methods and literature studies. The problematic nature of this effort to put law on a scientific basis is contrasted by Thomas with what turns out to be the equally problematic claims of those who look to literature or "rhetoric" (understood here as the entirety of discursive relations) to discover the ways in which language creates human practices including legal ones. Thomas proposes that thinkers such as James Boyd White go too far in their prescriptions of a "*prope*r use of legal rhetoric" (529) to foster public ethical debate. This sense of rhetoric includes a notion of creating community through rhetoric so as to alter social practice.

In his *Acts of Hope: Creating Authority in Literature, Law, and Politics* (1994), James Boyd White reads texts ranging from Shakespeare's *Richard II* through Lincoln's Second Inaugural Address to Nelson Mandela's speech to the dock during his sabotage trial in order to demonstrate how such texts create "ethical meaning." In this concept White includes both the changes which such texts may bring about in language, by for instance destroying divisions between 'us' and 'them' linguistically, and in so doing thereby creating a new kind of ethical community: "And this achievement is not one that takes place at the level of theory or proposition, but is performed in the text itself, ethically, as he [in this case Lincoln] acts upon his language and audience" (1994b: 285). The changes created by the texts of Mandela and Lincoln have the power to transform the way individuals relate to the authorities that have power over them. Audiences may take on a new set of meanings created by these uniquely productive texts.[35]

For Thomas, White overstates the case for literature's ability to cure the abuses committed by legal authority. Some division between the actual practice of law and the study of rhetoric, he insists, remains: "Whereas Posner's strict instrumentalism neglects the social dimension of rhetoric and authorship, White's stress on the performative aspect of legal rhetoric minimizes its necessarily instrumental function" (529). According to Thomas, both Posner's instrumentalist view of law and White's notion of reformist rhetoric fail to address the claims of equity in actual legal decisions and in discourse about law.

Equity, it may be remembered, is both a legal institution in England (that was immortalized in the negative by Dickens's *Bleak House*) and a concept to describe the mitigating situational circumstances that must be brought into play to counteract a narrowly legalist understanding of law.[36] Thomas attempts to bring equity back into the courtroom and law-and-literature classroom using the vehicle of supplemental, meant now in the Derridean sense, literature. Advocating the usefulness of paradoxical and dialogical literature which does not necessarily teach ethics to (implicitly) nasty lawyers, Thomas suggests that literature may indeed demonstrate the lack of community and the lack of representation of repressed voices in a culture at a given moment. Hence literature does not merge with law as Weisberg would have it or reinvent systems of authority as White might wish it to do, but offers an additional and necessary critical reading of cultural and legal processes:

> Indeed, when it comes to questions of governing societies ruled by law, the most literature can hope for is a supplementary role. It is precisely in such societies, however, that maintaining literature's supplementary role takes on added importance. This is because whereas they can conceive of no system more just than rule by law, they are also forced to confront the failure of their particular set of laws to be truly representative. By using literary texts to cross-examine particular laws at particular historical moments, the law and literature movement has helped raise important questions about the representativeness of such laws. (Thomas 1991: 539)

While this view seems balanced and conciliatory, it may strike a false note for those who understand literature as a productive discourse that contributes to material culture, a lesson teachers such as Michel Foucault and Raymond Williams have taught us. The notion that literature may at best point out the gaps that occur in the rule of law appears disconcerting. The marginalization (and inherent feminization) of

---

35 Cf., for instance, the Afterword to *Acts of Hope* (1994a: 303-7): However, readers may find the formulation of White's ethical philosophy in "The Ethics of Meaning" (1994b) more accessible.

36 Cf. Ziolkowski's brief history of equity in Elizabethan England (1997:167-74); or Kayman (2002: 14-16); for an extended analysis of equity in eighteenth and nineteenth-century British legal practice and in fiction, see Polloczek (1999).

literature, familiar from Posner, takes place in the context of the foregrounding of the rough-and-ready world of law.[37]

On another note, the last sentence of the passage quoted above bespeaks an awareness of history in Thomas's work on Law and Literature, which he has intensified in his monograph on writings from the American Renaissance (*Cross-Examinations of Law and Literature: Cooper, Hawthorne, Stowe, and Melville*, 1987). On the premise that law and literature both work within the framework of the stories a culture tells about itself, Thomas reads historical literary texts to address questions about legal ideology. Thus he shows that an interest in literature's effect on legal practice and vice versa did not begin with the literature-and-law movement of the 1970s. This diachronic approach to law-and-literature studies has been followed by Wai Chee Dimock in her juxtaposition of nineteenth-century American literary texts with both contemporary legal cases and a selection of philosophical theories about justice; her point is that literature expresses that which remains residual and unresolved in notions of commensurate justice (1996). Even more ambitiously, Jörg Schönert, instituting a German research group, has attempted to construct a historical typology of the overlap between penal laws and literary treatments of criminality in France, Germany, and Britain in the period between 1790 and 1920 (Schönert et al. 1983, 1991). Also following the historical trajectory of literature-and-law scholarship, Uwe Böker and his team have in a number of publications examined the effect of law on literature as well as other forms of public communication. Their research historically places legal discourses within the larger frameworks of institutionalized cultures of modernity (Böker et al.1996, 2001, 2002a, 2002b).

After an introduction to the variety of standpoints on Law and Literature, notice must be taken of how literature-and-law studies differ across national borders. Differences in recent historical developments and contemporary judicial systems have, for instance, led to contrasting foci in American and British law-and-literature scholarship. In the United States the perception that legal theories were extremist and either radically left (critical legal studies) or conservative and pseudo-scientific (law-and-economics movement) led many legal practitioners to seek a third, less partisan, way to understand law that was not so subject to ideological claims (Kayman 2002: 6). A middle ground was found in Law and Literature.[38]

The necessity of applying insights from literature-and-law scholarship made itself felt in another arena as well. With his appointment by President Reagan to the Supreme Court in 1986, William Rehnquist ushered in a newly conservative era in United States' judicial practice and interpretation. One of the major debates that has marked the Rehnquist era has been whether the Constitution should be interpreted in the manner its authors wrote it 'originally' or as a 'living' document that may be interpreted to effect social change as circumstances in the United States alter. Issues familiar from literary studies such as the question of author intentionality, the

37 Kayman also makes this point, although with reference to White and Ward (2002: 7).

38 This last point brings up a criticism that, with its liberal tendencies, law-and-literature scholarship may not show enough teeth in its political stance (cf. Dolin 1999: 9).

partiality of interpretation, and the impossibility of a 'literal' interpretation of texts have thus entered American Constitutional debate (cf. Levinson 1988).[39]

In comparison to its American counterpart, British legal debate is far less concerned with the correct interpretation of the Constitution, because there is no Supreme Court to declare laws unconstitutional. The more loosely structured common law tradition encourages discussion of the validity of particular bills and their precedents.[40] Yet as Kayman points out, Britain's increasing legal integration with the European Union may have caused its tradition-bound judiciary to be forced into a "deferred critical encounter with theory" (2002: 5). This turn to theory has been carried out by postmodern thinkers, who stress the linguistic quality of law as well as the need to test law and legal institutions on the basis of their ethical treatment of the individual who enters their grasp. Summarizing this type of work, Costas Douzinas, Peter Goodrich, and Yifat Hachamovitch write: "In the most synoptic of terms, we may say that language and ethics precede the law in the precise sense that justice, the right to a hearing, to a day in court, to judgment, is the precondition for the appearance of law" (Douzinas et al. 1994: 22). Peter Goodrich, in particular, has opened up a new form of critical inquiry with his insistence that the language of law contains a hidden reservoir of emotions and passions that are generally repressed but become concretized in legal facts (1990, 1994). This intertwining of linguistic and psychoanalytical method to approach legal texts presents yet a new type of interdisciplinary research.

This overview of Law and Literature has demonstrated a lack of consensus between the movements' leading proponents about what is the ultimate purpose of this interdiscipline. Some practitioners see literature as ancillary and of little actual importance to legal practice or Constitutional interpretation. For these thinkers, one can read literature to muse about problems in the human condition that are dealt with practically in adjudication. Still others in the CLS movement understand law as a practice that supports racist and sexist status quo power arrangements; hence critical interpretation of legal language, texts, and practices must be enacted to aid the disadvantaged. For them, applying critical reading strategies to legal texts is a vital political practice. Weisberg and White both understand literature to teach law about ethics. Ward, by contrast, wants literature to supplement narrow rule-governed learning in law school, and Thomas looks to literature to teach law about the processes of equity. Finally, postmodern research studies the language of legal texts to highlight how unconscious motivations have been repressed in social-scientific theories of law.

The range of ways to practice literature-and-law studies remains a broad church then. A sense of the importance to decide on the relations between literature, text, and law also remains fervent. In a much-quoted extreme statement of the one indissoluble difference between literary and legal practices, Robert M. Cover writes: "We begin,

---

39 Essays in this volume on *Caleb Williams* and contemporary linguistic theories as well as on the High Treason Trials of 1794 will show that debates about the degree to which individual legal texts and words themselves have concrete or alterable meanings were already pertinent in late eighteenth-century England and did not arise newly in the United States.

40 Cf. Levinson (1988: 156); Kayman (2002: 5); Murphy (1994).

then, not with what the judges say, but with what they do. The judges deal pain and death" (1986: 1609). Cover reminds the reader that judges perform speech acts: they commit actions with their words. In contrast to Cover, Weisberg states that without a sense of ethics won from an understanding of the textual unity of meaning and form, lawyers and judges may commit acts of cruelty. Relying on a sense of their own "legal professionalism" (Weisberg 1992: 145), lawyers in Vichy France overzealously interpreted German racial laws to cause the unnecessary deaths of tens of thousands of Jews. This might have been avoided if a respect for the foundational principles of French constitutional law had been remembered. Hence the danger of a formalistic application of the law lies in forgetting that "justice and words must be linked" (10). Thus Weisberg asserts that "[t]he battleground for us is the battleground of texts, not of situationalist theory" (175). As we explore the texts dealing with tribunals and incarceration in this volume, it is important to recall that our interpretive decisions may have social and ethical implications. But this, Ladies and Gentleman of the jury, remains in your hands to decide.

5. Overview of the Volume

This volume is divided into two parts, to which sections two (on trials) and three (on prisons) of this introduction are intended to serve as prefaces. While reading this book, the reader may gain the impression that some of the essays which appear here are in active dialogue with one another. This dialogic quality of the essays attests to what we believe is characteristic of the overlapping of legal, historical, and political themes in law-and-literature studies. Furthermore, the interplay of sometimes quite contradictory perspectives on the same material has made this volume a pleasure to edit and, we believe, will enrich its audience's reading experience.

The first part of the volume addresses trials and their textual treatments. The reader may be surprised that the essays do not follow chronologically on the basis of their historical subject matter. For instance, the discussion of judicial tribunals begins with Anna-Christina Giovanopoulos's essay on the trials of Captain Kidd and the impeachment proceedings against his Whig backers which took place on the cusp of the eighteenth century ("Captain Kidd and the King: Piracy and Politics in Restoration England"). Because it addresses impeachment as well as trial litigation and discusses the nexus between trial reports and criminal biographies within a wider political context, we believe that this essay provides an effective opening to many issues that will be explored in this volume. Specifically, Giovanopoulos begins by differentiating between internal and external legal cultures and various forms of political power. She goes on to illustrate how the trials of Kidd and the impeachment proceedings against his financial backers were used to carry out larger political battles for influence between the Commons, the House of Lords, and King William III. Comparing trial reports about and criminal biographies of Kidd, the author demonstrates how the texts she cites contributed to spreading norms that had been enforced in the courtroom to a larger audience.

The discussion of trials continues with three papers that have literary texts as their primary focus. Here we do proceed chronologically. Thomas Lederer explores the depiction in hagiographies (or saint's lives) of heresy trials that occurred during the period of religious upheaval following Henry VIII's break with Rome ("'Thereupon There Were Produced Three False Witnesses...': Trial Scenes in Elizabethan Sacred Biography"). Lederer begins by reminding the reader of the particulars of contemporary trial procedure including a lack of counsel for the defendant. He goes on to show how Protestant and Catholic hagiographers employed different discursive strategies to venerate the saintly protagonists of their narratives and to vilify those who persecuted, tried, and sentenced them. Since the saints' enemies were invested with legal authority, denigrating these officials became a form of institutional critique in which the saints' stance suggests, as does Antigone's defense, that there is a higher form of justice than that of the laws enforced by monarchs and their minions. Most interestingly for the general reader, perhaps, is Lederer's analysis of assertions made by some hagiographers that trials by jury – that most English of institutions – were in fact un-English, due to their having been introduced by the Norman King William the Conqueror.

Greta Olson's analysis of a variety of trial scenes in Shakespeare's plays attempts to counter readings of the playwright's oeuvre as either propagandistic or strictly subversive of monarchal authority ("Law as Thought Pattern and Ordering Principle in Shakespeare's Trial Scenes"). These depictions show how trials may either be abused by the powerful or, by contrast, be employed as a strategy for resolving crises and moral dilemmas. By exploring scenes in which trials are enacted in spectacular public forums and those in which the specifics of trial procedure are copied by individuals during private moments of crises, she shows that judicial forms and court procedures have been internalized by Shakespearean characters as patterns of thought. Olson finishes the essay with a typology of Shakespearean trial scenes that may be applied to other narratives.

The next paper provides a different typology of trial scenes, in this case those in twentieth-century British courtroom dramas. Outlining both the characteristics and the history of the genre she explicates, Beatrix Hesse distinguishes three phases of courtroom dramas ("Representations of the British Legal System in Twentieth-Century Popular Courtroom Drama"). These develop from being affirmative of the legal apparatus in the 1930s, to skeptical of the same in the 1950s and 1960s, and then downright ridiculing of the law by the 1970s. Hesse also notes how courtroom dramas were supplanted at this point by the popularity of televised crime and court dramas. A return to more naturalist depictions of court trials occurred in the genre during the 1980s and 1990s in which issues such as euthanasia and police tolerance of racism were explored.

The following essay returns us from the twentieth century to the close of the eighteenth. With its primary focus on William Godwin's *Caleb Williams*, Martin A. Kayman's contribution provides the volume with its final treatment of a fictional trial ("Trials of Law and Language: *Caleb Williams* and John Horne Tooke"). On the other hand, this essay opens up theoretical issues in connection with the law-and-literature debate by showing how the novel's multiple endings and beginnings may be seen either as an indictment of the power abuses that led to the trials of reformers for treason in 1794 or a literary illustration of the indeterminate truth of all narratives. By juxtaposing Caleb's desire to write an etymology with similar efforts by contemporary writers such as Eugene Aram and John Horne Tooke (a defendant in the High Treason Trials), Kayman paints a much broader picture of a historical move towards "a project for a natural science on which to ground both thought and justice" in so-called linguistic certainty.

The final essay in the trial section provides a contextualization of Kayman's article. In his analysis of the legal culture that surrounded the High Treason Trials of 1794, Christoph Houswitschka's primary interest is in tracing the interplay between the trials themselves and the texts that surrounded them ("Circulating Ideas of Democracy: The Legal Culture of the High Treason Trials of 1794"). Houswitschka describes the fate of the fictional Caleb Williams in the hands of his prosecutors as an illustration of what contemporary writers saw as the danger of the government's using literary techniques to devise a narrative of the defendants' treasonous acts. These authors countered the Crown's narrative with a counter-narrative about the government's conspiracy to create a fictional story of 'constructive' treason. Not only did reformist narratives influence the outcome of the trials before they began, but populist and highbrow publications written after the trials constructed them as a turning point in British history. Several of the texts which Houswitschka describes provide a further interesting counter-narrative to that of the hagiographic writers discussed by Lederer. Many of the texts written after the Treason Trials describe trial by jury as the most intrinsically British of all institutions and identify it as responsible for saving the defendants from execution.

With the trial and jailing of defendants in the High Treason Trials serving as a thematic bridge between Parts I and II of this volume, we now turn to the subject of imprisonment. The contributions in Part II are likewise arranged thematically. Frank Lauterbach's essay on prison autobiographies opens the dialogue about prisons and imprisonment by providing a surprising counter-narrative to two predominant analyses of prisoner texts ("Errands into the Carceral Wilderness: Fictions of Imprisonment as Narratives of Social Alterity"). Critics have traditionally stressed the subjectivity and personal suffering of the incarcerated individual and hence viewed such narratives as a kind of social critique; conversely, they have pointed out how the prison may be described by the prisoner as a site of liberation and transcendence. In contrast to these critics, Lauterbach understands the prison to be a symbolic boundary that is drawn by autobiographical writers between themselves and whatever they intuit as "other." Most often these others – whom the writer considers to have been rightly imprisoned – are described in terms of their animality or wildness. Importantly, and here Lauterbach's article has a clearly political thrust, this process of definition is undertaken to maintain status quo power relations.

Monika Fludernik's essay on carceral imagery explores those literary metaphors that use the image of imprisonment to describe an array of confining situations and moods ("Prison Metaphors – The Carceral Imaginary?"). Carceral metaphors and similes depend on prevalent notions of prison and imprisonment, hence the changing realities of prisons need to be taken into account. Fludernik's essay also provides an introduction to metaphor studies, employing techniques from cognitive metaphor analysis to describe source and target domains and processes of blending. After an initial description of the primary carceral images such as the dungeon, barrenness, and confinement with its related metonyms (chains and bars), the essay analyzes the complex trains of metaphorical images in *Les Misérables* to show how they serve to deconstruct the novel's moral oppositions. She concludes by describing the tendency of prison metaphors to concentrate on the spatially envisioned perspective of the incarcerated, rather than on the social alterity of the imprisoned (cf. Lauterbach).

Appropriately, the essay on carceral imagery is the first in a row of texts that deal with particular visions of imprisonment in novels. The next four essays whose subjects are primarily literary are positioned in the chronological order of the texts they examine. In his lyrical analysis of *Little Dorrit,* Harry E. Shaw explores how this novel combines "two ways of imagining the prison and its relation to everyday life" that had been familiar to British fiction since the eighteenth century ("Realities of the Prison: Dickens, Scott, and the Secularization of their Eighteenth-Century Inheritance"). One mode, defined by Fielding, envisions the prison as an extension of everyday life; the other mode, developed by Richardson, paints the prison as a site where quasi-religious transcendence of the carceral predicament may occur. Both novelists associate the prison with "female debasement" which Shaw argues is a regular motif in prison literature. Shaw then goes on to show how *The Heart of Mid-Lothian* also combines the two visions of the prison and depicts the process of modernization by historicizing the image of prison as a site of transcendence.

Whereas Shaw analyzes *Little Dorrit* within the context of the eighteenth-century prison novels that preceded it, Carol Colatrella parses the novel for its exploration of the theme of the innocent convict ("The Innocent Convict: Character, Reader Sympathy, and the Nineteenth-Century Prison in *Little Dorrit*"). Citing examples from other Victorian novels, Colatrella demonstrates the contemporary preoccupation with wrongful convictions and cruel prison conditions. She illustrates the variety of social, psychological, and institutional prisons in Dickens's novel. Finally, Colatrella links Little Dorrit to the tantalizing figure of another innocent convict in the novel, Arthur's biological mother.

Heidi Slettedahl Macpherson's essay takes us from the nineteenth century into the twentieth and back again ("Prison, Passion, and the Female Gaze: Twentieth-Century Representations of Nineteenth-Century Panopticons"). Her essay on twentieth-century novelistic treatments of nineteenth-century panopticons begins with a explanation of Michel Foucault's interpretation of Jeremy Bentham's prison model in which the incarcerated would be subject to the warden's gaze at all times. Macpherson demonstrates how the image of the panopticon – as explicated by Foucault – with its omnipresent male warden's gaze upon its inmates has been subverted in Angela Carter's *Nights at the Circus*, Margaret Atwood's *Alias Grace*, and Sarah Waters's *Affinity*. In these novels by women writers, inmates respond to surveillance with touch, by taking control of the objectifying gaze that attempts to control them visually, and finally by escaping panoptic boundaries.

Jacqueline Berben-Masi also makes reference to the panopticon in her description of the structure of the prison novel she discusses ("Percival Everett's *Glyph*: Prisons of the Body Physical, Political, and Academic"). Her essay introduces the reader to Percival Everett's postmodern novel *Glyph* and analyses it as an indictment of the systematic racism in American society and penal practice. Despite these heavy-weight themes, the novel is nevertheless humorous, playful, and parodic. Berben-Masi's essay uses John Edgar Wideman's description of his brother Robby's imprisonment in *Brothers and Keepers* as an intertextual tool for opening up the novel's theme of how African Americans are made infantile captives in the system that imprisons them. Everett employs mimicry, deconstruction, and a variety of text types in a 'performance' rather than an analysis of the predicament of the genius child Ralph who finally must disguise his talents to avoid imprisonment.

Foucault's *Discipline and Punish* (1979) again informs the essay on British and American prison films that follows the one on *Glyph.* Jan Alber extends Foucault's analysis of disciplinary techniques as a "technology of power over the body" to describe four types of corporal experiences of imprisonment that occur in prison movies and, with the exception of 'the hole,' in real prisons as well: these are the bodily experience of the guards, that of the regular inmates, the prisoner's experience of solitary confinement, and what he feels when he is put in 'the hole' ("Bodies Behind Bars: The Disciplining of the Prisoner's Body in British and American Prison Movies"). Each of these categories describes an increasingly harsh set of circumstances in which punishment is experienced as a form of sensory deprivation. Alber's analysis of prison films is relevant to a critique of contemporary penal institutions because, for better or worse, most individuals now gain their knowledge of prisons from movies or fictional television shows about them.

The last essay in our volume describes real experiences of being confined in 'a hole,' in this case South Africa's Robben Island, where opponents of apartheid were imprisoned as quasi slave laborers ("Caliban Revisited: Robben Island in the Autobiographical Record"). Monika Fludernik's essay on autobiographical accounts of imprisonment on Robben Island shows how the island has come to be at once an image of "the worst excesses of the apartheid state" and conversely a mythic symbol of "African resistance," a site where prisoners supported and educated each other collectively. The essay points out that Robben Island prison memoirs display more of the topoi of holocaust or gulag literature than those of other prison autobiographies. Although humiliation tactics and other inhumane abuses of the prisoners are recorded in these memoirs, their emphasis is on endurance rather than individual suffering. Fludernik uses Caliban's story to disclose the way in which the Robben Island memoirs represent an analogue of the Shakespearean colonial scenario. In this version of the story Caliban is first punished with enslavement for trying to rebel against Prospero. Yet the record he writes of his sufferings under Prospero helps to awaken the world to his plight and ultimately aids him in throwing off the bonds of apartheid.

6. Closing Remarks

Before turning to the essays themselves, we wish to briefly review how these texts 'do Law and Literature' in the variety of ways that were described in conjunction with critical legal studies and Posner's typology of law-and-literature studies. All of the essays printed here undertake to read literary texts in terms of their implications for cultural practices (and not, and here we differ with Posner, as metaphorical reflections on legal antimonies). Rather than seeing the 'reflection' of law in literature, contributors treat primary texts as vehicles for cultural production and exchange. This is true, for instance, of Houswitschka's analysis of the literary and legal discourses surrounding the High Treason Trials of 1794, just as it is for Lauterbach's study of the construction of social identities in Victorian prison texts. Fludernik's essay on South African accounts of imprisonment likewise presents a direct challenge to Posner's assertion that literature is of only marginal interest to the law. The autobiographical writings she analyzes contributed to international awareness and even the eventual dismantling of the systemized injustice and cruelty of apartheid. Affirming an insight made by Bruce Rockwood, her contribution shows that "in many nations and cultures without a functioning democratic life, writers are the only political opposition" (1998: 24).

Making a methodological move familiar from critical legal studies, a number of contributors to this volume expand the realm of texts considered pertinent to law to include a wider range of discursive practices. Lederer, Lauterbach, and Fludernik in her essay on Robben Island as well as Berben-Masi with reference to Wideman, all work with forms of life-writing (hagiography, biography, and autobiography) as supplements to those texts now considered canonical in literature-and-law studies, such as Shakespeare's *Measure for Measure* (1604), *The Merchant of Venice* (1596-97), Charles Dickens's *Bleak House* (1852-53), and Herman Melville's *Billy Budd* (1891/1924). Furthermore, in his study of US prison films Alber expands the boundaries of Law and Literature to include non-print media.

Following another trajectory of CLS, Lauterbach's contribution justifies the assertion that legal institutions serve to reify social divisions based on class, race, and ethnicity. His essay goes beyond unearthing hitherto suppressed stories about the suffering of the incarcerated. Instead, prisoners in their autobiographical self-representations may in fact contribute to cultural practices of stigmatizing other inmates as criminal, by arguing that they themselves are radically different from those who 'deserve' to be in jail.

Like Alan Hyde (CLS), Houswitschka and Kayman demonstrate with their essays the overlaps and points of mutual influence between legal and fictional texts. Their treatments of *Caleb Williams* also address questions of legal censorship of literature (Posner's fourth category). Both essays demonstrate that the end of the eighteenth century marked a period in which notions of fictionality, legality, and the authority of narratives were being fought out in the novel as well as the courtroom. Kayman's essay in particular reveals how law and literature were in a state of flux in their relation to one another at the close of the century. Moreover, this contribution incorporates insights of postmodern critical legal scholars by scrutinizing the linguistic underpinnings of law. Additionally, Giovanopoulos, Houswitschka, and Kayman read legal texts through the lenses of critical textual method. Hence their work conforms to what Posner categorizes as the second form of law-and-literature scholarship. Whereas Posner dismisses the usefulness of this type of work, these contributors discover political, historical, and literary implications in their parsing of eighteenth-century legal trial and impeachment documents and thereby amply justify this approach.

Those essays that roughly correspond with Posner's first category – that is, they treat literary texts with legal themes – do more than highlight the difference between, for example, positive and natural law. When literature is interpreted in light of how it reacts to contemporary legal practices, as in Hesse's article on British courtroom dramas, then it is viewed as a manifestation of larger cultural trends and attitudes towards legal institutions. Hence Colatrella's reading of *Little Dorrit* also records the general nineteenth-century fear that innocent citizens could be victimized by a legal machinery that was clearly fallible. Olson's reading of Shakespeare's trial scenes likewise suggests that institutional forms of authority were, during the early modern period, being internalized by individual people in their cognitive schemata. The same is true of the analyses by Macpherson and Berben-Masi. Macpherson's paper documents twentieth-century feminist reactions to masculinized power structures of an earlier era, while Berben-Masi's essay on *Glyph* shows the novel to be a parodic response to the variety of ways in which African-American men perceive themselves to be incarcerated in and by American society. Shaw's analysis of changing visions of the prison also provides a contribution to cultural history in that it highlights the symbolic qualities of these portrayals and their implications for the process of modernization. Finally, Fludernik's essay on carceral metaphors uncovers the myriad ways in which images and aspects of imprisonment inform and are projected onto experiences that are seen as restrictive or confining. All these essays elude Posner's first category – literature merely mimetically reflecting the law as it occurs in real-life contexts – in that they read the instances of real-world legal practices in the texts they treat within the wider horizon of discursive, psychological, political, and imaginative epistemes (to use a Foucauldian term).

This takes us to the subject of Foucault and the panopticon, a concept that has been nearly all-powerful in analyses of the prison and other disciplinary practices in the past twenty years (Foucault 1979; Bender 1987). It may have struck readers as odd that the introduction did not place more emphasis on Foucault's work or on Jeremy Bentham's original proposals for an architectural solution to prison discipline and criminal reform. In fact, only Macpherson's paper in this volume is directly inspired by Bentham's model and its repercussions in the cultural imaginary of the twentieth century. This is perhaps the place to explain why so few of the essays have turned to Foucault or to Bentham for their theoretical framework. We believe that the answer to this question lies in the fact that nearly all of the analyses of incarceration conducted in this volume attempt to refine and modify Foucauldian insights either by indirection or by complementation. Thus, although the disciplining of prisoners is clearly central to Alber's paper, he describes much more radical ways of disciplining than those envisaged by Foucault, who was after all discussing the late eighteenth and early nineteenth centuries in his study. Many essays also take account of the fact that panoptic prisons did not actually exist in England, even though some of Bentham's ideas fed into early to mid-Victorian prison architecture. Most contributors are also more interested in literary and thematic aspects of texts about imprisonment, focusing on the innocent accused or wrongfully convicted inmate, on prison metaphors, the individual artist's representation of incarceration, and on the wider social and societal significance of this theme. Such wider repercussions of imprisonment need not necessarily take the shape of Foucauldian epistemes. What the essays in this collection imply is that Foucault needs to be supplemented by a series of studies that enquire into the representations of criminality and imprisonment and into their discursive functions and ideological commitments. These insights will ultimately have to be re-aligned with levels of discursive formations that are comparable with Foucault's theses, but for the moment are not yet as clearly placeable within Foucault's account of successive discourse formations in *The Order of Things* (1970).

The ghost of Foucault also accounts for the manifestly political nature of the contributions in this volume. From this perspective, we are therefore closer to critical legal studies than to more traditional versions of law-and-literature or literature-and-law as instantiated by Posner and Weisberg, respectively. On the other hand, these historical and political interventions are deeply embedded in attentive readings of the discursive (and mostly) literary surface structure of the texts treated in the various papers of this volume. The ideological purport of these texts and their real-world referents and effects cannot, indeed, be responsibly discussed outside their generic, linguistic, stylistic, rhetorical, metaphorical, and topical manifestation. Our conviction is not only that legal texts and legal frameworks depend on language, whether in their textuality or in their speech act function, but that literature participates in ideological and discursive moves that invoke the norms and traditions of legal practices and that literary discourse may be complicit in creating images of exclusion, even while it at the same time allows for the subversive undermining of these very norms and traditions. As Margaret Cavendish, Duchess of Newcastle, put it in 1664:

> The truth is, it [i.e. Eloquence] can make Men like Gods or Devils, as having a Power beyond Nature, Custom and Force, for many times the Tongue hath been too Strong for the Sword, and often carried away the Victory; also it hath been too Subtil for the Laws as to Banish Right, and to Condemn Truth; and too hard for the Natures of Men, making their Passions its Prisoners: and since Eloquence hath such Power over Arms, and Laws, and Men, as to make Peace or War, to Compose or Dissolve Commonwealths, to Dispose of Souls and Bodies of Mankind, wherefore those men that are indued with such Eloquence and overflowing Wit, are both to be Fear'd and Lov'd, to be highly Advanced or utterly Banished; for those whose Eloquent Wit out-runs their Honesty, are to be Punished, but those that employ their Eloquent Wit and Elegant Graces, to the service of the Commonwealth, are to be Esteemed, Respected, and Relied upon, as Pillars of the Commonwealth. (Cavendish 1664: 54-55; qtd. Fitzmaurice 2002: 187-88)

This passage from Margaret Cavendish's *Social Letters* expatiates on the topic of eloquence, contrasting legitimate and illegitimate persuasion in the figures of angelic voices and devilish strategies of deception. Yet her account can also be applied to the ideological manipulation of discourse at large. The extract furthermore mirrors the central scenarios of trial and punishment. It calls for the reward of the virtuous and the punishment of the wicked, idealizing the wise and the just (the godly figure of the judge) while at the same time criminalizing those that hinder the course of justice. Conversely, eloquence – what we have called discourse – enthralls the listener, keeping its audience captive. Like the law, language (which in Cavendish's account should serve the law and the commonwealth) much like Sin in orthodox Christian accounts imprisons men (or, rather, their passions). It is a dangerous supplement to the law, to justice, and to reason; it is the instrument of the wicked but also the lifeline of the innocent. (Remember St. Thomas More's memorable metaphor in Robert Bolt's *A Man for All Seasons* [premiered 1960], where he compares the law to a forest whose trees shield him from the rough wind. Yet later that very same law was manipulated by the minions of Henry VIII and ultimately felled him.) Like the relationship of literature and the law, the marriage of law and language can be represented as an apotheosis fraught with the threat of its own subversion. Goldilocks's defense lawyer might plead for mercy and sing the praises of charity to the destitute. Her prosecutor, on the other hand, might well call for retribution, invoking the wrath of the law and the jury's justified outrage at her crimes. According to the prosecution's closing remarks, the jury members are 'the just' and need no forgiveness themselves. Hence they do not need to "forgive those that trespass against us."

Works Cited

Abbott, Jack Henry (1982 [1981]) *In the Belly of the Beast: Letters from Prison*. Intr. Norman Mailer. New York: Random House.

Amnesty International (1998) *USA: Hüter der Menschenrechte*. Bonn: AI, Sektion der Bundesrepublik Deutschland.

Amnesty International (2003) "Guantánamo Bay: Justice for All at Camp Delta." *Amnesty International News Release*. 24 October 2003. <http://www.amnestyusa.org/news/ 2003/uk07182003.html>.

Armstrong, Ken and Steve Mills (1999a) "Death Row Justice Derailed: Bias, Errors and Incompetence in Capital Cases have Turned Illinois' Harshest Punishment into its Least Credible." The Failure of the Death Penalty in Illinois, 2. *Chicago Tribune*, (14 November): 1.

Armstrong, Ken and Steve Mills (1999b) "Inept Defenses Cloud Verdicts with their Lives at Stake, Defendants in Illinois Capital Trials Need the Best Attorneys Available." The Failure of the Death Penalty in Illinois, 2. *Chicago Tribune* (15 November): 1.

Armstrong, Ken and Steve Mills (1999c) "The Inside Informant." The Failure of the Death Penalty in Illinois, 3. *Chicago Tribune* (16 November): 1.

Armstrong, Ken and Steve Mills (1999d) "A Tortured Path to Death Row." The Failure of the Death Penalty in Illinois, 4. *Chicago Tribune* (17 November): 1.

Armstrong, Ken and Steve Mills (1999e) "Convicted by a Hair." The Failure of the Death Penalty in Illinois, 5. *Chicago Tribune* (18 November): 1.

Ball, Milner S. (1999) "All the Law's a Stage." *Cardozo Studies in Law and Literature* 11.2: 215-21.

Bell, Derrick (1999) "The Power of Narrative." *Legal Studies Forum* 23. 3: 315-48; also available at Law in Popular Culture Collection – E-texts. 10 November 2003. <http://tarlton.law. utexas.edu/ lpop/etext/lsf/bell23.htm>.

Bell, Ian (1991) *Literature and Crime in Augustan England.* London: Routledge.

Bender, John (1987) *Imagining the Penitentiary: Fiction and the Architecture of Mind in Eighteenth-Century England.* Chicago, IL and London: Chicago Univ. Press.

Böker, Uwe und Christoph Houswitschka, ed (1996) *Literatur, Kriminalität und Rechtskultur im 17. und 18. Jahrhundert. Tagung am 17. und 18. Juni 1994 an der Technischen Universität Dresden.* Essen: Die Blaue Eule.

Böker, Uwe and Julie A. Hibbard ed. (2001) *Processes of Institutionalisation: Case Studies in Law, Prison and Censorship.* Essen: Die Blaue Eule.

Böker, Uwe, Richard Corballis and Julie A. Hibbard, ed. (2002a) *The Importance of Reinventing Oscar: Versions of Wilde during the Last 100 Years.* Amsterdam and New York: Rodopi.

Böker, Uwe and Julie A. Hibbard ed. (2002b) Sites of Discourse – Public and Private Spheres – Legal Culture. Amsterdam and New York: Rodopi.

Brombert, Victor (1978) *The Romantic Prison. The French Tradition* [*La prison romantique. Essai sur l'imaginaire. 1975*]. Baltimore, MD: Johns Hopkins Univ. Press.

Buffard, Simone (1973) *Le froid pénitentiaire. L'impossible réforme des prisons.* Paris: Seuil.

Cavendish, Margaret (1664) *CCXI Sociable Letters, written by the Thrice Noble, Illustrious, and Excellent Princess, the Marchioness of Newcastle.* London: William Wilson.

Campbell, Duncan. "Anger Grows as US Jails its Two Millionth Inmate." *The Guardian* 15. Feb. 2000. 5 February 2001. <www.guardian.co.uk/Archive/Article/0,4273,396344,00_html>.

Cardozo, Benjamin N. (1947 [1925]) "Law and Literature." *Selected Writings of Benjamin Nathan Cardozo.* Ed. Margaret Hall. New York: Fallon.

Christie, Nils (1993) *Crime Control as Industry: Towards GULAGS, Western Style?* London: Routledge.

Churchill, Ward (1992) "The Third World at Home: Political Prisons and Prisoners in the United States." *Cages of Steel: The Politics of Imprisonment in the United States.* Ed. Ward Churchill and J. J. Vander Wall. Washington, DC: Maisonneuve Press. 1-21.

Cotterill, Janet (2003) *Language and Power in Court: A Linguistic Analysis of the O. J. Simpson Trial.* Houndmills: Palgrave.

Cover, Robert M. (1986) "Violence and the World." *Yale Law Journal 95.* 1601-1629.

Denvir, John (2000 [1997]) "Law, Lawyers, Film & Television." *Law and Popular Culture.* – E-texts. 10 November 2003. <http://www.law.utexas.edu/lpop/etext/lsf/denvir24.htm>.

Dickens, Charles (1996 [1852-52]) *Bleak House.* Oxford: Oxford Univ. Press.

Dickens, Charles (1996 [1860-61]) *Great Expectations.* Boston and New York: Bedford Books of St. Martin's Press.

Dickens, Charles (1997 [1850]) *David Copperfield.* Oxford and New York: Oxford Univ. Press.

Dimock, Wai Chee (1996) *Residues of Justice: Literature, Law, Philosophy.* Berkeley, CA: California Univ. Press.

Dolin, Kieran (1999) *Fiction and the Law: Legal Discourse in Victorian and Modernist Literature*. Cambridge: Cambridge Univ. Press.

Douzinas, Costas, Peter Goodrich and Yifat Hachamovitch, ed. (1994) "Introduction: Politics, Ethics and the Legality of the Contingent." *Politics, Postmodernity and Critical Legal Studies*. London and New York: Routledge. 1-31.

Duncan, Grace Martha (1996) *Romantic Outlaws, Beloved Prisons. The Unconscious Meanings of Crime and Punishment*. New York: New York Univ. Press.

Faller, Lincoln B. (1993) *Crime and Defoe: A New Kind of Writing*. Cambridge: Cambridge Univ. Press.

Fitzmaurice, Susan M. (2002) *The Familiar Letter in Early Modern English. A Pragmatic Approach*. Pragmatics & Beyond. NS, 95. Amsterdam: John Benjamins.

Fludernik, Monika (1999) "Carceral Topography: Spatiality and Liminality in the Literary Prison." *Textual Practice*, 13.1: 43-77.

Fludernik, Monika (2003a) "Literarische Funktionen von Kriminalität." Ed. Michael Walter, Hans-Jörg Albrecht, and Harald Kania. *Alltagsvorstellungen von Kriminalität*. Münster: Lit. (in print).

Fludernik, Monika (2003b) "The Prison as World – The World as Prison: Theoretical and Historical Aspects of two Recurrent Topoi." *Symbolism* 3: 145-90.

Fludernik, Monika (forthcoming) "'Stone Walls Do Not a Prison Make': Rhetorical Strategies and Sentimentalism in the Representation of the Victorian Prison Experience." *Captivating Subjects: Writing Confinement, Citizenship and Nationhood in the Nineteenth Century*. Ed. Julia Wright and Jason Haslam. Toronto: Univ. of Toronto Press.

Foucault, Michel (1970 [1966]) *The Order Of Things: An Archeology of the Human Sciences*. New York: Vintage.

Foucault, Michel (1979 [1975].) *Discipline and Punish. The Birth of the Prison* New York: Vintage.

Galsworthy, John (1911[1910]) *Justice: A Tragedy in Four Acts*. London: Duckworth.

Garland, David (2000) "The Culture of High Crime Societies. Some Preconditions of Recent 'Law and Order' Policies." *British Journal of Criminology* 40: 347-75.

Garland, David (2001) *The Culture of Control. Crime and Social Order in Contemporary Society*. Oxford: Oxford Univ. Press.

Gladfelder, Hal (1997) "Criminal Trials and Narrative Realism, 1650-1750." *Prose Studies* 20.3: 21-48.

Goodrich, Peter (1990) *Languages of Law: From Logics of Memory to Nomadic Masks*. London: Weidenfeld and Nicolson.

Goodrich, Peter (1994) "*Jani Anglorum*: Signs, Symptoms, Slips and Interpretation in Law." *Politics, Postmodernity and Critical Legal Studies*. London and New York: Routledge. 107-44

Grey, Thomas C. (1991) *The Wallace Stevens Case: Law and the Practice of Poetry*. Cambridge, MA: Harvard Univ. Press.

Grisham, John (1993) *The Client*. New York: Doubleday.

Grossheim, Lucius (2001) "Beispiele für Aussagen US-amerikanischer Gefängnisinsassen im Internet." *Deutsch-Amerikanischer Almanach* 10: Der amerikanische Strafvollzug. 24 October. <http://daa.amerikanistik.net/daa10/ aussagen.html>.

Grossman, Jonathan (2002) *The Art of Alibi: English Law Courts and the Novel.* Baltimore, MD and London: Johns Hopkins Univ. Press.

Hallinan, Joseph T. (2001) *Going up the River: Travels in a Prison Nation.* New York: Random House.

Heger, Sabine (2001) "Die Debatte um die Struktur und Organisation moderner Frauengefängnisse in den USA." *Deutsch-Amerikanischer Almanach* 10: Der amerikanische Strafvollzug. 24 October 2003. <http://daa.amerikanistik.net/daa10/frauengefaengnisse.html>.

Highfield, Roger (2003) "Nobel Prize Winner to Fight US Terror Rules." *The Daily Telegraph* (9 October). 23 November 2003. <http://www.telegraph.co.uk/news/main.jhtml?xml=/news/2003/10/09/wnobel09.xml&sSheet=/news/2003/10/09/ixworld.html>.

Hyde, Alan (1997) *Bodies of Law.* Princeton, NJ: Princeton Univ. Press.

Grigg-Spall, Ian and Paddy Ireland (1992) "Introduction." *Critical Lawyers Handbook* Vol 1. Ed. London: Pluto, 1992. 3 November 2003 <http://freespace.virgin.net/suzanne.boyce/ files/book1/introduction.htm>.

Joyce, James (1974 [1916]) *A Portrait of the Artist as a Young* Man. Harmondsworth: Penguin.

Kastan, David Scott (1986) "Proud Majesty Made a Subject: Shakespeare and the Spectacle of Rule." *Shakespeare Quarterly* 37: 459-75.

Kayman, Martin A. (2002) "Law-and-Literature: Questions of Jurisdiction." *REAL Yearbook of Research in English and American Literature 18: Law and Literature*. Ed. Brook Thomas. Tübingen: Gunter Narr Verlag. 1-20.

Kennedy, Duncan (1983) "Legal Education as Training for Hierachy." *Legal Education and the Reproduction of Hierarchy: A Polemic Against the System.* Cambridge: Afar. 3 November 2003. <http://www.nclg.mcmail. com/23.htm>.

Kidd, Colin (2003) "Smut-Finder General." *London Review of Books* 25.18 (25 September): 11-12. [= review of James Morone, *Hellfire Nation: The Politics of Sin in American History*. New Haven, CT: Yale University Press, 2003.]

Kornstein, Daniel J. (1994) *Kill All the Lawyers? Shakespeare's Legal Appeal.* Princeton, MA: Princeton Univ. Press.

Lakoff, George (1994) *Women, Fire, and Dangerous Things: What Categories Reveal about the Mind.* Chicago, IL: Univ. of Chicago Press.

Lakoff, George and Mark Johnson (1980) *Metaphors We Live By*. Chicago, IL: Univ. of Chicago Press.

Langbein, John (1978) "The Criminal Trial Before the Lawyers." *The University of Chicago Law Review* 45.2: 263-316.

Langbein, John (2002) *The Origins of Adversary Criminal Trial.* Oxford: Oxford Univ. Press.

Laqueur, Thomas (2000) "Festival of Punishment." *London Review of Books* (5 October): 17-24.

Lauterbach, Frank (forthcoming) "'From the Slums *to* the Slums': The Delimitation of Social Identity in Late Victorian Prison Narratives." *Captivating Subjects: Writing Confinement, Citizenship and Nationhood in the Nineteenth Century.* Ed. Julia Wright and Jason Haslam. Toronto: Univ. of Toronto Press.

Legally Blonde (2001) Dir. Robert Luketic. MGM.

Legally Blonde (2003) Dir. Charles Herman-Wurmfeld. MGM.

Levinson, Sanford (1988) "Law as Literature." *Interpreting Law and Literature: A Hermeneutic Reader*. Ed. Sanford Levinson and Steven Mailloux. Evanston, IL: Northwestern Univ. Press: 155-73.

Lupa, Karsten (2001) "Haftbedingungen in US-Gefängnissen." *Deutsch-Amerikanischer Almanach* 10: Der amerikanische Strafvollzug. 24 October 2003. <http://daa.amerikanistik.net/daa10/haftbedingungen.html>.

Melossi, Dario and Massimo Pavarini (1981 [1977]) *The Prison and the Factory: Origins of the Penitentiary System*. Trans. Glynis Cousin. London: Macmillan, 1981.

Murphy, Tim (1994) "As If: *Camera Juridical*." *Politics, Postmodernity and Critical Legal Studies*. Ed Douzinas et al. London and New York: Routledge. 69-106.

Nussbaum, Martha C. (1995) *Poetic Justice: The Literary Imagination and Public Life*. Boston, MA: Beacon Press.

Polloczek, Dieter Paul (1999) *Literature and Legal Discourse: Equity and Ethics from Sterne to Conrad*. Cambridge: Cambridge Univ. Press.

Posner, Richard (1998 [1988]) *Law and Literature: A Misunderstood Relation*. Revised and Enlarged Ed. Cambridge, MA: Harvard Univ. Press.

Pratt, John (2000) "The Return of the Wheelbarrow Men; or, the Arrival of Postmodern Penalty." *British Journal of Criminology* 40: 127-45.

Ranney, Frances (1999) "Posner on Legal Texts: Law, Literature (Economics), and 'Welcome Harassment.'" *Un-Disciplining Literature*. Studies in the Postmodern Theory of Education. Ed. Kostas and Linda Myrsiades. New York and Berne: Lang. 94-116.

Richardson, Samuel (1833 [1751]) *The Works of Samuel Richardson*. Ed. Leslie Stephen. Vol. 3: *The History of Clarissa Harlowe*. London: Henry Sotheran.

Richetti, J. J. (1992) *Popular Fiction Before Richardson, Narrative Patterns, 1700-1739*. Oxford: Clarendon.

Rockwood, Bruce L. (1998 [1996]) "Introduction: On Doing Law and Literature." *Law and Literature Perspectives*. Critic of Institutions. Ed. Bruce L. Rockwood. New York: Lang. 1-37.

Schönert, Jörg et al. (1983) *Literatur und Kriminalität. Die gesellschaftliche Erfahrung von Verbrechen und Strafverfolgung als Gegenstand des Erzählens. Deutschland, England, Frankreich 1850-1880*. Tübingen. Niemeyer.

Schönert, Jörg et al. (1991) *Erzählte Kriminalität: Zur Typologie und Funktion von narrativen Darstellungen in Strafrechtspflege, Publizistik und Literatur*. Tübingen: Niemeyer.

Sedley, Stephen (2003) "Howzat?" *London Review of Books* (25 September): 15-17.

Shichor, David and Dale K. Sechrest ed. (1996) *Three Strikes and You're Out: Vengeance as Public Policy*. Thousand Oaks, CA: Sage.

Steiner, George (1984) *Antigones*. Oxford: Oxford Univ. Press.

The Verdict (1982). Dir. Sidney Lumet. Starring Paul Newman. Twentieth Century Fox.

Thomas, Brook (1991) "Reflections on the Law and Literature Revival." *Critical Inquiry* 17 (Spring): 510-39.

Thomas, Brook (1987) *Cross-Examinations of Law and Literature: Cooper, Hawthorne, Stowe, and Melville.* Cambridge: Cambridge Univ. Press.

To Kill a Mockingbird. (1962) Dir. Robert Mulligan, Universal.

Tonry, Michael ed. (1998) *The Handbook of Crime and Punishment.* New York/Oxford: Oxford Univ. Press.

Turner, Victor (1986) *The Anthropology of Performance.* New York: PAJ Publications.

U.S. Census Bureau (June 2001) *Introduction to Census 2000 Data Products.* 24 October 2003. <www.census.gov/prod/2001pubs/mso-01icdp.pdf>.

Ward, Ian (1995) *Law and Literature: Possibilities and Perspectives.* Cambridge: Cambridge Univ. Press.

Watt, Ian (1957) *The Rise of the Novel: Studies in Defoe, Richardson, and Fielding.* Berkeley, CA: California Univ. Press.

Webster, John (1986 [1612]) *The White Devil.* London: Methuen.

Weisberg, Richard (1988) "Coming of Age Some More: 'Law and Literature' Beyond the Cradle." *Nova Law Review* 13.1: 107-24.

Weisberg, Richard (1992) *Poethics, and Other Strategies of Law and Literature.* Columbia, NY: Columbia Univ. Press.

White, James Boyd (1994a) *Acts of Hope: Creating Authority in Literature, Law, and Politics.* Chicago, IL and London: Chicago Univ. Press.

White, James Boyd (1994b) "The Ethics of Meaning." *The Happy Couple: Law and Literature.* Ed. J. Neville Tuner and Pamela Williams. Sydney: Federation Press. 286-95.

Williams, Patricia (1991) *The Alchemy of Race and Rights.* Cambridge, MA: Harvard Univ. Press.

Wordsworth, William (1947 [1839]) "Sonnets Upon the Punishment of Death." *The Poetical Works of William Wordsworth. Vol. V.*. Ed. Ernest de Selincourt and Helen Darbishire. Oxford: Clarendon. 135-41.

Ziolkowski, Theodore (1997) *The Mirror of Justice: Literary Reflections of Legal Crises.* Princeton, NJ: Princeton Univ. Press.

PART ONE: TRIALS

"DO YOU PROMISE TO TELL THE TRUTH, THE HALF TRUTH OR NOTHING ABOUT THE TRUTH.....?"

Captain Kidd and the King: Piracy and Politics in Restoration England

Anna-Christina Giovanopoulos

Introduction

One film has gained the approval of mass audiences around the world in the mostly uneventful cinematic summer of 2003: *Pirates of the Caribbean: The Curse of the Black Pearl* (USA 2003). This blockbuster adapts the genre of the pirate movie for the twenty-first century, but it is witness to the continued fascination with a (romanticised) vision of piracy. This fascination is nothing new. In 1724, the enigmatic 'Captain Johnson' published his *General History of the Pirates* in London. This compilation, a sub-genre of the criminal biography, described the careers of some fifteen pirates and their crews. An immediate popular success, it went into several revisions, and, in 1728, a second volume appeared. According to critic J.A. Moore, the *History* "has created the modern conception of pirates" (Moore 1939: 127). Such famous characters as Captain Teach, alias Blackbeard, feature prominently. Yet among the pirates that twenty-first century readers and movie-goers most readily recognize, Captain Kidd takes pride of place. However, in his time, William Kidd was more than the archetypal pirate. He was used as a tool in the fierce political struggles between Whigs and Tories in the late 1690s and early 1700s.[1] The opposition exploited the fact that Whig politicians, among them Lord Somers of the leading Whig 'Junto,' had financed Kidd in 1695 to fight pirates. When Kidd became a pirate himself, the opposition attempted to prove in law courts that he had done so under Whig orders. The Kidd affair made 'much noise in the world' (*Bloody Register* 1999: 55). In May 1701, the captain was finally tried at the Old Bailey for murder and piracy. He was convicted and executed. Lord Somers, by contrast, was tried by his peers in Westminster Hall and found not guilty in June 1701.

After introducing the concept of law and literature, I will first describe the historical context of Captain Kidd's trials. Then I will discuss how the events leading to these trials were represented by eighteenth-century criminal biographies, namely by the *General History of the Pirates* (1728) and by the *Bloody Register* (1764). Next, I will analyze how the legal system was (ab)used for the purpose of ousting political rivals within the context of the Kidd affair. To illustrate this thesis I will analyze (a)

1 Modern scholarship reasserts the importance of divisions between Whigs and Tories under William (Holmes 1993: 335-336).

the controversial case of Captain Kidd, tried in four separate trials, and (b) two impeachments for High Crimes and Misdemeanors of the Whig lords Orford and Somers by the House of Commons in 1701. I will focus on the economic and political interests involved. It will be shown that, by implicating King William III in the proceedings, the Commons attempted to curb royal prerogative and to advance their powers. In conclusion, I will assess how the literary texts and the trial reports intersect with law and politics.

The pervasiveness of the law in the eighteenth century has been noted by scholars such as J. A. Sharpe (1984) or E. P. Thompson (1975). But in order to analyze the precise circulation processes between law, literature, and politics, it is useful to differentiate between internal and external legal cultures (Friedman 1975). The internal legal culture is characterized by a high degree of institutionalization and, as a specialized system, is concerned with law and legal practice. Circulation processes between the internal legal culture and other social systems create the external legal culture. To achieve political and social stability, the norms and values of the internal legal culture need to become an integral part of the external legal culture. This is accomplished through processes of habitualization. *Rechtsbegleitende Literatur* (see Drexler 1991), i.e. literature that accompanies and comments on legal decisions, plays an important part in this effort. While the law could be inscribed on the body through the spectacle of punishment, a wider audience was reached through literary texts, such as 'last dying speeches' and criminal biographies. Especially after the lapse of the licensing act in 1695, the print market grew rapidly, and cultural knowledge could circulate more widely. Heteroglossic literature did not, however, necessarily stabilize norms: "Literature's role in society is thus never simply passive, recording or documenting practices and procedures, but always interventionist, seeking to stabilize or destabilize the prevailing distribution of power and allocation of meanings" (Bell 1991: 229).

While analyzing the function of 'law' in criminal biographies and in trial reports, political and economic issues need to be addressed which manifest themselves in terms of power struggles between various players. Göhler (1997)[2] distinguishes between transitive and intransitive power based on the concepts of 'power over' and 'power to' (Pitkin 1972: 276-78). 'Power over' means the ability of one person to impose his/her intentions on another person, thereby limiting the latter's options to act (40; Weber 1976: I § 16). However, transitive power should not be confused with 'violence' (Arendt 1970), i.e. unmitigated control. When one person exerts power, the other person is not powerless; there may even be a balance whereby the actors limit each other's power. Values and regulatory principles are generated in interactions that enable and guide communication and, ultimately, create society (Göhler 1997: 43). To attain permanence these common values must be expressed symbolically. Only when they become permanent and visible (as they do, for instance, in criminal biographies) do they attain integrative power (44). 'Power to,' or intransitive power, on the other

2 Göhler, who specializes in political theory, develops a model to analyze (contemporary) political structures; his typology of power, however, also helps to explain eighteenth-century society on an abstract level.

hand, is concerned with the community itself; it comprises an ensemble of relations that transform a group of people into a community (41). Intransitive power such as the law may be generated through transitive power, i.e., it takes its origins in individuals' interactions; but transitive power is self-referential, and this communicative model is the precondition for entering into social relations (see Arendt 1970: 45).

Based on such concepts, power struggles are discussed in this paper: in the criminal biographies, narrators exert their powers as the presenters of evidence; in the trials and in the impeachment proceedings power becomes highly visible, although actors try to deny their power objectives by referring to the intransitive power of the 'law.' In late seventeenth- and early eighteenth-century England, political institutions were struggling to solidify their positions; asymmetrical power relations determined the interactions between King and Parliament, Commons and Lords, and, especially in the courtroom, between judges, prosecutors and defendants. Stephen Greenblatt has shown the importance of theatricality for the exercise of power (Greenblatt 1999: 46, 50). In the drama of the courtroom the "privileged visibility" of power becomes obvious. However, Greenblatt has also pointed out that power produces its own ambiguities and tensions, in fact, that the "apparent production of subversion is [...] the very condition of power" (65; see 136). Greenblatt has identified three modes of subversion and their containment: testing (of cultural fears), recording (of conflicting voices) and explaining (64). In the courtroom as in the literary accounts analyzed in this paper, I will focus on the mode of recording. Power records multiple voices because it

> [...] is not monolithic and hence may encounter and record in one of its functions materials that can threaten another of its functions; in part that power thrives on vigilance, and human beings are vigilant if they sense a threat; in part that power defines itself in relation to such threats or simply to that which is not identical with it. (37)

In the analysis of the legal trials, two additional forms of power will emerge: the power of (re)definition and the power of obstruction. In the trials of Captain Kidd, the power over evidence and the definition of meaning provides the analytical focus; in the impeachment proceedings against Lord Somers, the Lords proved their ability to resist by obstructing the Commons.

Historical Background: Piracy and Trade

In the late seventeenth century, piracy was a threat to English trade and to the reputation of England. Especially important trading partners from the Mughal Empire, ruled by Emperor Aurengzeb, readily accepted the view spread by England's economic rivals, France and Holland, that all pirates were English and that the East India Company was in collusion with them (Ritchie 1986: 107). Trade was vital for the development of England's military power (Brewer 1994: xx), and trading companies constituted an important economic force. The (Old) East India Company was among the most powerful institutions (Miege 1703: 246). However, the Company suffered heavily from piracy in the Red Sea and in the Indian Ocean. Whenever there was a new attack, the Indian rulers of the Mughal Empire closed trading posts temporarily (Winston 1969: 116), imprisoned Company representatives for certain periods, and imposed fines. Aurengzeb repeatedly approached the English merchants to demand compensation for losses suffered from pirates and to ensure protection from future attacks. Finally, the Company pressed the English government for action (Ritchie 1986: 137). However, Company interests collided with the interests of colonial governors in America. Due to the restrictions imposed by the Navigation Acts,[3] piracy became an economic factor, and colonial merchants traded regularly with Madagascar-based pirates who attacked the prosperous trade in the Indian Ocean (Winston 1969: 33).

The Admiralty, whom the East India Company asked for support, was caught between conflicting interests. Moreover, during the Nine Years' War the Admiralty did not have enough ships to assist the Company (Winston 1969: 117). They might have commissioned a privately financed ship. Yet in defense to the charge that they had obstructed the fight against pirates, the Admiralty claimed that it was not possible to commission privateers to fight pirates (Hargrave 1777: 342). 'Privateers' received a 'letter of marque' that allowed them to attack enemy ships legally. To keep privateers within the bounds of law, they were forbidden to appropriate booty for their own use prior to 'legal condemnation': captured ships and goods had to be presented to an Admiralty court where the prizes were valued; goods were returned to owners if possible, and the rest was distributed among Admiralty, King, and privateers (Winston 1969: 17-18). This rule made privateering an interesting economic venture.

When the government did not fund a ship to hunt the pirates in 1695, some Whig politicians stepped in and employed Kidd as captain. However, in mid-1697 Kidd became a pirate himself, and the East India Company had even more reason than usual to complain to the Government. The Company knew that some anonymous, probably Whig, financiers were involved. Trade and politics were intimately linked, and the (Old) East India Company was associated with the Tory interest, while the government at that time was dominated by Whigs who supported William. By collecting evidence against Kidd, the Company (Ritchie 1986: 137, 186-187) not only prevented future economic loss, but also succeeded in casting the Whigs in a bad light. The political opposition took up the issue and attempted to use the Company's evidence in the campaign to remove the Whig Junto from its position of power.

A General History of the Pirates

In the early eighteenth century, the difference between fact and fiction was not clearly established (see Davis 1983). While fiction carried negative associations, "the respectable use of narrative was in history, in all its guises. If an author wished to

---

3 The various Navigation Acts (of 1651, 1660, 1662; see also 1696) were designed to uphold a "national monopoly of the internal carrying trade and of colonial markets" (Brewer 1994:168), thus reducing Dutch hegemony. Basically, the acts required ships carrying goods between the American colonies and England to be English-built and -owned. In addition, three-quarters of the crew had to be English (Holmes 1993: 440-441).

fabulate in narrative [...] he had to cloak his artistry, conceal his creative presence behind a mask of literal verisimilitude" (Boardman 1983: 2). Thus, compilers of criminal biographies and early novelists emphasized the truth of their accounts, and, as in a legal trial, supported their claims with 'evidence,' such as eye-witness accounts and confessions of criminals. The *General History of the Pirates* follows this paradigm (*History* 1999: 7-8; see McKeon 2002: 100). But first, a note on attribution must be made: The Defoe scholar J. A. Moore wrote in 1939 that the *History* "was substantially Defoe's work throughout" (Furbank/Owens 1988: 133-34). However, Furbank and Owens, who have radically revised the Defoe canon (see 14-15), find no evidence that the work really is Defoe's.[4] Nevertheless, Gladfelder believes that if the stylistic characteristics used by previous bibliographers to determine Defoe's authorship are not singularly attributable to Defoe, then other authors were influenced by his "nuanced, elaborate representations of criminal subjectivities" (Gladfelder 2001: 98).

The *History* tells how Kidd was employed to fight pirates and on what legal grounds his commissions stood (*History* 1999: 1728: 440-42); then the focus turns on Kidd's voyage and piratical exploits (442-48). The narrative concludes with a highly condensed report from the trials (448-51). This structure already points to the hybridity of the account: historical documents are either summarized or quoted in full length, but a coherent narrative at the center avoids the monotony of a trial account that seeks to reconstruct the 'truth.' Instead, the reader is presented with a lively narrative characterized by stylistic variation and value judgments that are sometimes at odds with the professed aim of exposing the pirate.

In the opening paragraph, the narrator states that Kidd is known as a famous pirate. However, the public "could [not] account for his turning Pyrate" (*History* 1999: 440). This statement promises that the narrator will reveal Kidd's motives, thus creating suspense. Kidd is introduced as a "brave Man" who proved his worth as a seaman in 'King William's War' (1689-1697), alternatively known as the 'Nine Years' War.' As pirates became a threat to English ships, Lord Bellomont, styled the "Governor of Barbadoes," and "several other persons" who are not named, suggested that the government employ Kidd to fight the pirates because he was "acquainted with all their lurking Places" (ibid.). However, the government did not act, and the narrator criticizes "the Politicks" for their reluctance to combat piracy (ibid.). Instead, private enterprise took the initiative. Yet the narrator finds fault with this solution, stating that "the Lord *Bellomont* and some others" acted not for the public good but to increase their property, knowing "what a prodigious wealth must be in their [the pirates'] possession." Kidd's financial backers wanted to fight the pirates merely to get access to the booty which they planned to keep. "[T]o give the Thing a greater Reputation" (441), a 'King's Commission' (26 January 1696) was procured, which is quoted in full (441-42). Kidd had already received one commission by the Admiralty that enabled him to attack enemy trade; William now commissioned him to capture pirates as well as their booty.

---

4 See Cordingly (1998), esp. notes pp. 365-366 for a discussion of the maritime knowledge of 'Captain Johnson.' See also Schonhorn (1999: 709-712).

How does the *History* deal with Kidd's process of turning a pirate? Initially (1695), Kidd acted honorably; he sailed to New York (1696) where he hired more men. No reason is given why Kidd first went to New York and not to Madagascar where the pirates he was charged to hunt had their base. The narrator stresses that until Kidd reached the Indian Ocean (1697) it did "not appear [...] that he had the least Design of turning Pyrate"; he "did not offer the least Violence, tho' he was strong enough to have done what he pleas'd" with rich Indian ships (443). The narrator acts like a judge who carefully investigates the evidence. He grants: "[T]he first Outrage of Depredation I find he [Kidd] committed upon Mankind" was to rob natives of corn at "*Mabbee*, upon the *Red Sea*" (ibid.). Later, the narrator intervenes again: He repeats that Kidd "first meant well" and planned to pursue pirates, but when he did not find them, his mood changed. The narrator unequivocally casts Kidd's unnamed backers as the actual villains. He alleges that Kidd was afraid of the financial consortium that had fitted out his ship:

> [...] weary of ill Success, and fearing least [sic] his Owner, out of Humour at their great Expences, should dismiss him, and he should want Employment, and be mark'd out for an unlucky Man; rather, I say, than run the Hazard of Poverty, he resolved to do his Business one Way, since he could not do it another. (444)

Yet the narrator does not accept this as mitigating evidence.

The narrative continues with Kidd's murder of his gunner Moore and describes the attacks on ships of several nationalities, culminating in the capture of the *Quedah Merchant*, a "Moorish Ship of 400 Tuns richly loaden" (446). The biography resumes the story with Kidd's return from Madagascar (where he had befriended pirates) to New England (1699). Now the narrator criticizes Kidd and imposes his moral authority: he questions Kidd's judgment and claims that he wrongly relied on the protection of Lord Bellomont and on "one or two" French passes (448) allegedly found aboard the prizes.[5] Yet the narrator does not believe Kidd's version of events. He further asserts that Kidd assumed the profit he had made would "gain him new Friends" (ibid.), i.e., more protection from prosecution for piratical offences. Instead, Bellomont arrested Kidd immediately on his arrival in New York. Kidd was taken to London (1700) and tried in May 1701, over a year after his capture (ibid.). This lengthy imprisonment was unusual and points to the existence of political entanglements that delayed the trials.

In the last part of the text, the narrator relies on published trial reports. However, he changes the order of events: he begins with the acquittal of three minor characters, providing two paragraphs on legal detail. Then he turns to Kidd and those men of his who were found guilty of all offences. Here the focus is on the verdicts, and the narrator chooses a few passages in which legal views are explained (449). Kidd's trial for the murder of Moore is noted in one short sentence (ibid.). Kidd's defense to the five charges of piracy is condensed (450), and his use of character witnesses is

5 The presence of the French passes would have proven that Kidd had attacked only enemy ships, which he was entitled to do as a privateer. For an explication of the legal argument see below.

mentioned (450-51). The report ends with re-asserting the power of the judges' story and the narrator's dictum: "[T]he Evidence being full and particular against him, he was found guilty as beforementioned" (451). The account concludes with Kidd's claim that "he had been sworn against by perjured wicked People," and a laconic sentence about Kidd's execution. According to common use, his body was hung up in chains (ibid.). Authority was thus re-established.

The Bloody Register

The *Bloody Register* focuses not on piracy but on politics. Political entanglements are noted frequently, and even the names of Kidd's financial backers are revealed. The account begins with Kidd's conviction for piracy in 1701 and then carefully constructs a negative image of Kidd, who is described as a "very insignificant fellow." Slurs are made on his birth, his talents and his physical appearance: he looks "rather like a butcher than a seaman; and his manners were brutal to an uncommon degree." From the beginning, Kidd is excluded as the criminal 'other' who warrants no admiration. Kidd's morals are also exposed to criticism: he only claimed to be honest while he was actually consorting with pirates before he officially became one of them several years later (*Bloody Register* 1999: 55). To further illustrate Kidd's subversive potential, the narrator establishes that only Kidd was responsible for any repercussions on his backers, i.e., for their impeachment by the House of Commons: "[...] his foolish and vicious behaviour drew a great deal of trouble upon those who honoured him with their protection" (ibid.).

A few events from Kidd's piratical career are briefly summarized in a matter-of-fact manner. Then the account turns to politics. The narrator boldly states that the charges brought against Somers, one of Kidd's financiers, were "intended purely to hurt that lord's character, and render it impossible for his majesty to employ him longer in his service" (61). The narrator then returns to Kidd and quotes from the Ordinary's Account. There is a reference to Kidd's last dying speech and a description of his behavior during his execution. Executions and last dying speeches can be interpreted as ways to re-integrate the criminal into society and to contain their subversive potential. Kidd, however, refused to oblige: He became "inflamed with drink, which had so discomposed his mind, that it was very unfit for the great work before him, and not so concerned and affected as he ought to have been" (*Bloody Register* 1999: 62). The ordinary was dissatisfied with the sinner who was "unwilling to own the justness of his condemnation." However, when the rope broke in the first attempt to hang Kidd, the ordinary again urged Kidd to repent; Kidd allegedly cooperated (63). Thus, finally, power over even as dangerous a criminal as Kidd was restored.

In the preceding analyses I have focused on the economic and political issues that were involved in the 'Kidd affair.' I will now discuss Kidd's actions and his connections with the Whigs. As Hayden White has pointed out, historians, like authors, construct a narrative; however, whereas the narrators discussed above were not limited to facts, historians base their stories on verifiable documents and archival sources (see Fludernik 2001: 88-89). On the other hand, biographies cannot be used as historical sources without accounting for their bias and narrative strategies.

Politics

Two key questions emerge: why were powerful Whig politicians pursued so vigorously by the opposition; and why did the Whigs become so vulnerable to attacks by the opposition, who had to win a majority in the House of Commons before they could initiate legal proceedings against Somers and others on the grounds of – essentially – corruption. In 1688-1689, Parliament *de facto* deposed James II, brother of Charles II; James II fled to France. William of Orange, married to Charles II's eldest daughter Mary, ascended the throne. Soon after his accession, he was threatened by James II and his French troops. In 1689, William joined the League of Augsburg, an anti-French alliance comprised of the United Provinces ('Holland'), Spain, Austria and lesser German states. William declared war on France, which was to last until 1697. The Nine Years' War formally ended with the Treaty of Ryswick. However, the balance of power in Europe was still not decided. In an attempt to further limit the influence of Louis XIV, a secret 'Partition Treaty' was negotiated in 1698 between Britain, France and the United Provinces. One of the issues settled in the treaty was the succession to the Spanish throne: Joseph Ferdinand, Electoral Prince of Bavaria, was to become king of Spain rather than the Duke of Anjou, grandson of Louis XIV. After the death of Prince Ferdinand, a second Partition Treaty (1700) was signed between the three parties; now Archduke Charles (of Austria) was to receive Spain after the death of the present king (see Holmes 1993: 229-233).

In contrast to many of his continental counterparts, William could not rule independently of Parliament. As military leader the king was absent from London for much of his reign; thus he relied on ministerial government. Yet whenever he believed ministers to be falling short of his expectations, he exchanged them (Jones 1991: 257). Even though he tried to limit the power of parties, during the war he needed the support of the Whigs, who were usually successfully managed by the so-called 'Junto.' The Junto featured several talents: John Somers, Charles Montagu, Edward Russell, Charles Spencer, and Thomas Wharton. One of the most brilliant constitutional lawyers of his time (Nenner 1995: 107), John Somers "brought to their partnership peerless intellect and great moral strength," and was, furthermore one of the Lords Justices responsible for the kingdom when William was abroad. Charles Montagu, First Earl of Halifax, saw to the financial side and was a renowned orator (Holmes 1993: 345). Edward Russell, 1st Earl of Orford, had served as an Admiral and was the navy administrator (345-346). Charles Spencer, 3rd Earl of Sunderland, excelled in "energy, drive and manipulative skills" (346), and Thomas Wharton (elevated to the ranks of earl and later marquess) was an indispensable party manager (346).[6] Since the Junto had secured the funding for the war during the period of 1693-1697, they became associated with it and were criticized for the negative effects of taxation and

---

6 The first three were impeached by the Commons in 1701.

the maintenance of a standing army. These financial requirements were seen as a burden especially on the landowners; a standing army was associated with the 'despotism' of France and was perceived as an infringement on the rights of the people. A firm 'country' opposition, as it is termed, made up of Tories and opposition Whigs, emerged (Jones 1991: 271). In the parliamentary session 1697-1698, it became obvious that the Junto's sway over parliament had declined. Since William believed that the Junto had failed in securing his privileges in Parliament, he stopped supporting it, and its members resigned one by one (278).

In 1700, France refused to honor the (second) Partition Treaty; instead, Louis XIV claimed the Spanish throne for his grandson, thus raising fears among other nations that France would reach hegemony in Europe. Further, in 1701 France supported the claims of Charles, son of James II, to the English throne. A new war (England, the United Provinces and Austria against France) became imminent (Miege 1703: 344-45), but Parliament had to agree to finance this undertaking. However, power relations within Parliament changed in favor of the Tories who gained in the elections of January 1701. To secure their goodwill, William had to make certain concessions. For example, he had to withdraw his protection of former confidants (see Oldmixon 1716: 54; Holmes 1993: 200). Thus, by early 1701, the Tories were strong enough to challenge the power of the Whigs. One of their tactics involved voicing the allegation that Somers and others had supported Kidd's piratical exploits for personal financial gain.

Kidd and the Whigs

Let me now turn to Kidd's piratical career[7] and his association with the Whigs. William Kidd was born in Scotland. He became a respectable citizen of New York where he was entangled in Whig politics (Ritchie 1986: 34-35, 39-49). In 1695, Kidd went to London to obtain command of a ship in the navy, but without success. Instead he met Robert Livingston, who wanted to get back possessions he had lost in New York during the upheavals of the Glorious Revolution. Livingston learned that the Earl of Bellomont, backed by the Whigs, had been appointed as governor to Massachusetts initially and later also to New York (Ritchie 1986: 48). Bellomont wanted to prove his worth by fighting pirates. As Livingston needed Bellomont's good will to retrieve his property, he told the new governor of Kidd, who knew most of the "Chief Pyrates" and their haunts (Oldmixon 1716: 78). The idea was to fund a privateer and to be rewarded by the prizes Kidd would capture. Bellomont, Livingston, and Kidd entered into a contract or 'agreement' (10 October 1695; see Ritchie 1986: 52). To raise capital, Bellomont included the merchant Sir Edward Harrison (53). In a second version of the contract, more partners appeared who also sought to make money. However, these partners did not give their real names; instead, the names of surrogates "were used in Trust" (Hargrave 1777: 335). Thus, the new backers hoped to remain anonymous. But their hopes were in vain, and their identity

7 For details see Brooks (1930); Winston (1969); Ritchie (1986); Zacks (2002).

was finally revealed. They were prominent Whigs: Lord John Somers (then Lord Keeper of the Great Seal), the Duke of Shrewsbury (then Secretary of State), Edward Russell, Earl of Orford (then First Lord of the Admiralty), and Henry Sidney, Earl of Romney (then Master General of the Ordnance) (Winston 1969: 117). Kidd sailed under the two commissions mentioned in the *History*: the Admiralty Commission entitled him to attack the French as enemy trade (11 December 1695; Hargrave 1777: 307-308), and the King's Commission instructed Kidd to hunt the Red Sea for other pirates (26 January 1696; 308-309). Kidd was to keep an exact record of his actions in a journal and was supposed to bring the pirates to legal trial. However, the consortium could not simply keep all the prizes taken by Kidd. Only William III could grant this privilege of retaining the booty in full. To induce the king to agree to the deal, Shrewsbury suggested that William reserve a share of ten percent for himself. The deal was established privately, without the involvement of the usual administrative channels (Ritchie 1986: 54), thus creating a further reason for laying the transaction open to censure by parliament.

Kidd first went to New York. On the way to America, he captured a French prize, the only legal one he ever took. After the interlude in New York, Kidd sailed to the Indian Ocean where he attacked several ships. These acts of piracy as well as several other actions led to indictments against Kidd and were reflected in the specific charges made against him in his four trials. Kidd's first (successful) piratical act was – as was also recorded by the *History* – to forcefully enlist Captain Parker as his pilot and a Portuguese sailor as an interpreter (6 September 1697; 3rd indictment, 3rd trial). Kidd then killed his gunner William Moore in an argument (1st indictment, 1st trial). Later Kidd attacked several ships of various nationalities. No French-owned ship was among them, the only ships that he as an English privateer might lawfully attack. Instead, Kidd turned mostly against 'Moorish' ships. First was the *Maiden* (27 November 1697; 4th indictment, 3rd trial), a 'Moorish' ship captained by a Dutchman; second a 'Moorish ketch' (28 December 1697; 5th indictment, 4th trial); and third, one 'Portuguese ship' in January 1698 (6th indictment, 4th trial). On 30 January 1698, Kidd's actions culminated in his seizing the *Quedah Merchant* (2nd indictment, 2nd trial). In May 1698, Kidd arrived at Madagascar, the base of the Red Sea pirates, where instead of attacking the pirates, he fraternized with them. This episode was discussed during the trials as a proof of Kidd's amicable disposition towards pirates. Kidd remained at St. Marie, a settlement on the island, until late 1698.

The first authentic news of Kidd's activities reached London in August 1698. On 23 November 1698, the East India Company complained to the Lords Justices (Brooks 1930: 26), who instructed colonial governors to arrest Kidd (Ritchie 1986: 165). While at Madagascar, Kidd learned that he had been exposed as a pirate and sought to extricate himself by agreeing with his loyal men on an exculpatory narrative. In June 1699, Kidd arrived in America and started negotiations with Bellomont, who arrested the pirate in July and not immediately on his return to New England as claimed by the criminal biographies.

While Kidd had been to the Indian Ocean, the climate towards his patrons had worsened in London. The Junto realized that the East India Company was moving against Kidd, and by November 1698, it began taking action (Ritchie 1986: 187; 189-

191). Complex measures and countermeasures were introduced in and out of Parliament. Now the public learnt of William's grant of the booty to some unknown backers: The "*Faction* immediately clamour'd against the *Illegality* of the Commission and Grant, and would fain have had it believ'd that the Grantees were Confederates with the *Pyrate* Kidd" (Oldmixon 1716: 81). In December 1699, Robert Harley's[8] attempts to question the legality of the grants were defeated. But his view that "the Grant was dishonourable to the King, against the Law of Nations, contrary to the Laws and Statutes of this Realm, Invasive of Property, and Destructive of Trade and Commerce" (ibid.) appeared in the articles of impeachment drafted by the House of Commons against Somers and Orford in 1701. Hectic pre-trial events took place in connection with Kidd, with Tories and Whigs attempting to gain control over the evidence (Ritchie 1986: 193, 197; Oldmixon 1716: 82). Kidd was taken to England and kept in Newgate (April 1700-May 1701), for most of the time under close confinement (Ritchie 1986: 198).

In March 1701, the Kidd issue resurfaced, and as the Commons investigated the alleged affair, Kidd was interviewed twice in May (Ritchie 1986: 203). He "had nothing to say, which in any sort answer'd the Expectations of those who gave the Information [that Kidd would give evidence against the Whigs], or were so forward to send for him" (Oldmixon 1716: 84; see 85-86, 87-88). As he showed himself unwilling and incapable of offering proof against the Whig lords, the Commons lost interest in him. However, they continued to impeach several Whig lords and included the association between Kidd and the Junto in one of the 'articles,' i.e., accusations (83-84). These proceedings were pivotal in English political history as they ended the confused period in William's reign in which allegiances had cut across party lines (Speck 1994: 8). But before articles of impeachment were exhibited, the trials of the uncooperative Kidd took place on 8 and 9 May 1701.

The Trials of Captain Kid

The following sections are based on the 1777 edition of the *State Trials*. These verbatim reports of procedures do not belong to the internal legal culture. Rather they represent an important medium for the circulation of norms as they are directed at the external legal culture. Readers who did not turn to the more lurid examples of the criminal biography could find instruction and probably entertainment in the *State Trials* (see also Langbein 1978: 264-67).

Kidd was tried on five indictments in four trials held on two days (see above). One indictment was for murder (Kidd had killed his gunner); the other indictments against Kidd and nine of his men were for piracy. The trials feature much repetition; the reiteration of evidence was inevitable because the admiralty presented the same two witnesses to different juries. The witnesses were two former crew members of Kidd, Bradinham and Palmer, who had left their captain at Madagascar in 1698. They were

8 Due to a Tory/Court Whig alliance, Harley became Speaker of the House of Commons in February 1701 (Speck 1994: 23). Harley later led Anne's government; Daniel Defoe was closely associated with Harley (Sill 1983: 56-58).

promised a royal pardon, which they received after Kidd's trial (Ritchie 1986: 207; 291-92). It was customary for one jury to retire to consider the verdict while another trial began. Thus, the prosecution offered the same contextual evidence in all trials, even though different leaders for the prosecution appeared. The capture of the *Quedah Merchant* had caused many problems for the East India Company, because the ship had been leased to a close friend of Emperor Aurengzeb. Hence Kidd became the symbol of all the problems the Company was having with the pirates and the Mughal Empire (Ritchie 1986: 135). Thus, the Company had a great interest in gaining a conviction against Kidd and proving to Aurengzeb that they were serious about their war against pirates. Acknowledging the importance of the *Quedah Merchant* affair, the prosecution planned to begin proceedings against Kidd with charges connected to this piratical act. However, when Kidd successfully pleaded that he needed more time to prepare his defense, the trial for the murder of Moore was moved ahead (see Hargrave 1777: 290). The events surrounding the *Quedah Merchant* trial and the way the trial was staged clearly show the intersection between politics, trade, and law. For this reason, I focus on this trial in the following.

All the trials of Captain Kidd (and his men) involved an impressive array of judges and prosecutors. Renowned judges and admiralty lawyers united their talents, and through number and knowledge the prosecutors established their dominance. The trial for piratical acts against the *Quedah Merchant* was well managed. As Sir Charles Hedges, Chief Judge of the High Court of Admiralty, had warned earlier:

> Since Foreigners look upon Decrees of our Courts of Justice as the Sense and Judgement of the whole Nation, our Enemies will be glad to find an Occasion to say, that such Miscreants [...] are out of the Protection of all Laws [...]. The barbarous Nations will reproach us as being a Harbour, Receptacle, and a Nest of Pirates. (Ritchie 1986: 136)

In the *Quedah Merchant* trial, the prosecution showed more enthusiasm than in the trial for the murder of Moore. Dr. Newton made the opening speech for the prosecution and revealed himself to be a skilled orator. He lent much more flourish to the proceedings than his colleague in the first trial, an indication of how important convicting Kidd was. Newton implied that Kidd had never intended to act honestly according to his commissions – thus implicitly exonerating his financial backers – and he presented his claim with a well-developed sense of suspense (once even in Homeric dactyls); his narrative was lively, but was characterized by omissions, simplifications and generalizations (Hargrave 1777: 299-300). Newton unfolded all of Kidd's actions, even though the second indictment was only concerned with the *Quedah Merchant*. Thus, he emphasized Kidd's negative impact on trade and foreign relations. In finding Kidd guilty, the jury would convict a person "than whom no one in this Age has done more Mischief" (300), and

> [...] do Justice to the injured world, the *English* Nation (our common Country), whose Interest and Welfare so much depend on the Encrease and Security of Trade, and, lastly, to yourselves, whom the Law has made Judges of the Fact. (Ibid.)

Another member of the prosecution team, 'Crown Counsel' Coniers, directed the evidence and led his two witnesses through the whole narrative. The prosecution had great leeway in reconstructing Kidd's deeds. Only rarely did Justice Powell ask Coniers to stick to the specific indictment and not to get carried away with discussing further piratical acts (302). However, the relationship between Kidd and the pirate Culliford was analyzed in detail. Capturing the pirate would have been a task covered by the second commission, even though Kidd was not formally charged with anything in this connection. By constantly referring to the amity between Culliford and Kidd, the prosecution tried to establish the latter's piratical intentions.

Kidd's lack of control over the evidence was aggravated by the fact that according to legal rules he could not give evidence on his behalf nor could he use his men as witnesses while they were being tried under the same indictment (Brooks 1930: 43; see Langbein 1978). All he could do was to point out contradictions by cross-examining witnesses for the prosecution, relying on character witnesses and, in the few instances when a legal point could be made, using lawyers. In matters of fact, Kidd stood on thin ice: he could not prove witnesses for the prosecution were lying, and his own narrative was not believed. The Admiralty's witnesses remained unperturbed throughout Kidd's attacks on their honesty. Kidd relied in his defense on the fact that the *Quedah Merchant* had carried a French pass, which he claimed made her a French ship and therefore a legal prize (see also *History* 1999: 448). But as Kidd was unable to produce the French passes or at least bring forth witnesses that these papers had ever existed (see Hargrave 1777: 307, 309), his defense remained unconvincing.

The issue of the passes displays how evidence could be tampered with during pre-trial events when power relations came into play. Kidd gave the two French passes to Bellomont who sent them to Secretary Vernon, a Whig; the passes appeared among the papers delivered to the Commons. On Kidd's request, the Commons allowed him to receive his papers, but the passes were not among them. According to Ritchie's assessment, Vernon might have kept the passes deliberately to prevent Kidd from defending himself properly. Had Kidd produced the passes, this might have made his conviction more difficult; an acquittal would have sent out the wrong signal to Aurengzeb. Kidd's claim, that "Bellomont stript me of ye French passes, frightened and wheedled some of my men to misrepresent me, and by his Letters to his friends here Advised them to admit me a pyrate" (quoted in Ritchie 1986: 209) seems exaggerated. Closer to the point was this charge:

> If ye design I was sent upon, be illegal, or of ill consequence to ye trade of ye Nation, my Owners who knew ye Laws, ought to suffer for It, and not I, whom they made ye Tool of their Covetousnesse. Some great men would have me dye for Solving their Honor, and others to pacify ye Mogull for injuryes done by other men. (210)

Having failed twice to provide the Tories with any evidence against the Whig lords, Kidd could not count on politicians to help him. Further, it should be noted that even though the French passes were considered material to Kidd's defense both by himself and by the prosecution, the actual value of the passes is doubtful (Brooks 1930: 43-45,

47). It was common practice for merchant ships to carry a number of passes enabling them to assume nationalities as circumstance warranted. When Kidd approached ships flying a French flag and produced a French member of his crew as captain, as he did in one instance, his victims had to suppose that they were being attacked by a French privateer; they therefore responded by assuming a French identity (Brooks 1930: 45). Even if the French passes might have changed the verdicts in two cases, the absence of the papers did not influence the verdict in the other cases.

The juries found Kidd guilty in all four trials. All Kidd had to say in the end was: "My Lord, It is a very hard Sentence: For my Part, I am the innocentest Person of them all, only I have been sworn against by Perjured Persons" (Hargrave 1777: 338). His final attempt to obtain the attention of Robert Harley failed (Ritchie 1986: 221). On 10 May Judge Oxenden saw King William who decided that Kidd should hang while the others awaited a pardon (220-221). Kidd was executed on 23 May 1701. With him out of the way, the impeachment proceedings could gain pace.

Impeachments

'Impeachments' (see Jones 1991: 32) were criminal proceedings initiated by Parliament, typically against royal ministers. Impeachments were used regularly in the seventeenth and early eighteenth centuries to check the power of ministers. After 1678 the King could not reverse the judgment of Parliament. The importance of such trials declined towards the end of the eighteenth century, as shortcomings of the procedure became obvious during the impeachment of Warren Hastings (1788-1795). That "Impeachments are in themselves proper and necessary Checks to arbitrary Ministers" (*Method* 1715: 65) was a truth beyond dispute in the late seventeenth and early eighteenth centuries. Yet contemporaries were quick to add that often

> [...] the Differences which have happened between the two Houses of Parliament in the Course of Impeachments, have proceeded more from the Temper of some leading Men on each Side than the Nature of the Impeachments themselves. (66-67)

A more balanced assessment is offered by Geoffrey Holmes, who finds that in the three decades after the Revolution politicians did not favor compromise. Their dedication to a cause explains the "ferocity of warfare" in politics at that time (Holmes 1993: 346). But it was important to give actions the "color of law," and law became "a weapon that both sides [Whigs and Tories] used in the political battles [...]; control of the law was the political prize for which both sides fought" (Nenner 1995: 255). The House of Commons had "to Redress Grievances, and Ease the People of Oppressions" through the "Grand Inquest of the Realm" (Miege 1703: 419), i.e., through impeachments, which made "*Parliaments* to be a great Check to Men in Authority, and consequently abhorred by Delinquents" (420). The Commons was responsible for charges and evidence, the lords acted as judges: "And such is the Priviledge of the House of Commons in this Particular, that they may impeach the highest Lord in the Kingdom, either Spiritual or Temporal" (ibid.).

In the impeachments of 1701, the Commons criticized close advisors to William. However, the attacks were not carried out vigorously. The Commons was apparently mostly content to voice their opinion. They engaged with the Lords in power struggles over the respective rights of the two Houses and over the definition of legal concepts. The only impeachment procedure that reached the trial stage was that of Somers. The accusations concerned his behavior in the negotiations of the Partition Treaties that regulated the succession to the Spanish throne. King William had been the prime mover in these negotiations; he had by-passed Parliament and thus had not followed the principles established in the Glorious Revolution. But the Commons could not attack the King himself as that would have constituted the crime of High Treason, which was punishable by death. Instead, they concentrated on Lord Somers, who repeatedly pointed out his passive role in the negotiations. In the following section of the paper, I will focus on the impeachment articles relating to Captain Kidd in the proceedings against Orford and Somers.

The proper procedures began on 1 April 1701 with the impeachments of Portland,[9] Somers, Orford and Halifax (Hargrave 1777: 339). The House of Lords immediately asked the king "not to pass any Censure upon them [the four lords], until they are tried upon the same Impeachments, and Judgment be given according to the Usage of Parliament and the Laws of the Land" (340). A long round of exchanges between the Lords and the Commons began: the Lords urged the Commons to exhibit articles of impeachment or to finally make good the charges, while the Commons pointed to their privileges as prosecutors: they insisted on deciding without interference from the Lords when to deliver their accusations and deliberately took their time to draft the articles. When the articles against Orford finally arrived on 9 May (the second day of Kidd's trials), article 5 related to Kidd: it was claimed that Orford had refused to grant "Letters of Mart" (i.e., letters of marque to commission privateers) to those who wanted to suppress pirates in the Red Sea, but had instead used Kidd "who was known to be a Person of ill Fame and Reputation." This remark clearly documents the involvement of the East India Company in the impeachment proceedings. Kidd had embarked on piratical acts "being thereunto encouraged thro' the Hopes of being protected by the High Station and Interest of the said Earl, in Violation of the Law of Nations, and the Interruption and Discouragement of the Trade of *England*" (341). Orford denied all charges on 14 May. As to Kidd, Orford claimed that the Board of Admiralty had no authority to grant letters of marque and that he had informed the East India Company accordingly. The grant of goods to Kidd and his backers was not against the law, and the expedition had been intended for the public good; Kidd had not been known to be "of ill Fame and Reputation," and Orford had neither encouraged Kidd to commit piracies nor promised his protection (342). Somers replied to his articles of impeachment on 14 May. The thirteenth article referring to Kidd established the same facts as article 5 of the impeachments against Orford. Kidd was described as a "Person of evil Fame and Reputation, and since that time convicted of Piracy" for whom Orford, Bellomont, Somers and "others then in high Stations, and

9 No articles against Portland were presented: the impeachment was used as a lever against William who withdrew silently because he needed the support of the Tories.

in great Power and Authority" had procured a commission to seize pirates and their goods (ibid.). The grant received from William to keep the goods

> [...] manifestly tended to the Obstruction and discouragement of Trade and Navigation, the great Loss and Prejudice of Merchants and others [...], and the Dishonour of the King and Kingdom; and the said Lord *Sommers* was, by procuring and passing the said Grant, Guilty of a notorious Breach of his duty. (355)

Somers maintained that in 1695 nothing negative had been known about Kidd (354). As to the grant, the safeguard of keeping an account had been included, and the whole enterprise was undertaken for the public good (356). Also, the king would have received a tenth of the proceeds, proof of the honesty of the enterprise. As Kidd had betrayed the trust of his patrons, no one had gained anything (ibid.).

The proceedings became characterized by a series of increasingly acrimonious exchanges between the Commons and the Lords. The Lords wanted quick trials. The Commons, however, was adamant in claiming its right to decide when and whom to put to trial. Here the problems only began. Both Houses had to decide on proper legal procedures and needed to look for precedents. Finally, the Lords displayed their power over the Commons by setting 17 June 1701 as the date for Somers's trial. They informed the Commons and notified witnesses (374). Also, the king told the Lords that he tried to be helpful in finding papers relating to the "Original [Partition] Treaties." Yet as he did not have them, he "would do what he could towards it" (ibid.).

The Commons, however, did not attend the trial and the Lords did not object; a proclamation was made for the Commons to come forward and make good their charge (375-76). Westminster Hall was cleared, the Lords were called and the articles of impeachment were read with the answers. The House "was ready to hear the evidence." In the absence of accusers, the case was dismissed (378, votes 377-78). The Whigs had won after all, and Parliament turned to more pressing matters such as the impending war with France. A contemporary source reports on William's reaction to the trouble the Whig lords experienced in the wake of the Kidd affair: "That if by the Law of *England* he [William] could be a Witness, he could of his own Knowledge justify the lords concern'd in all they had done in that Affair" (Oldmixon 1716: 90).

Conclusion

Let us turn to the question of how the trial reports and the criminal biographies intersect with law and politics, and thus, with power. The narrators of the *History* and of the *Bloody Register* asseverate the veracity and authenticity of their accounts. Their 'true histories' were written in retrospect and are mainly based on the conflicting narratives presented by Kidd and his various accusers in the actual trials. 'Critical Legal Studies' have pointed out that "law is primarily a language, an interpretative and rhetorical enterprise like literature" (Dolin 1999: 8). Thus, the legal trial can be considered as a hermeneutic mode. Gladfelder argues that "[p]rinted trials reassembled the materials of legal inquiry and judgment into narrative demonstrations of the law's power to locate truth and repair the effects of transgression" (Gladfelder

2001: 59). However, the trials also record dissent: the parties involved are not objective and the law takes a partisan stance. Narrators of the criminal biographies work in a similar manner.

Through the trial reports, both the prosecution and the defense gained a voice. But the asymmetrical distribution of transitive power made Kidd's attempts to legitimate his actions impossible: his version was recorded yet it was already contained in the court room: The prosecution drove home the accusations and proved them to the satisfaction of the jury, and the judges summed up the evidence in the end, while Kidd struggled to extricate himself without success. Even though the judges appear to have wanted to be impartial, their 'charges to the jury' lent greater authority to the stories of the prosecution than to Kidd's narrative. One important difference between interpretation in law and in literature should be noted, namely that "the production and reception of texts within the law takes place within a context of the systemic application of state-sanctioned force" (Dolin 1999: 10). When the jury found against Kidd, he was executed. The only way Kidd might have escaped the repercussions of his piratical actions would have been through the help of the Whigs or the Tories who were struggling for political power. However, Kidd refused to (wrongly) accuse Somers and his other financial backers of any transgressions, thus causing some members of the House of Commons to note with disdain his apparent mental derangement after his long imprisonment in Newgate.

King William's implication in the affair is recorded in the impeachment proceedings against Lord Somers. The Commons carefully drafted articles of impeachment that reflected implicitly on King William's practices; as a more lurid example of corruption, it was alleged that Kidd had been sent on his piratical enterprises to the detriment of English trade. One of the accused lords pointed out that the King was to receive a share of Kidd's booty, proof of the honesty of the undertaking. But this fact is only mentioned in the *Bloody Register* (57), not in the *History* that excluded political complications. However, politics and power struggles did play the overwhelming role in bringing Kidd to trial. The proceedings against Somers were motivated, among other reasons, by dissatisfaction with William's autocratic style and his repeated attempts to bypass Parliament. The fact that the Partition Treaties had been negotiated in secret was used by the Commons to gain a lever against him through accusations of his advisers. Eventually, the House of Lords used their superior power as judges to either acquit or dismiss these charges. They invoked the intransitive power of the law and thus gave 'color of law' to what actually was a fierce political fight. But their victory was ambiguous, because the House of Commons established the legitimate right to criticize the King indirectly in the impeachment proceedings. Furthermore, a wider audience was reached through the publication of the proceedings. To prevent future monarchs from adopting William's independent style of government, several safeguards to curb royal prerogative were included in the 'Act of Settlement' of 1701; limitation of royal power was thus formalized in written law.

The trial reports relating to Captain Kidd established certain facts. Kidd's version that he had only attacked legal prizes and had merely consorted with the pirate Culliford out of fear for his life, was either disregarded or dismissed as 'fiction' by the criminal biographies. The evidence collected by the East India Company who had an axe to grind against the pirate Kidd on economic grounds and against the Whig lords on political grounds, proved superior to anything Kidd could offer.

Once the prosecutors' version of events was established, it was transferred to the external legal culture and taken up in ballads and popular literature. One biography ignored fact almost completely and simple reworked the pirate myth of Captain Morgan (Smith 1719). Yet the two narratives analyzed in this paper fashioned historical facts into selective accounts. Their different aims led to the choices of 'facts' and modes of presentation. The *History* focused on piracy, the *Bloody Register* on political implications. Even though the former appears less biased in its initial refusal to represent Kidd as the villain, it still affirmed his guilt.[10] The *Bloody Register*, on the other hand, followed the lead of Kidd's prosecutors to exonerate his financial backers implicitly. To this end, the narrator excluded Kidd as the criminal 'other' and re-instituted the power of the law. However, the instrumental role of the East India Company was not mentioned.

The comparison of the trial literature with the two biographies has shown how the legal culture expended its influence in literary texts. Eventually, however, politics and economics were marginalized, and the *History*, one of the most influential criminal biographies of Kidd, focused on adventure and entertaining narrative. After all, by the mid-Eighteenth century the political repercussions of the Kidd affair were becoming obsolete.

Works Cited

Arendt, Hannah (1967) *Macht und Gewalt*. München: Piper.

Bell, Ian (1991) *Literature and Crime in Augustan England*. London: Routledge.

Bloody Register (1999 [1764]) *The Bloody Register: A Select and Judicious Collection of the Most Remarkable Trials, for Murder, Treason, [...] and other high Crimes and Misdemeanors. From the Year 1700 to the Year 1764 inclusive*. Vol. 3. Ed. Nick Groom. London: Routledge.

Boardman, Michael M. (1983) *Defoe and the Uses of Narrative*. New Brunswick, NJ: Rutgers Univ. Press.

Brewer, John (1994 [1989]) *The Sinews of Power: War, Money and the English State 1688-1783*. London. Reprint.

Brooks, Graham, ed. (1930) *The Trial of Captain Kidd*. Edinburgh: Hodge.

10 I argue for the containment of subversion in Kidd's biography. An analysis of the complete *General History of the Pirates*, however, would show a tendency towards destabilizing authority.

Cordingly, David (1998) "Introduction." Captain Charles Johnson, *A General History of the Robberies & Murders of the Most Notorious Pirates*. London: Conway. vii-xiv.

Davis, Lennard J. (1983) *Factual Fictions: The Origins of the English Novel*. New York: Columbia Univ. Press.

Dolin, Kieran (1999) *Fiction and the Law: Legal Discourse in Victorian and Modernist Literature*. Cambridge: Cambridge Univ. Press.

Drexler, Peter (1991) *Literatur, Recht, Kriminalität: Untersuchungen zur Vorgeschichte des englischen Detektivromans 1830-1890*. Frankfurt/Main: Lang.

Fludernik, Monika (2001) "Fiction vs. Non-Fiction: Narratological Difference." Jörg Helbig, ed., *Erzählen und Erzähltheorie im 20. Jahrhundert*. Heidelberg: Winter" 85-103.

Friedman, Lawrence M. (1975) *The Legal System. A Social Perspective*. New York: Russell Sage.

Furbank, P. N., and W. R. Owens (1988) *The Canonisation of Daniel Defoe*. New Haven, CT: Yale Univ. Press.

Gladfelder, Hal (2001) *Criminality and Narrative in Eighteenth-Century England: Beyond the Law*. Baltimore: Johns Hopkins Univ. Press.

Göhler, Gerhard (1997) "Der Zusammenhang von Institution, Macht und Repräsentation." Gerhard Göhler et al., ed., *Institution – Macht – Repräsentation: Wofür politische Institutionen stehen und wie sie wirken*. Baden-Baden: Nomos. 11-62.

Greenblatt, Stephen (1999 [1988]) *Shakespearean Negotiations. The Circulation of Social Energy in Renaissance England*. Oxford: Clarendon.

Hargrave, Francis Ed. (1777) *A Complete Collection of State-Trials, and Proceedings for High-Treason, And other Crimes and Misdemeanors*. Volume 5. Fourth Edition. London: T. Wright.

History (1999 [1724-1728]) *A General History of the Pyrates*. [By 'Captain Charles Johnson'; attributed to Defoe by J.A. Moore; de-attributed by Furbank/Owens (1988)]. Ed. Manuel Schonhorn. Revised edition of the 1972 edition. Mineola, NY: Dover Publications.

Holmes, Geoffrey (1993) *The Making of a Great Power. Late Stuart and Early Georgian Britain 1660-1722*. London: Longman.

Jones, J. R. (1993 [1978]) *Country and Court: England 1658-1714*. London: Arnold.

Langbein, John (1978) "The Criminal Trial Before the Lawyers." *The University of Chicago Law Journal* 45: 263-316.

McKeon, Michael (2002 [1987]) *The Origins of the English Novel, 1600-1740*. Baltimore: Johns Hopkins Univ. Press.

Method (1715) *The Method of the Proceedings in the House of Lords and Commons in Cases of Impeachments for High Treason*. London: Roberts.

Miege, Guy (1703) *The New State of England, Under Our Sovereign, Queen Anne, in three parts*. (The 5th edition, with great alterations). London: n. publ.

Moore, John A. (1939) *Defoe in the Pillory and Other Studies*. Bloomington, IN: Indiana Univ. Press.

Nenner, Howard (1995) *The Right to be King. The Succession to the Crown of England, 1603-1714*. London: Macmillan.

Oldmixon, John (1716) *Memoirs of the Life of John Lord Somers*. London. n.p.

Pitkin, Hanna F. (1972) *Wittgenstein and Justice*. Berkeley, Los Angeles, London: Univ. of California Press.

Ritchie, Robert C. (1986) *Captain Kidd and the War Against Pirates*. Cambridge, MA: Harvard Univ. Press.

Schonhorn, Manuel (1999) "Introduction." *History* (1999): xi-xlviii.

Sharpe, J. A. (1984) *Crime in Early Modern England, 1550-1750*. London: Longman.

Smith, Captain Alexander (1926 [1719]) *A Complete History of the Lives and Robberies of the Most Notorious Highwaymen* [...]. Ed. Arthur L. Hayward. Fifth revised edition of the 1714 edition. London: Routledge.

Speck, W. A. (1994) *The Birth of Britain. A New Nation 1700-1710*. Oxford: Blackwell.

Thompson, E. P. (1990) *Whigs and Hunters. The Origin of the Black Act*. Reprint of the 1975 edition. Harmondsworth: Penguin.

Weber, Max (1976 [1922]) *Wirtschaft und Gesellschaft*. Ed. J. Winckelmann. Tübingen: Mohr.

Winston, Alexander (1969) *No Man Knows My Grave: Sir Henry Morgan, Captain William Kidd, Captain Woodes Rogers in the Great Age of the Privateers and Pirates 1665-1715*. Boston: Houghton Mifflin.

Zacks, Richard (2002) *The Pirate Hunter: The True Story of Captain Kidd*. New York: Hyperion.

"Thereupon There Were Produced Three False Witnesses...": Trial Scenes in Elizabethan Sacred Biography

Thomas Lederer

This essay concerns itself with trial scenes in hagiographic texts – i.e. 'saints' lives' in the broadest sense – from the Elizabethan period. Ever since the establishment of the literary genre of Christian sacred biography, trials, courtroom, and interrogation scenes have been a standard, indeed an integral, element of these narratives (Buschmann 1994: 77-78). They usually follow a relatively straightforward scheme: The hostile (pagan or worldly) authority challenges the saint to disown his or her faith. This prompts the saint to express an ardent defense of Christianity, often on the basis of theological and philosophical reasoning. The outcome may be a prolonged disputation on religion between the indomitable saint and the 'theologizing' judge (Günter 1949: 148), which gives the hagiographer an opportunity to air doctrinal statements. In an emotionally charged surrounding, the truth of Christian orthodoxy is opposed to the tenets of the tyrant and thus highlighted for the audience and made more memorable.

Since they are confrontations of the saints and the sinners in which the issue of crime vs. faith is particularly evident, trial scenes are especially appropriate for bringing out mutual structures of demonization and condemnation. In their redaction of trials and judicial executions of martyrs, the writers of sacred biography were centrally concerned with their subjects' presumed criminality. This dilemma of condemnation and veneration is as old as the genre itself. "The concept of martyrdom," writes David M. Loades, "has always presented problems to the Church" (1993: xv). The first men and women invoked as saints were Christian martyrs, who were put to violent death on account of their transgression of the set norms of the Roman state, and because of their refusal, even under severe pressure, to denounce their opinions. Thus, they placed themselves outside the rules respected by most of their contemporaries. Moreover, this process loaded their fellow Christians with the considerable burden of inheriting a tradition that suggested that Christianity meant hostility to legitimate authorities. And yet persecution was soon to become the constitutive act of the young community of believers in a process that may be called the 'dialectics of martyrdom.' Whereas judicial torturing and killing – often deliberately carried out before the public gaze – was generally designed to crush the victims' spirit of resistance and to terrorize others into conformity, it considerably shaped and heightened early Christians' sense of identity. Those whom the authorities expected to be demoralized by illegality and oppression in fact turned out to interpret their position as the winning one, even though all odds seemed to be against them. Defiantly, if paradoxically, Paul proclaimed, "Therefore I take pleasure in infirmities, in reproaches, in necessities, in persecutions, in distresses for Christ's sake: for when I am weak, then am I strong" (2Co 12:10). Tertullian's equally famous dictum about the blood of the martyrs being the seed of the Church – "semen est sanguis Christianorum" (Tert. apol. 50, 13) – defines this paradox in a no less forceful manner. If therefore in the Judeo-Christian tradition the antagonism between the martyr and the persecutor is conceived of as a struggle between truth and power (Dehandschutter 1989), then the martyrs' death is indeed the triumph of truth. It signifies that the follower of God's word has not submitted to the threats of the representatives of worldly domination. These 'dialectics of martyrdom' are reflected in Christian sacred biographies from the Apostles' days to the modern period, whenever saints are presented as defending themselves before institutions of the secular power.

The controversial period in England – the time of religious unrest after Henry VIII's breach with Rome in 1534 – provided hagiographers of either denomination with ample opportunity for telling tales of saints' endurance in trials, be these 'heresy' trials or 'popery' trials. Their situation was not too dissimilar to that of the authors of early Christian sacred biographies. As was the case with the Church's first martyrs and their conflict with the Roman state, the victims of the denominational struggle in Henrician, Marian, Elizabethan, and Jacobean England were indicted for their opposition to the commonweal. Legal proceedings against the heterodox were first and foremost political acts, in which, as in the executions which almost inevitably followed them, the near-absolute power of the secular authority was exerted, even inscribed, on the bodies of its hapless victims – a process by which sovereignty sought to maintain and reaffirm itself (see Foucault 1979: 3-69). Heresy trials in early modern England may actually be, however anachronistically, called 'show trials,' in which the law became, in the words of Margery and Frederick Schauer, a terrifying "engine of state."

This essay explores the narrative strategies employed by hagiographers of the four Elizabethan decades – both Protestant and Roman Catholic –for turning the defendants, prisoners, accused, and executed into the shining heroes of their tales. In the overwhelming majority of accounts they primarily achieve this goal by an inversion of the usual trial-and-condemnation paradigm. This is not surprising, since it is by now almost a truism that the staging of trials and the rituals of punishment contain an inherent potential of subversion and inversion: "In these executions, which ought to show only the terrorizing power of the prince, there was a whole aspect of the carnival, in which rules were inverted, authority mocked and criminals transformed into heroes" (Foucault 1979: 61). Therefore, deliberate inversion of legal power is hardly peculiar to sacred biographies. Rather, a distinguishing feature of trial scenes in saints' legends is the *double* inversion that took place in them. The mere transforming of the criminals into "heroes" which Foucault illustrated in the case of judicial executions in the eighteenth century, was not sufficient for the writers of saints' lives. They needed to criminalize the authority responsible for the saints' persecutions to a degree that far exceeded a simple "mocking" of state power. Hagiography virtually depends on the opposition between saint and anti-saint, a dichotomy that is intrinsic to the text type.

I divide my essay into four sections: After briefly discussing a selection of texts in which the legal procedures in heresy trials and the very institution of English common law are challenged (1), I turn to analyzing the narrative strategies of canonization and demonization employed in Protestant hagiographic trial scenes (2) and their Roman Catholic counterparts (3). The final section summarizes my findings (4). I have chosen highly representative text samples in order to highlight the general tendencies of Tudor sacred biography. There are, of course, cases in which the rhetorical strategies of canonization and demonization appear less clearly outlined and well defined than in these ones. Hagiography, like any other text type, resists all too rigorous categorization.

1. Challenging Legal Procedures and the Common Law

A very interesting type of condemnation occurs when the law itself is considered to be the source of sin. This of course accords with the dualistic thinking and argumentative strategies of hagiographic writers; but viewed in the context of the Renaissance it is far from typical and therefore deserves special attention. Let me begin this section with a brief outline of Elizabethan conventions of trials to ease understanding of the examples to be discussed.

In England, criminal cases were settled through *trial by jury* even before the sixteenth century. On the Continent, jurisdiction was dominated by the principles of Roman law. Most countries of western Europe had adopted a modified version of the Justinian code as part of their national law in the late fifteenth and early sixteenth centuries. Their turn toward Roman law brought with it inquisitorial practices, such as relying on written evidence and confessions extracted under torture, together with the wringing of procedural offices from the hands of laypersons and a thorough 'professionalization' of legal affairs. Yet in England, as opposed to these developments, medieval common law prevailed together with its pattern of criminal trials. J. H. Baker, on whose exhaustive essay on "Criminal Courts and Procedure at Common Law 1550-1800" (1977) I rely in this and the following paragraphs, sketches the latter as follows: "Under the common-law system, the judge merely presided over a public inquest by twelve ordinary folk sworn to find the truth, before whom the accuser and the accused pleaded to issue and produced their evidence and arguments much as they would in a civil suit" (21). The system of trial by jury, in other words, was characterized by public and oral proceedings, examination and cross-examination of witnesses to corroborate the truth of evidence, and a jury of twelve, the defendant's peers,[1] to decide on guilt or innocence.

1 "Peers, for this purpose [scil. a jury], were of two classes only: temporal lords of parliament, and commoners. [...] There was no age limit, but women were by custom excluded. The jurors did not have to be 'peers' of the accused in any particular sense: an esquire could be tried by merchants" (Baker 1977: 23).

Trials took place at the general sessions of the peace, usually called 'quarter sessions,' since they took place four times a year: at Michaelmas (September 29), Epiphany, Easter, and the Translation of Saint Thomas (July 7). They were characterized by the great swiftness with which they were carried out. A case did not usually last more than a couple of hours, and adjournment overnight was virtually unknown before the eighteenth century. This is partly due to certain peculiarities of these trials: Prisoners indicted for felony were usually denied any counsel or legal assistance, i.e. they had to defend their case themselves. Even witnesses for the defense were sometimes considered to be "no more permissible than counsel, because the prosecution case ought to be unanswerable" (38). The purpose of the jury was merely to pronounce the verdict (guilty vs. not guilty) at the end of the trial; judgment itself was not given at once, but at the end of the sessions. One reason for this custom was "neither to allow the judge time to reflect nor the prisoner to squirm, but to allow time to secure a pardon or prepare a motion in arrest of judgment" (40). Even after sentence was passed, the convict might still avert capital punishment, for instance by claiming "benefit of the clergy," i.e. the standard mitigation usually awarded to persons who were able to prove their literacy by reading out a number of verses from the Psalter.

That this order of trials was in accordance with the laws of God and men and judicial sentences were therefore intrinsically legitimate and also just, were well accepted by virtually all authors of the sixteenth century. A fundamental critique of criminal procedure on account of their injustice is hence hardly to be expected in Tudor trial accounts, even those embedded in sacred biography. Suggestive questions by the court, such as the so-called "Bloody Question," are often narrated, yet not commented upon, let alone criticized.[2] The better-known exception to the rule is found in the narratives of Sir Thomas More's trial: the defendant – himself a lawyer – recurrently refers to the illegitimate nature of the proceedings taken against him, a point gratefully taken up by his hagiographers.[3]

Therefore the rare cases in which denominational polemicists do thematize the established rules of legal procedures against 'traitors' and 'heretics' are all the more remarkable. In those cases the authors use two major points of attack. Occasionally, writers comment upon the corruption of individual judges and upon procedural details that are directed against the defendants and make it all but impossible for one indicted for a religious misdemeanor to escape the grip of the law. More rarely, the polemicists' venom is directed at the legal system itself, denouncing it as intrinsically wrong, worthless and actually criminal.

---

2 The "Bloody Question" is most usually the proposing of the following hypothetical case: If the pope deposed Queen Elizabeth, and if he, or any other by his appointment, such as the king of Spain, invaded England, whose side ought a good subject to take then? Such questions concerning the pope's secular power were traps for Catholic defendants, for "because of the different postulates of the accuser and the accused, it was morally impossible for a Catholic to answer them in such a way as to satisfy the judges" (Clancy 1964: 137-38).

3 On the deflections from course of justice during the trials of More and John, Cardinal Fisher see, among others, Schulte Herbrüggen (1978).

Let us first take a brief look at two Elizabethan documents that raise the issue of procedural propriety and judicial misdemeanor, one Roman Catholic, one Protestant. The first of these is *A Treatise Touching the Imprisonment and Indictments of Mr. Francis Tregian, Esquire* (Morris 1872: 65-140). This text is concerned with the fate of a Catholic landed gentleman, who lost his property and was exiled on account of his faith. It contains an interesting passage where the hagiographer reflects on the illegal nature of actions taken against the saint *qua* defendant. Tregian, we read, is accused, imprisoned and tried as a 'papist.' A short time afterwards the still imprisoned Tregian is brought to London to be tried again:

> Now, notwithstanding those other prisoners have been purposely brought, as we have before declared, out of Cornwall to receive their trial in the King's Bench, being only there arraigned; without any more ado, against all order of law, they were also, with Mr. Tregian, sent back to the place from whence they came, that they might there now once again receive trial under the same indictment whereof and wherefore they had once before received judgment. Sic lex lege caret, legumque invertitur ordo.
>
> Thus wholesome laws of States they stay,
> The use of Laws doth lack;
> Thus, thus all order is untwined,
> Which breedeth woeful wrack. (Morris 1872: 108)

In this text the anti-saintly judges violate the legal principle of *ne bis in idem* ('not twice for the same'), one of the basic premises of the English judicial system. The hagiographer scolds them for twisting the established order of things and for upsetting the foundations of procedural law: "Thus, the law lacks legality, the order of laws is overthrown." By actively influencing the legal procedure to the disadvantage of the defendant and by assuming power which they do not have, the authorities inflect the course of justice and deprive the defendant of his rights. In the same vein John Foxe criminalizes Edmund Bonner, the Marian bishop of London, and Nicholas Harpsfield, the archdeacon of Canterbury, two model oppressors representative of Foxean anti-hagiography. In a famous passage of *Actes and Monuments*, he describes how as inquisitors they ruthlessly take advantage of their position, not caring for either decency or custom in their treatment of Protestant defendants. As they interrogate Thomas Hinshaw, a nineteen-year old Protestant, they transgress their legal competency by performing a highly irregular feat of uncontrolled and arbitrary malice:

> Then Harpsfield, being in a mighty rage, told the bishop thereof; whereat the bishop fumed and fretted, that scant for anger being able to speak, he said, "Dost thou answer my archdeacon so, thou naughty boy? I shall handle thee well enough, be assured." So he sent for a couple of rods and caused him to kneel against a long bench in an arbour of his garden, where the said Thomas, without any enforcement of his part, offered himself to the beating, and did abide the fury of the said Bonner, so long as the fat-paunched bishop could endure with breath, and till for weariness he was fain to cease, and give place to his shameful act. He had two willow rods, but he wasted but one, and so left off. (Foxe 1965: VIII, 483-84)

Such critiques of judges' unjust behavior are rare, however. In the eyes of a twenty-first century beholder they appear only too rare. Many of the details of Renaissance criminal trials – e.g. the partiality of the judges, the use of the defendants' statements after their apprehension as evidence against them, and indeed the fact that it was all but impossible that the defendant might be acquitted[4] – may seem outrageous in the light of our own notions of justice. And yet they were perfectly acceptable practices in Tudor England, and therefore received little or no attention by hagiographers concerned with trials. On Anne Boleyn's trial for instance, Schauer and Schauer comment that the queen indeed received what might be called a fair trial by the standards of her own time, and her plight "was one shared with everyone so unfortunate as to be charged with a crime in [...] sixteenth-century England" (1980: 77). There is, they say, practically no evidence "that the rules of the time were in any way bent in order to assure Anne Boleyn's conviction. There was no need to tamper with rules that guaranteed the desired result" (80).

The second point of polemical attack, beyond the corruption and misdemeanor of single judges portrayed as sinner, concerns the very fundament of the legal system on which these treason and religion trials were grounded. The example I want to look at in this context is a passage from the formidable history of the English Reformation by the missioner Father Robert Persons (Parsons), *Certamen ecclesiae Anglicanae*, where the pugnacious Jesuit chastises the institutionalized injustice he observes in Elizabethan heresy trials. Persons lists the defects he sees in his country's judicial system.[5] These are precisely the characteristics of Tudor trials which Baker outlines and which Schauer and Schauer highlight critically in Anne Boleyn's case: The English courts, Persons argues, have hardly ever acquitted a defendant in several centuries ("vix unquam multis saeculis absolvitur aliquis qui ad istiusmodi iudicium producitur"). The prosecutors' role ("accusatorum partes") is played by servants of the king, by royal prebendaries and officials. For stating their case the prosecutors are allowed seemingly unlimited time. The defendant is not given nor permitted any legal help ("neque ullus reo procurator, advocatus vel iurisperitus [...] permittitur").[6] Overloaded with responsibility, defendants are accordingly hardly able to vindicate themselves, and, over and above that, they are under permanent threat of instant death ("mortisque periculo territus").

What Persons regards as a particularly serious defect of English law is the institution of trial by jury, and the abuse this system made possible. Particularly in the reign of Henry VIII, the influence of the crown in common law trials increased

---

4 Baker, however, suggests that in criminal (not 'treason' and 'heresy' – therefore state – trials) the percentage of actual convictions ranked between 10 % and 20 % between 1550 and 1800 (1977: 43).

5 I quote the relevant passage from Joseph Simons's edition of parts from Persons's manuscript (1965: 260).

6 "Contemporaries might well have argued, as we now argue in relation to pre-trial interrogation, that the innocent man has nothing to lose, everything to gain, from telling his story himself. But the denial of counsel seems to have been unfair in Tudor and Stuart state trials, when the Crown was defended by the best advocates of the day" (Baker 1977: 37).

considerably.[7] In Persons's eyes, this is the primary reason for the injustice that characterizes so many sentences. He scourges the pressure exerted by the crown and by powerful individuals upon judges and barristers, and by the judges upon the (unlearned) juries, whose decision became dependent on either royal favor or wrath: "For a jury to be punished (summarily or at a later proceeding) by fine or imprisonment for what was thought to be the wrong verdict was not unknown" (Schauer/Schauer 1980: 78).[8] Such abuses seem to have been common practice in the sixteenth and well into the seventeenth centuries. Witness another Catholic controversialist hagiographer, Thomas Worthington. In his biography of John Rigbie, a gentleman who was hung, drawn, and quartered in 1600 as the result of (alleged) treacherous behavior, we read of Rigbie's trial. After the interrogations are completed, the judge informs the jury that the verdict expected of them was to pronounce the defendant guilty, for, as he says, "you cannot but find it treason by the law." In a marginal note, Worthington ostracizes this blatant and illegitimate exertion of influence: "*Where els in the whole world, doth the Iudge tel the Inquisiters of truth, what they must find to be the truth?*" (Worthington 1601: 21; italics in the original).[9]

Persons's most remarkable argument is the claim that the common law of Tudor England, which he vituperates in some detail, is not indigenously English but rather has been imposed on the country by a foreign invader, the Norman William the Conqueror:

> Indeed, this form of trial had been introduced by William, duke of Normandy, whom they call the Conqueror, at the time when he had acquired the English crown by force of arms, so that after having subjugated them, he might also eliminate the English on the strength of his arbitrary decision, but especially gentlemen and grandees. Since this form of trial continues to the present day, everybody's life and death is entirely in the hands of the monarch, and everything depends on his decision. (Simons 1965: 260; my translation)[10]

Persons's text, a sixteenth-century evocation of the "Norman yoke," brings the issue of nationality into the discourse of religious denominations.[11] The polemicist questions the system of common law in England on the pretext of its alleged un-Englishness -- it

---

7 On Shakespeare's critique (in *Henry VIII*) of royal interference in felony trials see Wegemer (2000).

8 See also Clancy (1964: 114).

9 On the Catholic critique of interrogatory torture in Elizabethan England see Hanson (1991).

10 "Erat quidem introducta haec iudicii forma a Gulielmo duce Normandiae, quem Conquestorem vocant, tum cum Angliae regnum armis acquisiverat, ut Anglos, quos vi subiugaverat, pro arbitrio etiam quos vellet e medio tolleret, praecipue vero nobiles atque optimates. Quae quidem iudicii forma cum hodie etiam permaneat, penes principem est vita morsque omnium et ab eius arbitrio pendent universa."

11 The "Norman Yoke" theory is of course not an original contribution of Persons to the debate on the origins and nature of English common law. Despite his evident interest in using the idea of the law's un-English roots against the Protestant authorities, Persons "was only repeating what he found in the chronicles" (Clancy 1964: 113), e.g. Polydore Vergil and Reginald, Cardinal Pole.

is, he claims, a foreign concept that is alien to his free-born nation.[12] By doing so, he manages to implicitly demonize the oppressors of the Catholic mission by styling them as agents of a Continental tyrant's blood-stained legacy. Association of sinners with un-Englishness, particularly (Norman) French foreignness, existed in sacred biography even before the Renaissance.[13]

During the period of controversy, the mutual accusations of disloyalty to the realm and the monarch reached unsurpassed intensity. Loyal Catholics could contend that Protestantism was not only a 'heretical' challenge to the established religion but also an imported one. Denominational conservatism "combined with the ingrained xenophobia of Henrician Englishmen to demand a highly cautious approach to the continental Reformation" (Dickens 1964: 179). On the other hand, fear of Continental institutions and the importation of threatening foreign customs was equally strong on the Protestant side. It goes without saying that Persons's argument is a clean inversion of the cardinal accusations raised against the Jesuits in the national and religious discourse of Tudor England – un-Englishness and allegiance to a foreign tyrant: "None that prayeth for the Queen's enemies are the Queen's friends; but you Papists pray for the Pope, which is the Queen's enemy, for this is your prayer, so you are not the Queen's friends, but her enemies, and traitors" (Morris 1877: 78-79).

2. Trial Scenes in Protestant Sacred Biography

The central text of this section is a short narrative about the imprisonment and the interrogation of the martyr Anne Askew (Ayscough). I follow the text of John Louth, the sixteenth-century archdeacon of Nottingham, as printed in John Gough Nichols's compilation of Reformation narratives (1859). Askew was the wife of a Lincolnshire gentleman, John Kyme. Driven away on religious pretexts by her husband, she sought in vain to get a divorce, and subsequently settled in London where she became a member of the Protestant circle around Henry VIII's last queen, Catherine Parr. Arrested in March 1545, she was subjected to various examinations, also under torture, before she was burned at Smithfield in July 1546. Her crime had been her refusal to accept the official Church's doctrine on the nature of the Eucharist, the *shibboleth* as it were of sixteenth-century religious disputations and interrogations.[14]

Louth's text is a description of Askew's hearing by the Privy Council in May, 1546. He renders a scene from the official interrogation that indeed shows the subversive "aspect of the carnival" Foucault sees as being potentially present in so

12 Contrarily, in the eighteenth century trial by jury was defended as the *most English* of all legal institutions. See Houswitschka's paper in this volume.

13 The late medieval *South English Legendary*, for instance, contains a tale in which the Devil, trying to coax a saint (Theophilus of Cilicia) into an infernal pact, betrays his foreignness, and thus his wickedness, by courtly phrases in Norman French that punctuate his speech (D'Evelyn/Mill 1956: 222).

14 On biographical details, and for a discussion of Anne Askew's memoirs, and of the representation of her trial by John Bale, the first martyrologist of the English Reformation, see Knott (1993: 46-59).

many pre-modern and early modern judicial events. Its contents are as follows: The Lord Mayor of London, Sir Martin Bowes, one of the members of the interrogating Council, undertakes a theological dispute with the prisoner about the subject of the transubstantiation. He clumsily indulges in scholastic ratiocination and immediately reveals bizarre ignorance of the subject, thus giving Askew the chance to demonstrate not only her firm trust in her Reformed religion but also her argumentative superiority. That the defendant speaks about the Protestant doctrine of the Lord's Supper in precise and well-balanced words that may well be intended to serve for the edification of the text's devout readers is typical of the genre and not really remarkable. But the abstruse gallimaufry uttered by the prosecutor does deserve our attention. It provides a grotesque foil to the Protestant tenets presented in the text, and at the same time reduces Catholic beliefs to complete absurdity. Furthermore, it serves to enhance the portrait of Askew as a figure of light that is brilliantly set against the anti-saint trapped in the mists of his own ignorance:

> My lorde mayre, sir M. Bowes, syttyng with the cownsell, as moste meetest for his wysdome, and seeing hur standyng apon lyff and dethe, "I pray yow, (quod he,) my lordes, gyve me leave to talke with this woman." Leave was granted. *Lord Maiore*. Thou folyshe woman, sayest thow that the prestes can not make the body of Chryste? *A. Askowghe*. I say so, my lorde, for I have redd that God mayd man; but that man can make God I never yet redd, nor I suppose ever shall red yt. *L. Maiore*. No? yow folyshe woman: after the wordes of consecratione, ys it not the Lordes body? *A. Askowghe*. No, it ys bot consecrated bredd, or sacramentall bredd. *L. Maior*. What, yf a mowse eate yt after the consecratione, what shalbecome of the mowse? What sayeste thow, thow folyshe woman? *A. Askowghe*. What shall become of hur say yow, my lorde? *L. Maior*. I say that the mowse is damned. *A. Askew*. Alacke, poore mowse! By this tyme the lordes had ynowghe of my lorde maiores divinitie, and perceavyng that some cowld not keape in theyr lawghyng, proceeded to the butchery and slawter that they entended afore thei came thither. (Nichols 1968: 41)

Bowes's words, as has been said, are a parodic travesty of the Roman Catholic doctrine of the sacrament.[15] Without difficulties, Askew dumbfounds the man who attempts to intimidate her, and turns Bowes's iterated accusation of foolishness entirely against himself. "If the documents present anything like an accurate picture," A. G. Dickens remarked, "this daughter of a Lincolnshire knight proved herself an educated, pert and formidable disputant" (Dickens 1964: 194). The prosecutor – i.e.

---

15 He quotes one of the stereotypical Protestant arguments against transubstantiation, namely the claim that the dogma implies that priests 'make' Christ in the liturgy of Mass. Thus he inadvertently acts against his own case. John Louth himself ironically refers to a priest preparing for the ceremony with the derisory words that "he was abowte to make his God" (37). Afterwards, Bowes awkwardly alludes to a textbook question of medieval transubstantiation theology: What happens when the consecrated host – by its substance Christ's *verum corpus*! – is eaten by a mouse? Does it 'retransubstantiate' to be mere bread, or is Christ's body subsequently contained within the animal? Pope Gregory XI had, in 1371, prohibited the belief in a 'retransubstantiation' on pains of excommunication. Bowes, however, misapprehends the point and assumes that it is the *mouse* who merits condemnation by eating the host. Perhaps he is also thinking of Paul's admonition: "For he that eateth and drinketh unworthily, eateth and drinketh damnation to himself, not discerning the Lord's body" (1Co 11:29).

the anti-saint – appears as a conceited dunce who is not able to think for himself or to gain insight into religious truths. With his maladroit reference to authoritarian schoolmanship, he counter-acts the Reformed ideal of the responsible Christian layperson. The passage's concluding sentence contains a further strategy of criminalizing the representatives of the law. It delineates the Catholic oppressors as hardened sinners, obtuse and yet truculent, who proceed to "butchery and slawter" after having enjoyed their laugh.

Let me supply two further instances from one of the English Reformation's central texts, John Foxe's *Actes and Monuments* (*Book of Martyrs*), where the hagiographer denigrates the functionaries of law and hierarchy by attributing certain vices to them. The first one is a description of Stephen Gardiner, Roman Catholic Bishop of Winchester, Queen Mary's Lord Chancellor and a leading Counter-Reformer, who in Foxe's eyes is nothing but an "enemy of God's word." The self-complacency that dominates Louth's portrait of Sir Martin Bowes reappears as Gardiner's worst trait, yet his vainglory is more dangerous and less scurrilous than that of the Lord Mayor:

> He was of a proud stomach, and high-minded, in his own opinion and conceit flattering himself too much; in wit, crafty and subtle; toward his superiors flattering and fair spoken; to his inferiors fierce, against his equals stout and envious, namely, if in judgment and sentence he any thing withstood him [...]. (Foxe 1965: VII, 585)

Similarly, in a second passage, Foxe ascribes features of malignity to those that represent the secular authorities. In this case the sinners come from another social stratum than the callous men of the Council that Louth had sketched in his account of Anne Askew's trial. Moreover, their debauchery is of a completely different kind. The text is taken from Foxe's account of the execution of Dr. Rowland Taylor, the rector of Hadleigh in Sussex, who suffered martyrdom on February 9, 1555. Foxe takes care to present the headsmen as outcasts who would much rather deserve judicial punishment than the saintly man of God whom they torment. Taylor suffers at the hands of four utter rogues, namely

> [...] one Mulleie, of Kersey, a man for his virtues fit to be a hangman, and Soyce a very drunkard, and Warwick, who, in the commotion time in king Edward's days, lost one of his ears for his seditious talk; amongst whom also was one Robert King, deviser of interludes, who albeit was there present, and had doing there with the gunpowder: what he meant and did therein (he himself saith he did it for the best, and for quick despatch) the Lord knoweth, which shall judge all: more of this I have not to say. (VI, 699)

So much for this memorable if paraliptic portrayal of four desperados, whose status and background alone brands them as marginal figures, and whose infamous reputation adds to the thoroughly negative picture they offer. Soyce for instance is an alcoholic, Warwick a would-be revolutionary, King is not much more than a mountebank. That the hagiographer dwells with so much detail on these fellows who serve as the deputies of the law that put Taylor to death by analogy has the effect of elevating the saint in the eyes of the audience.

In these brief passages we have seen how the central strategy employed by Elizabethan Protestant hagiographers to turn the defendants into the heroes of trial accounts is to demonize the prosecutors. They do so by describing them as incapable of fulfilling societal expectations and as deviating from social norms. In these narratives, the representatives of judicial power fail to live up to some of those standards of godliness and good citizenship that since Max Weber (1920) have been known as the Protestant ethic. Among these standards are industriousness, temperance, frugality, rational-utilitarian stewardship (i.e. rightful use of one's talents), submission under authorities, honesty, and learning. Such a tactic may be observed in a large number of Reformed sacred biographies, especially after Protestantism had been firmly established in England both as a system of beliefs and thoughts and as a social institution. In precisely the same vein e.g. John Bunyan criminalizes the jury that pronounce the deadly verdict over Faithful, one of the most radiantly saintly characters of *The Pilgrim's Progress*, as reprobates in the sense of the Protestant ethic:

> Then went the Jury out, whose names were, Mr *Blind-man,* Mr *No-good,* Mr *Malice,* Mr *Love-lust,* Mr *Live-loose,* Mr *Heady,* Mr *High-mind,* Mr *Enmity,* Mr *Lyar,* Mr *Cruelty,* Mr *Hate-Light,* and Mr *Implacable;* who every one gave in his private Verdict against him among themselves, and afterwards unanimously concluded to bring him in guilty before the Judge. (Bunyan 1909: 101-2; italics in the original)

3. Trial Scenes in Roman Catholic Sacred Biography

My central example of Elizabethan Recusant[16] hagiographic prose is Father John Mush's *Life of Margaret Clitherow*. It is the biography of a butcher's wife from York, who was arrested, tried, and sentenced to death on account of having "harboured and maintained Jesuit and Seminary priests, traitors to the Queen's Majesty" in her house (Morris 1877: 413). She was subjected to the *peine forte et dure*, in other words, half-starved and crushed beneath a door panel loaded with rocks, and died on March 25, 1586.[17] Throughout his text, Mush, who had been Clitherow's confessor, never tires of highlighting her sanctity against the backdrop of her adversaries' paradigmatic ungodliness. The following passage, which I consider highly representative, is taken from his account of the saint's interrogations after she has been arraigned for treacherous behavior. In the Common Hall in York, "two judges, Mr. Clinch and Mr. Rhodes, and divers of the Council," first explain to the prisoner with what she is charged.

---

16 Recusant: "One, especially a Roman Catholic (*Popish recusant*), who refused to attend the services of the Church of England" (*OED*). From 1559 onward, recusancy was a crime punishable by fines and imprisonment (Palliser 1992: 385).

17 For details of her trial see Cross (1993). Margaret Clitherow was officially canonized by Pope Paul VI in 1970. Baker (1977: 34) calls the *peine forte et dure* "the most barbaric feature of common-law procedure."

> Then they brought forth two chalices, divers pictures, and in mockery put two vestments and other church gear upon two lewd fellows' backs, and in derision the one began to pull and dally with the other, scoffing on the bench before the judges, and holding up singing breads,[18] said to the martyr: "Behold thy gods in whom thou believest." They asked her how she liked those vestments. The martyr said: "I like them well, if they were on their backs that know to use them to God's honour, as they were made." Then Judge Clinch stood up and asked her: "In whom believe you?" "I believe," quoth the martyr, "in God." "In what God?" quoth the judge. "I believe," quoth the martyr, "in God the Father, in God the Son, and God the Holy Ghost; in these Three Persons and One I fully believe, and that by the passion, death, and merits of Christ Jesu I must be saved." The judge said: "You say well;" and said no more. [...] The judge said: "We must proceed by law against you, which will condemn you to a sharp death for want of trial." The martyr said cheerfully: "God's will be done: I think I may suffer any death for this good cause." (413-14)

The martyr[19] avoids making any statement that could be considered a direct confession – in the judicial praxis of the early modern period, this is an indispensable requirement for a condemnation (van Dülmen 1985: 24). She replies curtly, precisely, without trying to appease the interrogators by dissimulating her beliefs and without zealous or emotional bluster. What is of interest in this context is primarily the denigration of those who are in possession of secular power. The judges' paramount care is to convince the defendant that her persisting in her Catholic beliefs is idolatrous and traitorous. Yet they are incapable of bringing forth reasonable arguments. Thus, they rely on blasphemy in order to break their victim. Two "lewd fellows" are produced, who perform sacrilegious abuses of Catholic liturgical vestments and vessels, even of the host, in order to express their scorn for Clitherow's religion. But in contrast to the frantic raillery of her tormentors, the defendant remains composed and determined. Quietly, even serenely, she accepts the capital sentence, which arrives with relentless promptitude, pronounced by judges who indeed represent the law as a compliant "engine of state."

Mush's rhetorical canonization of Clitherow culminates in his description of her death. After she has spent her last night in prayer, she is dragged to the place of execution, the tollbooth at the bridge over the river Ouse, where she undergoes the *peine forte et dure*. The hagiographer spares his readers no painful detail of his protagonist's slow, humiliating death.[20] He carries the effective antagonism between

---

18 Singing bread (or singing cake): "The wafer used in the celebration of the mass" (*OED*).

19 Mush's use of the word 'martyr' in a literary canonization is subtly instrumentalized. For one, the increasingly frequent application of the term to Clitherow towards the end of her trial (and with over-abundance in the account of her execution) corroborates his point that his heroine is one of the long row of Christian martyrs who die for the true religion. At the same time, his use of the term in the examination scene plays on the word's etymology (Greek *martús*), which encompasses both the meanings 'judicial witness' and 'blood-witness of God.'

20 Her hagiographer suggests that Clitherow might have been pregnant at the time of her death and that the judges, although suspecting her state, deny her "the benefit of [her] condition" (Morris 1877: 421). This "benefit" is well-known to readers of e.g. Defoe's *Moll Flanders*: "If a female convict was quick with child, the judge was bound to respite judgment of death until after delivery; her condition was tried by a jury of matrons, and [...] such juries were usually

the piety of the saint and the criminal energy of the ungodly to the utmost extreme by attributing to Clitherow traits that are directly reminiscent of those of the suffering Christ:

> The door was laid upon her, her hands she joined towards her face. Then the sheriff said, "Nay, you must have your hands bound." The martyr put forth her hands over the door still joined. Then two sergeants parted them, and with the inkle strings, which she had prepared for that purpose bound them to two posts, so that her body and her arms made a perfect cross. They willed her again to ask the Queen's Majesty's forgiveness, and to pray for her. The martyr said she had prayed for her. They also willed her to ask her husband's forgiveness. The martyr said, "If ever I have offended him, but for my conscience, I ask him forgiveness."
>
> After this they laid weight upon her, which when she first felt, she said, "Jesu! Jesu! Jesu! have mercy upon me!" which were the last words she was heard to speak. (Morris 1877: 431-32)

Although never explicitly stated, Clitherow's Christ-like traits are so conspicuous that they hardly need pointing out. She, for instance, prays for "them which despitefully use" her (Lk 6:28) as Christ had pronounced words of forgiveness on the cross (Lk 23:34),[21] and she does so even before the anti-saints request her to. A striking detail is that Clitherow suffers with her arms outstretched, in the shape of "a perfect cross," in other words, in the cruciform position of the dying Christ. The semi-liturgical triple invocation of the Lord's name that concludes the passage rounds off and corroborates the numerous details given in the previous paragraph that suggest parallels between Clitherow's execution and that of Christ. Mush further supports these hints by stating later in the text that Clitherow's body remained "in the press" from nine o'clock in the morning till three in the afternoon (432), the time of the day that is traditionally associated with Christ's death. "Hath not God turned everything in this your horrible murther, to the most honour of His saint?" he rhetorically asks the judges (439), before he makes it clear that Clitherow died not only on a Roman Catholic holy day – the Annunciation – but that this day actually coincided with Good Friday, "wherein all Christendom celebrateth the memory of Christ's death and piteously lamenteth His pains suffered this day, for our offences" (440).

I want to take up the point of Margaret Clitherow's Christ-like traits and quote once more from is *A Treatise Touching the Imprisonment and Indictments of Mr. Francis Tregian, Esquire*. In one passage of this narrative we read about the imprisonment and trial of Father Cuthbert Maine (Mayne), Tregian's friend and the first Jesuit seminarian who was put to death in England (November 29, 1577). His prosecutors, who are painted in odious colors, are not able to find any legal ground for the accusations of treason which they raise against the priest. The hagiographer achieves his goal of criminalizing them and at the same time of canonizing Maine by pointing out that the position of secular authority's representatives is essentially the same as that of the "chief priests, and elders" responsible for Christ's death. Of these Matthew says that they eagerly search premises in order to sentence Christ, but lack

---

favourable whenever possible" (Baker 1977: 44). Again, judicial misdemeanor is attacked, albeit tentatively and indirectly.

21 Cf. the dying words of the Church's protomartyr, Stephen (Ac 7:60).

grounds on which to base their accusation (Mt 26:59-61). This is the case with Maine's accusers. First, they resort to the questionable clue that they have found with the defendant "a void piece of paper printed at Douay," i.e. at one of the English Catholics' exile colleges on the Continent, which they interpret as circumstantial evidence against him, just as a murderer "may be found out by having bloody weapons." But this tactic does not yield the expected success, since Maine's case, as the hagiographer remarks with grim irony, still "doth as much resemble that case of murder, as the Judge's nose was like a shoeing-horn" (Morris 1872: 80). Hence the sinful judges, like the Gospel's "chief priests, and elders," have to rely on calumniators for corroborating their claim that Maine is a traitor:

> Thereupon there were produced three false witnesses (not much unlike to those who accused our Saviour Christ) testifying upon their oaths that [...] he, amongst many other speeches used unto them, should deny that the Queen was Supreme Head of the Church of England [...]. (81)

The Recusant hagiographer explicitly emphasizes the parallel between his protagonist and Christ. But whereas Matthew merely speaks of "two false witnesses" (Mt 26:60),[22] and Mark is content with the indifferent statement that "there arose certain [scil. individuals]" (Mk 14:57) who were willing to traduce Christ, Maine's hagiographer cites no less than three slanderers, who 'testify' against the missioner to send him to the scaffold.

Maine's trial is but one of many in which Roman Catholic writers of sacred biography seek to denigrate their saints' adversaries by comparing them to those who killed Christ. An anonymous Elizabethan Catholic diarist – known only as the Yorkshire Recusant – deals a sweeping attack against the Elizabethan religious authorities. He scornfully calls them "gross Puritans" and blames them for desiring the complete eradication of the English Catholics. The following sentence concludes his tirade:

> But He that patiently sustained the like villanies [sic] of the Jews, hanging upon the cross for our redemption and example, assisteth us with His grace, that in this hour our meekness, joy, and peace of heart are manifest, to the confusion of our adversaries and the godly edification of all charitable beholders. (Morris 1877: 97)

As these selective examples illustrate, the anti-saints of Catholic hagiographic trial scenes are often characterized by their failure to humbly conform to the "positive concept of rules and roles" (Sullivan 1995: 87) set by the hierarchical Church. Such an obstinate refusal of submission is understood as being tantamount to forswearing God and throwing oneself to the powers of hell. This happens explicitly in Sir Thomas More's comments on the polemical writings of the Reformers when he says that that "the deuyll hath now taught hys dysciples, the dyuysers of these heresyes, to make many shorte treatyses" (More 1947: 440). The Yorkshire Recusant uses the same

22 Several "false witnesses" also speak out against Stephen (Ac 6:13). Cf. the "two lewd fellows" that are hired to mock Margaret Clitherow.

image when he writes about Henry Hastings, Earl of Huntingdon, the Lord President of the North and an ardent Protestant, that he "proveth himself to be not only a most wicked and malicious limb of Satan, but also a most injurious and a violent tyrant" (Morris 1877: 73). More commonly, demoniac traits – features that characterize them as acting under the influence of hellish spirits – are only implicitly ascribed to those in possession of secular power. Authorities are condemned as a corollary effect of the overt canonization of their victims, so to speak, to whom distinct Christ-like traits are attributed. Innocent saints are tried, condemned, and executed by sinners who speak and act like the slanderous accusers described in the biblical passion narratives. The relationship between canonization and denigration is reciprocal here: the brighter the saint shines, the more wicked the anti-saint appears.

4. Summary and Outlook

From Christianity's earliest days, hagiographers had operated on what Aron Gurevich calls a "pair of opposing concepts, *fidelis – perfidus*" (1988: 57). Consequently, they always had occasion for powerful strategies of demonizing the Other – the prosecutor, the judge, the headsman. Moreover, their rhetoric needed to transform the powers-that-be, in the figure of their representative (judge, torturer, executor), not merely into a puny bugbear but actually into a forceful sinner figure, an active perpetrator with criminal energy of his own. In hagiographic trial and execution narratives, therefore, the defendant becomes the hero by virtue of his/her exemplary godliness, i.e. his/her fulfillment of religious norms and expectations, and/or by virtue of the divine favor (grace) that rests upon him/her (Scharfe 1969: 96). The prosecutor, in his (I deliberately use the masculine pronoun) role as the opponent of the saint, was denigrated, condemned, indeed criminalized, through traits of his character that counteract precisely those norms and expectations fulfilled and over-fulfilled by the saint. Hagiographers argued that although society, through the deputies of its legal institutions, had pronounced its deadly verdict on the martyrs, society did *not* actually possess the competency to judge them rightfully. In the words of Northrop Frye: "It [i.e. society] has no standards in itself, for distinguishing what is below the law from what is above it: it cannot tell a prophet from a blasphemer, a saint from a witch, a philosopher from a teacher of subversive doctrines" (1991: 11).

One phenomenon addressed in this paper, the direct critique of legal institutions is comparably rare both in sacred biography and in Renaissance texts in general; however, it occurs in several Protestant and Roman Catholic writings of the Elizabethan period. In some cases individuals' misdemeanors, such as the partiality of judges, is reprobated. This entails describing these men in their role as representatives of authority as if they were criminals. Catholic Recusants denounce individual judges on account of their partiality and incompetence; Foxe vilifies Marian counter-Reformers as spiteful sadists. In other cases, the institution of the common law itself is critiqued. Robert Persons interprets the common law as the portentous legacy of a tyrannical autocrat, characterizing it as un-English. He is one of many who criticize

English law on account of its alleged foreignness, and one of even more who employ foreignness as a negative attribution in the denominational conflict.[23]

As is to be expected, there are slight differences between the argumentative techniques used by the opposing denominations: "Every martyrology," Helen C. White writes, "has its types and its patterns" (1963: 236). Consequently, hagiographers of both denominational affiliations have their preferred strategies to create opposing pairs of saints and anti-saints, to canonize and to demonize antagonists. These strategies depend on the norms and expectations shared by the respective denominations. With a grain of salt, we may say that after the establishment of institutionalized Protestantism and the ensuing come-uppance of the moral code that constitutes Weber's "Protestant ethic," Protestant polemicists tended to demonize the prosecutors in hagiographic trial scenes by pointing at their lack of precisely this type of morality.

Catholic polemicists, on the other hand, generally tended towards a more overt demonization of their opponents by emphasizing the palpably 'evil' (i.e. demoniac) traits of the prosecutors. The Christ-like qualities that many Catholic hagiographers bestow upon the martyrs in their texts analogously influence the image of the prosecutors, implicitly yet forcefully demonizing them. It becomes clear that these mechanisms of attributing criminality and sanctity are among the most urgent concerns of the hagiographers and that they account for some features of the text type not discussed in this paper. Trial accounts in English Renaissance sacred biography, for instance, teem with doctrinaire disputations, which, if Stephen Greenblatt is right, "are in fact shadow arguments, as in a ritual or a play, for actual persuasion is out of the question: the heretic will either abjure for fear of punishment or stand firm and be punished" (1980: 77). What such logomachies achieve, however, is precisely a fashioning of the contrasted characters of saints and anti-saints.

The predominance of 'practical' arguments in Protestant texts may be set in direct correlation with the increasing reluctance to see transcendental powers at work which came in the wake of the Reformation, a consequence of what Max Weber felicitously dubbed the world's disenchantment (*Entzauberung*). This process, he argues, began with the rationalizing prophecies of the Old Testament, was influenced by Hellenist scientific thought, and found its climax in the seventeenth century (Weber 1981: 123). Miracles, for instance, part and parcel of Roman Catholic sacred biography, play a considerably less significant role in Reformed writings as early as in the sixteenth century. Protestant divines taught that the "Apostles, and perhaps a few subsequent generations, had been given the power to perform miracles in order to establish the Christian religion; once this had been achieved, miracles were purposeless" (Walker 1981: 66). The difference between the Protestant ethic and its Roman Catholic

23 Thomas H. Clancy remarked upon the significance of Persons's stricture: "The whole interest of Persons' insistence on the Norman origin of the common law is that it keeps alive a theme on which the lawyers will spill barrels of ink and which will be developed later on by the Levellers as a basis for a thoroughgoing criticism of the English legal system" (1964: 113). On the continuation of this discourse in seventeenth-century heresy trials, and on a Quaker critique of the administration of "the laws of England," especially of procedural regulations, see Böker (2002).

alternative has left its distinct mark on sacred biography and still informs our cultures significantly.

Trial scenes, as I said above, are showpieces of confrontation that provide hagiographers with the opportunity to portray their subjects as villainous perpetrators and saintly heroes. Writing the hagiography of an individual put to death by the law of the land was a challenge to the writers that allowed them to elaborate artfully on the 'dialectics of martyrdom' and to effectively utilize these for their purpose. Indeed, we may safely assume that hagiographers of the Elizabethan period and throughout the history of Christianity did not merely take refuge in strategies of double inversion of the trial-and-condemnation paradigm as a desperate means of exculpating their subjects and thereby their religion. Rather, they interpreted conflict with the world and with worldly power – represented by the authorities – as no less than a hallmark of the elect. Convinced of the ultimate rightness of their protagonists' actions, they outlined them as innocent and shining victims of state oppression.[24] In his *Pensées*, Blaise Pascal meditates on precisely this close affinity between judicial persecution and religious salvation or glorification: "Jesus Christ did not want to be killed without legal procedure, for it is far more disgraceful to die at the hands of the law than in an unlawful revolt" (1976: 457, my translation).[25]

Works Cited

Baker, J. H. (1977) "Criminal Courts and Procedure at Common Law 1550-1800." *Crime in England 1550-1800*. Ed. J. S. Cockburn. London: Methuen & Co. 15-48.

Böker, Uwe (2002) "Institutionalised Rules of Discourse and the Court Room as a Site of the Public Sphere." *Sites of Discourse – Public and Private Spheres – Legal Culture: Papers from a Conference Held at the Technical University of Dresden, December 2001*. Ed. Uwe Böker and Julie A. Hibbard. Internationale Forschungen zur Allgemeinen und Vergleichenden Literaturwissenschaft, 64. Amsterdam; New York: Rodopi. 35-66.

Bunyan, John (1909 [1678]) *The Pilgrim's Progress*. Ed. Charles W. Eliot. The Harvard Classics; 15. New York: Collier.

Buschmann, Gerd (1994) *Martyrium Polycarpi – eine formgeschichtliche Studie: Ein Beitrag zur Frage nach der Entstehung der Gattung Märtyrerakte*. Beihefte zur

24 This actually allows comparison with religious and political suicide bombers of today, whose opposition to what they perceive to be an evil imposition of power structures, and in particular willingness to sacrifice themselves for their convictions, often earns them the status of 'martyrs' in the eyes of their fellow believers or supporters.

25 "Jésus-Christ n'a pas voulu être tué sans les formes de la justice, car il est bien plus ignominieux de mourir par justice que par une sédition injuste."

Zeitschrift für die Neutestamentliche Wissenschaft und die Kunde der älteren Kirche, 70. Berlin; New York: De Gruyter.

Clancy, Thomas H. (1964) *Papist Pamphleteers: The Allen-Persons Party and the Political Thought of the Counter-Reformation in England, 1572-1615*. Jesuit Studies, 18. Chicago, IL: Loyola Univ. Press.

Cross, Claire (1993) "An Elizabethan Martyrologist and his Martyr: John Mush and Margaret Clitherow." Wood 1993: 271-81.

Dehandschutter, B. A. G. M. (1989) "Martyrium und Agon: Über die Wurzeln der Vorstellung vom ΑΓΩΝ im Vierten Makkabäerbuch." *Die Entstehung der jüdischen Martyrologie*. Ed. J. W. van Henten, B. A. G. M. Dehandschutter, and H. J. W. van der Klaauw. Studia post-biblica, 38. Leiden et al.: E. J. Brill. 215-19.

D'Evelyn, Charlotte, and Anna J. Mill, ed. (1956) *The South English Legendary*. EETS O.S., 235, 236. London: Oxford Univ. Press.

Dickens, A. G. (1964) *The English Reformation*. London: B. T. Batsford.

Foucault, Michel (1979 [1975]) *Discipline and Punish: The Birth of the Prison*. New York: Vintage Books.

Foxe, John (1965 [1570]) *Actes and Monuments of these Latter and Perilous Dayes, touching Matters of the Church* [...]. 8 vols. Ed. George Townsend, 1841. New York: AMS Press. Reprint.

Frye, Northrop (1991) "Crime and Sin in the Bible." *Rough Justice: Essays on Crime in Literature*. Ed. M. L. Friedland Toronto, Ont.; Buffalo, NY; London: Univ. of Toronto Press. 3-18.

Greenblatt, Stephen (1980) *Renaissance Self-Fashioning: From More to Shakespeare*. Chicago, IL; London: Univ. of Chicago Press.

Günter, Heinrich (1949) *Psychologie der Legende: Studien zu einer wissenschaftlichen Heiligen-Geschichte*. Freiburg (Breisgau): Herder.

Gurevich, Aron (1988) *Medieval Popular Culture: Problems of Belief and Perception*. Cambridge Studies in Oral and Literate Culture, 14. Cambridge et al.: Cambridge Univ. Press; Paris: Editions de la Maison des Sciences de l'Homme.

Hanson, Elizabeth (1991) "Torture and Truth in Renaissance England." *Representations* 34: 53-84.

Knott, John R. (1993) *Discourses of Martyrdom in English Literature 1563-1694*. Cambridge: Cambridge Univ. Press.

Loades, David (1993) "Introduction." Wood 1993: xv-xviii.

More, Sir Thomas (1947 [1533]) "A Letter of syr Tho. More Knyght impugnynge the erronyouse wrytyng of John Fryth agaynst the blessed sacrament of the aultare." *The Correspondence of Sir Thomas More*. Ed. Elizabeth Frances Rogers. Princeton, NJ: Princeton Univ. Press. 439-64.

Morris, John, ed. (1872) *The Troubles of our Catholic Forefathers: Related by Themselves*. First Series. London: Burns & Oates.

Morris, John, ed. (1877) *The Troubles of our Catholic Forefathers: Related by Themselves*. Third Series. London: Burns & Oates.

Nichols, John Gough, ed. (1968 [1859]) *Narratives of the Days of the Reformation: Chiefly from the Manuscripts of John Foxe the Martyrologist*. New York; London: AMS Press. Reprint.

Palliser, D. M. (1992) *The Age of Elizabeth: England under the Later Tudors, 1547-1603*. London; New York: Longman.

Pascal, Blaise (1976 [posth. 1670]) *Pensées: Nouvelle édition établie pour la première fois d'après la copie de référence de Gilberte Pascal*. Ed. Philippe Sellier. Paris: Mercure de France.

Scharfe, Martin (1969) "Der Heilige in der protestantischen Volksfrömmigkeit." *Hessische Blätter für Volkskunde* 60: 93-106.

Schauer, Margery Stone, and Frederick Schauer (1980) "Law as the Engine of State: The Trial of Anne Boleyn." *William and Mary Law Review* 22: 49-84.

Schulte Herbrüggen, Hubertus (1978) "Mores Prozeß und Hinrichtung." *500 Jahre Thomas Morus: Humanist, Staatsmann, Märtyrer*. Ed. Hermann Boventer. Bensberger Protokolle, 22. Bergisch Gladbach: Thomas-Morus-Akademie Bensberg. 187-205.

Simons, Joseph Servatius Franciscus (1965) *Robert Persons S.J.: Certamen ecclesiae Anglicanae*. Assen: Van Gorcum & Comp.; Prakke & Prakke.

Sullivan, Ceri (1995) *Dismembered Rhetoric: English Recusant Writing, 1580 to 1603*. Madison, WI: Fairleigh Dickinson Univ. Press; London: Associated Univ. Presses.

Tertullianus, Q. Septimius Florens (1984) *Apologeticum*. Ed. Carl Becker. Munich: Kösel.

van Dülmen, Richard (1985) *Theater des Schreckens: Gerichtspraxis und Strafrituale in der frühen Neuzeit*. Munich: C. H. Beck.

Walker, D. P. (1981) *Unclean Spirits: Possession and Exorcism in France and England in the Late Sixteenth and Early Seventeenth Centuries*. London: Scolar Press.

Weber, Max (1981 [1920]) *Die protestantische Ethik I: Eine Aufsatzsammlung*. Ed. Johannes Winckelmann. Gütersloher Taschenbücher Siebenstern, 53. Gütersloh: Mohn.

Wegemer, Gerard (2000) "Henry VIII on Trial: Confronting Malice and Conscience in Shakespeare's *All Is True*." *Renascence* 52: 111-30.

White, Helen C. (1963) *Tudor Books of Saints and Martyrs*. Madison, WI: Univ. of Wisconsin Press.

Wood, Diana, ed. (1993) *Martyrs and Martyrologies: Papers Read at the 1992 Summer Meeting and the 1993 Winter Meeting of the Ecclesiastical History Society*. Studies in Church History, 30. Oxford: Blackwell.

Worthington, Thomas (1601) *A Relation of sixtene Martyrs: Glorified in England in twelve Monethes*. Douai: Widow of Iames Boscard.

Law as Thought Pattern and Ordering Principle in Shakespeare's Trial Scenes

Greta Olson

Shakespeare's facility with legal themes, references, and phraseology has been noted again and again.[1] Whether the playwright was an apprentice to a lawyer during his 'lost' pre-London years or simply was forced to comprehend and make use of the law to find his way in the world as an intelligent and highly-verbal young man without many useful connections, we do not conclusively know. Certainly, Shakespeare was involved in lawsuits in which he had to testify or tried to recover money he had lent to others (Duncan-Jones 2001: 213-14, 241-44; Kornstein 15-21). That highly specific judicial terminology appears in scenes of great feeling speaks for his having perhaps internalized this vocabulary into his own emotional framework.[2] At times this language seems excessively formal and may even hinder the emotional impact of a given scene. For instance, Romeo entitles his last kiss to Juliet as "A dateless bargain to engrossing Death" (1594-96: V. iii. 115), suggesting that he has just signed a contract or bond rather than lost his beloved young wife. Whatever Shakespeare's practical experience with law was, legal terms and procedures permeate his work and are used to address fundamental conflicts in human interaction and impose order over their resultant crises. As Ervene Gulley asserts, Shakespeare's plays reveal "a sense of law as both method and metaphor by which western civilization organizes and evaluates human behavior" (1998: 53).

This essay extends Gulley's reading of the trial scene in *Measure for Measure* (1604) as an illustration of law "as an ordering and conserving social construct" (68) to interpret a variety of related scenes in Shakespeare's plays. As I will argue, 'trial scenes' of many types abound in Shakespeare's plays. In these tribunals principal characters' fates are pondered over and dramatized, trial procedure is depicted in minute detail and critically questioned, and judicial vocabulary is adopted. By moving through a range of scenes that are ordered on the basis of their increasingly explicit depictions of judicial examination before a judge and a jury, I want to demonstrate how Shakespearean characters employ trial procedures to respond to personal failure and to create order out of their chaotic circumstances. Moreover, the playwright uses

---

1 For an early example, see John Lord Campbell's *Shakespeare's Legal Acquirements Considered* (1859); for a recent treatment of this subject, see Daniel J. Kornstein's *Kill All the Lawyers? Shakespeare's Legal Appeal* (1994).

2 Duncan-Jones (2001: 23) quotes Edgar Fripp's *Shakespeare's Haunts Near Stratford* (1929).

these forums to illustrate the power of trials as public, cathartic rituals as well as to highlight the danger of their being abused by the powerful. Not only are trial scenes internalized by individual characters as models of coping behavior, but they are also employed to lend wider meaning to private conflict and to interrogate law as a means of enacting justice.

My conclusions are followed by a form of postscript. The final section of this paper consists of a schematic analysis of the trial scenes discussed earlier and presents a typology of fictional trials. With this schema I wish to point out how structural differences between the trial scenes accompany and underline their functional variations.

Shakespeare's Varied Use of Trial Scenes

In this essay I distinguish between five types of trial scenes on the basis of how explicitly they enact legal trial procedures. On one end of the scale, 'real' trial scenes occur in which a jury is present and judgment (now called a sentence) is actually spoken and given effect. On the other end of the scale, 'implicit' trial scenes mimic the trappings and language of trial proceedings, but remain empty of legal authority. Both real trials and their pretend counterparts enable participants to understand their individual predicaments and to analyze their experiences using legal paradigms.

Invoking a form of trial that was introduced after the Norman Conquest, Shakespeare stages public trials between men warring for power in historical settings (category one). Resting on the medieval belief that God would help the 'better' man to win in a duel, trials by battle often decide questions of succession and inheritance. One of these is Edgar's defeat of his evil brother Edmund in *King Lear* (1605-6). Here, the former swears upon his oath and honor that his brother will be proven a traitor in battle (V. iii). Another trial by battle is undertaken by Mowbray and Bolingbroke in *Richard II* (1595). The Marshall initiates this hugely public battle with the words:

> Harry of Herford, Lancaster, and Derby,
> Stands here, for God, his sovereign, and himself,
> On pain to be found false and recreant,
> To prove the Duke of Norfolk, Thomas Mowbray,
> A traitor to his God, his king, and him,
> And dares him to set forward to the fight. (I. iii. 104-9)

In trials by arms God takes the place of a judge as the arbiter of justice, and a judgment is spoken in the form of one of the dueling parties being injured or killed. In the scene quoted from here, Richard Plantagenet exercises his royal prerogative to end the trial by combat, before God, as adjudicator, has determined the combatants' fates. While their procedures differ from those of trial by jury, trials by arms also function as ritualized resolutions of conflict. Like the trial of Queen Katherine in *Henry VIII* (1612-13), which is attended by doctors of law, bishops, priests, officers, and noblemen, such trials by battle are highly public and have eminently political purposes. Witnesses to these battles take over the functions of jurors in trials by jury.

Explicit trial scenes conform to actual court sessions (category two): One of these is the trial scene at the end of *Measure for Measure* in which the Duke acts as the judge and jury of peers for Angelo, his corrupt deputy. Another is Katherine's trial scene in *Henry VIII*, in which the Queen defends herself in front of the court as a good, if neglected, wife and rejects her prosecutor Cardinal Wolsey's 'arguments' for the dissolution of the marriage between the king and her (II. iv). These scenes display Shakespeare's interest in the pomp and circumstance of law. Trials are enacted by him as spectacular pieces of theater.

Apart from 'realistic' enactments of court sessions and trials by battle, Shakespeare also invents mock trial scenes such as the one in *King Lear*, Act III, scene vi (category three). In a humble farmhouse, the formerly powerful king asks a presumed madman and the fool to act as his justices. The impoverished and disillusioned Lear then indicts his elder daughters for treason and sentences Regan in proxy using a joint stool and a bench to serve for a court. In this scene pomp disappears; the trial proceeds using the simplest of means and settings. Moreover, the roles of appellant, appellee, witness, and judge are merged in Lear's person.

Furthermore, Shakespeare composes scenes in which trial procedures and vocabulary are conceived of privately by individuals in an effort to organize their disturbed thoughts and perceptions (category four). Prominent among these scenes, which I call implicit trials, is Richard III's imaginary indictment of himself for murder at the end of the play (1592-93: IV. v). Here, Richard assumes the parts of the prosecutor who arraigns himself as well as the accused who defends himself against this charge. This last scene provides an example of how legal vocabulary and public trial procedure are internalized by an individual and employed as a coping mechanism in moments of crisis.

On a more abstract level, one might also call those many moments of conscious meditation and self-questioning in which legal terminology is adopted by Shakespeare's protagonists 'trials' (category 5).[3] However, in this essay I want to concentrate on only those types of scenes in which trial procedures are sequentially enacted or made repeated reference to (categories two through four). In what follows I trace the movement from Richard III's imagined trial of himself to Lear's semi-public mock trial of his daughters to the highly explicit and public trial of Angelo in *Measure for Measure*. These scenes dramatize human conflict and demonstrate how trials may be subject to corruption and foul play. In addition, they depict how individuals refer to trial elements and to impose order on their chaotic thoughts and experiences.

Before delving into these texts, it seems necessary to briefly describe early modern English trial procedure. As Debora Shuger explains, "[s]ixteenth-century English monarchs did not act as judges, at least not on any regular basis" (2001: 82). Rather than presiding over court sessions themselves, monarchs had representatives in

---

3 For instance, in his soliloquy at the end of Act II, scene ii of *Measure for Measure*, Angelo notes with surprise that he is subject to the same lust for which he, as the instrument of law, is putting Claudio to death. His meditation takes on a polyphonic quality that resembles Richard III's seemingly schizophrenic adoptions of the voices of the prosecution and defense in his implicit trial scene. Hamlet's various examinations of his motives for revenge could also be termed trials of conscience, as could Macbeth's frequent voicing of a sense of guilt.

the Chancery for civil cases and in the King's Council in Westminster, or Star Chamber, for criminal ones who acted as judges for them. Furthermore, assizes and ecclesiastical courts addressed felonies and misdemeanors on a local level. All these courts derived their authority on the basis of the monarch's prerogative to dispense justice (82-83). Trial by jury or by one's peers for lords of Parliament became a defendant's right with the Magna Carta in 1215. However, juried trials were not conducted universally nor necessarily fairly (Baker 1977: 19-23).

A minute account of the Duke of Buckingham's trial for treason in Westminster Hall in *Henry VIII* (II. i) serves as an example of a criminal trial carried out on the highest level. It is important to note that treason trials were notable for the monarch's power to have his aims enacted by his hand-picked judiciary.[4] Indeed, in Shakespeare's play, Henry VIII stages several highly stilted trials to railroad his wishes (Wegemer 112). Reporting on the Duke's trial for treason, one gentleman who witnessed the proceedings tells another about what he experienced:

> [...] The great Duke
> Came to the bar, where to his accusations
> He pleads still not guilty, and alleged
> Many sharp reasons to defeat the law.
> The King's attorney, on the contrary,
> Urged on the examinations, proofs, confessions,
> Of diverse witnesses, which the Duke desired
> To have brought *viva voce* to his face;
> At which appeared against him his surveyor,
> Sir Gilbert Park his chancellor, and John Court,
> Confessor to him, with that devil monk,
> Hopkins, that made this mischief.
>
> [..]
> All these accused him strongly, which he fain
> Would have flung from him, but indeed he could not.
> And so his peers, upon his evidence,
> Have found him guilty of high treason. (II. i. 11-22, 24-27)

Those unfamiliar with early modern English law may be surprised by the familiarity of the vocabulary and procedures in this trial scene which, written at the beginning of the sixteenth century, dramatizes events that had occurred nearly a century before then. Similarities between current Anglo-American trials and this one include "the bar" to demarcate the area where the justice or justices are seated facing the defendant; formal charges being spoken against the defendant (arraignment), the identification of the defendant as the person accused of the crime when charges are spoken; the defendant's plea to the charges made against him; the presentation of the case by the prosecution and the introduction of Crown (or prosecutor's) witnesses; the announcement of a verdict by the jury of peers (jurors for commoners); and the

4 For an account of Tudor legal procedures see Schauer and Schauer (1980) and Lederer's discussion of heresy trials after 1534 in this volume.

pronouncing of judgment by the judge that follows just after the lines quoted above.[5] Many of these elements will appear in the trial scenes discussed in the following sections.

Notably lacking from this trial from a twenty-first century point of view is a counsel for the defendant, who might have counter-examined the prosecution's witnesses and questioned its evidence, brought evidence to attest for the defendant's innocence, and introduced witnesses that would have denied the claims made by the prosecution.[6] That trial procedure could be used to effect injustice is an obvious theme in Shakespeare's dramatization of trials held during Henry VIII's reign. While not questioning the legality of how Buckingham has been tried, the gentleman does note that he was virtually powerless to defend himself. Within the context of the king's carefully orchestrated public ritual, the defendant's efforts to contravene the "proofs, confessions" of the Crown witnesses have no real effect. This question of whether individuals can receive justice in trials that are organized by and presided over by those who hold power will be pursued in the trial scenes described below.

Richard III: The Villain Tries Himself for Villainy

The imaginary trial scene in *Richard III* is so brief that it can be quoted in full. On the eve of his battle with Henry, Earl of Richmond, the future King Henry VII, Richard falls into uneasy sleep and is visited by the victims of his many crimes. He proceeds to interpret these visitations using the language of a trial (Act V, scene iii). He takes the eleven ghosts of his murdered victims to be witnesses for the prosecution who testify against him and charge him with murder. The appearance of each new ghost verifies and builds upon the testimony of the last. Although Shakespeare's major source text, Sir Thomas More's *History*, had dramatically emphasized Richard's inability to sleep peacefully after he had ordered his nephews – the princes in the Tower – to be murdered, it was entirely Shakespeare's invention to couch Richard's sleepless crises of conscience in terms of a trial by law:[7]

---

5 For a detailed discussion of the various trial types and procedures, see Baker (1977).

6 Baker notes that there were few "rules of evidence" and no notion of hearsay during the period (1977: 38-40). As Schauer and Schauer point out, the burden of proof lay on the defendant in trials for treason and major felonies during the Tudor period. An adversarial notion of truth that could be won by comparing the prosecution's and the defense's interpretations of evidence and testimony presented to the court was not yet in place (1980: 77). On the evolution of the notion of narrative truth won through adversarial argument, see Kayman in this volume.

7 "I have harde by credible reporte of suche as were secrete with his chamberers that after this abhominable deed done, he never was quiet in his mynde he never thought him selfe sure where he wente abroade, his body prively feinted, his eyen wherled aboute, his hande ever on his dagger, his countenaunce and maner lyke alwaies to stricke againe, he toke evill reste on nightes, laye long wakyng and musyng, forweried with care and watche, rather slombred then slept, troubled with fearefull dreames, sodeinly somtyme stert up, leapte out of his bed and loked about the chamber, so was his restless harte continually tossed and tombled with the tedious impression and strormy remembraunce of his abhominable murther and execrable tyrannye" (More's *The History of King Richard*; quoted in Hall's *Union* 363). Anne has prepared the audience for this

> What do I fear? Myself? There's none else by;
> Richard loves Richard, that is, I and I.
> Is there a murderer here? No. Yes, I am!
> Then fly. What, from myself? Great reason why,
> Lest I revenge? What, myself upon myself?
> Alack, I love myself. Wherefore? For any good
> That I myself have done unto myself?
> O no, alas, I rather hate myself
> For hateful deeds committed by myself.
> I am a villain, – yet I lie, I am not.
> Fool, of thyself speak well! Fool, do not flatter.
> My conscience hath a thousand several tongues,
> And every tongue brings in a several tale,
> And every tale condemns me for a villain:
> Perjury, perjury, in the highest degree;
> Murder, stern murder, in the direst degree;
> All several sins, all us'd in each degree,
> Throng to the bar, crying all, 'Guilty, guilty!' (V. iii. 183-200)

Anticipating Bakhtinian polyphony and Freudian divisions of the self, Richard takes on a variety of roles and voices in his imaginary trial of himself. First he attempts, like a clerk in a court session to identify the accused formally and read the indictment against him: "Is there a murderer here?" The answer is both a plea of 'not guilty' and a confession of the indictment: "No. Yes, I am!" Serving as the equivalent of a Crown witness, Richard then brings in evidence against himself: "For hateful deeds committed by myself. / I am a villain." He then responds as an accused person might do to contradict the Crown witnesses' testimony: "– yet I lie, I am not. / Fool, of thyself speak well!"[8]

Yet it would appear that more witnesses are waiting to support the Crown's indictment for murder: Richard's conscience has "a thousand several tongues. / And every tongue brings in a several tale." These 'tongues' – a metonymy for the witnesses – reiterate the prosecution's charges. Clearly, Richard identifies the 'tale' bringers with the victims of his crimes who have just disturbed his sleep. Each one "brings in" the evidence and "[t]hrong[s] to the bar, crying all, 'Guilty, guilty!'"[9] Simultaneously, a defiant Richard, speaking as the accused who refuses to accept the charge against him, counters this evidence with the charge of "Perjury, perjury in the high'st degree!" Realizing that sentencing would surely result in a verdict of guilty and a judgment of execution, Richard despairs; he envisions a death in which he will be missed and mourned by no one. This presents no alternative to his wretched life. In this moment

---

scene with her mention of Richard's "timorous dreams" (IV. i. 84) in her last scene while living as well as during her communication to Richard from the dead (V. iii. 160-67).

8 Baker points out that a running debate between the accused and his accusers was still common in the late sixteenth century (1977: 38, 305).

9 Significantly, 'brings in' is used in the same way as in Lear's mock trial scene (1605-6: III. vi. 35), and this is the first recorded usage of this legalistic meaning of the prepositional verb (*Richard III* 2000: 344, Note 173).

of self-recognition, Richard anticipates the verdict, conviction, and execution of judgment that will be carried out on the battle field the next day (Clemen 307).

Interestingly, Richard appears to create the notion of various degrees of legal culpability in this scene when he refers to the "highest degree!" of crime committed against him (perjury) and the "direst degree" of how he has committed murder, much as a contemporary speaker would differentiate between first (premeditated) and second-degree (reckless) murder and manslaughter. According to the textual notes to the play in the Oxford edition, this specifically legal usage of the term was not "recorded before 1676" (2000: 344, Note 176). However, Shakespeare appears to anticipate an understanding of law in which a given crime can be characterized as more or less reprehensible and subject to harsh judgment.

By taking himself to court, so to say, Richard affirms the validity of trial procedure as a manner of redressing conflict. It is striking that Richard never questions whether natural succession is the right way to impose authority in the realm; instead, as William Carroll asserts, he simply removes everyone between himself and his own 'natural' place in the line up to the crown (1992). Similarly, although Richard is guilty of a variety of crimes, he nevertheless resorts to legal procedure to address the issue of a judgment over his past actions. He identifies and arraigns himself, brings in evidence against himself, offers a defense based on the prosecution's false witnesses, and finally pronounces a verdict.

Like the major protagonists in the other trial scenes discussed here, Richard also gets lawyerly when he insists on receiving due process before the law. He violently protests against his being made the object of judicial foul play (perjury). Stylizing himself as a wronged innocent, he alludes to the fact that arraignments for murder may well be based on reports by false witnesses. With his counter-charge of perjury, Richard puts himself on the side of those who are penalized by the misuse of law in the trial scenes discussed below: the disempowered Lear, and Isabella and Mariana.

This internalized trial scene marks a turning point in Richard's characterization. The would-be villain who has walked over the bodies of children and widows to gain the crown now calls on law to enact justice and uses legal forms in the debate with himself. Heretofore shown to be a dynamic Machiavellian without scruple, he now appears as a man ridden with self-doubt. The lack of resolution to this internal trial scene – the judgment is only imagined – is answered in the following act. There, in another trial by battle, the great warrior Richard is slain with spectacular publicity by his rival Henry Tudor, Earl of Richmond.

Conventional readings of the so-called dream or ghost scene suggest that it is a comic variant of Shakespeare's later introspective soliloquies and it enacts Richard's role as a Machiavellian ruler (Sanders 1968: 106-8); alternatively the scene is viewed as a repetition of Richard's stichomythic dialogues with characters like Anne, in which he takes on both opposing parts (Braunmuller 1984: 121), or a symbolic war between Richard and his reluctant conscience after he has succeeded in becoming the villain he set out to be in his first soliloquy (Frisch 1993: 279-80; Van Laan 1978: 146-47). Finally, the scene is read as an enactment of the schism in Richard's personality (Neill 1975: 123-24; Ornstein 1972: 78-79; Iser 1993; Pearlman 1992: 66-67).

While such readings convincingly explain Richard's adopting multiple voices in this scene, they fail to comment on the specificity of his use of legal terminology and insistence on due process. Again, judicial vocabulary and process are absent in the source text for this scene. Thus Shakespeare's introduction of them in this dramatization of events from 1485 has particular meaning. In a moment of severe crisis Richard adopts elements of trial procedure to cope with his loss of confidence in his heretofore unvanquished effort to gain and consolidate power. Law provides him with a way to interpret the visitation from the dead and gives him words with and a form in which to defend himself against their charges. That an individual awakening from a nightmare uses highly specific legal vocabulary and alludes to trial procedures suggests that trials are not just showy rituals of power but have also become internalized psychological parameters for interpreting the world.

Imagining that he is without his power as king to tell his justices how to pass sentence, Richard stylizes himself as a potential victim of the law. He thus places himself on the side of the defendant who would be more or less powerless in the face a court in which the king had the power to determine the verdict. In so doing he disassociates himself from his own power as arbiter of justice and identifies himself with those who are judged over. Thus he points out the fundamental ambivalence of trials as methods to achieve justice.

King Lear: Madmen and Fools Play at Going to the Bar

Far more explicit than Richard's imaginary trial of himself for murder is Lear's mock trial of Goneril and Regan for treason.[10] At the beginning of the play the King stages a symbolic trial of love amongst his three daughters in which they had to give verbal testimony about their affection for him. Lear acts as a misguided judge when he awards his kingdom to Goneril and Regan and disowns his youngest child Cordelia (Act I, scene i).[11] Lear soon learns about the effects of his rash mistake when he is insulted and disempowered by Goneril (Act I, scene iv) and refused a home by Regan (Act II, scene ii). Stripped of power and honor and having torn off his own robes, Lear proceeds during the third act to wander the heath and storm at fate and himself for having made such drastic mistakes.

While taking rest in a farmhouse Lear attempts to impose some order on a world that has been turned upside down due to his own fallibility by enacting an imaginary trial of his daughters. First he announces his intention to make his daughters stand trial by proxy: "I will arraign them straight" (III. vi. 20). He then formally greets the two pseudo-justices, Edgar and the fool, by assigning them places in the courtroom (III. vi. 21-22). George Keeton reads Lear's calling of the "robed man of justice" and "his yoke-fellow of equity" as an allusion to a sovereign's bringing together a special

10 On the omission of the trial scene from the folio edition of the play, see Warren (1983), who argues that Shakespeare himself cut the scene due to difficulties that occurred in performing it. See also Lusardi, who on the contrary argues for its dramatic importance to the play's development (1988).

11 For a reading of the play as a series of symbolic trial scenes, see Hockey (1959).

session that would include the Courts of Common Law and the Chancellor's Court (1967: 33), thus emphasizing the specificity of Lear's legal vocabulary and allusion to contemporary judicial practices and highlighting the seriousness of the case to be heard.

Lear pronounces his wish to witness the trial with his own eyes, to see justice enacted as it were, and asks that the formal evidence of the witnesses be brought against the accused: "I'll see their trial first. Bring in their evidence" (III. vi. 35). Edgar and the fool then take on their roles as the king's commissioned deputies of justice and lend legitimacy to these imagined trial proceedings when Edgar announces: "Let us deal justly" (III. vi. 40). He then recites a ditty about an absentee shepherd, whose sheep are susceptible to harm, which serves as an obvious allegory to Lear's having poorly stewarded his flock and people by divesting himself of power in favor of his two unscrupulous daughters (Lockhart 1975: 470-71).

"Arraign her first, 'tis Goneril" (III. vi. 46), Lear demands, suggesting that his first daughter is the primary culprit. Like Richard III's allusion to a maximum degree to which perjury and murder can be committed, Lear suggests here that the defendants are culpable to different degrees. Goneril is indeed the child who has thrown her father and king out of his former home and was the first to show him complete disrespect: she "kicked the poor King her father" (III. vi. 47-48) This line is alternately read as an illustration of Lear's "*personal* anguish" (Kronenfeld 1988: 210) — an indication of his interest in his personal sufferings rather than the larger abuse of justice that has occurred — or as evidence that Lear has been subject to actual physical abuse (Lusardi 1988: 132). Taking over the role of the Crown counsel or a doctor of law, the fool questions the fictive Goneril and demands that she identify herself: "Is your name Goneril?" (III. vi. 49). Thus an identification of the accused takes place after the formal arraignment. When Goneril fails to respond, the fool insults her by apologizing for having mistaken her for a footstool.

Acting as a Crown witness, Lear testifies to his second daughter Regan's guilt on the evidence of her "warped looks" (III. vi. 52). In the role of the incensed appellant who watches with consternation as the defendant goes free, he then charges the court with foul play for allowing Regan to escape from her trial: "[C]orruption in the place! / False justicer, why hast thou let her 'scape?" (III. vi. 54-55). Regan's imaginary flight brings the trial to an abrupt close. Its fantastic quality is commented upon by Edgar's ironic "Bless thy five wits" (III. vi. 56).

Lear assumes various roles in the court session. Playing the parts of the plaintiff, he acts as the victim of filial ingratitude and lack of charity; as the Crown counsel and prosecutor's witness, he accuses the defendants of crimes and appeals to a higher authority for justice: those earthly justices who would let Regan walk free must be false ones. Additionally, he adopts the roles of the jury and judge. Although the mock trial has been cut off abruptly, it does in fact climax in a form of verdict and judgment when Lear announces that Regan should be "anatomize[d]" (III. vi. 73).

Lear's attempt to enact justice in a world in which he has become powerless by borrowing forms from trials by jury is highly significant in this scene. No codified law can address the wrongs that have occurred and will continue to occur in this mythic Britain (Oppel 1968: 359). And the three exiled men who act as justices, accusers, and witnesses in this treason trial are without the power to impose a verdict. Yet walking through the procedures of arraigning and identifying the defendants and hearing the testimony against them appears to calm Lear enough to allow him to sleep. As in Richard's implicit trial scene, law functions for a deeply troubled individual as an ordering principle, even when it is merely symbolic. Identified and indicted, the accused are formally 'brought to the bar' by having the fool and Edgar pretend to create the space of a courtroom. When justice appears to be being impeded, Lear accuses the justices of having been bribed. He then identifies and indicts Regan and pronounces judgment over her. Having lost everything – power, his daughters' love and respect, his ability to defend himself militarily, the right to act as a justice – Lear creates an imaginary trial in which the wrongs done to him can be addressed and his daughters can be indicted for treason.

Lear's mock trial in which the guilty parties would be convicted if the justices had power stands in radical contrast to the scene of cruel military-style justice that follows it. Accused of treason by Cornwall and Regan, Gloucester is summarily punished by having his eyes gauged out of their sockets (III. vii). Here an innocent is destroyed in a farce of justice carried out by the powerful. Reading the play as a series of trials, one could say that the trial masque is followed by a scene of miscarried justice (Oppel 368). If some larger trial by God is carried out in this bleak and grand play, as it is in *Richard III*, then the judgment is spoken and the punishment occurs when Regan and Goneril destroy each other due to their sexual jealousy concerning Edmund.

The mock trial scene brings Goneril and Regan to the bar; yet ultimately this scene constitutes a trial of Lear for his having unwisely chosen to give up the power that would in fact have allowed him to put into practice his wish to try his daughters for treason. Lear acts both as a private person or plaintiff and as the public incarnation of justice, the former king. Not only does Lear – here the impoverished outsider – accuse the justice of being corrupt in allowing Regan to escape and hence allude to the potential for the miscarriage of justice by the powerful against the weak, but he also indirectly arraigns himself for having failed in his former role as a just king and benevolent judge. Lear's indictment of justice and the abuse of legal proceedings by the powerful will continue in Act IV, scene vi.

This mock and semi-public trial represents a fantastic realization of Lear's internal need to sue his daughters for treason in a manner as public and spectacular as the Duke of Buckingham's trial in *Henry VIII*. The parodic and, at times, disorderly and chaotic quality of the trial emphasizes the functions of trials in general, namely that of responding to crises with ritualistic and orderly performances.[12] As in the last scene of *Measure for Measure*, the enactment of a trial in *King Lear* is shown to be a form of ritualized redress of private wrongs. Even if the trial Lear enacts has no public consequences other than for his small on-stage audience, it demonstrates to the audience that the trappings of law may be used successfully by individuals to make order of chaos and resolve conflict.

---

12 Adopting the anthropologist Victor Turner's analysis of drama as a form of ritual, Lusardi reads the mock trial scene as the group's, and not only Lear's, effort to try to re-impose meaning and order on their chaotic circumstances (1988:133).

Measure for Measure: A Fallen Angel and Women on Trial

The trial scene that constitutes the last act of *Measure for Measure* is similar to Shakespeare's most famous trial, Act IV, scene i from *The Merchant of Venice* (1596-97). Both trials are rich in dramatic twists and turns and cliff-hangers. Before justice is enacted the villain appears to get off scot-free and innocent victims are maltreated.[13]

Similar to those fictional trial scenes one views in contemporary television dramas, tension has to be built up before some measure of justice – if it is justice – is enacted. The plot twists that precede the trial in *Measure for Measure* account partially for its spectacular, unexpected quality. Having been criticized for executing law too leniently in a Vienna that has become filled with brothels and corruption, the Duke departs from his city, leaving authority in the hands of the young, apparently incorruptible nobleman Angelo, whose very name seems to tell the audience what it needs to know about him. Obeying the Duke's command that he institute a stricter policy of law enforcement, Angelo revives a law against "fornication"[14] that has fallen into disuse. He uses the young nobleman Claudio, who has impregnated his fiancée, to set up a precedent. After enduring public penance,[15] Claudio is put in prison and sentenced to death. Insisting on his role as an impartial instrument of the law rather than an executive of worldly power, Angelo claims that he would convict him even if he were his own close relation:

> It is the law, not I, condemn your brother;
> Were he my kinsman, brother, or my son,
> It should be thus with him. He must die tomorrow. (II. ii. 80-82)

Angelo invokes a vision of law as an impartial abstraction that cannot be influenced by human ties or emotions. Yet his actions directly contradict this vision: he will attempt to bully Claudio's sister into having sex with him in return for her brother's life and will nevertheless command his execution.

At the end of the play Angelo is tried for his crimes in a spectacular demonstration of the Duke's power. Importantly, the contemporary vision of the king at the beginning of the Jacobean period was as a benevolent deputy of divine justice in a world in which the disenfranchised were likely to be abused (Shuger 2001: 74). When

---

13 I do not explicate *The Merchant of Venice*'s trial scene here, because one element of its structure differs considerably from the other trials discussed here. Portia, as a disguised doctor of law, first appears to support Shylock's claim to have his bond fulfilled and then invents or remembers the ancient law that hinders him from collecting the interest on it. It is her and not the ruler of Venice, the Duke, who acts as attorney and jury. She also orchestrates the trial, not the Duke. Hence the issues of royal authority and the dual role of the ruler as a private and public person with regard to the law are not addressed in the play.

14 Hayne points out that one of the issues being explored in the play is the lack of words to describe different types of illicit sex other than "fornication" (1999: 162).

15 Offenders could be punished by having to appear in church or in the market place dressed in a white sheet, standing in the pillory, being whipped, and of course by getting married (Bawcutt 1991: 11).

enacting justice and enforcing laws as "God's substitutes" in a faulted world, rulers were permitted to resort to using extraordinary measures (Pope 1970: 57). Hence the Duke's setting up of Angelo in the trial scene is presumably meant to serve the ends of the weaker members of his city such as Claudio, Isabella, and Mariana.

Vincentio has ordered Angelo to meet him at the gates of the city where the city's nobleman and officers are gathered, providing a jury of peers. Ironically, Vincentio opens the scene by loading praise on Angelo for his reported integrity and good service:

> [...] we hear
> Such goodness of your justice that our soul
> Cannot but yield you forth to public thanks (V. i. 5-7)

This initial legitimation of Angelo's actions renders the fact that he is subsequently charged with and convicted for his crimes all the more dramatic. After the Duke's speech Isabella makes a dramatic entrance. As instructed by Friar Lodowick (i.e. the Duke in disguise), she demands that the Duke fulfill his role as the incarnation of justice now that he has returned to his city. She cries out to him:

> [...] dishonour not your eye
> By throwing it on any other object,
> Till you have heard me in my true complaint,
> And given me justice! Justice! Justice! Justice! (V. i. 23-26)

Thus Isabella – under direction – turns the Duke's formal reassumption of power into a criminal court session. As an appellant she sues Angelo in person, accusing him of deceit, murder, fornication, and rape (arraignment):

> That Angelo's forsworn, is it not strange?
> That Angelo's a murderer, is't not strange?
> That Angelo is an adulterous thief,
> An hypocrite, a virgin-violator,
> Is it not strange, and strange? (V. i. 40-44)

The repetitions of "that Angelo is" and "is it not strange" stress the contradiction between Angelo's name and his deeds and betray Isabella's awareness that the revelation of Angelo's true character will come as a great surprise to her audience and may be greeted with suspicion. Furthermore, the repetitions of the deputy's proper name serve as a formal identification of the criminal. It is ironic here or typically Shakespearean that in stating her accusations Isabella perjures and slanders herself. At the behest of the disguised Duke, she had convinced Angelo's former fiancée to have sex with him under the cover of darkness in her place.

What follows reminds the contemporary reader of many a rape trial scene in which the victim turns into the accused.[16] Angelo responds to Isabella's first accusation by suggesting that she is mad with grief (V. i. 35-37). Afterwards, the Duke and Friar Peter gang up to discredit Isabella's word and she is carted off to prison. Mariana is then brought in as a witness for Angelo's character. She swears that Angelo, who abandoned her several years before, did not bed Isabella but herself. Now Angelo joins the other men in helping to discredit the woman's testimony. He claims that it was not the loss of her dowry that made him desert his fiancée but rather her sexual impurity (V. i. 215-23).

Playing with his victim, the Duke twice insists that Angelo should preside over the decision of how the two women should be punished: "be you judge / of your own cause" (V. i. 168-69, 255-56). Underlining the play's juxtaposition of enforcing the law to the letter versus applying judgment in an equitable fashion, this speech also echoes Christ's charge to those who would stone the adulteress: that he should throw the first stone who is himself blameless (John 8:7). As the Duke and the audience well know, Angelo is ill-fit to pass judgment on women he has victimized.

Departing and then reentering in his disguise as the friar, the Duke claims that Vienna's court is guilty of judicial malpractice, if, as it appears, the Duke has left the act of coming to a verdict to the perpetrator of the crime, Angelo:

> [...] the Duke's unjust
> Thus to retort your manifest appeal,
> And put your trial in the villain's mouth
> Which here you come to accuse. (V. i. 298-301)

This speech constitutes the moment in which the court in the person of the Duke is accused of foul play. Interestingly, the Duke takes on several roles here. He is at once a private individual who demands justice from dishonest authorities and the public figure of the seemingly absent, negligent ruler who has left presiding over a criminal case to the very deputy who is accused of crimes.[17]

Importantly, Shakespeare acknowledges the danger of abusing legal forms to further individual interests. Characters' insistence that trial procedure should be fair demonstrates both their faith in the institution as a source of public authority as well as their reliance upon it to settle conflict. Moments in which trial procedure is questioned also demonstrate individuals' ready knowledge of judicial forms and awareness of the related potential abuses of power.

After the outspoken Friar has caused as much disruption as the unruly women who preceded him, Escalus orders that he also be taken off to prison like the "giglets" (V. i. 345), or prostitutes, who have conspired with him. Significantly, in a play about the meanings and results of illegal forms of sexuality, the seeming friar and the novice – both figures of abstinence – are here associated with loose women. This association

---

16 See, for instance, Alice Sebold's account of her rape and the subsequent trial of her attacker in *Lucky* (1999).

17 For an extended analysis of the Duke's role-playing see Gless (1979: 116-43).

brings the play's exploration of sexual politics to the forefront in two different ways. On the one hand, the powerlessness of sexually stigmatized women in the Duke's Vienna is highlighted in this speech. To disturb the proceedings of the court as the Friar has done is to make oneself – like a prostitute – into an undesirable who should be carted off to jail, just as the brothels should be moved outside the city. On the other hand Escalus's speech points out the problems involved in making allegations of sexual wrongdoing. Would-be Puritans like Angelo are shown to be subject to the messy movements of desire. And individuals such as Claudio, Isabella, and Mariana may be inappropriately punished for actions involving sex.

When the 'friar' resists, his hood is removed, and in a spectacular dénouement, he is revealed to be the Duke. Angelo instantly expresses the wish to be executed rather than have the Duke preside over his trial. Re-instated in power, the Duke then begins setting various wrongs aright in an elaborate rapid-fire sentencing and pardoning ceremony. Angelo's, Claudio's and Lucio's sentences to enter hastily performed marriages to women with whom they have 'fornicated' transform *Measure for Measure* from what appeared to be a tragedy in the third act into a not-terribly-funny comedy. Lucio complains that having to marry "a punk" (V. i. 520) is a fate worse than torture and execution. Surely, this will be a marriage without affection. Similarly, Angelo states that he would have preferred death to the 'merciful' punishment of an enforced marriage (V. i. 472-75). He, too, will make an ambivalent husband to the woman he once abandoned. Finally, Isabella is 'rewarded by' or punished with a marriage proposal from the Duke. This proposal might be a reward for her having generously pleaded for Angelo's life while she still believed him to have been the cause of her brother's death. Alternately – but the issue is left unresolved – the proposal may be a form of punishment for the sense of morality that made Isabella's choice early in the play to protect her honor rather than her brother's life a patently clear one. The Duke's having 'saved' her brother as well as her virginity may compel her to enter a marital union with him. Effectively, she may become subject to a form of coercion involving her body and emotions that differs little from what she was subject to under Angelo except that it will be sanctified by the church and state. Finally, the Duke, who condemned the laxity of law enforcement in Vienna, breaks the law himself by behaving like a bawd to convince the presumably virginal Mariana to pretend to be someone else and engage in illicit sex. Ultimately, the critics agree that the trial scene contributes largely to this problem play's resistance to closure.

Positive interpretations of the trial see it as a dramatic debate between the claims of strict common law practice and the alternate claims of the court of equity. The Duke uses artifice, what was known legally as a *dolus bonus* (a good trick), in order to aid the claims of the weaker party in the play and to achieve a form of "Christian social justice" in the end (Shuger 2001: 94, 98). According to this reading, the Duke's actions correspond to an understanding of the monarch as one who protects the interests of the powerless (here, women) against those of the powerful (101). Another critic, Barbara Everett, understands the play and its culminating trial as a depiction of the humanization of justice and the growth of self-knowledge in the individual who has been appointed the difficult task of enforcing the law:

> Authority and goodness are essentially amateur, hypothetical, circumstantial: they are that which does not despise, at need, squalid shifts like bed tricks or humping about the head of a dead pirate. They are also, since the Duke corrects only that action which he himself initiated, something like an inward process of responsible self-knowledge, self-discovery. (2003: 24)

More critical readings view the play and its trial as a demonstration of the Duke's (and perhaps the newly-crowned James I's) abuse of judicial procedures during the treason trials at the beginning of his reign (Bernthal 1992). Harriet Hawkins stresses the ambivalence the audience feels about the Duke's having forced a comic ending (marriage) on the development of events and characters (Angelo and Isabella), whose personalities would more coherently have called for a tragic ending involving death (1987: 87-88).

Whether one condones the Duke's schemes and surprise last-minute acquittals remains a question of interpretation. Leaving this issue open, I wish to bring out four aspects of the trial scene. First, it functions as a clear demonstration of how Shakespeare's rulers exercise the law in order to signify their power. In the trial the Duke reveals that he has been present all along and has – if we follow the positive interpretations – made certain that tragic events like Claudio's beheading and Isabella's loss of honor did not occur. The Duke has scripted an elaborate play in which the actors deal with problems of real crimes and abstract notions of law in the most public of settings, a royal trial in the open air.[18] He resolves tensions between abstract law and real circumstances as well as a number of seemingly irresolvable moral dilemmas in this scene. In his dual roles as friar and ruler, Duke Vincentio demonstrates his god-like knowledge of and authority over his subjects.

Second, the scene demonstrates the extent to which trials function as highly dramatic forums: Numerous unveilings occur in this scene: Mariana "unmask[s]" (V. i. 205) and reveals herself as Angelo's wife by right; Lucio forcibly removes the friar's hood and uncovers the Duke; the criminal thought to be the murderer Bernadine is "unmuffle[d]" (V. i. 487) to reveal Claudio, who all but the Duke thought was dead. In the hands of a masterful director such as the Duke, trials make for exciting theater.

Third, the scene illustrates how private conflicts can be publicized and resolved in the courtroom, when Isabella brings the coercion to which she has been subject to light and reveals Angelo's anything but angelic character. If a tribunal is unbiased by the machinations of the powerful, victimized individuals may make use of them to criticize corrupt public authority and to give voice to their hurts. Furthermore, injuries done in private take on public meanings and may be ritualistically healed through the judicial process.

Finally, the scene addresses the possibility of the abuse of legal forms by corrupt officials. If no Duke Vincentio is waiting in the wings to put wrongs aright, judicial authority can be used as an instrument of injustice, either to impose a blindly legalistic notion of law that would put a Claudio to death for fornication or to act as an

---

18 I am following Gulley's reading of the play in which he concludes: "[...] the layering of competing scripts that defines the play's structure suggests that law in practice is inevitably performance and, further, that only through performance can the shape of law be determined" (1996: 68).

instrument of corruption. In sum, trials then are shown to be powerful public rituals and avenues for conflict resolution that may also be perverted to advance immoral ends.

Conclusion

The trial scenes discussed above range from the implicit, private, and imaginary to the explicit and public. At one end of this range, verdicts and judgments are envisioned and an image of the courtroom is invoked, at the other end, trial procedure is followed, and the presence of jurors ensure that punishments will be carried out. These scenes demonstrate how Shakespearean characters make reference to trial procedure or actually enact mock trials to redress wrongs and pattern their actions in the face of troubling circumstances. Less than as documentations of the specifics of Elizabethan and Jacobean law, I read these scenes more as indications that Shakespeare regarded trial procedure to be a model of behavior, if an imperfect one, which individuals internalize and refer to when in crisis.

Elements of trials in these scenes include arraignments, identifications of the accused, pleas, the bringing in of evidence, witnesses, verdicts, convictions, and judgments. These structures inform the reflections of individuals when they are alone, like Richard, or in small groups, like Lear. Even when no one is present to witness a trial, its forms manifest themselves as meaningful for the individual who pictures or mimics them. Trial procedures become organizational principles that individuals apply to their disordered thoughts and worlds, even when they themselves are the causes of that disorder. In their adoption of judicial forms and procedures and legal vocabulary, Shakespearean characters subject their private experiences to public practices of authority. They impose the discipline of trial procedure upon themselves to become, in fact, their own jurors and justices.[19]

Despite its ambiguities, the explicit trial scene in *Measure for Measure* demonstrates the enactment of law as a successful form of public, political authority. Concurrently, this explicit trial scene shows law to be no simple business. Duke Vincentio commits crimes in order to avoid larger wrongs. He prostitutes Mariana to save Isabella's virginity. Regarding this act cynically, we can surmise that he saves the pleasure for himself. He lies to Isabella and causes her inordinate pain by making her believe that her brother has been executed. He also forces Isabella to perjure herself in order to set up the courtroom setting that will bring about Angelo's dramatic fall from power and respectability.

Yet the Duke also plays the part of the subversive Friar in order to accuse himself of misusing his power by allowing Angelo to preside over the case against him. Ultimately, he saves the day by showing himself to be both aware of potential power abuses – due to Angelo's corruption and the Duke's apparent neglect of affairs – and ready to allot justice in a measured and merciful way. Moreover, the claims of private

---

19 Arguably, Shakespeare anticipates Michel Foucault's thesis that external sources of authority were internalized into the individual as methods of self-surveillance in modernity (*Discipline and Punish: The Birth of the Prison*, 1979).

persons, wronged women like Mariana and Isabella, are given public redress and are publicly righted in the Duke's elaborately staged trial scene. Law as an instrument that can either be abused by the powerful or may vindicate the claims of the powerless is itself brought to court in *Measure for Measure*'s final act.

Lear's mock trial in front of a fool and a pretended madman shows how the individual, here the disempowered king, resorts to legal procedures when under duress to address his having been wronged. The drama of this scene arises out of the former incarnation of justice, the King, now acting as a private person, who arraigns those who have wronged him in a trial scene that is without public consequence due to the King's banishment and the jurors' dubious status. Furthermore, Lear's trial becomes a trial of himself as a king and father who made fatal mistakes of judgment and gave his power away imprudently.

Richard's internal, imaginary trial scene illustrates how public practices of authority are adopted in the individual's mind, here a tyrannical ruler in dialog with himself. Richard has shown himself to be eminently criminal. Yet when pressed by the appearance of his dead victims into a fear of punishment he uses the procedures of a trial to try to clear his sense of confusion and quiet his doubts. Richard's miserable failure at the battle of Bosworth Field represents a carrying out of the imaginary jury's verdict of guilty which he, as his own jury, has pronounced against himself. The legitimacy of legal process is underlined by the offender's punishment by death in a trial by battle. This battle ends with Henry Tudor, Earl of Richmond, who serves as the personification of justice and the good king, winning the show and restoring peace to war-scarred England.

In these trial scenes judicial authority is put on trial. The potential for legal abuse by the powerful of the weak – women in *Measure for Measure*, a homeless and impoverished old man in *King Lear*, perhaps even Richard in his fashioning of himself as the perennially unloved man – is shown to be a far-reaching problem. Thus Shakespeare in his trial scenes explores the issue of law as an instrument of injustice as well as justice. The dangers of powerful individuals' abuse of judicial procedure are dramatized as is the possibility that the weak may gain a voice and ultimately be recompensed with the aid of law. That a Duke, a former ruler, and a present king set up the trial scenes described here demonstrates an awareness of the awful power invested in monarchs as arbiters of justice. Simultaneously, their appearances in these scenes as private individuals who demand due procedure for themselves and their confederates show trials to be rituals in which crises may be resolved and justice enacted. That Richard, Lear, and Vincentio all adopt numerous roles – as judges, witnesses, jurors, and defendants – in the trial scenes they imagine or actually cause to transpire shows their familiarity with and facility for employing legal procedures. Moreover, the way in which they tailor trial elements to fit their individual circumstances and fulfill their psychological needs, demonstrates the degree to which law structures their thought and colors their perceptions.

Whether Shakespeare intended his trials to reflect on 'real' contemporary legal proceedings, or to be instances of social criticism or flattering testimonials to his monarchs' judicial practices, or, far more likely, as some combination of the above, remains open to interpretation.[20] However that may be, Shakespeare's trial scenes and their ritualized treatment of human conflicts make for consummate theater. Moreover, they show that the trappings of law inform human experience and thought both inside and outside the courtroom.

Typology of trial scenes

The following typology is intended as a schematic interpretation of the prototypical trial scenes described above. My intention is to show whether the trials take place as public rituals or as privately enacted patterns of dealing with duress, to explore to what degree they adhere to actual jury trial procedure, and what their outcomes are. Significantly, the play's ruler or former ruler acts as judge in these trials and functions as a director within these scenes as pieces of ritualized theater.

Level of explicitness in terms of adherence to trial procedure and judicial vocabulary	**implicit** Richard III's imaginary trial of himself for murder (V. iii. 183-200)	**semi-explicit** Lear's mock trial of Goneril and Regan for treason (III. vi.)	**explicit** Duke Vincentio's public trial of Angelo for perjury, intended murder, and fornication in *Measure for Measure* (V. i)
Publicness	private, Richard is alone	semi-private: Lear is with the Fool and Edgar who is pre-tending to be a mad beggar	public, in court in the presence of the monarch, nobility and clergyman
Number of participants in trial	one	three individuals, all divested of power	crowd of peers and commoners
Outcome	verdict of guilty, which is perhaps transferred into a judgment in the trial by battle that follows	spoken judgment of "anatomization": Regan is later poisoned by her sister who then stabs herself.	Angelo's actual and intended crimes are revealed. He is convicted and subsequently pardoned.

This typology might be put to use in several ways which I will describe sequentially. In a first step, it could be employed to characterize the myriad of other trial scenes

20 Ian Ward summarizes developments in Shakespeare criticism since Trilling to see the Bard either as a propagandist for his monarchs, as a social subversive, or as an apolitical man of theater (1995: 67-68).

from Shakespeare's plays that for lack of space could not be discussed in this paper; it could thus be determined whether these scenes serve similar functions as in the plays analyzed above. Significantly, only the trial scene from *Measure for Measure* depicts an actual court session. Otherwise, characters like Richard and Lear fashion themselves as litigants to enact trials privately or semi-privately. These less explicit trial scenes demonstrate, as I have argued, the degree to which law and its specific manifestations in trial procedure have been internalized by individuals as a pattern of thought and an ordering principle. Thus in a second step, one could apply the categories described above to other Renaissance dramas in which trial scenes of various types are depicted to discover whether the same process of internalizing structures of public judicial authority also occur in them. In a third step one might take a diachronic approach to dramatic trial scenes to see how attitudes towards and familiarity with trial procedure are reflected in the degree to which their characters make private reference to and use of them. Finally, one might apply the criteria of explicit adherence to trial procedure and internalization of judicial proceedings to other genre such as the novel to explore the functions that trial scenes serve there.

Works Cited

Baker, J. H. (1977) "Criminal Courts and Procedure at Common Law 1550-1800." *Crime in England 1550-1800.* Ed. J. S. Cockburn. London: Methuen. 15-48.

Bawcutt, N. W. (1991) "Introduction." *Measure for Measure.* Ed. N. W. Bawcutt. Oxford: Clarendon Press.

Bernthal, Craig A. (1992) "Staging Justice: James I and the Trial Scenes of *Measure for Measure.*" *Studies in English Literature* 32: 247-69.

Braunmuller, A. R. (1984) "Early Shakespearian Tragedy and its Contemporary Context: Cause and Emotion in Titus Andronicus, Richard III, and The Rape of Lucrece." *Shakespearian Tragedy.* Stratford-upon-Avon Studies, 20. London: Edward Arnold. 97-128.

Campbell, John Lord (2001 [1859]) *Shakespeare's Legal Acquirements Considered.* London: Jon Murray. *Shakespeare Law Library.* August 8, 2003. <http://www.sourcetext.com /lawlibrary/campbell/00.htm>.

Carroll, William C. (1992) "'The Form of Law': Ritual and Succession in *Richard III.*" *True Rites and Maimed Rites.* Ed. Linda Woodbridge and Edward Berry. Urbana, IL: Illinois Univ. Press.

Clemen, Wolfgang (1957) *Kommentar zu Shakespeares* Richard III. Göttingen: Vandenhoeck & Ruprecht.

Duncan-Jones, Katherine (2001) *Ungentle Shakespeare: Scenes from His Life.* London: Arden Shakespeare.

Everett, Barbara (2003) "A Dream of Passion: Barbara Everett on the Peculiar Comedy of Measure for Measure." *London Review of Books* 25. 1C (2 January): 23-26.

Foucault, Michel (1991 [1975]) *Discipline and Punish: The Birth of the Prison*. Trans. Alan Sheridan. London: Penguin.

Frisch, Morton J. (1993) "Shakespeare's Richard III and the Soul of the Tyrant." *Interpretation: A Journal of Political Philosophy* 20: 275-84.

Gless, Darryl J. (1979) *Measure for Measure, the Law, and the Convent*. Princeton, MA: Princeton Univ. Press.

Gulley, Ervene (1998) "'Dressed in a little Brief Authority': Law as Theater in *Measure for Measure*." *Law and Literature Perspectives*. Ed. Bruce L. Rockwood. New York: Lang. 53-69.

Hall, Edward (1981) *The Union of the Two Noble and Illustrate Famelies of Lancastre and York*. 1548. Appendix III: Source Materials. *King Richard III* (1981) Ed. Antony Hammond. London: Methuen. 341-74.

Hawkins, Harriet (1987) "'On the other hand': Justice and Mercy in *Measure for Measure*." *Measure for Measure*. Brighton: Harvester Press. 43-88.

Hayne, Victoria (1999) "Performing Social Practice: The Example of *Measure for Measure*." *Critical Essays on Shakespeare's* Measure for Measure. Ed. Richard Wheeler. New York: Hall. 145-77.

Hockey, Dorothy C. (1959) "The Trial Pattern in *King Lear*." *Shakespeare Quarterly* 10: 389-95.

Iser, Wolfgang (1993) *Staging Politics: The Lasting Impact of Shakespeare's Histories*. New York: Columbia Univ. Press.

Keeton, George W. (1967) *Shakespeare's Legal and Political Background*. London: Pitman & Sons.

Kornstein, Daniel J. (1994) *Kill All the Lawyers? Shakespeare's Legal Appeal*. Princeton, MA: Princeton Univ. Press.

Kronenfeld, Judy (1988) *King Lear and the Naked Truth: Rethinking the Language of Religion and Resistance*. Durham NC: Duke Univ. Press.

Lockhart, Adrienne (1975) "The Cat is Grey: *King Lear*'s Mad Trial Scene." *Shakespeare Quarterly* 26: 469-71.

Lusardi, James P. (1988) "Lear's Mock Trial." *Shakespeare on Television: An Anthology of Essays and Reviews*. Hanover, NH: New England Univ. Press. 130-39.

More, Sir Thomas. *The History of King Richard the thirde*. Appendix III: Source Materials. *King Richard III* (1981) Ed. Antony Hammond. London: Methuen. 342-63.

Neill, Michael (1975) "Shakespeare's Halle of Mirrors: Play, Politics, and Psychology in *Richard III*." *Shakespeare Studies* 8: 99-129.

Ornstein, Robert (1972) *A Kingdom for a Stage: The Achievement of Shakespeare's History Plays*. Cambridge, MA: Harvard Univ. Press.

Oppel, Horst (1968) *Die Gerichtsszene in* King Lear. Mainz: Akademie der Wissenschaften und der Literatur.

Pearlman, E. (1992) *William Shakespeare: The History Plays*. New York: Twayne.

Pope, Elizabeth Marie (1970) "The Renaissance Background of *Measure for Measure*." *Twentieth-Century Interpretations of Measure for Measure: A Collection of Critical Essays*. Ed. George L. Geckle. Englewood Cliffs, NJ: Prentice-Hall. 50-72.

Sanders, Wilbur (1968) *The Dramatist and the Received Idea: Studies in the Plays of Marlowe and Shakespeare*. Cambridge: Cambridge Univ. Press.

Schauer, Margery Stone, and Frederick Schauer (1980) "Law as the Engine of State: The Trial of Anne Boleyn." *William and Mary Law Review* 22: 49-84.

Sebold, Alice. *Lucky*. Scribner: New York, 1999.

Shakespeare, William (1955) *The Merchant of Venice*. 1596-97. Ed. John Russell Brown. The Arden Edition of the Works of William Shakespeare. London: Methuen.

Shakespeare, William (1993) *Measure for Measure*. 1604. Ed. Jane Coles and Rex Gibson. Cambridge School Shakespeare. Cambridge: Cambridge Univ. Press.

Shakespeare, William (1980) *Romeo and Juliet*. 1594-96. Ed. Brian Gibbons. The Arden Edition of the Works of William Shakespeare. London/New York: Methuen.

Shakespeare, William (1981) *Richard III*. 1592-93. Ed. Antony Hammond. The Arden Edition of the Works of William Shakespeare. London/New York: Methuen.

Shakespeare, William (1982) *King Richard the Second*. 1595. Ed. Peter Ure. The Arden Edition of the Works of William Shakespeare. London/New York: Methuen.

Shakespeare, William (1997) *King Lear*. 1605-6. Ed. R. A. Foakes. The Arden Edition of the Works of William Shakespeare. Walton-on-Thames: Thomas Nelson and Sons.

Shakespeare, William (2000) *The Tragedy of King Richard III*. 1592-93. Ed. John Jowett. Oxford: Oxford Univ. Press.

Shakespeare, William, and John Fletcher (2000) *King Henry VIII (All is True)*. Ed. Gordon McMullan. The Arden Edition of the Works of William Shakespeare. London: Thomson Learning.

Shuger, Debora Kuller (2001) *Political Theologies in Shakespeare's England: The Sacred and the State in Measure for Measure*. Houndsmills: Palgrave.

Van Laan, Thomas F. (1978) *Role-playing in Shakespeare*. Toronto: Toronto Univ. Press.

Ward, Ian (1995) *Law and Literature: Possibilities and Perspectives*. Cambridge: Cambridge Univ. Press.

Warren, Roger (1983) "The Folio Omission of the Mock Trial: Motives and Consequences." *The Division of the Kingdoms: Shakespeare's Two Versions of King Lear*. Ed. Gary Taylor and Michael Warren. Oxford: Clarendon.

Wegemer, Gerard (2000) "Henry VIII on Trial: Confronting Malice and Conscience in Shakespeare's *All Is True*." *Renascence* 52: 111-30.

Representations of the British Legal System in Twentieth-Century Popular Courtroom Drama

Beatrix Hesse

Courtroom Drama

This paper will be concerned with the analysis of some representative examples of British courtroom drama, outlining its most conspicuous recurrent features such as the convention of the innocent suspect and the problem of the production of truth. Furthermore, the three historical phases of courtroom drama and their respective forms of social criticism will be outlined on the basis of plays typical to them. My essay will end with a discussion of plays that depart from the formula to some extent.

For the purposes of this paper, "courtroom drama" will be defined as a play of which a major portion consists of a court trial. A typical courtroom drama plot revolves around an accused whose innocence is revealed in the course of the trial while the real culprit is unmasked und punished. In this respect, courtroom drama belongs to the more extensive class of crime plays. From the four-part sequence of events from crime through detection and trial to punishment, courtroom drama concentrates on the penultimate stage, while other types of crime play focus on crime and detection or on imprisonment. It should be noted that very few plays attempt to sketch the whole sequence of events from incitement to crime to eventual punishment. Although the crime play is an extremely popular and long-lived British genre, it has attracted astonishingly little critical interest, particularly considering the large amount of criticism produced in the related field of the twentieth-century detective novel. What Charles LaBorde remarked about the crime play in 1976 still applies today: "It remains a major twentieth-century theatre form without detailed scholarly analyses of either its history, development, or structure" (1976: 3).

The few critics that have devoted attention to the crime play as a genre agree with Frank Rahill's historical outline according to which the twentieth-century crime play first evolved in the US. The earliest example mentioned is *The Argyle Case* by Harvey J. O'Higgins and Harriet Ford, first performed in 1912, quickly followed by the two earliest examples of courtroom drama, Elmer Rice's *On Trial* of 1914 and Bayard Veiller's *The Trial of Mary Dugan* of 1917. While Rice's play is usually noted mainly because it made use of the flashback technique, a device which, though common in film, is rare on stage, it is *The Trial of Mary Dugan* which is usually considered to be the prototype of all courtroom plays to follow, as for instance by Erdmut August in his dissertation *Dramaturgie des Kriminalstücks* (1976). The play's plot runs as follows:

Chorus girl Mary Dugan is accused of having murdered her married lover, bank director Rice. Her attorney, Edward West, seems helpless as well as useless, but fortunately in the course of the action he is replaced by Mary's long-lost brother Jimmy who studied law with Mary's financial support. The real culprit turns out to be West, who was the lover of Mrs. Rice and with her aid murdered her husband. This short plot synopsis reveals the courtroom play's twin interests in the discovery of true guilt and the revelation of true innocence. In his discussion of *The Trial of Mary Dugan*, August also notes the inherent theatricality of any court trial: a trial necessarily involves suspense about the verdict, it consists of a structured sequence of events prescribed by the legal code, and it provides opportunities for spectacular entrances and exits. Each participant in a trial is allotted a specific part, and the techniques of interrogation and cross-examination correspond nicely to a drama's need to unfold its action in dialogical form (1976: 77-81). The theatricality of the court trial is a feature highlighted in several courtroom dramas of the 1950s.

However, not only its natural affinity to the theater has made courtroom drama a popular theatre form. As J. S. R. Goodlad has suggested in *A Sociology of Popular Drama*, "popular drama is concerned with the survival of the social system [and hence] may serve as a vehicle by which a community repeatedly instructs its members in correct behaviour" (Goodlad 1972: 7). Courtroom drama with its sharp juxtaposition of the guilty and the innocent would seem a most appropriate tool for doing so. An analysis of popular courtroom drama may also reveal to what extent audiences are ready to trust in the efficiency and fairness of their own legal system. Although courtroom drama tends to end happily, with the punishment of the guilty and the revelation of innocence misprized, the happy outcome may sometimes be a result of individual initiative rather than the reliability of the system. Since attitudes to their respective legal systems may be expected to differ between British and American audiences, I will limit my study to the analysis of British courtroom drama. (Incidentally, very few courtroom plays ever successfully crossed the Atlantic.) British courtroom dramas, like crime plays, evolved later than their American counterparts and developed a different format.

I will begin by discussing two relatively early examples of the British variety of the courtroom play, Barringer's *Inquest* and Wooll's *Libel!*, both from the 1930s, and continue with an analysis of plays from the genre's Golden Age, the 1950s: the spectacularly successful *Witness for the Prosecution* (1953) by Agatha Christie; *Hostile Witness* (1965) by Jack Roffey; as well as stage adaptations of novels by the lawyer Henry Cecil. The continuing appeal of the format will be documented by an analysis of a more recent example, Jeffrey Archer's *Beyond Reasonable Doubt* (1987). Finally, some attention will be devoted to courtroom plays that depart from the traditional "whodunit" formula by writers of considerable critical acclaim, such as John Galsworthy, Terence Rattigan, John Mortimer, and David Hare.

1930s' Courtroom Drama of Identity: *Inquest* and *Libel!*

The two earliest British courtroom whodunits which a reasonably thorough search has unearthed are *Inquest* by Michael Barringer, first performed in 1931, and *Libel!* (1934) by Edward Wooll. In both cases the action revolves around an exchange of identities. Although the very term "whodunit" suggests a question of mystery and puzzle solving, the plays of Barringer and Wooll are primarily concerned with character revelation and this to an even greater extent than most other crime plays.

The earlier play is the less interesting of the two. Nor is it a courtroom drama in the strict sense of the word, being set in an improvised coroner's court in a country school. The plot is based on the central idea of an exchange of identities between presumed murderer and supposed victim, thus providing a complete reversal of expectations in the last scenes. The dead body over which the inquest of the title is held is not that of the presumed victim but his stepfather, whom the "victim" shot in an act of self-defense. The culprit's wife and mother try to shield him, even though the wife has a new lover and therefore for some time comes under suspicion of having disposed of her husband herself. The truth is revealed when the women learn that the murderer has recently died in a distant sanatorium. Some comic relief is provided by the conflict between the local coroner and the lawyer representing the prime suspect, who is used to more professional conduct in court. As this short plot synopsis shows, this play departs from the model of *The Trial of Mary Dugan* in several respects. Firstly, the central question is not that of guilt and innocence, but that of the identity of the characters – not "whodunit," but "who is who"? Secondly, justice is brought about by the incidental death of the culprit and not by the proceedings in court. And finally, court procedure itself is the target of mild ridicule. We will encounter each of these features again in the analyses of the following plays.

In *Libel!*, the theme of the exchange of identities is even more pronounced As the title suggests, in this play the court trial starts as a case of libel against a newspaper. In the course of the trial it becomes obvious, however, that unless his case is defended, the plaintiff will face a murder charge. The initial stage direction contains "General Directions for Court Deportment," reflecting the author's observations on the behavior of individuals involved in a court trial in a mildly humorous manner, noting for instance that "(a)bout two-thirds of the jury manage to affect a sustained interest in the case. The rest oscillate for much of the time between vacuity and involuntary slumber" and "[t]he Associate and Usher throughout affect no interest and completely identify themselves with the respective roles of immobile and mobile human furniture" (Wooll 1934: 5). The play's plot revolves around the predicament of Sir Mark Loddon, who has to prove that he is indeed Sir Mark returned home from World War I, suffering from severe amnesia, and not a daring impostor who has done away with the real Sir Mark. In a confrontation with another potential self – a character called merely "number 15" who has lost all claim to humanity through being reduced to mere animal functions – the protagonist finally regains his sense of identity. Twenty-five years after its first performance, this striking play was filmed by Anthony Asquith (1959).

The continuing vitality of the play testifies to the quasi-mythical character of its plot, which is strongly indebted to Victorian melodrama. As Douglas Woodruff remarks in *The Tichborne Claimant – A Victorian Mystery*, the Victorian stage

> [...] used no plot more frequently than the story of the long-lost heir coming into great possessions, which were equated with happiness for the final curtain. Nearly all the comic operas of Gilbert and Sullivan, the splendid series which began in 1878 (just as the Tichborne agitation was dying away), have for their plot the discovery of a rightful heir, some question of mistaken or concealed identity, with property and position involved. (Woodruff 1957: xv)

Although the motif of the claimant was borrowed from Victorian literature, the concept of identity had undergone a substantial change. This becomes evident if we consider for instance the example of the villain in Wilkie Collins's *The Woman in White*, an impostor who inflicts an exchange of identities on his innocent wife and a chance witness in order to protect his dreadful secret and increase his property. Sir Percival Glyde's secret is that he is "not himself" in the sense of having no claim to the title since he was born out of wedlock. In *Libel!*, this Victorian concept of identity based on patrilinear inheritance is combined with a more modern understanding of identity as psychological integrity. Sir Mark is "not himself" because he has lost his memory due to a traumatic experience.

The myth of a man asked to prove that he is indeed himself later formed the core of a succession of highly popular films based on the case of Martin Guerre, reported in François Gayot de Pitaval's *Causes célèbres* (1764-1771), a popular collection of exceptional and interesting law cases. The French film *Le retour de Martin Guerre* (1982) and the American film *Sommersby* (1993) explore the problem of identity in the light of yet another basic human experience, that of change. Since a man who returns home after years cannot be expected to be the man he used to be, how do his relatives establish that he is indeed the man who went away? As in the case of Martin Guerre, the wife of the protagonist in *Libel!* commits an important error concerning her husband's identity. But although witnesses therefore cannot always be trusted, the trial turns out to be an appropriate means of bringing out the truth: through the cathartic experience of accusation and confrontation, Sir Mark regains his sense of self, just as at the end of *Inquest* the victim and the culprit are disentangled and labeled.

In comparison to the American format, which focuses on guilt and innocence, the early British courtroom whodunit differs strikingly in stressing questions of identity: the court trial not only allows one to distinguish between the innocent and the guilty, it serves as a quasi-religious purification rite that lends human beings a sense of their self. This somewhat optimistic attitude towards the healing power of the legal ritual was sharply questioned in the 1950s and 1960s, the period in which British courtroom drama flourished.

The Golden Age of Courtroom Drama: From the Early 1950s to the Late 1960s – Christie, Roffey, and Henry Cecil

In his book *A Sociology of Popular Drama*, J. S. R. Goodlad lists the thirty-five most popular stage plays between 1955 and 1965, among them Agatha Christie's *Witness for the Prosecution* and Jack Roffey's *Hostile Witness*. Both plays ran for over 400 performances and achieved estimated audience sizes of over a million (Christie) and nearly half a million (Roffey). Produced by Peter Saunders, *Witness for the Prosecution* opened at the Winter Garden in 1953 and was later successfully transferred to New York. It was Saunders who first suggested to Christie that she adapt her short story "Witness for the Prosecution" from the collection *The Hound of Death* for the stage. Christie was reluctant, doubting her ability to write a successful courtroom drama. After reading about trial transcripts and discussing court procedure with barristers and solicitors, she wrote the play very quickly, changing the ending to make it "more visually dramatic and violent" (Haining 1990: 30). The author was very satisfied with the finished work and reportedly considered it her best play. In the Christie canon, however, the success of *Witness for the Prosecution* tends to be overlooked because of the immense popularity of *The Mousetrap*, which is still running today. Besides, *Witness for the Prosecution* is now better known for the film version (1957), which stars Charles Laughton and introduces a humorous subplot of comic banter between Sir Wilfrid and his nurse.

Although the plot has become widely familiar due to the film, a short synopsis shall be provided. Leonard Vole, a rather likeable but slightly unstable young man, is accused of having murdered Emily French, an elderly acquaintance of his, who left him her considerable fortune. Vole is defended by Sir Wilfrid Robarts, who soon realizes that Vole's acquittal depends on the alibi his mysterious foreign wife Romaine can supply. To everybody's surprise, Romaine appears in court as witness for the prosecution and the evidence she gives is totally damning for Leonard. On the same evening, Sir Wilfrid is approached by another mysterious woman, a Cockney prostitute, who sells him a bundle of love letters, written by Romaine to her secret lover and in which she explains how she will get rid of Leonard. On this fresh evidence, Leonard is acquitted, but Sir Wilfrid learns to his surprise that the strange woman was no other than Romaine, who desperately loves her husband and therefore put on an act to provide him with a convincing alibi, even though she knew him to be the murderer. When she finds out that Leonard has betrayed her with a younger woman and intends to desert her, she stabs Leonard with the knife that killed Emily French.

What is most striking about this play is its sustained interest in theatricality, an element first introduced, it seems, by the professional actress Romaine Vole. In the course of the play, Romaine adopts several different roles, all based on stock characters from melodrama. In the first act, when she comes to consult Sir Wilfrid about her husband's prospects in the impending trial, she is calm, self-assured, mysterious and "cool as a cucumber," as Sir Wilfrid puts it. When she gives evidence in court in the second act, she is a frightened foreigner suddenly overcome with scruples, and her English has deteriorated to a remarkable extent. In the third act she first appears as a down-and-out prostitute speaking with a heavy Cockney accent and later, in court, as a communist agent who betrays herself in an outburst of fury.

Romaine's play-acting, however, only serves to highlight the amount of role-play already inherent in the court trial. Three of the five witnesses called, for instance, are expert witnesses: a police inspector, a police surgeon, and a laboratory assistant. Since both parties have had access to their reports, their cross-examination does not yield any new information; the dialogue between counsel and witness is performed solely for the benefit of the jury, their audience. "[I]f my learned friend is going to answer his own questions, the presence of the witness seems to be superfluous" (Christie 1993: 425), Sir Wilfrid quite appropriately remarks, even though he himself also prefers expert witnesses whose answers he can anticipate. He whispers his asides "audibly for the benefit of the jury" (434), as the stage direction prescribes, and the prosecuting counsel justly complains about his learned friend's "theatrical outbursts" (441). Romaine's masterpiece of dramatic art, the impersonation of a Cockney prostitute, is presented in III.i, and the act she puts on is slyly compared to Sir Wilfrid's act of playing the Queen's Coroner. "Didn't recognize you without your wig" (456), she purrs, a remark heavily loaded with irony, since Romaine herself is in this scene wearing a blonde wig that renders her unrecognizable. These sustained comparisons between courtroom procedure and theatrical performance serve to undermine the audience's faith in the fairness and efficacy of this procedure. Moreover, in *Witness for the Prosecution*, the criminal trial leads to a miscarriage of justice. What the play demonstrates is how a combination of legal knowledge and acting talent can completely manipulate the legal machinery, so that the criminal is brought to bay in the end not by the organs of institutionalized justice but by the revenge of a jealous woman.

While Christie made use of the convention of the innocent accused in order to subvert it, Jack Roffey's *Hostile Witness* (Haymarket, 1964) once again presented a straight treatment of the theme. The play begins with a major reversal of fortune: a respectable Queen's Coroner suddenly finds himself arrested for murder. Simon Crawford, an extremely self-reliant and independent man, is accused of having stabbed Judge Gregory – with fairly damning evidence against him. The police investigate on information received from a mysterious character called Armitage who successfully planted the evidence against Crawford and then disappeared. With the help of Sheila, junior counsel at his chambers, Crawford manages to identify "Armitage" as a criminal named Logan, who was once sentenced to life imprisonment by Judge Gregory and Crawford for the prosecution and swore to enact revenge on them. Since the conventions of the whodunit require that the criminal must be a character familiar to the reader/audience, it is obvious that Logan must be a close friend or colleague of Crawford's. (This convention first developed in the related field of detective fiction.) It turns out that he has been serving as a senior clerk in Crawford's chambers for the last fifteen years under the assumed name of Charles Milburn.

The most interesting aspect of the play is the humanizing effect the trial has on Crawford. When asked to describe him in the first act, Sheila gives the following unflattering portrayal: "I think he's intolerant, and a bully. He has an immense conceit and – because of this he is supremely self-sufficient. I think he's ambitious, and as far as his ambition is concerned, quite ruthless" (Roffey 1965: 25). Crawford's lack of interest in the members of his chambers as human beings almost brings about his downfall. The plot hinges on the possibility that a highly intelligent man may fail to notice that a person seeking employment in his firm is identical with a man whom he sent to prison for life six years earlier. Crawford, however, claims that "no Counsel can picture the man in the dock five minutes after the trial is over" (64), a statement that is allowed to stand uncorrected. Crawford's blindness towards the accused as a human being is mirrored by another kind of blindness: Milburn is color blind, and it is this handicap that brings about his identification. Having lost the support of his counsel and friend Sir Peter, Crawford has only Sheila to rely on. For the first time he learns what she really thinks of him. Nonetheless, he brings himself to appeal to her for help. The play's basic conflict between the need for mutual support and the desire for independence is humorously echoed in a short dialogue between widower Crawford and his bachelor colleague Gillespie:

> Gillespie: A solitary life still has its compensations.
> Crawford: Has it? I must confess that, so far, I have failed to rediscover a single one of any importance. (15)

While, in *Witness for the Prosecution*, a court trial was presented as an elaborate game of deception, Roffey's main criticism of the legal system seems to be that a career in the legal professions may emotionally cripple a man. In this respect, Crawford resembles not only Robarts, but also Carstairs (*Alibi for a Judge*), Sir Peter (*Murmuring Judges*), Sir Robert Morton (*The Winslow Boy*) and Sir Tommy Banter (*The Dock Brief*).[1] To judge from these plays, the typical lawyer undergoes a rigorous specialized training that provides him with a high social status, while rendering him almost perfectly incapable of relating to his fellow citizens as ordinary human beings.

Though the motif of acting and theatricality is by no means as pronounced as in Christie's play, Roffey also draws a parallel between the audience and the jury in his description of the courtroom set: "The Court is seen from the point of view of the jury – so that when Judge or Counsel address the jury they are in fact addressing the audience" (30). This effect was not lost on the audience, as a review of the opening performance shows, in which *Evening News* critic Felix Barker took up the comparison between audience and jury: "*Hostile Witness* [...] was tried before an enthusiastic jury at the Haymarket Theatre last night. The sentence of this court: a year at least" (Richards 1973: 207). Treating the audience as a jury is an interesting phenomenon: it does not merely ensure that a certain degree of audience involvement is achieved, it also specifies what type of audience reaction is expected. The audience is reassured that their opinion on the Right and Wrong of the case is valued within their legal system. However, the equation of audience and jury also implies that in a

---

1 The reference is to Henry Cecil's *Alibi for a Judge* (1967), David Hare's *Murmuring Judges* (1991), Terence Rattigan's *The Winslow Boy* (1991), and John Mortimer's *The Dock Brief* (1970).

court trial, laymen are strictly separated from professionals, with the professionals taking the active role and the laymen remaining largely passive.

When Roffey wrote *Hostile Witness* he had been employed at the the Old Bailey for almost twenty years and had already written another courtroom drama, *No Other Verdict*, which had had a short run at the Duchess in 1954. Barrister Henry Cecil also drew on his first hand knowledge of lawyers and the law in his novels and short stories. Not all of his works are detective stories, though they all deal with the law in one way or another. Several of his novels were adapted for the stage, and four of the dramatized versions were subsequently published. Three of them saw production in the London West End, while the fourth one, *Brothers in Law* (1957), a humorous play about a young lawyer finding his feet co-scripted by Ted Willis, did not survive its try-out run in Wimbledon. The three remaining plays are *Settled Out of Court* (adapted by Cecil and William Saroyan, Savoy, 1960), *Alibi for a Judge* (adapted by Cecil, Felicity Douglas and Basil Dawson, Savoy, 1965) and *According to the Evidence* (also adapted by Cecil, Douglas and Dawson, Savoy, 1967).

All three are concerned with alternative (and possibly superior) forms of establishing justice. As the title suggests, *Settled Out of Court* is set outside the courtroom, and the accused is allowed to manage the proceedings and guide the cross examination of the witnesses. *Alibi for a Judge* considers reducing the judge's supreme authority, and *According to the Evidence* suggests that it may be necessary to take the law into one's own hands. Moreover, the latter play reveals legal procedure to be culturally transmitted rather than absolute and immutable. The following short plot synopses of the three plays will show how these ideas are carried out in their respective plays.

Lonsdale Walsh, the protagonist of *Settled Out of Court*, has been sentenced to life imprisonment for murdering his business rival Adolphus Barnwell. He escapes from prison in order to prove his innocence – a variation of the popular motif of the innocent accused. With the help of master criminal Mr. I, he collects the witnesses from his trial in the house of the presiding judge, Sir George Halliday, for a mock re-trial. Gradually, Walsh manages to persuade Sir George that he was framed by Josephine, Barnwell's widow, who, however, is honestly convinced of Walsh's guilt. Realizing that the evidence has indeed been manipulated, Sir George recommends that the case be taken up again. In a final twist, Walsh, in a private conversation with Josephine, reveals that he did indeed murder Barnwell. Josephine swears that she will avenge herself on him, wherever he may hide. What begins as an apparent criticism of the British legal system turns into its vindication: the accused turns out to be guilty after all, and formal court procedure is thus proved to be superior to the unofficial re-trial, since it prevents the accused from manipulating the witnesses and jury.

The title character of *Alibi for a Judge*, Judge Gerald Carstairs, has a reputation for influencing the jury to get the verdict he believes to be right. After a particularly unfair trial against William Burford who is accused of bank robbery, the judge feels qualms of conscience and takes up his own investigation into the circumstances of the crime. Burford's charming but mendacious wife Lesley claims that Burford was framed by an old friend of his, one Thompson, whom she believes she has recognized on a racecourse. So the judge and Lesley start going to the races together, with

Lesley's objective apparently being to get them into a compromising position. However, Thompson is always a few steps ahead of them: Judge Carstairs is considering bringing formal action against Lesley for swindling money out of him under false pretences, when Thompson is finally found with the loot of the robbery hidden at his place. The hope that Carstairs will in the future abstain from influencing the jury, however, is not fulfilled. Cecil's interest in the legitimacy of the formalities of the British legal system is summed up in Lesley's remark: "You seem to think that justice can only be done by dressing up in eighteenth-century wigs in a courtroom" (Cecil/Douglas/Dawson 1967: 40).

While the starting point of *Alibi for a Judge* is an innocent man convicted for a crime he did not commit, the action of *According to the Evidence* is triggered off by the acquittal of a man who is obviously guilty. After a murderer has been acquitted, anthropologist Alec Morland decides to take the law into his own hands: he follows the suspect around and kills him just in time to prevent another murder. A friend of Morland's, Secret Service man Adam Low, tries to clear him by first getting him arrested and then acquitted, a motif probably borrowed from Agatha Christie's very first novel, *The Mysterious Affair at Styles* (1920). Cecil's interest in alternative forms of justice is humorously reflected in Morland's description of particularly strange forms of criminal law practiced by primitive societies – Morland's own decision to bring the murderer to justice, however, is viewed with approval.

As the above summaries show, all three plays deal with attempts by an individual to obtain justice where the judicial system has failed. This is not simply a personal preoccupation of Cecil's; J. S. R. Goodlad names the "control of desire for revenge" (9) as one of the five areas of living perceived as particularly problematic by the viewing public in Britain between 1955 and 1965. The urge to take the law into one's own hands, of course, is by no means a newly developed social problem. As research into the history of the crime play shows, the motif of revenge as "a kind of wild justice" is a particularly prominent motif in plays of the 1930s, such as Edgar Wallace's *The Green Pack* (Wyndham's, 1932), James Parish's *Distinguished Gathering* (Embassy, 1935) and Alec Coppel's *I Killed the Count!* (Whitehall, 1937). Cecil's plays as a rule approve of individual initiative in cases in which the legal machinery seems flawed. However, the legal system is still perceived as basically sound.

In contrast to Roffey, Cecil portrays his lawyers as fundamentally decent and likeable characters, even if they are occasionally overbearing and a little too sure of themselves. Although Cecil was doubtlessly much better acquainted with the peculiarities of the law and its representatives than Christie, his courtroom plays never gained the same amount of popularity as *Witness for the Prosecution*. This suggests that theater audiences largely shared Christie's skeptical view concerning the legal system's ability to discover the truth and establish justice.

Recent Courtroom Drama: Archer's *Beyond Reasonable Doubt* and Hare's *Murmuring Judges*

In the period after 1970, popular interest in the stage crime play rapidly declined, probably because the crime play proved such an attractive format for TV and could now be more comfortably consumed at home. Two relatively recent examples of courtroom drama, however, deserve to be mentioned: Jeffrey Archer's *Beyond Reasonable Doubt* (Queen's, 1987) and David Hare's *Murmuring Judges* (National, 1991). Archer's play deals with a case of euthanasia: Did Sir David Metcalfe QC poison his terminally ill wife Millicent or did he not? The theme of a mercy killing allows the playwright to present a murder mystery with the culprit as its central character without losing audience sympathies for his protagonist. And on stage, the active part of the criminal is necessarily more attractive than that of the detective who is "merely a critic." The first act of the play shows the trial against Sir David, who defends himself, with his old enemy Anthony Blair-Booth for the prosecution. The case for the prosecution rests mainly on the evidence of housekeeper Mrs. Rogers, who claims that the Metcalfes' marriage was unhappy and that she actually saw Sir David administer the fatal pill to Millicent. Immediately before the verdict the curtain falls. In the second act, a flashback to a time nine months earlier presents the Metcalfes as an affectionate couple who are severely depressed by Millicent's terminal illness. The last scene shows Sir David two weeks after his acquittal, sharing a bottle of wine with his intimate friend Lionel and confessing that he actually did kill his wife at her own request. Now he has obtained his freedom, he will, however, not return to the bar but commit suicide.

Archer's play clearly imitates *Witness for the Prosecution*, making use of the formula of the innocent accused only to subvert it. As in Christie's play, it is suggested that a singularly gifted individual may successfully manipulate the legal machinery according to his (or her) wishes. As the recent trial against Jeffrey Archer suggests, the writer indeed thought this a practicable proposition.[2] Media coverage of the Archer trial also concentrated on another aspect central to *Beyond Reasonable Doubt*: the fact that the truth about a marriage is known only to the two partners. As a whole, the real life trial against Archer contained all the necessary ingredients of a successful courtroom play: the motif of the "eternal triangle," the reversal of fortune that turns the plaintiff in a libel case into the accused, and the courageous wife who stands by her husband. The appeal the case had for the media is therefore hardly surprising.

The motif of the mercy killing was taken up again in another recent courtroom drama, Terence Frisby's *Rough Justice* (Apollo, 1994). This play revolves around a father who claims the moral right to kill his severely handicapped child. *Rough Justice* contains a slight mystery element, since it is discovered in the course of the action that it was in fact the child's mother who committed the deed while her husband merely

2 In 1987, Jeffrey Archer sued the newspaper *Daily Star* for libel. The *Daily Star* had reported on Lord Archer's alleged association with a prostitute. Archer won his case and was awarded 500,000 pounds damages. Later, however, it turned out that he had presented a forged diary in court as his alibi for the dates in question. He was tried for perjury and sentenced to four years' imprisonment, of which he served two.

tried to protect her, but the main interest of the play resides in its discussion of the legitimacy of euthanasia. If critics of detective fiction are correct in supposing that the ideal victim in a detective plot must always somehow offend the social order,[3] the emergence of the theme of a mercy killing in the late twentieth century reveals a disturbing strain of hostility towards handicapped people in contemporary British society.

Though roughly contemporary to *Beyond Reasonable Doubt*, David Hare's *Murmuring Judges* could hardly have been a more different play. This may be due in part to the authors' political persuasions which radically differ from those of Jeffrey Archer. *Murmuring Judges* was the second play of Hare's trilogy on British institutions, appearing after *Racing Demon* (1990, performed Cottesloe, 1990), a play about the Church of England, and before *The Absence of War* (1993, performed Olivier, 1993), which was concerned with the political parties.[4] The play follows three young people through the British penal institutions of the police, the law court, and the prison. The young Irishman Gerard McKinnon, although a first time offender, is sentenced to five years' imprisonment after collaborating in a robbery. It turns out that two policemen eager for promotion – Barry Hopper and Jimmy Khan – planted drugs on McKinnon's accomplices in order to force a confession from them. Irina Platt, a junior lawyer in the chambers of conservative barrister Sir Peter Edgecombe, tries to make sure that McKinnon receives a fair trial in his appeal but finds that she is up against numerous time-honored rules of behavior and institutional loyalties. As a result of her efforts, McKinnon's sentence is reduced to four years and a half, but the whole affair has a number of more far-reaching consequences: Barry is promoted to the Flying Squad, but his girlfriend Sandra, a young police constable, decides to report him to the authorities; Irina quits her post in Sir Peter's office, and Gerard for the first time discovers his affinities with the Irish Republican Army. The fact that the female characters show a more marked tendency to act according to their conscience than their male counterparts would be open to criticism if it were not made abundantly clear that both Irina and Sandra find themselves outsiders in a male-dominated profession from the start.

Murmuring Judges is the rare case of a play that accompanies its characters through three different institutions of penal justice. Most other playwrights concerned with the theme of crime and punishment tend to concentrate either on police investigation (as John Hopkins in *This Story of Yours* (1969) or Barrie Keeffe in *Sus* (1979), on courtroom procedure like the plays discussed above, or on prison life (as for instance William Douglas Home in *"Now, Barabbas..."* (1947) and Ludovic Kennedy in *Murder Story* (1955)).

Yet Hare's play is not without precedent in this respect. John Galsworthy's *Justice*, first presented at the Duke of York's in 1910 (and thus an even earlier play than the American prototypes described in the first section of this paper) showed the discovery of a crime and its perpetrator, the trial and imprisonment of the culprit, and the

---

3 Cf. Grella (1988: 96-98).

4 This indicates that after the success of the first play of the trilogy, the National Theatre's management considered it fit to produce the two following plays in their largest auditorium.

situation in which he finds himself after his release from prison. Falder, a junior clerk in a solicitors' office, forges a check, but his crime is soon discovered by his employers. In the subsequent trial, Falder's young and inexperienced counsel unsuccessfully tries to get him acquitted on grounds of temporary insanity. The play's third act is set in prison, and the silent scene, III.iii, showing Falder in solitary confinement is reported to have been almost unbearably moving. After his release from prison, Falder approaches his former employers for help. When he finds himself threatened with renewed arrest for failing to report to his parole officer, he jumps to his death. *Justice* was the singular case of a courtroom play that actually brought about legal reform: young Winston Churchill was so impressed by it that he agreed to reduce the use of solitary confinement.

Critics have mainly praised the play's scrupulous fairness: "Galsworthy is not trapped into a cheap antithesis; his prison officers are decent chaps with the best intentions, and his convict is a moral weakling sent down for petty forgery. The wordless scene of Falder's solitary confinement harrows not because he is a victim of grotesque injustice but because we feel no penal system ought to treat a man this way" (Smith 1973: 75). Smith draws attention to the fact that the convention of the innocent accused is inappropriate if a playwright intends to write politically effective courtroom drama. A play obviously is more politically effective if it draws its audience's attention towards a general social ill – "no penal system ought to treat a man this way" – than when it deals with the exceptional case of an innocent man suffering in prison, which might be considered a personal tragedy but not a social injustice that needs to be remedied. Accordingly, Hare imitated Galsworthy's model and dispensed with the convention of the innocent suspect.

Serious courtroom plays like *Murmuring Judges* and *Justice* differ from the popular variety in three essential aspects: they use a far wider range of settings, they do not make use of the convention of the innocent accused, and they do not involve a mystery about the identity of the culprit. While gaining in critical acclaim, these plays run the danger of being less popular and thus less financially successful than their counterparts. (Though it was no mean feat for *Murmuring Judges* to fill the National Theatre's Olivier.) Both Hare and Galsworthy wrote suspenseful courtroom drama while at the same time departing from the whodunit structure. The suspense created in these two plays does not relate to the question of whether the legal machinery will get hold of the true culprit, but what the legal machinery will do to the culprit who has already been caught. This shift of focus permits a more profound insight into the very workings of this machinery, which proves that it may occasionally be helpful to depart from the basic formula. In the last section of my paper, I would like to discuss a handful of courtroom plays that also reject the whodunit format and use the genre of the courtroom drama for other ends.

Terence Rattigan's Courtroom Plays and John Mortimer's *The Dock Brief*

Author of numerous well-made plays, Terence Rattigan began writing in a period in which well-madeness was a token of quality in a stage play and wrote his last works in an era that considered "well-made" a derogatory term, a process outlined by John

Russell Taylor in *The Rise and Fall of the Well-Made Play*. Two of Rattigan's plays make extensive use of the courtroom setting: *The Winslow Boy* (Lyric, 1946) and *Cause Célèbre* (Her Majesty's, 1977). Both are based on famous court cases, *The Winslow Boy* on the Archer-Shee trial of 1910 and *Cause Célèbre* on the notorious Rattenbury murder case of 1935. Accordingly, the amount of suspense created is minimal, since audiences could reasonably be expected to know about the outcome of the two trials. In both plays, Rattigan makes use of the court trial in order to expose the inner mechanisms of family life, which also sheds light on the relationship between private life and behavior in the public or political realm.

The Winslow Boy revolves around a fourteen-year-old naval cadet accused of having stolen a classmate's five-shilling postal order. The boy's father, determined to see justice done, engages the help of famous barrister Sir Robert Morton. The whole family makes substantial financial and personal sacrifices in order to see their youngest member cleared of suspicion. The real revelation of the ending, however, is not that of the boy's innocence, which is taken for granted from the end of Act II onwards, but the discovery of Sir Robert's humanity concealed beneath his fish-like exterior. As in *Libel!* and *Hostile Witness*, the trial is conceived in terms of an ordeal that brings about character revelation or even self-discovery. The play's continuing vitality was demonstrated by the very recent (1999) film version directed by American playwright David Mamet.

The most striking aspect of *Cause Célèbre* is that the focus of interest is not on the accused couple but on the effect her participation in the trial has on a female member of the jury, one Mrs. Davenport. Alma Rattenbury was accused of having murdered her elderly husband with the help of her eighteen-year-old houseboy with whom she had been conducting an affair. Mrs. Davenport, from whose perspective the trial is witnessed, is at first reluctant to sit on the jury since she is very much aware of her prejudices against Rattenbury. These prejudices are occasioned not by the murder charge but by Rattenbury's sexual misdemeanors, particularly her seduction of a minor – Davenport has a son approximately the same age as Rattenbury's lover. Thus the Rattenbury and Davenport subplots are linked by their common theme of hypocrisy in sexual matters. In particular, the denial of normal sexual appetites in male adolescents by middle-class women's morality is attacked. As in *The Winslow Boy*, the court trial brings about character revelation, but the character concerned is not that of the accused. This ascribes an almost magical power to the proceedings in the courtroom, which seem to be capable of bringing out the truth about everybody who happens to enter its sacred space.

Cause Célèbre had originally been produced by BBC Radio 4 in 1975. Likewise, John Mortimer's *The Dock Brief* (Garrick, 1958) was originally written for radio and presented by BBC 3 in 1957. A paper on the British courtroom play would hardly be complete without mention of *The Dock Brief*, first, because of its popularity, and second, because its approach to the legal professions is one of undiluted satire. After years of waiting, failed barrister Morgenhall finally gets his first "dock brief,"[5] having

5 The term "dock brief" refers to the ancient practice in British law of allowing prisoners too poor to pay a lawyer to select one at random by pointing at him or her from the dock.

been selected at random by a penniless prisoner. The accused, a meek little man called Fowle, however, is rather uncooperative, admitting cheerfully that he has indeed killed his wife since he could no longer endure her hearty sense of humor. Morgenhall persuades Fowle to put up a fight and in extensive role-play they rehearse the impending trial. The theater metaphor is thus even more pronounced than in *Witness for the Prosecution*. However, when the great moment comes, Morgenhall is so overcome with panic that he doesn't manage to utter a word. The incompetence of his counsel grants Fowle a reprieve. Interestingly, the trial itself is not shown; the play's two scenes are set in Fowle's cell immediately before and after the courtroom action. In his introduction to *Five Plays*, Mortimer stated that he had attempted "to chart the tottering course of British middle-class attitudes in decline" (Mortimer 1970: 7). His vivid verbal images in *The Dock Brief*, for instance the character sketch of a judge and the description of the atmosphere in a court of appeal, testify to this intention:

> Sir Tommy Banter, living with a widowed sister in a draughty great morgue on Wimbledon Common. Digestion, bad. Politics, an Independent Moral Conservative. Favourite author, doesn't read. Diversions, snooker in the basement of the morgue, peeping at lovers on the Common and money being given away on the television. In love with capital punishment, corporal punishment, and a younger brother who is accomplished at embroidery. A small, alarmed man frightened of the great dog he lives with to give him the air of a country squire. Served with distinction in the Great War at sentencing soldiers to long terms of imprisonment. A man without friends, unexpectedly adored by a great-niece, three years old. (26)

> A big, quiet Court in the early Summer afternoon. Piles of books, and when you put one down the dust and powdered leather rises and makes the ushers sneeze. The clock ticks. Three old judges in scarlet take snuff with trembling hands. You'll sit in the dock and not follow a legal word. And I'll give them all my Law and get you off on a technicality. (43)

These two typical passages are characterized by a pervasive imagery of cold, fear, death and decay and, above all, of immobility. Mortimer's sketch of legal procedure and the representatives of the legal system of all the plays surveyed in this essay clearly reveal the most skeptical attitude towards the Law. It is also the play that most notably departs from the traditional whodunit plot structure. This suggests that the extent to which a courtroom drama affirms the existing legal system may actually be gauged from the extent to which it conforms to the traditional format: a whodunit concerned with the exculpation of an innocent suspect is highly affirmative, whereas a courtroom drama that clarifies the identity of the culprit from the outset and then shows him being processed through the legal machinery tends to be highly critical of that procedure.

Characteristics and Modifications of the Format of Courtroom Drama – A Summary

All the plays surveyed share characteristic concerns and techniques. The most important element of the courtroom drama would seem to be the character of the innocent suspect, who is forced to confront the whole of his community single-handedly. This endows him with heroic stature (even if he eventually turns out to be guilty after all, as in *Witness for the Prosecution* or *Beyond Reasonable Doubt*). The trial itself is frequently perceived as an ordeal in which truth is revealed miraculously and justice established by some other means than ordinary court procedure. Of the authors quoted, only Cecil seems to trust to some extent in the efficiency and fairness of the rules of court procedure.

Though one would assume that the central concern of courtroom drama is the guilt or innocence of the accused, this is rarely the case in the plays analyzed in this survey. British courtroom drama has been interested in the identity of the accused (*Inquest*, *Libel!*) or in revealing the true character of the other participants in the trial, whether witness (*Witness for the Prosecution*), defense counsel (*The Winslow Boy*), judge (*Alibi for a Judge*) or jury member (*Cause Célèbre*). Only *Hostile Witness*, *Settled Out of Court* and *Beyond Reasonable Doubt* revolve around the guilt or innocence of the accused. In each of these plays, however, the protagonist fulfills an actantial role apart from that of the accused. The central characters of *Hostile Witness* and *Beyond Reasonable Doubt* are lawyers defending themselves, while the hero of *Settled Out of Court* manages the entire court proceedings. Roffey, Cecil and Archer allow their heroes to retain some degree of initiative – turning them into completely passive victims of the legal apparatus apparently would make the plays unbearable to watch.

Outside courtroom drama, the crime play hardly ever shows the culprit being processed through the legal machinery. Once caught, the culprit is often allowed to commit suicide or is punished by other forms of poetic justice. Accordingly, a crime play will either show the detection of a crime or a court trial and the punishment of the culprit, but hardly ever present the whole sequence of events from crime through detection and trial to punishment. Where the whole series of events is portrayed, as in Galsworthy's *Justice*, the play usually intends to criticize legal practice. Besides, a number of crime plays quite openly view individual initiative to take the law into one's own hands with approval, a tendency also in evidence in the courtroom plays *Beyond Reasonable Doubt* and *Rough Justice*. These observations suggest that courtroom drama does not really lend itself to a celebration of the legal system; it is clearly not accidental that nearly all courtroom plays are concerned with the very real danger of a miscarriage of justice.

In the development of British courtroom drama, three major phases may be discerned. Plays of the first phase around 1930 (for instance *Libel!*) take an affirmative attitude to the legal system: though errors may occasionally occur, the system itself is basically sound. The next phase, represented for example by *Witness for the Prosecution* of 1953, is characterized by greater skepticism, or, as in the case of John Mortimer's *The Dock Brief*, downright ridicule. This trend corresponds to an overall skepticism towards established institutions that can be observed in postwar British drama in general. The neo-Conservative 1980s and 1990s saw the return of a type of naturalistic courtroom drama that occasionally even attempted to engage in contemporary political debates, most notably Hare's *Murmuring Judges*, which is clearly indebted to the problem plays of Galsworthy.

The trend towards realism and immediate political relevance reached its climax in the 1999 production of Richard Norton-Taylor's *The Colour of Justice* (Victoria

Palace). This is not a courtroom drama in the traditional sense, since it is based entirely on the actual trial transcripts of the Stephen Lawrence Inquiry, which investigated the unprofessional and inefficient action taken by the police force following a racist attack on and subsequent death of a teenage boy. This is about as far as docudrama can go. Yet it must be kept in mind that the transcripts of course had been edited and that *The Colour of Justice*, after all, was not a real court inquiry but a Westend entertainment like all of the fictional courtroom dramas before it.

It would be wrong to assume, however, that this type of hyper-realistic courtroom drama has completely superseded the "Mary-Dugan" formula. The story of the innocent accused who is saved by the action of a heroic lawyer is still regularly retold to TV audiences all over the world in programs like the Matlock and Perry Mason series. While these programs purport to present exceptional cases, their regular repetition paradoxically suggests that the arrest and trial of an innocent man is nothing out of the ordinary. Although their political stance tends to be conservative, these programs surely do not help to increase faith in the fairness and efficacy of the judicial system. Such TV plays are generally consumed in the manner of children's bedtime stories; pleasure resides in the eternal retelling of the same plot. By contrast, plays like *The Colour of Justice* or *Murmuring Judges* offer their spectators an entirely different form of gratification. Claiming to be more than superficial representations of the collision between an individual and the legal apparatus, these plays promise to lift the lid off and give the viewer a glimpse of the very mechanism of the apparatus itself.

Works Cited

Archer, Jeffrey (1989) *Beyond Reasonable Doubt*. London: French.

August, Erdmut (1976) *Dramaturgie des Kriminalstücks*. Ph D Diss.: Berlin.

Barringer, Michael (1935) *Inquest*. London: Deane.

Cecil, Henry (1957) *Brothers in Law*. London: French.

Cecil, Henry, and William Saroyan (1962) *Settled Out of Court*. London: French.

Cecil, Henry, Felicity Douglas and Basil Dawson (1967) *Alibi for a Judge*. London: French.

Cecil, Henry, Felicity Douglas and Basil Dawson (1967) *According to the Evidence*. London: French.

Christie, Agatha (1920) *The Mysterious Affair at Styles*. London: Lane.

Christie, Agatha (1993) *Witness for the Prosecution. The Mousetrap and Other Plays*. (Ed. Ira Levin) New York: Harper.

Coppel, Alec (1938) *I Killed the Count!*. London: Heinemann.

Frisby, Terence (1995) *Rough Justice*. London: French.

Galsworthy, John (1910) *Justice*. London: Duckworth.

Goodlad, J. S. R. (1972) *A Sociology of Popular Drama*. Totowa, NJ: Rowman and Littlefield.
Grella, George (1988 [1980]) "The Formal Detective Novel." *Detective Fiction: A Collection of Critical Essays*. Ed. Robin W. Winks. Woodstock, VT: The Countryman Press. 84-102.
Haining, Peter (1990) *Agatha Christie: Murder in Four Acts*. London: Virgin.
Hare, David (1990) *Racing Demon*. London: Faber and Faber.
Hare, David (1991) *Murmuring Judges*. London: Faber and Faber.
Hare, David (1993) *The Absence of War*. London: Faber and Faber.
Home, William Douglas (1947) *"Now, Barabbas..."*. London: Longmans.
Hopkins, John (1969) *This Story of Yours*. Harmondsworth: Penguin.
Keeffe, Barrie (1979) *Sus*. London: Methuen.
Kennedy, Ludovic (1955) *Murder Story*. London: Evans.
LaBorde, Charles (1976) *Form and Formula in Detective Drama*. Ph D Diss.: Ohio State.
Le retour de Martin Guerre. Dir. Daniel Vigne. Nimbus, 1982.
Libel! Dir. Anthony Asquith. MGM, 1959.
Mortimer, John (1970) *The Dock Brief. Five Plays*. London: Methuen.
Norton-Taylor, Richard (1999) *The Colour of Justice*. London: Oberon.
O'Higgins, Harvey J, and Harriet Ford (1927) *The Argyle Case*. London and New York: French.
Parish, James (1936) *Distinguished Gathering*. London: French.
Pitaval, Gayot de (1764-1771) *Causes célèbres et interessantes*. Amsterdam: Chatelain.
Rahill, Frank (1967) *The World of Melodrama*. University Park and London: Pennsylvania State Univ. Press.
Rattigan, Terence (1978) *Cause Célèbre*. London: Hamilton.
Rattigan, Terence (1994) *The Winslow Boy*. London: Nick Hern.
Rice, Elmer (1919) *On Trial*. London and New York: French.
Richards, Stanley (1973) *10 Classic Mystery and Suspense Plays of the Modern Theatre*. New York: Dodd.
Roffey, Jack (1965) *Hostile Witness*. London: Evans.
Smith, James L (1973) *Melodrama*. London: Methuen.
Sommersby. Dir. Jon Amiel. Warner Brothers, 1993.
Taylor, John Russell (1967) *The Rise and Fall of the Well-made Play*. London: Methuen.
Veiller, Bayard (1928) *The Trial of Mary Dugan*. London and New York: French.
Wallace, Edgar Horatio (1933) *The Green Pack*. London: French.
Witness for the Prosecution. Dir. Billy Wilder. United Artists, 1957.
Woodruff, Douglas (1957) *The Tichborne Claimant – A Victorian Mystery*. London: Hollis and Carter.
Wooll, Edward (1934) *Libel!*. London: Heinemann.

Trials of Law and Language: *Caleb Williams* and John Horne Tooke*

Martin A. Kayman

I. The End

William Godwin's *Caleb Williams*, written on the eve of the trials in 1794, in which a number of his fellow radicals were accused of high treason,[1] is itself punctuated by a series of trials or courtroom hearings, of varying degrees of formality, and which culminate in the confrontation between Caleb and Falkland which closes the novel. In accord with the legal preoccupations of the narrative, the text is particularly attentive to its evidentiary paradigms – as Caleb, the first-person narrator, reports at the beginning of Volume II:

> I have stated the narrative of Mr. Collins, interspersed with such other information as I was able to collect, with all the exactness that my memory, assisted by certain memorandums I made at the time, will afford. I do not pretend to warrant the authenticity of any part of these memoirs except so much as fell under my own knowledge, and that part shall be stated with the same simplicity and accuracy that I would observe towards a court which was to decide in the last resort upon everything that was dear to me. (Godwin 1982: 106)[2]

The consistent involvement of the narrative with criminal proceedings and legal paradigms suggests that something more is at play here than strategies of novelistic realism. *Caleb Williams* is a text that, both formally and thematically, raises critical issues concerning relations between literature and the law. In this article, by reading *Caleb Williams* alongside a case closely related to the contemporary treason trials, I shall discuss the way relations between literary and legal narratives are destabilized and eventually dislocated in both novel and court in the late eighteenth century. At the same time, I shall examine the significance of Caleb Williams's strange decision, at an important stage of the novel, to write "an etymological analysis of the English

---

* My thanks to Sharon Ragaz and Helen Worthington, for their assistance in approaching Tooke and Aram, respectively.

1 Against the background of the French Revolution, in 1794 the government unsuccessfully brought charges of treason against a number of leading figures in the movement for parliamentary reform. For accounts of the 1794 trials, see Barrell (2000) and Wharam (1992).

2 Future references to this edition will be given in the text.

language" (294) – a text which for us remains a blank, since, as the novel speeds towards its conclusion, Caleb is obliged to abandon his project. I shall conclude, however, by suggesting that in this apparently incidental digression, we in fact find the sign of an important shift in the relationship between law and literature at the turn of the century.

As the preoccupation with legal hearings and evidence indicates, one of the central questions of "law and literature" in the novel is the complications that rhetoric inevitably brings to the trial process. Thus, for example, on the eve of Caleb's first trial for theft, Mr. Forester advises him:

> Make the best story you can for yourself; true, if truth, as I hope, will serve your purpose; but, if not, the most plausible and ingenious you can invent. That is what self-defence requires from every man where, as it always happens to a man upon his trial, he has the whole world against him, and has his own battle to fight against the world. (162-63)

In the English courtroom, with its adversarial regime of trial rather than the inquisitorial "quest for truth" of Continental law, the literary is already always present, in the question of the distinction between truth and invention, between legal and literary narration.

What determines the truth of a trial is, in legal terms, the verdict given at the end, which retrospectively reinterprets hitherto ambivalent or conflicting evidence into a singular meaning which is inscribed as history. In a preface written in 1832 for the Standard Novels edition of another of his works, *Fleetwood*, Godwin provides the following testimony regarding the composition of *Caleb Williams*:

> I formed a conception of a book of fictitious adventure, that should in some way be distinguished by a very powerful interest. Pursuing this idea, I invented first the third volume of my tale, then the second, and last of all the first. I bent myself to the conception of a series of adventures of flight and pursuit… (Godwin 1982: 336-37)

This supposedly original form of literary construction, writing from the "verdict" backwards to the beginning, allied particularly to the theme of "flight and pursuit," has contributed to the reputation of *Caleb Williams* as an early example of a popular "law and literature" genre, the detective novel.[3] The narrative is constituted by a paradoxical dynamic: as the writer writes backwards, the reader reads forward ("flight and pursuit"). Similarly, when he first escapes from prison, Caleb states that "I am writing my adventures and not my apology" (194). The forward movement of "adventures," a flight towards a meaning as yet unknown, is contrasted with the essential retrospective nature of an apology or confession (or, for that matter, a detective story), which reinterprets, from the truth of the present, the eventually mysterious or misleading events of the past.

---

3 Ousby (1976) devotes his second chapter to the pioneering nature of *Caleb Williams* in detective fiction. For Symons (1994: 29) it is above all the text's retrospective construction that determines its importance to the genre.

Yet, although rarely so explicit, this double dynamic is true of any narrative, the meaning of which is only given by the constantly deferred conclusion towards which the text impels the reader.[4] That there will be a conclusion that permits a coherent reading or readings is part of the contract narratives establish with readers – the sort of conclusion being a question of genre. To that extent, both law and literature depend on the promise of a "verdict" – although, outside a certain type of detective story or currently fashionable courtroom novel, the genre of "verdict" they offer is likely to be very different.

However, with Godwin's narrative, which here makes a point of its constructed status as a literary narrative (designed, that is, precisely for literary effect – "a very powerful interest"), this dynamic and its assurance of coherence is, in the end, radically disturbed. When the reader does arrive at the end of the novel – at least, in what might be considered its current "standard" edition for the "Oxford World's Classics" series – he or she finds that the published ending is not in fact that which Godwin originally wrote.[5] In the first version, it would appear, Caleb was to go mad – an ending which could not but retrospectively put in doubt the status of what he had written hitherto.[6]

In fact, most readings of *Caleb Williams* do grant the narrator the benefit of the doubt in the matter of Falkland's alleged murder of Tyrell; in other words, they come to a verdict. Whilst we are provided by Caleb with considerable circumstantial evidence, the direct and most compelling evidence of Falkland's guilt derives from his two confessions of the murder, the first made privately to Caleb, the second made publicly at the final legal hearing where, at the climax of the narrative, Caleb formally charges him with Tyrell's murder. In presenting his accusation to the court, however, what Caleb narrates is not the tale of the crime, but his own story, making the

---

4 Walter Benjamin (1999) provides the *locus classicus* for the retrospective nature of narrative, which is elaborated by Peter Brooks's *Reading for the Plot* (1984).

5 See Godwin (1982: 327), where the original ending is printed as an appendix, following the published "Postscript." For a full account of editorial alterations, see Pamela Clemit's edition (Godwin 1992a). Gary Kelly provides a persuasive account of the change (1976: 184-90).

6 The humble narrator and protagonist of *Caleb Williams* is employed as a secretary by Fernando Falkland, the romantic aristocrat who instantly becomes an object of his admiration and passionate curiosity. When a tyrannical squire with whom Falkland had publicly quarreled is found dead, Caleb decides that his master was responsible, although Hawkins and his son are hanged for the crime. However, after catching Caleb breaking into his trunk during a fire, Falkland confesses to Tyrrel's murder. When Caleb attempts to leave his service, Falkland accuses him of stealing valuable objects from the trunk. Caleb escapes from prison, only to be captured by a gang of thieves, led by the noble anarchist, Raymond. After leaving the gang and working for a while in London, Caleb is caught by Falkland's agent, Gines. Surprisingly, no evidence is given against him at this trial, and Caleb passes a period of peace in a rural retreat. However, wherever Caleb finds himself, sooner or later he is pursued by the suspicion of his crime. Realizing that Falkland will never allow him to leave the country, he finally goes to a magistrate and accuses his master of murder. In the published version, Falkland confesses his guilt in court. In the manuscript version, Caleb is imprisoned for forgery and goes mad. For a recent examination of the novel, which also provides an excellent guide to major traditions for reading it, see Fludernik (2001).

narrative of his adventures constitute the indictment. No evidence is given in support of Falkland's original confession; Caleb merely asserts that he confessed, embedding that confession, as happened on the first occasion, deep within his own narrative (321). In other words, the confession is essentially "hearsay" – its credibility depends on the reliability of Caleb's narrative. The ending which supports Falkland's guilt, then, is one that rests on hearsay evidence.

Although the reliability of first-person narrators is always an issue in literary narratives, it is of course crucially so in legal testimony. This was particularly the case during the period between the 1780s and the early 1800s, when, according to T. P. Gallanis (1999), modern evidentiary rules were in effect being established. Indeed, again because of its distinctive adversarial process, the rules governing the admissibility and exclusion of evidence are the defining peculiarity of English law (Gallanis: 500). The rule against hearsay – developed, according to Gallanis, through the increased involvement of legal counsel in criminal cases during this period – is the most important of the exclusionary protocols which define English legal practice at trial, "the centrepiece of modern evidentiary law" (503). Bearing in mind that Godwin's novel was published in the very midst of this period, the fluidity in notions of admissibility and the degree of judicial discretion described by Gallanis do much to explain the apparently arbitrary reluctance of magistrates in *Caleb Williams* to treat the accused felon Caleb as a competent witness against his accuser – thereby raising the question of his competence as a legal narrator in the text.

What, then, is the relation between Caleb's literary and legal narrative competence in the novel? Judging by the published conclusion, Caleb is presented as a competent literary narrator, in rhetorical terms at least – and this competence does appear to facilitate a true verdict. Although Caleb characterizes the version he gives to the court as non-literary – "a plain and unadulterated tale" (323) –, the truth of his accusation is in fact confirmed by its rhetorical effect, drawing a public confession from Falkland which is itself a result of the impact of Caleb's narrative on the court: as Falkland recognizes, it is because "the artless and manly story you have told, has carried conviction to every hearer" that he is moved to confess.

On the other hand, in the original conclusion, this literary competence offered no guarantee. In this version Caleb himself draws attention in advance to the importance of the rhetorical dimension of his testimony, at the same time implicitly associating it with the credibility of the novel itself: "I depended for my success upon the consistency and probability of my narrative" (328). However, while Falkland again acknowledges the compelling nature of the presentation, "told with great artifice and appearance of consistency," he here denounces it as a fiction (329). Rather than challenging Caleb's tale as evidence, Falkland invokes another order of legal truth: he "wages his law," as it were, against Caleb's narrative inventiveness, standing on his character as a guarantee of the "credit" of his assertion that "he had had no such confession to make" (329) and convincing the court without the aid of the customary twelve witnesses.[7]

So, in the end, is Caleb's narrative, as it turns from adventure story to indictment, true, or merely persuasive? Where truth is the result of a contest of narratives, how can one judge, especially when, as in this case, one narrative is embedded within the other? As we have observed, an important aid to assessing first-person testimony in an adversarial context – the verdict – has been complicated here by the ghost of an alternative ending which undermines the reliability not only of the homodiegetic narration (which is common enough), but also of the narrative structure as such (which is much rarer): it is as if the original verdict has been overturned, but without the same finality. The suppression of the original conclusion does not eliminate it entirely; it continues to be present not only in the pages of the modern published edition but also in the elements elsewhere in the text which had prepared for that conclusion.[8]

The contract of the coherent ending has, then, been structurally compromised by Godwin himself. So let us try another, more literary, approach. What of the promise that genre offers as a guide to the meaning of the text? Here again the situation is complicated, this time by the thematization of literature and the consequent foregrounding of genre in the novel. While the narrative is punctuated by a series of legal hearings or trials, "Caleb's actions," as Karl Simms points out, "invariably take place in the library or its annex" (Simms 1987: 348). Caleb apologizes in advance for himself as essentially a literary figure: "Though I was no stranger to books, I had no practical acquaintance with men" (5). Reading is presented as a key to character: Caleb's personality and his relationship with Falkland are explicitly conditioned by his own "invincible attachment to books of narrative and romance" (4) and by Falkland's similar enthusiasm for stories of "chivalry and romance" (10).[9]

The text not only draws attention to the formative nature of reading; it also emphasizes the pragmatic nature of writing. In the 1832 retrospective, Godwin also explains the genesis of the novel by informing us that "It was my fortune at that time to be obliged to consider my pen as the sole instrument for supplying my current expenses" (1982: 335). Likewise, when hiding in London, looking for ways of "earning for myself the means of existence," Caleb "determined that literature should be the field of my first experiment" (256-7). Such a workmanlike attitude leads him to turn his hand to a series of literary genres: poetry, moral essays, and finally "the

---

7 "Waging one's law" or "compurgation" was an ancient defence in which the accused would swear his innocence and call on twelve citizens to vouch for that oath. Although abolished in felony cases in the twelfth century, it remained a defence against debt until its abolition in 1833.

8 Thus, for example, in the penultimate chapter, as he explains his "writing of these memoirs" (303), Caleb confesses that "My sensations at certain periods amounted to insanity" (306). This is intensified when he discovers that Falkland will not allow him to leave the country, provoking "a new and terrible revolution of my fortune and my mind" (312).

9 The author too, in the 1832 preface, feels that his writing can be elucidated by his reading (Godwin 1982: 340). The list of works provided there is supplemented by his journals and proves a useful approach to reading the text for Gary Kelly (1976: 191-92) and Patricia Clemit (1993: 46, 54-56).

histories of celebrated robbers," plagiarized from the classic rogue literature he read as a youth (259).

This is the context in which early on, as we have seen, Caleb informs us that he is writing his "adventures," not his "apology." Given his acknowledged (if derivative) competence in the genre, this seems to provide a generic context in which we might read his narrative. However, just as the text has, in a sense, had two endings during its history, it has also had two titles – the legal token of a text's identity. Originally published as *Things as They Are; or, The Adventures of Caleb Williams*, the text became simply *Caleb Williams* in the Standard Edition of 1832. Although a conventional form of subtitling eighteenth-century novels, there is a sense here in which the "or" in the original title is entirely literal, taking this text ("Things as They Are") out of its stated generic context, and placing it precisely in opposition to the adventure genre – a move which is, at the same time, a sign of the novel's innovative nature as a different sort of narrative to those popular earlier in the century.[10]

In the third volume Caleb is pursued not only by Falkland's agent Gines, but precisely by a narrative of his (criminal) life, "the most wonderful and surprising history, and miraculous adventures of Caleb Williams" (268) or "the Wonderful and Surprising History of Caleb Williams" (301), written, Caleb tells us (273), by Gines himself. Indeed, the appearance and effect of Gines's narrative turn out to be the proximate occasion for the writing of *Things as They Are*: "I hasten to the conclusion of my melancholy story. I began to write soon after the period to which I have now conducted it" – in other words, when he was driven from the pastoral idyll he had been enjoying after London by the reappearance of the pamphlet tale (302). Caleb's life is already an adventure story which forms a sort of indictment against which he is forced to assert a rival narrative – what he presents as an account of "things as they are." The very title, then, denies the text's generic status, offering itself not as a conventional literary form, but as a transparent and true account of events. It is this disavowal of genre and of rhetoric ("a plain and unadulterated tale") that transforms his narrative into the legal indictment Caleb presents against his accuser.

We are back at the ending, then, to find that *Caleb Williams* appears in fact as an account of the genesis of itself as a response to a genre narrative which, at the same time, doubles as a legal indictment – literature, in a word, becoming law by claiming to escape the contingencies and partialities of genre.[11] Yet to state, as I did above, that the text has two endings is to underestimate the complexity of the matter. The rival conclusions to which I have been referring hitherto are not in fact endings but "postscripts." If the writing in effect ends (conventionally enough, one might say) with the decision to write – "I will unfold a tale –!" (314) – it also concludes with the

---

10 Jonathan Grossman (2002) analyzes how *Caleb Williams* enacts the transition from the Newgate Calendar structure of narrative to that of the modern novel. As the present article implies, highly suggestive though his argument is, he perhaps overstates the case when he grounds the paradigm of the modern novel directly in that of the modern trial.

11 As Goodrich (1996) points out, the denial, or "forgetting," of its own existence as a genre of writing is central to the construction of legal discourse as such (as it is to science). The literary reading of law is, thus, an act of restitution to the law of "that which law seeks to forget, namely, the ethic and desire of legality as genre and as text" (113).

recognition that, at the end, something essential remains unwritten: "The pen lingers in my fingers! – Is there any thing I have left unsaid?" (315). What can be missing in a "plain and unadulterated tale" which restores truth against the falsifications of genre literature? It turns out that, in this novel, even the narrative of indictment is predicated on the fantasy of another text that could underwrite it as a "true bill" of indictment – namely a written confession by Falkland contained, Caleb is now convinced, amongst "The contents of the fatal trunk from which my misfortunes originated."

The text thus returns us at the end to another beginning as its ground. The trunk Caleb refers to here is the one Falkland had caught him breaking into, thereby, allegedly, triggering his master's confession, and provoking the charge of theft against Caleb with which his "adventures" in effect began. Although he had failed to see its contents at the time, Caleb now finds himself convinced that what Falkland's trunk ("chest" in the first edition) really contained was "a faithful narrative of [the murder of Tyrrel] and its concomitant transactions" signed by Falkland himself (315).[12] Since, however, "such a narrative will probably never see the light [...] this story of mine may amply, severely [sic] perhaps, supply its place" (316). In the end, then, just as Caleb's story turns into an indictment, it also recognizes itself as the substitute for an inaccessible narrative of events whose existence it itself conjectures: it reveals itself, in other words, to be a fiction. For that reason, only the supplement of a "postscript" can prevent the text from dissolving into an ever-receding horizon of writing, where text refers only to text (cf. Simms: 357-58). What makes *Caleb Williams* even more interesting is that this vital supplement, in its own doubling, turns out, as we have seen, to be radically unstable, thereby making us even more aware of the way the meaning of the novel depends on its postscripts.

This instability is, of course, a particularly literary effect, and hence part of the fascination of the novel – and one that reminds us that a novel is not a trial, however much the text may thematize legal proceedings or frame itself in legal protocols. To that extent, literary narrative competence is distinguished here from legal competence not by the acceptance or not of rhetoric but by the novel's irreducible fictionality and its lawless instabilities of ending, genre and title – which this novel takes to extremes. However, this radical demarcation of the literary does not by any means release literature from the law; the two universes continue to encroach aggressively upon each other. In the case of *Caleb Williams*, the problematic relation between law and literature persists, as a question of interpretation – as one might say, from the start.

The Beginning

If determining the ending of Godwin's text is problematic, ascertaining its beginning is certainly no less so (cf. Simms 1987: 346). We have already seen that the very title is unstable – proposing an internal contest between the generic or rhetorical and "things

---

12 According to Falkland, it had contained the valuable objects which were later found amongst Caleb's possessions and formed the material evidence of his crime. In other words, in their impenetrability, "The contents of the [...] trunk" also contain the fundamental ambiguity of the competing narratives of the "Adventures" and "Things as they are."

as they are," before turning into the novelistic *Caleb Williams*. Following the title, however, Godwin does, apparently, offer a preface which, in the way of such things, should provide an explicit indication of how his innovative text might be read. But, if *Caleb Williams* ends with a postscript and its ghost, it starts with a preface even more radically doubled into a shadow of itself – and this not for literary, but for what are presented as legal reasons.

For readers of David McCracken's edition, the novel begins with a preface bearing the date of the first edition: May 12, 1794. Yet readers of the text based on that first edition printed by Pamela Clemit for the Pickering Masters's "Collected Novels and Memoirs of William Godwin" (Godwin 1992a) have a different reading experience, with the preface reduced to an endnote. A postscript is again required, in the published preface, dated October 29, 1795, to explain its simultaneous presence and absence as the opening of the novel by the fact that it had been withdrawn by the publishers for fear of prosecution by the law.

The original unprinted preface indicates that the text is intended as both a psychological study and a political indictment of the abuse of power. *Caleb Williams*, "a study and delineation of things passing in the moral world," is written in the context of contemporary debates over the reform of "the existing constitution of society," and proposes, more specifically, "a general review of the modes of domestic and unrecorded despotism, by which man becomes the destroyer of man" (Godwin 1982: 1). As the postscript testifies, the absence of the preface was itself *prima facie* evidence of that despotism: "Terror was the order of the day; and it was feared that even the humble novelist might be shown to be constructively a traitor" (2). At a time when the government was arraigning contemporary radical opinion for treason, the publishers withdrew the preface because they were anxious that the novel might be legally but illegitimately interpreted ("constructed" in legal jargon) as treasonable by the courts. On the other hand, the preface provides a legitimate (though, it fears, potentially illegal) reading of the novel as a critique of the despotic nature of the "existing constitution." In other words, the presence/absence of the preface and its coming (back) into being only through a postscript, testimony to the disturbance of the literary by the legal, raises the difficulty of determining the proper limits of literary and legal interpretation.

After all, *Caleb Williams*, like Godwin's *Enquiry Concerning Political Justice* published the previous year, reads as an explicit indictment of the legal system as the corrupt instrument of aristocratic power. Randa Helfield goes even further and makes a reasonable case for viewing *Caleb Williams* as a "Treasonous Construction": not only does Caleb's feudal disobedience contemplate and culminate, by his own confession, in the death of his master (a form of statutory "petty treason"), but his very endeavor to narrate Falkland's life can be viewed as a form of usurpation of his lord's sovereign authority over that life (Helfield 1995: 50-53). No doubt a story of treason, even one that invites the reader to refer it to contemporary society, is not of itself a treasonable story. But whether the text takes its denunciation of contemporary despotism to the point of treason or not is not the question here. What is at issue, as it was centrally in the treason trials, are the protocols of interpretation in a court of law. If the courts would be wrong to read this allegory of a revolt against despotism as a treasonous text, what might be a "lawful construction" of *Caleb Williams*? And, again, how could you tell?

Caleb Williams was published in May 1794; in October of the same year, Godwin made a direct intervention in the treason trial process with an anonymous pamphlet entitled *Cursory Strictures on the Charge Delivered by Lord Chief Justice Eyre to the Grand Jury* (Godwin 1794), which directed itself at the lawful interpretation of law. The offence of treason was statutorily defined as "compass[ing] or imagin[ing]" the death of the king (25 Edward III). The "imagining" had to be evidenced by some form of overt act – in other words, the application of the statute required a legal interpretation both of what "imagining the king's death" meant, and of what acts were evidence of such an imaginary crime. John Barrell (2000) has written a masterly study of the politics of the word "imagine" in relation to the statute and its application in the 1794 trials. But equally at issue is the question of *fiction* in law.

"Constructive treason" is a form of "legal fiction" in that it claims to interpret an ancient statute in such a way as to embrace modern circumstances which did not exist, and therefore could not be explicitly stated, at the time of the statute's creation. Although the Lord Chief Justice no doubt overstretched the process of interpretation here, legal fictions were routinely employed in the eighteenth century to enable English law to adapt to modern conditions, particularly those of emergent capitalism. Acts of legislation by parliament had an identifiable author and temporality, and could therefore be identified with particular contingencies and interests (especially, as the 1794 trials indicated, at a time when parliament was under intense assault for corruption). In contrast, the use of legal fictions appeared to preserve the continuity and anonymity of the "immemorial" Common Law.[13] While the great eighteenth-century jurisprudent and apologist for the Common Law, Sir William Blackstone (1723-80), recommended the development of legal fictions as a safer form of continuous legal development than originary legislation (Blackstone 1979: III, 268), Jeremy Bentham, in a move which helped initiate a decisive shift in thinking towards legal positivism, identified such fictions as the source of a judicial usurpation, on behalf of the aristocracy, of parliamentary sovereignty (Bentham 1988).

Godwin takes a firmly Benthamite line in his *Cursory Strictures*: the Chief Justice's interpretation of "the king" as embracing not just his person but his authority was seen by Godwin not as a legitimate and modernizing reading of the fourteenth-century statute but as a "new and portentous treason of his own mere creation" (Godwin 1794: 19). Indeed, it is not the business of judges to interpret the law, but to expound it: "The meaning [judges] found in the statute yesterday, that meaning, and no other, they are to find today" (25). Interpreting and thereby adapting the law meant in effect making new laws, and only parliament can do that. Such, indeed, said the original statute: "if in any future time it might be necessary to declare any new treasons, that should only be done by a direct proceeding of parliament for that special purpose" (8). According to Godwin, it was this deeply unliterary stability of meaning

---

13 For legal fictions, see Fuller (1967). The classic case is the expansion of the law of writ of *assumpsit* as a means of dealing with modern forms of contract. For this and other issues of the use of legal fictions in eighteenth-century commercial law, see Kayman (1997) and (2001).

and its built-in safeguard against the development of new meanings through interpretation that made the statute "one of the great palladiums of the English Constitution" (7). From the novelist's point of view, Eyre was in effect committing the crime of legal creativity. In that sense, one might almost say that, by using fiction to usurp the authority of the king-in-parliament to make law, it was the Chief Justice who had treasonous ambitions.

There is no doubt sound legal reasoning in Godwin's text, certainly in contrast to Eyre's attempt to broaden the crime; and it certainly establishes a stable model of writing and interpretation for the law which would contrast radically with the literary instabilities he exploits in *Caleb Williams*. However, in his distinction between "interpreting" and "expounding" and its invocation of the stability, literalness and transparency of legal discourse Godwin is being somewhat disingenuous. One can only assume that his argument was strategic – seeking rhetorical effect, rather than stating what he felt to be the truth. As Barrell points out, Godwin's defense here of the inalterability of the meaning of written law is in contradiction to his own comprehensive critique of law: "there was perhaps no law in the statute book which confirmed more readily than 25 Edward III the doctrine at the heart of the critique, in Godwin's *Political Justice*, of systems of established law: that 'Lawgivers have not the faculty of unlimited prescience, and cannot define that which is infinite'" (Godwin 1794; quoted in Barrell 2000: 302-3).[14]

In fact, Godwin's vision of the law sees it as itself deeply unreliable, constantly self-undermined by its constitutional inability to do justice. *Caleb Williams* itself dedicates much of its energies to both an implicit and an explicit critique of the law as an instrument of tyranny which massacres the innocent and protects the powerful. In his philosophical *Enquiry into Political Justice*, Godwin argues that justice is served not by law but by individual acts of judgment according to objective principles of reason informed by a maximum of knowledge – a principle which also informs the novel. In the political realm, accordingly,

> Legislation, as it has been usually understood, is not an affair of human competence. Immutable reason is the true legislator, and her decrees it behoves us to investigate. The functions of society extend, not to the making, but the interpreting of law [...]. (Godwin 1976: 236)

These interpretative acts, based on the law of reason, are private and particular, or performed casuistically by juries, not statutory or judicial. Parliamentary legislation and judicial rules present insuperable problems, since, by virtue of the maxim that "every case is a rule to itself" (quoted at 686), new cases will always reveal the deficiencies of the law's anticipatory powers. Either the law is "wrest[ed]" to fit the case (cf. Eyre?), or new law has to be made. But the latter solution is little better than the former: "it is therefore perpetually necessary to make new laws." Law becomes "a labyrinth without end [...] a mass of contradictions that cannot be untangled" (687), another unstable economy of postscripts.

---

14 Barrell is quoting from Godwin's first (1793) edition of *Political Justice*; the third (1798) edition edited by Kramnick gives "boundless" for "infinite" (Godwin 1985: 686).

Godwin's principle is, then, a general one, directed explicitly against law, contract and promises. Reasonable and just acts of private judgment depend on the flow of information. The problem with all forms of rule or commitment, he explains, is that they foreclose the possibility of knowledge: "we abridge, and that in the most essential point, the time of gaining information, if we bind ourselves today to the conduct we will observe two months hence" (1976: 220). The preface to the third edition of *Political Justice* is itself a sign of this, as Godwin explains that, during the publishing history of his treatise:

> The ideas of the author became more perspicuous and digested as his enquiries advanced. The longer he considered the subject, the more clearly he seemed to understand it. This circumstance has led him into some inaccuracies of language and reasoning [...]. (68)

Another example of the consequences of the principle, necessarily, is the last-minute revision of the ending of *Caleb Williams*.

A Pastoral Etymology

In *Political Justice*, Godwin would have us believe that his universe of particular judgments is stabilized and rendered just by a universal law of reason. But his rejection of promise and contract in favor of particularity and an ever-receding horizon of knowledge makes for a radical lack of stability, a constitutive lawlessness, which is endemic to both his textual and his legal world. Even the iron rule of reason argued in *Political Justice* is compromised in *Caleb Williams* by a dynamic of sympathy and benevolence, while the unreliability of the evidence frustrates the notion of informed and reasoned private judgment. In the novel, the truth relies on an inaccessible text buried in the subject's "chest," while, in the *Cursory Strictures*, the claim to the eternal stability of the written law appears to be just a rhetorical move in a legal debate about political meaning, and hence evidence itself of the contingency of meaning. By the same token, as we have seen in the discussion of the postscripts with which *Caleb Williams* both ends and begins, even as the novel draws attention to its inseparability from the law, the narrative is framed by episodes which display the instabilities of both the literary and the legal. So, again, how is one to judge, to arrive at a just construction or interpretation of texts, be they legal or literary? This, the relation between theories of meaning and of textuality in law and literature, is the very question which has, hitherto, driven many of the concerns of the "law-and-literature" movement, unsettling faith in the law of reason and the reason of the law at the same time as it raises the question of the authority and ambit of literary theory.[15] *Caleb Williams* is, in this sense, perhaps rather than as an anticipation of the detective novel, an exemplary text of "law-and-literature."

---

15 For an introduction to the concerns of the "law-and-literature" movement, see, for example, Levinson and Mailloux (1988) and Thomas (1991); for the question of the claims of literary theory as a theory of textuality in general, see Kayman (2002).

In this context, I want then to turn now to the other form of writing I mentioned at the opening in which Caleb, rather puzzlingly perhaps, engages. During his pastoral interlude, whilst working as an "instructor in mathematics and its practical application" (Godwin 1982: 289), Caleb decides "to attempt, at least for my own use, an etymological analysis of the English language" (294). This is the only writing he does which has no other purpose than his own satisfaction. When he leaves the village, driven out by Gines's tale, he leaves behind him his etymological studies, which, like Falkland's "faithful narrative," remain lost. Caleb links the abandoning of his etymological "apparatus" with the beginning of the present narrative, which is, of course, the last piece of writing he performs.

What is this about? What is the significance of this apparently inconsequential enquiry into *language*, bracketed and abandoned in this way, in this rural tranquility between Caleb's literary career in London and the transformation of his adventures into the legal indictment of his oppressor? I will suggest that the episode points, characteristically for this novel, in two directions, one literary and the other legal, and that it is here, in the difference between them, that we find the dislocation of the relations between law and literature that, through these allusions, *Caleb Williams* opens up.

The most obvious association for Caleb's etymological studies is the figure of Eugene Aram, who is mentioned earlier, in a footnote by Godwin to Raymond's discussion with Caleb about the law (228).[16] He is cited, however, as an example of the injustice of the legal system, not as an etymologist. Nonetheless, Aram was a schoolteacher, mathematician and self-taught linguist, who was executed in 1759 for a murder committed fourteen years earlier. Since the murder he had led a respectable and scholarly life and, apparently, written an etymological dictionary, or, as the version of his life in the *Newgate Calendar* says more accurately, a "comparative lexicon" ([Anon.] 1926: 271).

Aram, whose story was fictionalized by Bulwer-Lytton in 1830, is certainly a fascinating case. Judging by a pamphlet published at the time and reedited, ostensibly in a more complete form, in the nineteenth century ([Fryer] 1842), his self-defense in court was remarkable. Conducting his own defense, and making a point of his lack of forensic skill, Aram demolished the charge with a learned critique of the evidence (complete with footnotes), which drew extensively on his antiquarian studies regarding saints and hermits to demonstrate that the finding of bones in a cave was no evidence that a crime had in fact taken place.[17] The judge, however, had no time for this, turning cultural knowledge back into rhetoric:

---

16 The footnote directs us to the *Annual Register for 1759*. This was the first of a series founded and edited by Edmund Burke, dedicated to events in politics and literature. Curiously for the case I discuss below, the 1776 edition included the first book publication of the American Declaration of Independence.

17 Like Caleb, Aram defended himself also by accusing his accuser, his alleged accomplice, Richard Houseman, who, having been acquitted for lack of evidence, had been the principal witness against him. See [Fryer] (1842: 19-20).

> [...] the defence was certainly a most learned, subtle, and eloquent composition [...] but he thought it partook little of real feeling – that it strongly resembled, in style, the pleading of a practised rhetorician, who had no interest in the transaction, but took up the case solely for the purpose of displaying his own ingenuity. ([Fryer] 1842: 45-46)

Following the verdict, as a sort of postscript, Aram also made a "Confession," but, while narrating the story of his life, he does not actually confess the offence. Rather, he gives an account of his intriguing linguistic project.[18] Like Caleb's, Aram's "etymological study" is also lost, but the "Essay towards a Lexicon Upon an Entirely New Plan" that he wrote whilst awaiting execution proclaims a revision of linguistic history, based hitherto on the primacy of Latin and Greek. Rather, he claims, a comparative study of classical and Welsh vocabulary shows "that the original of both the Latin and the Greek is, in a great measure, Celtic, – that same Celtic, which, polished by Greece, and refined by Rome, – only with dialectical variation, – flowed from the lips of Virgil, and thundered from the mouth of Homer [...]" ([Fryer] 1842: 77). The key point is that Aram's etymology, in some ways an eccentric anticipation of nineteenth-century philology, conceives of language fundamentally in relation to literary and cultural history, mixing Classical and Biblical narratives with historical toponyms and traditional folk practices. As such, his speculations take us away from the legal concerns of *Caleb Williams* and locate the study of etymology itself in the same sort of bracketed space as Caleb's pastoral retreat (it should be observed that the latter does write his etymological study in Wales) – an interlude in the instabilities of law and literature that make up the text. However, as I suggested above, Aram is not the only etymologist the text may be alluding to. In the second part of this article, I will discuss the other etymological study which I propose is brought into play by *Caleb Williams*, one in a different genre, with rather more theoretical, and political, impact.

II. Trying language

According to Godwin's memoirs, John Horne Tooke, the second of the "conspirators" to be tried for treason in 1794, whom Godwin had met two years previously, maintained that Godwin's *Cursory Strictures* (Godwin 1794) had saved his life (Godwin 1992b: 50).[19] Again Barrell has provided a thorough account of Tooke's trial for treason, and particularly of the eventual importance to Godwin's contribution to his acquittal (2000: 366-91). But it is in fact an earlier case that I want to suggest is relevant here: Tooke's trial in 1777, under his original name of John Horne, for

18 The "Confession" is addressed, coincidentally, to "the Reverend Mr. Collins" ([Fryer] 1842: 49), the name of Caleb's original patron and surrogate father (Godwin 1982: 309).

19 In his footnotes to the discussion of law, Godwin refers to a second case in the *Annual Register* where the culprit was tried many years after the offence, the notorious murderer William Andrew Horne (no relation to this John Horne [Tooke]).

seditious libel.[20] Seditious libel is clearly of interest because, while treason need not involve writings, this offence is strictly related to the interpretation of words. Furthermore, it is an offence whose complicated development depended on legal constructions or fictions, extending the act of personal defamation of a private individual to the seditious defamation of the king, to that of his magistrates or individual ministers, and finally, in the early eighteenth century, to the government in general (see Hamburger 1985). This last 'constructive' reading is not dissimilar to Eyre's attempt in 1794 to extend the meaning of a conspiracy against the king's person so as to embrace a conspiracy against his authority.

Tooke's trial is of interest here in the first place because, like Godwin in his novel, Tooke enacts, in the courtroom, a critique of the law as an instrument of state tyranny by turning the accusation against him into an indictment of his accusers. Furthermore, he does so by using literary and theatrical strategies to destabilize the trial genre itself. Defending himself (a man barred by his priesthood from becoming a lawyer as he wished), he proceeded, in a dramatic and often comic manner, to subvert the assumed distinctions between the various agents in the process (judge/jury and prosecution/defense) and to disrupt the temporal structure of the trial. Indeed, for the Attorney General, Edward Thurlow, Tooke's real offence was actually a fundamental contempt for the law, paradoxically expressed by obedience to the law of authorship itself. By signing his name to the seditious advertisement, rather than hiding behind anonymity, Thurlow argued, Tooke was issuing a challenge to the very rule of law: "Either prosecute this, or never prosecute again as long as you live, is the true language of this advertisement" (Howell 1814: 753).[21] Certainly, Tooke's strategy of undermining so many structural features of the trial constitutes a profound practical critique of the institution – at least under the contemporary regime.

As soon as the charge was read, Tooke's opening act in the trial was to make a point of order – a sort of legal preface – which immediately disturbed the distinction between judge and jury and challenged the convention barring defendants from addressing the jury directly. Having obtained permission from Lord Mansfield to make his point, Tooke began: "Gentlemen of the jury [...]" (660). When stopped by the judge ("No. Not to the jury. If you make an objection to the irregularity of the proceedings you must address me."), Tooke replied: "I am well aware of it: and I hope that your lordship will, upon this and other occasions, hear me before you suppose me to be in the wrong." All he was going to do, he explained, was to ask the jury to pay attention to the point he was about to make to the judge. Yet by this maneuver Tooke had from the very start raised the issue of the neutrality of the judge. Being tried by a "Special Jury" (a jury of supposed experts), he was also in due course (686-87) to challenge the process of jury selection as practiced by Mansfield's court, thereby

---

20 Horne took his surname from his late benefactor, William Tooke. The charge of seditious libel was brought by the Attorney General for an advertisement Tooke had published in 1775 to raise funds in support of the widows of American revolutionaries. The defendant made much of the fact that the charge had taken two years to come to court.

21 Future references to this report are given in the text.

putting in question what Blackstone (1979: III, 379) had designated as "the glory of the English law," trial by one's peers.[22]

Tooke's initial anticipatory move also profoundly disrupted the fundamental narrative sequence of the trial, the ways in which they are supposed to begin and end. With this point of order, Tooke managed to open his defense before the Attorney General had presented any evidence against him, whilst the objection itself challenged precisely the prosecution's privilege of speaking last. Thus, when Mansfield upheld the Attorney General's right to have the last word, Tooke accused the judge of conniving with the prosecution to commit an injustice, turning the prosecutor and the judge themselves into defendants and his defense into that of a victim of the state and its judicial lackeys (665-66). The maneuver served as a preface to an on-going attack on the Attorney General as a political, rather than legal, protagonist. Following the latter's presentation of the case, in which Thurlow made the mistake of protesting against the "slander" uttered by the defendant in his initial objection, the latter remarked, convincingly enough: "If a man in the court who had not known that I was the defendant had come in at the time that that gentleman was talking of his integrity, his conscience, and his duty; I ask, would he not immediately have concluded that Mr. Attorney General was the defendant then making his defence" (679).[23]

This was, as I say, all very theatrical. Tooke ended his own defense with an equally unsettling – and no less theatrical – gesture. No sooner had Thurlow begun his reply than the defendant rose again: "My lord, I don't mean to interrupt the Attorney General: but, my lord, my haste, and the shame I feel for having made any defence to such a kind of charge, made me forget to examine my witnesses [...]." (740). After a short debate over the admissibility of witnesses to a libel defense, Mansfield told Tooke to call his witnesses: "I call the Attorney General." Although the Chief Justice did not allow the testimony, Tooke was nonetheless able to register his objection to the process whereby he was charged according to an "information" (i.e. on the Attorney General's initiative) rather than by indictment by a Grand Jury. Thurlow was no doubt correct when he complained that Tooke "has proceeded in as singular a way as I believe ever any cause was conducted that was ever tried in any court of justice" (745): his defense consisted "in abusing me; the judge; the jury; the Crown-office; the law as it now stands; the counsel that appeared for the printers [...] and the solicitor of the Treasury!" (753).

"Singular" it may have been; but it was not, however, abuse, and it was not personal; Tooke's theatrical approach put in question a number of the basic conventions of the trial genre in order to reveal how they were being manipulated by a despotic government. His strategy was, however, unsuccessful. Again, as in *Caleb Williams*, Tooke's trial narrative required a postscript. After he was found guilty, Tooke made a motion "in arrest of judgment," a form of appeal, in which, no less

22 Again Tooke had a good point; just as he was charged by information (i.e. on evidence from the Attorney General) rather than indictment (by a Grand Jury), the Special Jury by which he was tried was carefully selected to represent loyal burghers from London.

23 Tooke does not spare the Attorney-General's "client" (as it were), the House of Commons, "the most corrupt assembly of men that ever existed upon the face of the earth" (Howell 1814: 696).

dramatically, he challenged the very existence of the charge that had initiated the trial against him. This is where the ultimate significance of his trial resides. Whereas his defense had used literary strategies to focus aspects of legal form, the postscript to the verdict shifted focus to issues of language.

The information against him alleged that, in 1775, he had published a seditious libel "of and concerning" the government, by appealing for funds for "the relief of the widows, orphans, and aged parents of our beloved American fellow-subjects, who, faithful to the character of Englishmen, preferring death to slavery, were for that reason only inhumanly [sic] murdered by the king's troops at or near Lexington and Concord [...]" (653). In the face of this, Tooke asserted, in this appeal and the subsequent "writ of error" (a second appeal, to the House of Lords), that "I am not [...] charged with any crime" (764). The formal accusation had failed to explicitly specify the offense; although scrupulous in its traditional glossing of referents – "the king's (meaning his said majesty's) troops" – the charge had failed to assert crucial particulars of context that would ground the crime: that there had been an insurrection in America, that the troops had been acting under the government's orders, or indeed that there had in fact been any deaths (764). Without specifying the referents that would allow an interpretation of Tooke's words to be proved or challenged as words of sedition, the indictment was, potentially, a fiction:

> Gentlemen, I have no more asserted, that there were any persons murdered, than I have asserted that they have left behind them widows, orphans, or aged parents. Perhaps no persons were murdered, perhaps no persons were even killed at Lexington and Concord on the 19th of April 1775 [...]. There is indeed a description in the advertisement of certain persons for whose use the collection was made: if there are no such persons, the intended charity will not take place. (722-23)

In other words, having thoroughly disturbed the legal paradigm of his trial, Tooke's ultimate defense focused on how the language of the charge against him should be interpreted. Mansfield argued against the plea in arrest of judgment that "[i]t is the duty of the jury, to construe plain words and clear allusions to matters of universal notoriety, according to their obvious meaning, and as every body else who reads must understand them" (774). But Tooke maintained that "It would be no answer to say that all this was notorious," all the relevant facts had to be explicit in the charge (790) – otherwise it was (in the legal phrase) "innuendo," and would have to be proved in evidence.[24] Unlike literary fiction, the law did not allow for free interpretation of deictics and other referential elements.

The court was somewhat nonplussed by Tooke's insistence that the meaning of the charge was not clear, that "plain words" and "universal notoriety" could not supply what remained implicit or assumed in the information, indeed, that even the self-evident was linguistic and thus open to interpretation, and Tooke was fined £200 and sent to prison for a year. Like Aram, it was whilst in prison that Tooke began his

---

24 "[A]n innuendo was any word the referent for which was not immediately obvious when the word was taken out of context" (Kropf 1974/75: 159).

major etymological study of English, the *Diversions of Purley* (Tooke 1996), published in two volumes in 1786 and 1805. Whereas Aram's etymological project was incidental to his legal situation, Tooke's theory of language, as he explained in the "Letter to Mr. Dunning" (written to his counsel from prison in 1778 and included in the *Diversions*), was directly motivated by a demand for political justice. It was also markedly a linguistic, rather than a literary, project.

A Political Etymology

Referring to the charge against him and a precedent invoked against his appeal, Tooke complained as follows:

> But that the Conjunction THAT, and the Prepositions OF and CONCERNING (words which have hitherto been held to have NO meaning) should be made the abject instruments of my *civil extinction* [...] appeared to me to make my exit from civil life as degrading as if I had been brained by a lady's fan. For mankind in general are not sufficiently aware that words without meaning, or of equivocal meaning, are the everlasting engines of fraud and injustice [...]. (Tooke 1996: 1, 74)

Tooke argued that, contrary to common sense and the conservative grammarians, words had one invariable meaning which did not alter according to their place in the sentence. Grammarians believed that conjunctions, particles and articles were meaningless in themselves, representing only relational mental operations. For Tooke, meaning was a matter of etymology, not grammar; the word "that," like any other, "however used and employed, and however named and classed, always retains the one and the same signification" (II, 514).[25]

Misunderstandings arose because people were not aware of the linguistic operation that Tooke put at the center of his theory: the "abbreviation" which words undergo through time in the interests of efficient communication. Words were basically nouns (and eventually verbs) whose ultimate meaning was "the name of a sensation." For the sake of fluency, these were often "abbreviated" into abstractions and into other parts of speech which, like "that," were not signs of ideas, things or relationships, but merely signs of other signs. On the other hand, the original, and, from his etymological point of view, the actual meaning of an abbreviated term could always be traced back to its noun. In this case "that" meant "*Taken*, *Assumed*; being merely the past participle of the Anglo-Saxon verb Ðean, Ðeᵹan [...]; sumere, assumere, accipere [...] IT and THAT always refer to some thing or things, person or persons, *Taken*, *Assumed*, or *Spoken of* before [...]." (II, 62-63). That had been the problem at his trial: what was assumed had not been explicitly named.

---

25 The question of "that" referred to a precedent adduced by Mansfield to prove that it was not in fact necessary to specify such matters in an indictment; Tooke was outraged by this because, according to his theory, the word "that" did contain the relevant information (whereas Mansfield held it was meaningless, merely connecting clauses). Under the rules governing such appeals, Tooke could not challenge Mansfield's precedent in court. The "Letter to Dunning" was his response.

There is no need here to involve ourselves in the complexities of Tooke's critique of the indictment and the precedents cited against him.[26] The important point is that it was precisely the meaning of the apparently "meaningless" elements in language that Tooke made the key to its correct interpretation, at both the theoretical and the pragmatic level. By taking such a thoroughly *linguistic* view, Tooke dislocates the issue in court from an opposition of truth and rhetoric, to an opposition of truth and *misunderstanding*, which could be repaired through etymological analysis. Tooke's etymology, in contrast to Aram's, was not cultural or literary but based on contemporary canons of natural philosophy, founded in this case on the materialism of the noun (see Aarslef 1983: 88 et seq.). In other words, it presented itself as a science, a discourse, like law, which posits itself as independent of genre.

The importance of Tooke's contribution to the history of linguistics is a matter for debate. Godwin enticingly recalls: "I had become acquainted with a Mr. Horne Tooke, to whose etymological conversations and various talents I am proud to acknowledge myself greatly indebted; though these came too late to be of any use to me in the concoction of my own work [...]" (Godwin 1992b: 49). Olivia Smith (1984) has made a persuasive case for Tooke's contribution to the liberation of English, and its study, from classical models and particularly from a theory of language which mapped grammatical hierarchies onto mental and social ones. In his turn, Hans Aarslef (1983) draws attention to the role of Tooke's empiricist etymology in setting linguistics in the Britain on a scientific path, replacing the philosophical framework of the universal grammarians with the analytical methods of natural philosophy, comparable to those of the emergent science of chemistry (88-90). On the other hand, Aarslef also holds Tooke's "remarkable" (73) reputation responsible for keeping "England immune to the new philology" for thirty years.[27]

As far as this article is concerned, however, Tooke's importance lies precisely in the move towards the notion that problems of legal interpretation can be resolved through the instruments of a science of language, rather than through the conflicts of rhetoric and genre – a move from "law-and-literature," as it were, to "forensic linguistics."[28] Furthermore, the science in question was not, like Aram's, founded in cultural history, but in lexical analysis whose semantics transcended cultural specificity, being grounded in universal sensational experience. It is a move that was to be taken considerably further in the following century by Jeremy Bentham, another admirer of Tooke's linguistics. Driven by his repugnance at the Blackstonian theory of legal fictions referred to above, Bentham also developed an empiricist theory of language with the aim of exploding what he presented as the mystifying metaphysics

---

26 Helpful accounts of the "that" example may be found in Smith (1984: 113) and in Aarslef (1983: 54-55).

27 Aram's view of etymology as cultural history allied to myth and folk practices was in fact methodologically closer to what was to emerge as the philological paradigm.

28 For forensic linguistics, see, for example, the journal *Forensic Linguistics*, edited by Malcolm Coulthard *et al.* Janet Cotterill's methodologically "eclectic" study of the O. J. Simpson trial provides a good idea of the range of applied linguistics employed in the emerging discipline (Cotterill 2003). Its approach can be interestingly contrasted with the more "law-and-literature" study of the same trial by Shoshana Felman (2002).

of the Common Law and establishing a more just legal system on what he believed were scientifically reliable linguistic grounds (see, for example, Bentham 1962a, 1962b and Ogden 1932).

Tooke and Bentham also share the radical notion that Philosophy had been misled by Language (Tooke 1996: I, 14). Confusion over the nature of language had given rise to "a metaphysical jargon and a false morality, which can only be dissipated by etymology" (II,19) – a sort of deconstruction for the Enlightenment, unlikely as it may sound. For Tooke, rather than expressing or relating "ideas," "[t]he business of the mind, as far as it concerns Language, appears to me to be very simple. It extends no further than to receive impressions, that is, to have Sensations or Feelings. What are called its operations, are merely the operations of Language" (I, 49). This, he argued, was precisely the mistake Locke had made (Locke 1977); had he written the third volume of his *Essay Concerning Human Understanding* (the volume on language) earlier, he would have founded his entire philosophy on a theory of language, not a theory of ideas.

An idea of the implications – and limitations – of this linguistic philosophy can be found in the etymological analyses Tooke provides for some key words used in this article. Tooke derives "truth," for example, from the past participle of an Anglo-Saxon verb meaning "*To Think, To Believe firmly, To be thoroughly persuaded of, To Trow,*" and hence:

> TRUE, as we now write it; or TREW, as it was formerly written; means simply and merely – That which is TROWED. And, instead of its being a rare commodity upon earth; except only in words, there is nothing but TRUTH in the world [...]. There is therefore no such thing as eternal, immutable, everlasting TRUTH [...] Two persons may contradict each other, and yet both speak TRUTH: for the TRUTH of one person may be the opposite to the TRUTH of another. (II, 402-3)

(This is as good a summary of the adversarial system as any.) A similar linguistic relativism applies to the notion of "Right" – "no other than RECT-*um* (*Regitum*), the past participle of the Latin verb *Regere*" (II. 6). And, by the same token, Law:

> In our ancient books it was written *Laugh*, *Lagh*, *Lage*, and *Ley* [...].
>
> It is merely the past tense and past participle Laȝ or Læȝ, of the Gothic and Anglo-Saxon verb [...]: and it means (something or any thing, *Chose, Cosa, Aliquid*) *Laid down* – as a rule of conduct. (II, 8-9)

Thus, for example, "The RIGHT hand is, that which Custom and those who have brought us up have *Ordered* or *directed* us to use in preference, when one hand only is employed [...]" (10). The people of Melinda, who apparently use their left hand where Europeans use their right, are nonetheless, in their language, using their "right hand."

This example is not trivial, for the inevitable question of Tooke's opposition in the past to "what was *Ordered* and *commanded*" (II, 15), for which he was tried both in 1777 and 1794, precipitates a contradiction. As Tooke explains:

> A thing may be at the same time both RIGHT and WRONG, as well as RIGHT and LEFT. It may be *commanded* to be done, and *commanded* not to be done. The LAW, Læȝ, Laȝ, i.e. that which is

> *Laid down*, may be different by different authorities [...]. I follow the LAW of God [...] when I follow the LAWS of human nature [...] I revere the Constitution and the constitutional laws of England; because they are in conformity with the LAWS of God and nature: and upon these are founded the rational RIGHTS of Englishmen. (II. 15-16)

Just as the etymological method relies on an originary, "truthful" meaning which somehow survives hidden in current usage and can be scientifically recovered, so too the relativism of its linguistic philosophy is shown to rest finally on a transcendent and metaphysical law – not unlike Godwin's belief, in *Political Justice*, in a law of reason that guarantees the possibility of justice within the instabilities of narrative and judgment.

This reliance, again, on an absent truth which grounds justice constitutes, in the end, a critical gap in Tooke's theory. The *Diversions of Purley* is another text which fails to end where it finishes. Tooke reputedly wrote three volumes: the first two – which were published – were dedicated to a critique of dominant theories; but the third volume, containing his own positive linguistic philosophy, never saw the light of day. One does not know whether Tooke burnt the manuscript because, as Aarslef suspects, he found "himself in so hopeless a quandary over the ultimate foundation of his system that he despaired of ever finding the solution" (Aarslef: 68). But it is certainly the case that, here at least, the positive theory of language which held linguistics out as a law of correct interpretation remained, as it were, buried in "Falkland's chest." In short, it remained a fiction, like so many of the etymologies themselves. The gesture Godwin tentatively made towards etymology in *Caleb Williams*, as a fantasy of scholarship bracketed from the politics of literature and law, becomes in Tooke a project for a natural science on which to ground both thought and justice. And yet the foundations for the scientific laws of language themselves remain fictional – an imaginary narrative of meanings.

Nonetheless, the challenge had been issued: law-and-linguistics was now on the agenda, conjuring up, in contrast to the disruptions provoked by "law-and-literature," the reassuring promise of scientific certainty at the intersection of law and language. In the same way, I would suggest, contemporary literary theory, which has been so critically attentive to the discourses of the law over the last twenty or so years, needs now to address the increasing importance of linguistics and its claims to jurisdiction in relation to both law and literature.

Works Cited

Aarsleff, Hans (1983) *The Study of Language in England 1780-1860*. Minneapolis & London: Univ. of Minnesota Press & The Athlone Press.

[Anon.] (1926 [1760]) "Eugene Aram." *The Complete Newgate Calendar*. Ed. R. Sanders. London/ Austin, Texas: Navarre Society/ Tralton Law in Popular Culture Collection, pp. 270-284. 31 July 2003. <http://www.law.utexas.edu/ lpop/etext/ newgate3/aram.htm>.

Barrell, John (2000) *Imagining the King's Death: Figurative Treason, Fantasies of Regicide 1793-1796*. Oxford: Oxford Univ. Press.

Benjamin, Walter (1999) "The Art of the Storyteller." *Illuminations*. Ed. Hannah Arendt. Trans. Harry Zohn. London: Pimlico: 83-107.

Bentham, Jeremy (1962a) "Essay on Language." *The Works of Jeremy Bentham*. Ed. John Bowring. Vol. VIII: 294-338. New York: Russell & Russell.

Bentham, Jeremy (1962b) "Ontology." *The Works of Jeremy Bentham*. Ed. John Bowring. Vol. VIII: 194-211. New York: Russell & Russell.

Bentham, Jeremy (1988) *A Fragment on Government (1776)*. Cambridge: Cambridge Univ. Press.

Blackstone, William (1979) *Commentaries on the Laws of England (1765-69)*. 4 Volumes. Chicago, IL: Chicago Univ. Press.

Brooks, Peter (1984) *Reading for the Plot: Design and Intention in Narrative*. Oxford: Clarendon Press.

Bulwer-Lytton, Edward (2002 [1830]) *Eugene Aram*. Holicong, PA: Wildside Press.

Clemit, Pamela (1993) *The Godwinian Novel: The Rational Fictions of Godwin, Brockden Brown, Mary Shelley*. Oxford: Clarendon.

Cotterill, Janet (2003) *Language and Power in Court: A Linguistic Analysis of the O. J. Simpson Trial*. London: Palgrave.

Felman, Shoshana (2002) *The Juridical Unconscious: Trials and Traumas in the Twentieth Century*. Cambridge, MA: Harvard Univ. Press.

Fludernik, Monika (2001) "William Godwin's *Caleb Williams*: The Tarnishing of the Sublime." *ELH* 68.4: 857-96.

[Fryer, Michael] (1842) *The Trial and Life of Eugene Aram; Several of his Letters and Poems; and his Plan and Specimens of an Anglo-Celtic Lexicon*. Richmond.

Fuller, Lon L. (1967) *Legal Fictions*. Stanford, Calif: Stanford Univ. Press.

Gallanis, T. P. (1999) "The Rise of Modern Evidence Law." *Iowa Law Review* 84.3: 499-560.

Godwin, William (1794) *Cursory Strictures on the Charge Delivered by Lord Chief Justice Eyre to the Grand Jury, October 2, 1794*. London [n.publ.].

Godwin, William (1976 [1793]) *Enquiry Concerning Political Justice*. Harmondsworth: Penguin.

Godwin, William (1982 [1794]) *Things as They Are; or, The Adventures of Caleb Williams*. Ed. David McCracken. Oxford: Oxford Univ. Press.

Godwin, William (1985 [1798]) *Enquiry Concerning Political Justice*. Ed. Isaac Kramnick. Harmondsworth: Penguin.

Godwin, William (1992a [1794]) *Caleb Williams*. Ed. Pamela Clemit. London: William Pickering.

Godwin, William (1992b) "Autobiographical Fragments and Reflections." *Memoirs*. Ed. Mark Philp. London: William Pickering. 39-65.

Goodrich, Peter (1996) *Law in the Courts of Love : Literature and Other Minor Jurisprudences, Politics of Language*. London: Routledge.

Grossman, Jonathan H. (2002) *The Art of Alibi: English Law Courts and the Novel*. Baltimore, MD: Johns Hopkins Univ. Press.

Hamburger, Philip (1985) "The Development of the Law of Seditious Libel and the Control of the Press." *Stanford Law Review* 37. 661-765.

Helfield, Randa (1995) "Constructive Treason and Godwin's Treasonous Constructions." *Mosaic* 28.2: 43-62.

Howell, T. B. (ed.) (1814). "R vs. John Horne" (1777) *State Trials*. London: Hansard. Vol. XX: 651-797.

Kayman, Martin A. (1997) "The Reader and the Jury: Legal Fictions and the Making of Commercial Law in Eighteenth-Century England." *Eighteenth-Century Fiction* 9.4: 373-394.

Kayman, Martin A. (2001) "The 'New Sort of Speciality' and the 'New Province of Writing': Bank Notes, Fiction and the Law in *Tom Jones*." *ELH* 68: 633-53.

Kayman, Martin A. (2002) "Law-and-Literature: Questions of Jurisdiction." *REAL Yearbook of Research in English and American Literature 18: Law and Literature*. Ed. Brook Thomas. Tübingen: Gunter Narr Verlag. 1-20.

Kelly, Gary (1976) *The English Jacobin Novel 1780-1805*. Oxford: Clarendon.

Kropf, C. R. (1974/75) "Libel and Satire in the Eighteenth Century." *Eighteenth-Century Studies* 8.2 (Winter): 153-69.

Levinson, Sanford and Steven Mailloux, eds., (1988) *Interpreting Law and Literature: A Hermeneutic Reader*. Evanston, IL: Northwestern Univ. Press.

Locke, John (1977) *An Essay Concerning Human Understanding*. Harmondsworth: Penguin.

Ogden, C. K. (1932) *Bentham's Theory of Fictions*. London: Kegan Paul, Trench, Trübner.

Ousby, Ian (1976) *Bloodhounds of Heaven: The Detective in English Fiction from Godwin to Doyle*. Cambridge, MA: Harvard Univ. Press.

Simms, Karl N. (1987) "Caleb Williams' Godwin: Things as they Are Written." *Studies in Romanticism* 26 (Fall): 343-363.

Smith, Olivia (1984) *The Politics of Language 1791-1819*. Oxford: Clarendon Press.

Symons, Julian (1994) *Bloody Murder: From the Detective Story to the Crime Novel, a History*. London: Pan.

Thomas, Brook (1991) "Reflections on the Law and Literature Revival." *Critical Inquiry* 17 (Spring): 510-39.

Tooke, John Horne (1996) *Diversions of Purley*. London: Routledge/Thoemmes Press.

Wharam, Alan (1992) *The Treason Trials, 1794*. Leicester: Leicester Univ. Press.

Circulating Ideas of Democracy: The Legal Culture of the High Treason Trials of 1794

Christoph Houswitschka

The apprehension of leading members of the radical movement in London[1] in April 1794 and the ensuing Trials for High Treason represent a neglected chapter in both the political and literary history of England.[2] Studies which mainly regard these cases as an event in legal history (e.g. Wharam 1992) have failed to see the intricate relationships between politics, law and literary culture that were involved in them. In recent years, Thomas Pfau (1997), John Barrell (2000) and Michael Scrivener (2001) have shown that the High Treason Trials are among the most significant British cultural events in the period after the French Revolution.[3] For instance, in his study *Imagining the King's Death: Figurative Treason, Fantasies of Regicide, 1793-1796*, Barrell explains that a crucial literary concept like imagination, which shaped the literary genres at the end of the eighteenth century,[4] also had an enormous impact on

1 The reform movement was organized in so-called corresponding societies. For two comprehensive studies on the London Corresponding Society (LCS; founded in 1792), the Society for Constitutional Information (SCI; founded in 1780) and similar organizations, see Lottes (1979) and Goodwin (1979).

2 On 6 October, the Grand Jury confirmed an indictment of twelve reformers for high treason. See *A Copy of The Bill of Indictment* (1794) for the names of the accused reformers: Thomas Hardy, John Richter, Matthew Moore, John Thelwall, Richard Hodgson, John Baxter, John Horne Tooke, John August Bonney, Stewart Kyd, Jeremiah Joyce, Thomas Wardle and Thomas Holcroft. On 28 October, the trial was opened against Thomas Hardy by Lord Chief Justice James Eyre, who presided over the nine-hour long speech given by the attorney general, Sir John Scott, later Lord Eldon (1751-1838). The trial lasted an unusually long period of eight days, and the printed version of the account encompasses more than 2,000 pages. The sessions started at 8 o'clock in the morning and often lasted until well after midnight (Stryker 1949: 280-306; Goodwin 1979: 343-346; Hostettler 1996: 112-115; Bewley 1998: 173).

3 Also see my unpublished habilitation thesis: *Die Rechtskultur der High Treason Trials von 1794 und die Literatur der Demokratisierung* [The Legal Culture of the High Treason Trials of 1794 and the Literature of Democratization] (Dresden 2000).

4 See Barrell (2000) for a political definition of "imagination" as derived from Dugald Stewart's *Elements of the Philosophy of the Human Mind* (1792): "It may be a form of memory, the power which re-presents to the mind 'the images of things in the order and manner in which they were received by the senses'; but it can also combine those images 'in a new manner, and according to a different order': it has the 'singular power of fabricating images, without any foundation in reality.' This version of 'creative' imagination has the power of associating a vast range of ideas

contemporary political and legal reasoning. In 1350 the High Treason Statute of Edward III had ruled out "compassing and imagining" the King's death as a treasonable offence. Thus emerging theories about imagination helped the government to justify constructive treason, i.e., treason imputed to a person from his or her conduct or course of actions, though no separate action amounted in itself to treason.[5]

Pfau has convincingly shown that Godwin was among the first who understood that "the prepossession of the real by increasingly self-confirming disciplinary narratives" (1997: 44)[6] is the most effective way to determine what kind of opinions people develop about the reality they live in. It is no coincidence that Godwin destroyed the charge of constructive treason of the Secret Committee with the anonymous publication of *Cursory Strictures on the Charge delivered by Lord Chief Justice Eyre to the Grand Jury, October 2, 1794* (Godwin 1993a: II,77-105) even before the trial had begun.[7] The involvement of British writers and poets in the debate around the High Treason Trials testifies to the contest for a legitimate narrative to explain the impact of the French Revolution on Great Britain. This contest was closely linked to the question of who had the power to determine the distinction between a fictional narrative and a narrative construction of reality. Authors like Godwin refused to accept the government's creation of the legal fiction of a conspiracy with the help of literary techniques. In the High Treason Trials crucial cultural differentiations were being made between the literary and the political spheres. The High Treason Trials made the legal system the battle ground for these conflicts.

---

into a unitary design, of inventing, often intuitively, probable designs and structures by which apparently disparate ideas might be combined, or of projecting a complete design on the basis of an incomplete set of data or sequence of ideas" (Barrell 2000: 5; see ibid. for more research).

5 By the late eighteenth century the crime of treason as defined in 25 Edward III had been re-interpreted as a mental act of violence rather than a physical one (Barrell 1992: 122-123). In his charge to the Grand Jury, the Lord Chief Justice quoted from 25 Edward III: "These overt acts involve in them two distinct considerations: 1st, The matter of fact of which they consist; in the next place, the relation of that fact to the design" (*A Copy of The Bill of Indictment* 1794: ii). Chief Justice Sir James Eyre focused on the second aspect, the design. In his formulation of constructive treason, the "overt acts" tied to imagining or compassing the king's death include remote actions that could eventually bring about the King's death. The charge to the Grand Jury used "self-confirming, 'constructive,' and distinctly narrative modes of inferential legal argumentation," as Pfau explains (1997: 31).

6 Pfau quotes Forester who tells Caleb Williams: "[M]ake the best story you can for yourself, true, if truth, as I hope, will serve your purpose; but, if not, the most plausible and ingenious you can invent. That is what self-defence requires from every man, where, as it always happens to a man upon his trial, he has the whole world against him, and has his own battle to fight against the world" (Pfau 1997: 44; quoting Godwin 1982: 162-3).

7 William Godwin's *Cursory Strictures* is one of the few texts that has been analyzed by historians of the Treason Trials (Barrell 1992: 119-144; Helfield 1995; Pfau 1997: 42-46; Barrell 2000: 300-307). Many more commentaries of the legal proceedings (for instance Thelwall 1995a and Thelwall 1995) have been mentioned but never discussed in the context of the trials (Hampsher-Monk 1991). Hazlitt suggests that Godwin's "legal acuteness" may have saved the accused persons' lives (see Clemit 1993: 41). Barrell, however, calls *A Warning to Judges and Jurors on State Trials* (London: D.I. Eaton n.d.) "more influential on the conduct of the defence than the *Cursory Strictures*" (2000: 309).

The following essay is divided into three parts. In the first section, the relevance of the High Treason Trials for defining literature's function as well as demarcating the boundaries between the political and the literary systems will be described within the context of Godwin's contributions to this controversy. In the second section, various contributions to the legal culture of the High Treason Trials will be explored in more detail. The third section is concerned with the construction of a radical historiography in the legal culture of the Treason Trials.

Competitive Definitions of the Difference between Literary and Political Systems in the High Treason Trials of 1794

Samuel Taylor Coleridge confirmed Godwin's analysis of the charge made to the Grand Jury in his pamphlet "The Plot Discovered: Or An Address To The People, Against Ministerial Treason" (Bristol, 28 November 1795) by distinguishing between the law and commentary on the law. The commentary is the place where Crown lawyers usurp literary techniques in order to change the law: "The old Treason Laws are superseded by the exploded commentaries of obsequious Crown lawyers, the commentary has conspired against the text: a vile and useless slave has conspired to dethrone its venerable master" (Coleridge 1971: 288). Objecting to "an unparalleled mass of arbitrary constructions, of new fangled treasons, and doctrines equally inconsistent with history and themselves" (1993a: 82), Godwin comes to the conclusion that "this new imaginary treason is no treason by the laws of England" (85). As a novelist and an author, Godwin was sensitive to the danger of fictionalizing professional arguments constructed from within the legal system:

> [...] consider the unexplored country before us. Every paragraph now presents us with a new treason, real or imaginary, pretendedly direct, or avowedly constructive. Division and subdivision rise upon us, and almost every one is concluded with the awful denunciation of Treason. (Godwin 1993a: 86)

Legal fictions which blurred the distinction between fact and fiction in law threatened every citizen. In the preface to the 1794 edition of his novel *Caleb Williams*, which was subsequently withdrawn, Godwin wrote: "It is now known to philosophers that the spirit and character of the government intrudes itself into every rank of society. But this is a truth highly worthy to be communicated to persons whom books of philosophy and science are never likely to reach" (1982: 1).[8]

In other words, Godwin's successful novel is not only a popularized version of his *An Enquiry into Political Justice* (1793) but also a popularized rejection of the "unrecorded despotism, by which man becomes the destroyer of man" (1982: 1). The government's "unrecorded" hegemony within the sphere of literary construction rendered the necessity of defining the boundaries of the literary or aesthetic realm clear so as to rule out legal authors from misrepresenting reality to support their own

8 For an analysis of "Caleb Williams and the Treason Trials," see Philp (1986: 103-119).

specific political or legal interests. By analyzing the narrative regimes the government deployed to invent constructive treason, the radical opposition learnt how to use the power of its literary judgment. In this manner they attempted both to repel the attack on their rights and to influence the legal and political systems by establishing a counter-narrative to the charge of the Grand Jury.

Godwin's *Caleb Williams* is a different kind of attempt to do this. In the preface to the second edition, which was published shortly before the so-called *Two Gagging Acts* were passed in the Parliament, Godwin associated the novel's publication with the usurpation of literary techniques by the government. According to him, the political system had constructed conspiracy narratives in order to use them against intellectuals and literary people:

> Caleb Williams made his first appearance in the world, in the same month in which the sanguinary plot broke out against the liberties of Englishmen, which was happily terminated by the acquittal of its first intended victims, in the close of that year. Terror was the order of the day; and *it was feared that even the humble novelist might be shown to be constructively a traitor.* (1982: 1-2; my emphasis)

The text whose authors had used literary techniques to invent constructive treason was the report by the Secret Committee. This report had been debated in the two Houses during the spring of 1794 and was later published under the title *An Account of the Treason and Sedition* (1794). Anticipating all the major obstacles against the indictment for High Treason, the critics of the impending trials either argued against making the accusation in the first place or suggested that the reformers be charged with sedition instead. Opponents of the ensuing charge to the Grand Jury criticized the way the governmental committees had tried to re-define the status and function of published texts by using them as materials for their legal fictions.[9]

Among the opponents was Richard Brinsley Sheridan, whose statements (like those of many other Members of Parliament) are quoted in the *Debates on the Report of the Committee of Secrecy* (1794): "[A] number of copies of idle papers that had been printed, published, and circulated, some of them for the last two years, and all of them before the commencement of the last Session of Parliament" were used to justify this measure which was "founded upon a conviction on the minds of those who introduced and supported it." Yet the supposed treasonable acts did not exist (1794: 18), as the Earl of Lauderdale emphasized: "What were the materials that proved this

---

9 Burke himself was well aware of the arbitrary and constructivist nature of legal fictions in any society. In "An Appeal from the New to the Old Whigs" he wrote: "In a state of rude Nature there is no such thing as a people. A number of men in themselves have no collective capacity. The idea of a people is [...] wholly artificial, and made, like all other legal fictions, by common agreement" (1975: 169). The legal fiction fabricated by the government aimed at creating a collective identity for the radical movement by denouncing its members as conspirators and traitors; at the same time it attempted to secure a common agreement on this fiction by legitimizing this construction in court. For a study on legal fictions, see Fuller (1967). For the relationship of legal discourse and literature, see Polloczek (1999; for the eighteenth century, particularly 20-73).

dark and hidden conspiracy? Seditious papers, that had appeared in every newspaper in the country, and treasonable writings, that had everywhere been handed about, printed, published, and circulated for the last fourteenth months" (1794: 99).

In the period of Romanticism the concept of creative imagination[10] was not limited to the realm of literature. If unrelated ideas could be made part of a unitary design and applied to questions of law and politics, the imaginary could become institutionalized in the arguments of the prosecution. In *The Cursory Strictures*, Godwin expresses a fear that the law could become a matter of interpretation "shifting with every gale of accident" (1993a: 89), a thesis he later repeated in a letter to the imprisoned Thelwall.[11] Godwin believed that such legal interpretation might establish constructive treason and eventually be used at the trials to effect the execution of the prisoners (1993a: 100).

In an anonymous letter to the *Morning Chronicle*, Godwin addresses "such persons as may be appointed to serve upon juries for the trial of seditious and treasonable words." They ought to remember their responsibility for the freedom of the country and withdraw "from the current of popular and temporary passions" (Godwin 1993b: 24): "This man, though he differs from me, may yet be honest" (1993b: 26). Godwin warns his readers that failure to observe these maxims could turn England into a despot state like Russia or Morocco. He wonders whether England has not already changed for the worse: "I no longer know my country" (ibid.).[12] He goes on to remind his readers of the Glorious Revolution, fearing that the reformers' being sentenced to death could bring about civil war – a responsibility which the jurors should be aware of.

Godwin and Coleridge's criticism of the use of literary techniques by Crown lawyers was one attempt to use the power of written texts to subvert the constructions made by the legal system. In the following section, I shall discuss other interventionist contributions to the literature surrounding the High Treason Trials. The texts demonstrate that the literary culture of the 1790s played a major role in the Trials. When the Crown lawyers attempted to appropriate literary techniques for their purposes, literature reacted by transgressing the narrowly defined boundaries of the legal system.

The ensuing negotiations to determine the difference between the literary and the political spheres brought about greater democratic participation within the public sphere. Legal sociologists have described this process for modern societies. According to Lawrence Friedman, the making of law is the result of social forces which press upon the legal system and evoke legal acts – "when legal culture converts interests

10 Before the Romantic period one would not have used the term "creative imagination," but rather have spoken of wit and invention.

11 This letter, dated 18 September 1794, was published by Cecil Boyle Thelwall, the writer's second wife, in a biography of her husband (1837: 206-08).

12 Godwin pointed out that the state wanted to change 25 Edward III without passing a controversial law in Parliament. Cf. phrases such as "arraigned and capitally punished for a crime, that no law describes" (1993a: 83); "new constructions of old statutes" (82) and "the whole proceedings [...] are of the nature of an *ex post facto* law" (98).

into demands or permits this conversion" (1975: 194 and 1985: 192-93). The term "legal culture" then describes "public knowledge of and attitudes and behavior patterns toward the legal system" and the "long-term residue of social structure, representing old power and influence" (1975: 194). This definition covers two opposing perspectives which Friedman distinguishes as external and internal legal cultures:

> We can distinguish between an external and an internal legal culture. The external legal culture is the legal culture of the general population; the internal legal culture is the legal culture of those members of society who perform specialized legal tasks. (223)

The intervention of a small group of intellectuals and literary people in 1794 created an external legal culture with the help of mainly literary texts. This group wrote commentaries which influenced the findings of the law. As a whole, these commentaries can be regarded as a counter-narrative that rejects the Crown lawyers' charge to the Grand Jury. The narrative modes which were used in both cases are reminiscent of what Godwin achieved in his novel *Caleb Williams*.

Godwin distinguishes Caleb the "historian" (another term for "narrator"), who writes the narrative down after it has happened, from the "hero" (the person engaged in the action) (Godwin 1982: xiii). Both narrative positions can be found in the legal culture of the Treason Trials and reflect the common distinction of event and story, or, to use Koselleck's terminology, the uniqueness of the individual event as opposed to its meaningful position in a narrative. *In eventu* the structure of events is described as chronology. *Post eventu* these events are used to explain a historical development as *causae* (Koselleck 1992: 148-49). While events were unfolding into a story of opposition and prosecution, authors constructed themselves as the "heroes" of the Trials in order to participate in what was going on in the court room. Therefore, it is very important to determine at what particular moment during the trials a given contribution was intended to be made. After the Treason Trials the authors of legal culture became historians. They decided how to put together the individual textual contributions into a coherent narrative. Opposing narratives of the internal and the external legal cultures were negotiated in the court room and in the public sphere. The radical opposition had to react to the "Godwinian" narrative of the Crown lawyers who had anticipated the end of their story – a conspiracy of the radical movement – before they put together the charge to the Grand Jury.[13] Like the author of *Caleb Williams*, both the Crown lawyers and the radicals tried to "write a tale, that shall constitute an epoch in the mind of the reader, that no one, after he has read it, shall ever be exactly the same man that he was before" (Godwin 1982: 338). In the heated political debate of 1794, each group wanted their supporters to believe that a

---

13 See Godwin's "Account of the Composition of Caleb Willliams" as quoted from Godwin's preface to the "Standard Novels" edition of *Fleetwood* (London, November 20, 1832): "I formed a conception of a book of fictitious adventure, that should in some way be distinguished by a very powerful interest. Pursuing this idea, I invented first the third volume of my tale, then the second, and last of all the first" (Godwin 1982:336-37).

conspiracy was unfolding. For this reason, each side tried to suggest that the imminent dangers of the whole plot were still concealed. Crown lawyers thus argued that parliamentary reform was not the issue, and radical authors tried to convince their readers that the primary target was not the execution of Thomas Hardy and others for High Treason. Instead, both sides argued that the enemy was scheming to destroy the entire constitution.

The Making of Heroes and Martyrs in the Legal Culture of the Treason Trials

In more than fifty pages, the anonymous author of *A Calm Inquiry into the Office and Duties of Jurymen in Cases of High-Treason: with Seasonable Remarks. Earnestly Recommended to their Attention in the Present Crisis* (1794) explains why the outcome of the imminent Treason Trials depended on the jury's remaining impartial. Summoning a variety of rhetorical devices to make his argument, he endows the jurors with almost mythical functions as heroic guardians of the constitution. The jury thus comes to elicit an emotional rapport in the tract's audience.

The ideal juror ought to be a "person of the same condition with those whom he is to try" (*Calm Inquiry* 1794: 9). Whereas the judge represents the interests of the state, the juror has to know the feelings, the motives and intentions of the persons accused: "The jury are to consider themselves as invested with the solemn function of judging of the hearts of the persons accused" (12). Like Godwin, the author points out that "the crime of high-treason, so penal in its consequences, is clearly and unequivocally defined by the statute of 25th EDWARD III" (13). According to the *Calm Inquiry*, constructive treason was a crime only during the period from Henry IV's to Queen Mary's reign, especially during the reign of Henry VIII, who suspended Edward's statute law. Henry III was particularly creative about developing "the spirit of inventing new and strange treasons" (19).

The coherence of the narrative ought not to be established by the prosecution alone, but also by people who were in a position to judge the motives and intentions of the accused persons: "A charge of treason, it is to be recollected, has frequently been made an engine of political craft in the hands of designing men, and brought forward to serve a particular purpose" (29). The author sees a pattern behind reports about the Secret Committee "that we, as is commonly the case in the hour of excessive alarm, should endanger the very blessing we so much prize, by our too great anxiety to preserve it" (35). The fact that there is not "one great act of treason, but a variety of complicated charges, built upon one another" reflects this danger (39).

The danger reformers might pose to the public order is systematically played down by the author. He attests that they are political philosophers who, thinking too favourably of human nature, looked forward to an "æra of ideal perfection in society, which experience has hitherto shewn to be sufficiently remote" (41). In his view, the reformers are "admirers of a visionary republic," "who amused themselves in the retirement of their closets with forming theoretical plans of government" (ibid.). This was exactly what Burke had regarded as a major threat to the political institutions.

Both *The Cursory Strictures* and *Calm Inquiry* succeeded in circulating knowledge between the public and the legal system even before the trials had begun.

This was accomplished by casting the defendants and the jurors in the roles of heroes in the unfolding legal drama. Moreover, the texts argue that the representations of the political and social situation in a country are less likely to be fictitious when people of different opinions contribute to them. The authors warn that the government should not be allowed to write the narrative of the reform movement in the style of a conspiracy. Like Caleb Williams in Godwin's novel, they knew that the Crown lawyers' "diseased imagination" (Godwin 1982: 25) – like that of Mr. Tyrrel – had to be opposed with the composition of another story, their own narrative of the radical movement's campaign for democratization.

Even after the trials and the acquittal of the accused, there was a great interest in explanations of and commentaries on the Treason Trials. The character of these contributions changed from that of intervention and participation to a composition of history. For reasons of space I omit all the publications by the accused reformers in this discussion[14] as well as those lawyers and the attorney general who tried to justify their cases to the public. Let it suffice to show how the attorney general, Sir John Scott, tried in every way possible to lay the blame for his defeat on others:

> I therefore opened the Case and the Evidence at large in a Speech of nine hours – the Trial of Hardy, which came on first, lasted many days. [...] The Judge, who summed up the Evidence, after hearing both Sides, had more doubt whether the Case of high treason was made out, than he had when he attended the Privy Counsel. Erskine, and Gibbs, the Prisoner's Counsel ably took Advantage, particularly the latter, of the prejudices against what is called constructive Treason, the Jury fatigued and puzzled, and in the State, in which they were, it cannot be surprising that they acquitted the accused. (Eldon 1960: 57)

In this statement Sir John Scott acknowledges both that the narrative of the charge was too long and that the prevailing legal culture of the reform movement had an impact on judge Eyre and the jury. This is also confirmed by the analysis of Mark Wilks, a farmer, Baptist minister and radical orator who on 19 April 1795 delivered two sermons in St. Paul's Chapel, Norwich, under the single title *Athaliah; or the Tocsin sounded by Modern Alarmists* (1795).[15] These sermons touched on the fictitious character of the charge of constructive treason. In them Wilks tried to show that the

---

14 Hardy's autobiography has already been mentioned. Similar memoirs and defenses of their positions were published by Thelwall (1995a: 3-64), Joyce (1794), and Holcroft. Thelwall wrote prison poems (1795) and Horne Tooke wrote a diary (1995). Also see John Augustus Bonney's prison diary which was published by Nicholas Roe (2002: 120-40). For other sources on the legal culture surrounding the Treason Trials, see my forthcoming anthology *Freedom – Treason – Revolution. Uncollected Sources of the Political and Legal Culture of the London Treason Trials (1794).* In the account of his arrest, Joyce explains why he refused to answer any of his interrogators' questions: "I am sorry for it; but I do not think it right to set a precedent of an accused man answering any questions. This is my only reason" (1794: 38). Written by the accused reformers themselves, all of these publications are part of the legal culture that surrounded the Treason Trials; they constitute a group of texts which cannot be discussed in detail here.

15 See Barrell for more information on Wilks (2000: 409-10 and 433). Barrell also refers to his daughter Sarah's *Memoir of the Rev. Mark Wilks* (London: F. Westley, 1821).

whole legal construction of the case was based on an alarmist suspicion which denied others free access to information. "What! are we in Hanover? No," he demands provocatively. He then answers by claiming that the situation is worse in England, because the law in Hanover does not regard selling allegedly dangerous books as an act of high treason:

> And will any man dare to say, that the laws are more sanguinary in England than in Germany? If the offence of political inquiry, and of circulating pamphlets, can be atoned for in Hanover, by a few rix-dollars, shall it be punished in England with imprisonment and death? Besides, the circulation of a book, by no means proves an approbation of its principles. [...] Is every man who buys, lends, gives away, recommends, or any how circulates the testament, a Christian? [...] It is, in my opinion, impossible to judge of a man's principles, either by the books he reads or circulates. The only fair conclusion that can be drawn from the circulation of books, is, that those who circulate them, wish to promote a spirit of inquiry. (1795: 15-16)

Wilks's brilliant rhetoric shows how predictable the failure of the prosecution was after Members of Parliament such as Lauderdale and Sheridan as well as Godwin had criticized the charge of constructive treason's having been put together like a fictional narrative.

These examples also demonstrate that contributors to the legal culture surrounding the trials used literary techniques to stir up emotions against the government. At the same time they accused the government of using literary techniques to invent a fictional narrative. Whereas it was legitimate in their eyes to employ literary techniques in texts affecting the culture around the trial, this was not the case in legal texts which belonged to the realm of the law.

Some of the most conclusive publications which appeared after the Treason Trials embedded the trials' legal aspects in broader issues. Thus these texts profited from the interest in the Treason Trials and also attributed a historical significance to them which was expected to survive events themselves. George A. B. Dyer wrote *A Dissertation of the Theory and Practice of Benevolence* (1795) in order to advertise the need to support the acquitted reformers with donations. Dyer saw the reformers' political aspirations and hopes in the tradition of the optimistic world view of the eighteenth century.[16] For Dyer, benevolence is characterized by independence which "crowns the happiness of private life" (Dyer 1795: 6). Governments protecting this private virtue "produce publick happiness" and "procure moral freedom through the medium of political justice" (ibid.). Dyer sees the Treason Trials as an embarrassing example that the "state of society in a country may be so corrupt, that charitable as well as political institutions may be little more than publick exhibitions of mistakes, sources and vice" (1795: 36).

Dyer embeds the story of the Treason Trials in a philosophical theory so as to prove that the accused were victims rather than perpetrators. His book represents the

---

16 Nicholas Roe discusses the *Dissertation* in the context of "The politics of kindness in 'Tintern Abbey'" (2002: 36-42), which was conceived by Coleridge and Dyer in 1795: "Important here is Dyer's point that the natural environment may actively (it seems) encourage 'human conduct', and bring about the amelioration of society as a whole" (37).

accused reformers Thomas Hardy, John Horne Tooke[17] and John Thelwall (1795: 78-81) as "moral martyrs" who defended justice with their benevolence; their fates resembling those of characters from *Caleb Williams* like Emily Melvile or the Hawkins who are all brutally destroyed by Tyrrel (1982: 74-8 and 83-9). Dyer illustrates the destruction of man by man or "this phenomenon of man destroying man," as Thelwall says (1995a: 87). Thomas Hardy's wife lost her unborn child while escaping from loyalist rioters and died of wounds that were inflicted when she tried to climb through a window. Dyer comments: "there can be no calculation of damages, and no indemnification" (1795: 78). John Horne Tooke's ill state of health "rendered it probable, that he would not survive his imprisonment" (1795: 79). In order to illustrate Thelwall's suffering, Dyer prints one of the poems which he had written in prison, "On hearing, for certainty that we were to be tried for High Treason" (1795: 80-81). Dyer even asks his readers to buy Thelwall's books[18] to help support the author, who had lost all his money during imprisonment since he was not able to pursue his business (1795: 81-82). Thus Dyer transformed each accused radical from being a victim of the government's treason narrative into a hero whose tragic fate the reader could deplore like that of Caleb.

Whereas the author of *Calm Inquiry* and Dyer both addressed an educated readership, many songs and pamphlets concerning the Treason Trials were written for public meetings. These texts were intended to distribute legal knowledge to every group in society. The following songs and pamphlets were propaganda texts which did not try to re-write the government's narrative, but rather attacked the governmental authors of the Treason Trials. *The Book of Bobs. Being a Serious Caution to the Pensioned Tribe of Albo*, for instance, complains about the government's inattention to the widespread poverty in the country:

> But instead thereof, ye chastised them with whips and with scorpions, and gave their bread unto strangers, which fighteth for your lust, the gold and the silver, also hath thou taken from thy people, and given unto foreign Princes, as it pleaseth thee, [...] And the children of Albo, said unto thee REFORM, and ye hallowed out TREASON, TREASON! (*Book of Bobs* 1795: 5)

The anonymous author refers to Hessian soldiers who were stationed in England to fight against revolutionary France, something many radicals and Whigs had regarded as in breach of the constitution.[19] Alluding to the Treason Trials, *The Book of Bobs*'s

---

17 For Tooke's trial, see Stryker (1949: 307-37) and Bewley (1998: 170-89). There are also at least four different editions of the proceedings (Tooke 1794). Horne Tooke included his experiences of various trials in his etymological work *The Diversions of Purley*. See Martin A. Kayman in this volume and my article on "Der Hochverratsprozeß gegen John Horne Tooke (1794): der Sprachforscher als Verteidiger seiner Bürgerrechte" (1996: 262-81).

18 Dyer recommends purchasing Thelwall's *The Peripatetic*, *Essay towards the Definition of Animal Vitality*, and his *Political Lectures*.

19 In January 1794, Hessian troops landed in England and barracks were erected for them. See for instance "Address to the People of Great Britain and Ireland of the LCS, 20 January 1794" (quoted from *Trial of John Horne Tooke, November 1794. State Trials*, XXV, pp. 640-4), in: Cobban (1960: 313): "CITIZENS; – We have referred to Magna Charta, to the Bill of Rights, and

author blames the government for having imprisoned the reformers, "but the lord their God saw that they had done no evil, and so he delivered them from out of your hand, and from your wrath" (5). In a prophetic voice, the speaker reproaches the government for having betrayed the people and finds open resistance and defiance to be justifiable: "But because thou hath done this and was not ashamed, will the lord God cause the people whom thou hath opprest, to forsake thy laws, and resist from thy power for thou hath dealt wickedly with men" (5-6). Thus resistance even seems to be justified by God.

The Book of Bobs belongs to the more radical contributions to the legal culture surrounding the High Treason Trials. It states that every citizen should "bring down the kings [sic] house and the walls thereof, even unto the ground, and make the king to flee from their presence lest they smite him" (6-7). At the same time the speaker disingenuously claims to be "an enemy to riots, and tumults" who has been forced by circumstances to warn "the pensioned tribe to redress the grievances of the starving Swine, least the multitude devour them like hogs-wash" (8).[20] In contrast to this radical voice which constructed a justification for future political action, the majority of texts surrounding the High Treason Trials attempted to establish them as a distinctive event in the nation's history. This is particularly true of the poetry composed in connection with the Treason Trials and to which we now turn.

The Construction of a Radical Historiography and the External Legal Culture of the Treason Trials

One of the most impressive justifications of the historical significance of the Treason Trials is John Baxter's *New and Impartial History of England* (1796). On 830 pages, Baxter, one of the defendants in 1794, rewrites Britain's entire history and eventually arrives at the Treason Trials of 1794.[21] His concept of writing a history for the people and portraying the trials as a turning point was inspired by David Hume's *British*

---

to the Revolution and we certainly do find that our ancestors did establish wise and wholesome laws; but we as certainly find, that, of the venerable Constitution of our ancestors, hardly a vestige remains. [...] Will you wait till BARRACKS are erected in every village, and till subsidized Hessians and Hanoverians are upon us?" In the *State Trial of Thomas Hardy*, Erskine pointed out that some radicals might have purchased weapons to defend themselves against the Hessians rather than to threaten the government (Hardy 1794: I, 301-303). See also Barrell (2000: 182-230).

20 The allusion to Burke's "swinish multitude" was a popular motif in polemical writings of the radical movement. Burke coined the expression for the French revolutionaries in *Reflections on the Revolution in France*: "[...] learning will be cast into the mire and trodden down under the hoofs of a swinish multitude" (1981: 130). For the most popular radical replies to Burke, see Spence (1792) and Parkinson (1995).

21 Baxter shifted the historical center of gravity from the French Revolution to the Treason Trials. This appropriation of national history from the perspective of the Treason Trials is documented on the first page of the preface, where all twelve defendants are listed in capital letters. Various copper engravings represent Thomas Paine, John Horne Tooke, John Thelwall and Thomas Hardy along with kings and other great persons. The frontispiece serves to justify this selection: Liberty is pictured defending the British Constitution against anarchy and despotism.

History, which was widely read by the reformers. This construction of a radical historiography that depicts the Treason Trials as a crucial event can also be found in the following songs and poems.

The speaker of "Trial by Jury, A New Song" (1795) emphasizes in eight stanzas: "The sum of my lay/ Is 'Blest be the Day/ That a Trial by Jury remains'" (*Trial by Jury* 1795: 1). This song helped to shape the history of the Treason Trials from a radical point of view. It tells about the defeat of a state which has failed to forge chains for its citizens. The third stanza describes the system of spies the government invented to silence the reform movement (see Roe 1984: 46-50): "The mask is too thin/ To cover their sin,/ While a Trial by Jury remains" (*Trial by Jury* 1795: 1). Similar to the *Calm Inquiry*, the radical rhetoric of the text claims that the Grand Jury represents the people. The song re-defines an essential institution of the legal system as the last vestige of the old Anglo-Saxon constitution and claims it for the radical movement.[22]

The sixth stanza of "Trial by Jury" praises three English Kings, "NED, ALFRED, and WILL,/ Who brighten'd with Freedom our plains" (ibid.). Although, there is no explicit indication in the text of whether these names refer to specific kings, one can assume in the context of the Treason Trials that Ned refers to Edward III, who had abolished the charge of constructive treason; Alfred stands for the old Anglo-Saxon constitution[23] and the introduction of the trial by jury (see Hayley 1795: 13); and William of Orange is associated with the progress associated with the so-called Glorious Revolution and the Bill of Rights.

In the last two stanzas, freedom is once more directly linked to the Treason Trials and the trial by jury: "Let Freedom's fair name/ Each bosom enflame/ That fetters and slav'ry disdains;/ If Freedom be lost,/ No more may we boast,/ That a Trial by Jury remains" (*Trial by Jury* 1795: 1). The use of "no more" links the achievements of the three kings to the historical event of the Treason Trials. The speaker discusses their historical significance: If Hardy and the other radicals had been sentenced to death, the whole institution of Trial by Jury would have been destroyed. Fortunately, the bravery of the defendants succeeded in protecting the constitution: "That Freedom to save,/ All dangers we'll brave,/ And spend the last drop in our veins;/ That our children may say,/ 'O blest be the day/ That a Trial by Jury remains'" (*Trial by Jury* 1795: 2). In this song the legal institution of the Grand Jury is not only re-appropriated by the radical movement as that part of the constitution they want to defend, but the

---

22 According to radical ideology, the institution of the Grand Jury was an essential part of the so-called old Anglo-Saxon constitution which had not yet been corrupted by Norman feudalism, i.e. despotism. The Anglo-Saxon constitution was a myth used by the radical movement to justify their reforms. Bonwick explains the radicals' concern for the Anglo-Saxon constitution with their understanding of history: "History, they believed, had a powerful instrumental function to perform in the analysis of the contemporary world" (Bonwick 1977: 253). To demonstrate his identification with this tradition, Thomas Erskine made "Trial By Jury" his family motto (Hurst 1946: 27) and had it embossed on the buttons of his coat (Barrell 2000: 347).

23 Cf. Baxter's explanation in his *History*: "From these premises it will appear, our constitution is no more derived from the Norman Conquest, than from the Revolution, but from our Saxon ancestors, who had an active and an equal share in the making and administering of the laws" (1796: ix).

Treason Trials are integrated into the wider project of writing a radical history of England that claims to represent the history of the people. The reference to three kings who stand for this historical tradition is an implicit defense against the charge that the radical movement was anti-monarchical. The concise historical and legal ideology behind the lines of this song shows how important literature was as an instrument to position the radical movement in contradistinction to the government.

Iolo Morganwyg's "Trial by Jury, the Grand Palladium of British Liberty" (1795) also discusses crucial issues of the Treason Trials.[24] He celebrates Thomas Erskine and Vicary Gibbs as well as Thomas Hardy, John Horne Tooke and John Thelwall, whom he calls the "Triumphant Acquittals." In its choice of rhetorical devices this song is more artistic and literary than "Trial by Jury." It compares the reformers with solid rocks that defy storm and weather. The spies of the government who swore false oaths in court are ridiculed. Truth has prevailed thanks to the "JURIES OF BRITAIN." The last stanza concludes with a triumphant appropriation of the nation's rescue by the reform movement: "Boast, BRITAIN, thy JURIES! thy glory!" (Morganwyg 1795: 1). Only with the help of an Anglo-Saxon institution such as the jury could men like Erskine and Gibbs defend traditional rights:

> Far and wide as the light, of true FREEDOM the soul,
> Be thy BLEST INSTITUTION proclaim'd;
> With ERSKINE, with GIBBS, on Eternity's roll,
> In the language of Glory be nam'd. (Ibid.)

The Welsh bard, for one, legitimizes the reforms by authenticating their historical origins; secondly, he demands that reform ideas of participation be introduced into the institutions of the legal system, and, thirdly, represents the individual as a romantic hero or martyr who relinquishes his own interests to save the constitution.

Historical authentification and legitimation was also the prime motive for William Hayley (1745-1820) to write a poem he then dedicated to the advocates of the Treason Trials. *The National Advocates, a Poem. Affectionately inscribed to the Honourable Thomas Erskine and Vicary Gibbs, Esquire, in praise of their exertions in defence of Thomas Hardy, Horne Tooke and others*, is committed to attributing historical meaning to the Treason Trials. Published in London in 1795 by the radical bookseller J. Debrett, this 448-line-long epic poem came from the pen of a well-known author of his times, William Hayley. Avoiding involvement in the political struggles, Hayley introduces himself as an epic poet with a national agenda which dates back to the period of King Alfred, that is, to the time when the old constitution was believed to have been created. He shows a particular interest in the question of how national history, i.e. the reformer's view of national history, can be created and established in

---

24 The Welsh author Iolo Morganwyg (1746-1826), who also called himself Edward Williams of Flimstone and Ned Williams, Bard of Glamorgan, invented one of the best known Welsh festivals, the "Gorsedd." This festival was celebrated for the first time in London on Primrose Hill in 1792. For a reference to Morganwyg's song and the significance of the fact that only Erskine and Gibbs are mentioned by name in it but none of the defendants, see Barrell (2000: 403).

literature. Literature, in Hayley's view, ought to legitimize social and political reform as national progress. In Hayley's poem, the Treason Trials seem to play only a minor role. However, their historical significance motivated him to write the poem in the first place. Unlike other authors, Hayley does not explain legal proceedings or comment on their political meaning. The reformers' advocates are depicted by him as epic heroes: "ye Legal Heroes of my song" (1795: 29; l. 379). The speaker wants to contribute to the historical memory of the Treason Trials: "ERSKINE and GIBBS! whose names, to Nature dear,/ Ages unborn may gratefully revere" (31; ll. 417-8). Hayley sees the Treason Trials as a turning point in the process of reform and democratization.

London's role as a champion of freedom and democracy should inspire people across the world. "Britain's favour'd isle" (l. 15) is filled with the "sound of joy that town to town repeats,/ Circling from London and her crowded streets, [...] To every confine of th' enfranchis'd land, –" (2; ll. 19-22). Hayley has a teleological view of history. As he sees it, after the acquittals of 1794, the freedoms of the old Anglo-Saxon constitution are likely to be revived. "Assuring Britain, in her worst alarm,/ That Law's bright ægis blazes on her arm;/ That round her sons the snares of legal death/ Burst at the hallow'd touch of Virtue's breath" (4; ll. 37-40). Allegorical Britannia protects and defends the accused reformers against the dangers of being executed for treason.

Hayley suggests a link between King Alfred, the father of the old constitution, and the defense counsel: "The heart of Alfred still our love excites,/ He lives, he breathes in ev'ry Jury's rights!/ Though of his line no Prince upholds the name,/ He still exists the favourite of Fame!" (13; ll. 163-6). After Alfred, these constitutional rights were lost (cf. ll. 167-178) but can be regained with the help of their last bastion, the trial by jury: "Our guardian Juries, as the friends of life!" (12; l. 148).[25] Hayley wants King George III to become another King Alfred: "If England must perceive with fond regret/ The star of Brunswick is for ever set;/ A George with Alfred may this glory share,/ That Law's pure current was his sov'reign care" (14; ll. 185-8).

Hayley addresses the King in order to condemn the party politics of Pitt. He suggests that both the King and the poet stand above party politics and therefore may become protectors of the common weal as Erskine and Gibbs did:

> Verse undebas'd by adulation's art,
> Fresh from the fountain of a feeling heart,
> That scorns all Party rage of either side,
> Faction's fierce spleen, and Pow'r's suspicious pride,
> And, loving England, that her laws display
> The blest beneficence of temperate sway,
> Honours her advocates, whose truth and zeal
> Stand the firm pillars of the public weal: – (6; ll. 71-78)

---

25 In his autobiography, Hardy also claims that the jury saved eleven million Britons from losing their freedom (1977: 67).

Of course, Hayley is anything but an objective observer. He alludes to the fact that published texts were used as evidence against the reformers when he warns: "Unguarded Poet, in his troubled time,/ Beware, cries Caution, how you rant in rhime, [sic] / Lest you should find there's treason in the metre" (10; ll. 129-31). Here, the poet represents "the just offspring and the guard of law" who mediates between the monarch and the people: "The voice of England, her creative voice, / Hails in a King the ruler of her choice" (11; l. 136). The poet voices the sovereign rights of the people while not being a member of the reform movement himself.

Instead, Hayley describes the role of the epic poet during times of national crisis. The poet's muse is "Historic Truth" rendered in the form of "Moral Fiction" which works like a "mimic glass" (28; ll. 369-372). The poet protects his country from the "Lord of Hell" of French Revolution which would expel Britons from their paradise. Furthermore, the poet is a "potent mind" who serves "England's welfare" as a prophet of national history. He is a "national advocate" of constitutional rights and a mediator between King and people. Like a national poet, lawyers like Erskine and Gibbs are "void of fear,/ In conduct graceful, and in motive clear,/ They paid just homage to presiding Law,/ With manly deference, and decent awe" (30-1; ll. 393-416).

As we have seen, a wide range of political attitudes and affiliations are voiced in the external legal culture of the 1790s. Literary texts either help to convey political ideas into the internal legal culture or are used to appropriate well-known legal events for the radical agenda. Thus Jacobin literature proves to be a hotbed of ideas which encourage democratization rather than an isolated cultural phenomenon. The emerging narrative of the nation's traditions fictionalizes British history and legitimizes cultural and political change.

Conclusions

The literary and essayistic texts discussed above either attempt to explain the complex legal problems involved in the Treason Trials of 1794 or work to uncover the political interests behind these seemingly objective legal proceedings. The texts that constitute the legal culture surrounding the Treason Trials include fictional and non-fictional contributions. Published with a keen awareness of the link between the time of their publication and the Treason Trials, they try to exert influence on either the prosecution (Godwin) or the jury (*Calm Inquiry*). The theme of Treason Trials is used for ideological purposes, either to create solidarity and a common oppositional spirit (songs) or to fashion the prisoners into martyrs in order to denounce the current state of injustice (Godwin, Dyer). Texts written after the acquittal of the accused have a strong interest in according the trials historical significance (Hayley and Baxter) and in positioning the Treason Trials as a turning point in British history.

The authors of the legal culture surrounding the Treason Trials were encouraged by Godwin's success in destroying the prosecution's case before the trials. In the same year that *Caleb Williams* was published, Godwin was among those who analyzed the government's charges against the reformers from the perspective of an author of imaginary narratives. Thus Godwin's novel *Caleb Williams* helps the reader to understand the issues discussed in the legal culture surrounding the Treason Trials. As in the case of Falkland's persecution of Caleb, Godwin shows that "the grand and animating reveries of the imagination" can deteriorate into dangerous visions of "anguish and despair" (1982: 97) and create "a delusion of the imagination" (296), which threatens to destroy ordinary citizens. In parallel to Caleb, who is acquitted, the reformers were eventually exonerated from their alleged crimes.

However, the government and the radicals also depended on each other in a strange manner. Like Falkland and Caleb, they needed each other to justify their agendas. Without their respective enemies neither side could claim the existence of conspiracies and hidden narratives. Similarly, without the illegitimate narrative that the Crown lawyers compiled on the basis of radical publications, reformist authors could never have created heroes of jurors and martyrs of the defendants to influence the legal culture as they did.

Works Cited

Account of the Treason (1794) *An Account of the Treason and Sedition, Committed by the London Corresponding Society, the Society for Constitutional Information, the other Societies of London, [...]; and The Whole of the Two Reports, Presented to the Hon. House of Commons, by The Secret Committee*. London: Printed for J. Downes.

Barrell, John (1992) "Imaginary Treason, Imaginary Law: The State Trials of 1794." *The Birth of Pandora and the Division of Knowledge*. Basingstoke: Macmillan/ Philadelphia: Univ. of Pennsylvania Press. 119-143.

Barrell, John (2000) *Imagining the King's Death: Figurative Treason, Fantasies of Regicide, 1793-1796*. Oxford: Oxford Univ. Press.

Baxter, John (1796) *A New and Impartial History of England, from the most early period of genuine historical evidence to the present important and alarming crisis, a period pregnant with the fate of empires, kingdoms, and states.* [...] *By John Baxter, Member of the London Corresponding Society, and one of the twelve indicted and acquitted of high treason at the Old Bailey. Assisted by several gentlemen, distinguished friends to liberty and a parliamentary reform.* With plates. London: Printed for the Proprietors; and Sold by H. D. Symonds.

Bewley, Christina, and David Bewley (1998) *Gentleman Radical: A Life of John Horne Tooke 1736-1812*. London: Tauris Academic Studies/New York: St Martin's Press.

Bonwick, Colin (1977) *English Radicals and the American Revolution*. Chapel Hill: Univ. of North Carolina Press.

Book of Bobs (n.d. [1795]) *The Book of Bobs: Being a Serious Caution to the Pensioned Tribe of Albo.* London: Printed for R. Bedford, and Sold by all the Patriotic Booksellers.

Burke, Edmund (1975 [1791]) "An Appeal from the New to the Old Whigs, in Consequence of Some Late Discussions in Parliament Relative to the Reflections on the French Revolution." *The Works. Twelve Volumes in Six*, vol. 4. Hildesheim and New York: Georg Olms. 57-215.

Burke, Edmund (1981) "Reflections on the Revolutions in France." *The Writings and Speeches of Edmund Burke*, vol. 8. Ed. Paul Langford, L. G. Mitchell, William B. Todd. London: Clarendon Press. 53-293.

Calm Inquiry (1794) *A Calm Inquiry into the Office and Duties of Jurymen in Cases of High-Treason: with Seasonable Remarks. Earnestly Recommended to their Attention in the Present Crisis.* London: Printed for J.S. Jordan.

Clemit, Pamela (1993) *The Godwinian Novel.The Rational Fictions of Godwin, Brockden Brown, Mary Shelley.* Oxford: Clarendon Press.

Cobban, Alfred ed. (1960) *The Debate on the French Revolution, 1789-1800.* London: A. and C. Black.

Coleridge, Samuel Taylor (1971) "The Plot Discovered: Or An Address To The People, Against Ministerial Treason." *Lectures 1795 On Politics and Religion.* Ed. Lewis Patton and Peter Mann. London: Routledge and Kegan Paul. 287-291.

Copy of The Bill of Indictment (1794) *A Copy of The Bill of Indictment Found Against Thomas Hardy, Thomas Holcroft, John Horne Tooke, John Richter, John Augustus Bonney, Matthew Moore, Stewart Kyd, John Thelwall, Jeremiah Joyce, Richard Hodgson, Thomas Wardle, John Baxter For High Treason with A List of the Grand and Petty Jurors, and the Names of the Witnesses, Who Have been Subpœned on the Part of the Crown.* London: J.Bell. 9-112.

Debates on the Report of the Committee of Secrecy (1794) *Debates on the Report of the Committee of Secrecy in the House of Commons. On the 16th and 17th of May, and in the House of Lords, on the 17th and 19th and 22d of the same month, 1794, also the Speech of Mr. Booth, Member for Chester; and afterwards Lord Warrington, in 1681, on the violent proceedings of the Privy Council, in the Reign of Charles II, quoted by Mr. Jekyll, in his Speech on the 17th May 1794, and a List of the Minority in both Houses of the Parliament who voted against the Suspension of the Habeas Corpus Act, and the Protest of Earl Stanhope, &c. in the Houses of Lords. Edinburgh: J. Robertson,* [...] Where may be had, a great variety of Books, Pamphlets and Stationary, Important Debates in both Houses of Parliament, the Trials of Messrs. Muir, Palmer, Skirving, Margarot and Gerrald, &c &c. London: n.publ.

Dyer, George A.B. (1795) *A Dissertation of the Theory and Practice of Benevolence.* London: Printed for Kearsley.

Eldon, Sir John Scott, Earl of (1960 [1827]) *The Life, Political and Official, of John, Earl of Eldon, Late Lord High Chancellor of Great Britain, &c. &c.* London: Hunt and Clarke.

Friedman, Lawrence M. (1975) *The Legal System: A Social Perspective.* New York: Russell Sage Foundation. Friedman, Lawrence M. (1985) "Transformations in American Legal Culture 1800-1985." *Zeitschrift für Rechtssoziologie* 6:2.191-205.

Fuller, Lon L. (1967) *Legal Fictions.* Stanford: Stanford Univ. Press.

Godwin, William (1982 [1794]) *Caleb Williams.* Ed. David McCracken. Oxford: Oxford Univ. Press.

Godwin, William (1993a) "Cursory Strictures on the Charge delivered by Lord Chief Justice Eyre to the Grand Jury, October 2, 1794. First Published in the Morning Chronicle October 21." *Political and Philosophical Writings of William Godwin. Political Writings*, vol. 2. Ed. Mark Philp and Austin Gee. London: William Pickering. 77-105.

Godwin, William (1993b) "Letter 5: To such persons as may be appointed to serve upon juries for the trial of seditious and treasonable words." *Political and Philosophical Writings of William Godwin. Political Writings*, vol. 2. Ed. Mark Philp and Austin Gee. London: William Pickering. 24-27.

Goodwin, Albert (1979) *The Friends of Liberty: The English Democratic Movement in the Age of the French Revolution.* London: Alan Hutchinson.

Hampsher-Monk, Iain (1991) "John Thelwall and the Eighteenth-Century Radical Response to Political Economy." *Historical Journal* 34: 1-20.

Hardy, Thomas (1794) *The Trial of Thomas Hardy for High Treason, at the Sessions House in the Old Bailey.* Taken in Short-hand, by Joseph Gurney. London: Sold by Martha Gurney

Hardy, Thomas (1977) "Memoir of Thomas Hardy." *Testaments of Radicalism: Memoirs of Working Class Politicians 1790-1885.* Ed. David Vincent. London: Europa. 31-102.

Hayley, William (1795) *The National Advocates, a Poem. Affectionately inscribed to the Honourable Thomas Erskine and Vicary Gibbs, Esquire.* London: J. Debrett.

Helfield, Randa (1995) "Constructive Treason and Godwin's Treasonous Constructions." *Mosaic* 28. 2: 43-62.

Hostettler, John (1996) *Thomas Erskine and Trial by Jury.* Chichester: Barry Rose Law Publishers.

Houswitschka, Christoph (2000) "Die Rechtskultur der High Treason Trials von 1794 und die Literatur der Demokratisierung." Habilitationsschrift Dresden.

Houswitschka, Christoph (1996) "Der Hochverratsprozeß gegen John Horne Tooke (1794): Der Sprachforscher als Verteidiger seiner Bürgerrechte." *Literatur, Kriminalität und Rechtskultur im 17. und 18. Jahrhundert.* Ed. Uwe Böker and Christoph Houswitschka. Essen: Blaue Eule. 262-281.

Hurst, Gerald (1946) *A Short History of Lincoln's Inn.* London: Constable.

Joyce, Jeremiah (1794) *A Sermon Preached on Sunday, February the 23d, 1794. By Jeremiah Joyce, twenty-three Weeks a close Prisoner in the Tower of London, to which is added an appendix, containing an account of the author's arrest for "treasonable practices;" his examination before his Majesty's most honourable Privy Council; his commitment to the Tower, and subsequent treatment.* London: Printed for the Author, and Sold by J. Ridgway; H. D. Symonds; and D. Holt, Newark.

Koselleck, Reinhart (1992) "Darstellung, Ereignis und Struktur." *Vergangene Zukunft. Zur Semantik geschichtlicher Zeiten.* 2nd ed. Frankfurt/M.: Suhrkamp. 144-157.

Lottes, Günther (1979) *Politische Aufklärung und plebejisches Publikum. Zur Theorie und Praxis des englischen Radikalismus im späten 18. Jahrhundert.* Munich: Oldenbourg.

Morganwyg, Iolo (1795) *Trial by Jury, the Grand Palladium of British Liberty. A song, sung at the Crown and Anchor, Feb. 4 1795, in celebration of the late trials for High Treason, and Triumphant Acquittals of Thomas Hardy, John Horne Tooke, and John Thelwall; and in honour of their Counsel Thomas Erskine, and Vicary Gibbs. By Edward Williams, "author of Poems, lyric and Pastoral, lately published".* [London: n.publ.]

Parkinson, James (1995 [1793]) "An Address to the Hon. Edmund Burke from the Swinish Multitude." *Political Writings of the 1790s.* Vol 4: *Radicalism and Reform.* Ed. Gregory Claeys. London: William Pickering. 129-136.

Pfau, Thomas (1997) "Paranoia Historicized: Legal Fantasy, Social Change, and Satiric Meta-Commentary in the 1794 Treason Trials." *Romanticism, Radicalism, and the Press.* Ed. Stephen C. Behrendt. Detroit: Wayne State Univ. Press. 30-64.

Philp, Mark (1986) *Godwin's Political Justice.* London: Duckworth.

Polloczek, Dieter Paul (1999). *Literature and Legal Discourse: Equity and Ethics from Sterne to Conrad.* Cambridge Univ. Press.

Roe, Nicholas (1984) "Who Was Spy Nozy?" *The Wordsworth Circle* 15. 2: 46-50.

Roe, Nicholas (2002) *The Politics of Nature: William Wordsworth and Some* Contemporaries. 2nd ed. Houndmills: Palgrave.

Scrivener, Michael Henry (2001) *Seditious Allegories: John Thelwall and Jacobin Writing.* Philadelphia: Pennsylvania State Univ. Press.

Spence, Thomas (1792) *Burke's Address to the "Swinish Multitude" and The Swinish Multitude's Reply to Burke's Address.* London [n. publ.].

Stryker, Lloyd Paul (1947) *For the Defense: Thomas Erskine, the Most Enlightened Liberal of His Times, 1750-1823.* Garden City, NY: Doubleday.

Thelwall, Cecil Boyle (1837) *The Life of John Thelwall: By His Widow*, vol. 1. London: John Macrone.

Thelwall, John (1795) *Poems Written in Close Confinement in the Tower and Newgate, Under a Charge of High Treason.* London: J. Ridgway.

Thelwall, John (1995a [1795]) "The Natural and Constitutional Right of Britons to Annual Parliaments, Universal Suffrage, and the Freedom of Popular Association." *Politics of English Jacobinism: Writings of John Thelwall.* Ed. Gregory Claeys. Pennsylvania State Univ. Press. 3-64.

Thelwall, John (1995b [1796]) "The Rights of Nature, Against the Usurpations of Establishments." *Politics of English Jacobinism: Writings of John Thelwall.* Ed. Gregory Claeys. Pennsylvania State Univ. Press. 389-500.

Tooke, John Horne (1794) *The Trial of John Horne Tooke, on a Charge of High Treason: which Began at the Old Bailey, on Monday the 17th of November, 1794, and was Concluded on Saturday the 22d, when he was Acquitted.* Newcastle upon Tyne: Printed by M. Brown.

Tooke, John Horne (1995) *Prison Diary (16 May - 22 November, 1794) of John Horne Tooke*. Ed. A.V. Beedell and A.D. Harvey. Leeds: The Leeds Philosphical and Literary Society.

Trial by Jury (n.d. [1795]): *Trial by Jury: A New Song*. London: n.publ.

Wharam, Alan (1992) *The Treason Trials, 1794*. Leicester/London: Leicester Univ. Press.

Wilks, Mark (1795) *Athaliah; or the Tocsin sounded by modern alarmists: two collection sermons, towards defraying the expense of the defendants in the late trials for high treason: preached on the nineteenth of April, 1795, in St. Paul's*. London: n.publ.

PART TWO: PRISONS

"Question Authority" is **bad** advice.

Textual Errands into the Carceral Wilderness: Prison Autobiographies and the Construction of Cultural Hegemonies

Frank Lauterbach

In 1618, Geffray Mynshul described his imprisonment for debt in the King's Bench as an "East Indian voyage" (1821: 13) and a sojourn into a "wildernesse of wilde beasts" (38) – images which signal that the prison is doubly removed from those standards of civilization that Mynshul wishes to share with his readers. On the one hand, the jail is associated with fierce animals and, on the other hand, with a desolate and savage territory. The prison is represented as a domain that suspends ordinary experience, as a reality with which Mynshul does not wish to be associated. Though his imprisonment has, in fact, been caused by his lack of credit, he presents it as an almost voluntary exploration, now retold for the perusal of his readership. By textualizing his incarceration metaphorically as a kind of errand into a wilderness, Mynshul (like other prison writers of his time) retains the superior stance of a traveler who does not belong to the region he traverses as well as of a narrator who does not participate in what he narrates.[1] As I argue in what follows, most autobiographical writing that belongs to what I call the dominant mode of prison literature involves such textual errands into the carceral wilderness – even if the savagery (or "wildness") of this wilderness is rarely stated as explicitly as in Mynshul's account. Whatever other purposes they may serve (such as psychological survival, institutional reform, etc.), first-hand prison accounts regularly design the jail experience as a discursive icon, which establishes and maintains a variety of cultural hegemonies that are produced and manipulated in and through acts of narrative representation.

For this reason, the Puritan overtones of my title are deliberate. Possibly, few expressions can better convey the Protestant spirit of rhetorically fashioning the other in a way that allows for its hierarchical subordination than the title of Reverend Samuel Danforth's famous election sermon of 1670, *A Brief Recognition of New*

---

1 In 1617, William Fennor, for instance, styled himself an explorer of "an infernal island" (see the subtitle of his pamphlet *The Counter's Commonwealth: Or, A Voyage Made to an Infernal Island Discovered by Many Captains, Seafaring Men, Gentlemen, Merchants, and Other Tradesmen*), while Thomas Dekker, in 1614, "travelled" to the Bermudas and the antipodes (in Overbury 1936: 83, 84). Although some of these images are, of course, derived from Elizabethan and Jacobean stock clichés, they nevertheless support a powerful double commentary on both imprisonment and transatlantic colonialism.

England's Errand into the Wilderness. The co-existence of autochthonous cultures in America is anxiously sublimated by identifying them with a natural environment which, though hostile, can be dutifully subjected. Indigenous identities are discursively constructed as inferior, or rather excluded from the realm of "civilization." A similar move is reiterated in the dominant tradition of prison writing where the prison is used to establish a boundary designed to delimit and subordinate a particular inner-cultural – and, at times, intercultural – alterity. By introducing themselves as detached narrators, incarcerated authors can construct the jail rhetorically as the space of their other. Such rhetoric (like that of Danforth's title[2]) frequently involves a figurative depiction of either the prison or the inmates, which links the delimitations associated with the prison to generally accepted wider cultural demarcations.[3] In this sense, representations of the prison as a carceral wilderness automatically find themselves running a textual errand and, thus, participate in cultural discourses of hegemonial differentiation.

With its focus on rhetorical constructions of cultural otherness, my ensuing argument moves beyond most prior readings of literary imprisonment – whether post-Foucauldian or more traditional ones. Instead of asking how representations of the prison engage in (often conflictive) negotiations between legal, political, or ethical agendas and the mental or physical interests of an individual, I propose to focus on the cultural capital that textualized imprisonment accumulates for the construction – or deconstruction – of alterity. By looking at what types of textual errands are run into perceived carceral wildernesses, this essay adopts a bird's-eye view of penal institutions' collective significance as evoked through symbolic associations. It concentrates on autobiographical texts as a genre where the need for social self-assertion or strategic self-positioning is felt with particular urgency and the prison's symbolic value as a cultural icon is exploited most explicitly. In the first section, I illustrate my approach by analyzing the accounts by an insolvent debtor, a habitual petty criminal, and a religious prisoner of conscience. While these three texts all place their other on the far side of the boundary constructed through their representation of the prison, they exemplify three different types of alterity: the prison becomes the other of national political and economic interests, of assumptions of social and ethnic superiority, or of the spiritual inner self. Using the analysis of the three autobiographical examples as a point of departure, the second section of this essay outlines the theoretical basis of my argument in more general terms and is, thus, meant to be suggestive for further studies of literary imprisonment in a broader sense.

2 On the historical significance of Danforth's ambivalent image, see Miller (1956: 3-15).

3 This becomes most obvious when they (like Danforth) use images of colonial settlement or imperial conquest that assert the superiority of one's own culture. My interpretation of the culturally productive potential of such metaphors follows Roland Greene's persuasive reading of the powerful reconfiguration of Petrarca's imagery in the Italianite poetry of Mendoza, Camões, Wyatt, and others (see esp. Greene 1999: 141-46 for the early colonialist transformations of the pertinent seafaring metaphors of *Canzoniere* 189). See also Lauterbach (2003: 44-45) on how in early Spanish Renaissance love poetry an imperialist discourse emerges the moment courtly Aristotelean images of love are replaced by Italianite neo-Platonic metaphors.

I. Prison Autobiographies

The title of the rather inconspicuous 1691 prison tract *The Cry of the Oppressed: Being a True and Tragical Account of the Unparallel'd Sufferings of Multitudes of Poor Imprisoned Debtors, in most of the Gaols in England,* [...]*; Some of Them Being [...] Lodg'd with Hogs, Felons, and Condemn'd Persons,* [...]*; with Other Barbarous Cruelties, not to Be Parallel'd in Any History, or Nation* by one Moses Pitt offers its readers two general possibilities for approaching the actual text. First – and most overtly –, it points at the injustices and devastating effects of imprisonment for debt and, consequently, constitutes a social critique. The title leads us to expect an indictment of the cruel prison conditions in post-Restoration England. And, we are not disappointed on that count: throughout the book, the jail is presented as a place where an extraordinary amount of "Barbarities" (Pitt 1691: [viii]) are committed. Incarcerated debtors lie there "Starving, Rotting with Soars and Carbuncles, Devour'd with Vermin, Poisoned with Nasty Stinks, Knocked on the Head, and that for no Crimes, but for their Misfortunes, Miscarriages, and Losses, by Trade and Merchandizing, which in no Times or Ages could be avoided" ([vii]). Such depictions as well as the author's detailed account of his suffering and the inclusion of a large number of letters from all over England concerning abuses in local jails, make it easy to read the text as social criticism, as a reproach for oppressive imprisonment for debt. Indeed, as a petitioner to Parliament, Pitt was clearly interested in exposing and denouncing the cruelties and failures of the debtor's prisons.

Yet, while there can be no doubt about the validity of placing Pitt's tract in the context of a long tradition of first-hand attacks on prison conditions,[4] such a reading

---

4 See, for example, the anonymous Elizabethan tracts *The Lamentations of the Prisoners in Newgate and Other Gaols* (1565-66), *An Admonition to Cruel Jailors* (1569-70), *A New Ballad of a Prisoner Brought Home in a Coffin to Pay His Creditors* (1588-89), as well as William Wager's *The Cruel Debtor* (1566), John Pitts's *A Poor Man's Petition in Behalf of Poor Prisoners* (1579), Robert Southwell's *An Humble Supplication to Her Majesty* (1591), Luke Hutton's *Lamentation* (1596), Thomas Dekker's *Villainies Discovered* (1616), Mynshul's and Fennor's sketches mentioned above, Robert Speed's *The Counter Scuffle* (1621), Richard Brathwaite's *Whimzies* (1631), Thomas Dekker's *English Villainies* (1632), Nathaniel Wickins's *Woodstreet Counter's Plea for Its Prisoner* (1638), Thomas Grantham's *A Motion against Imprisonment* (1642), William Bagwell's *The Merchant Distressed* (1644), James Frese's *A Declaration and Appeal* (1645), Francis Mussell's *The Prisoner's Observation by Way of Complaint* (1645), John Lilburne's *The Oppressed Man's Oppression Declared* (1646), John Jones's *The Cry of Blood* (1651), John Lilburn's *The Upright Man's Vindication* (1653), William Pryor's *The Out-Cries of the Poor, Oppressed and Imprisoned* (1659), George Wither's *An Improvement of Imprisonment, The Prisoner's Plea* (both 1661), and *A Proclamation in the Name of the King of Kings* (1662), Samuel Speed's *The Prisoner's Complaint* (1673), Charles Cotton's *The Confinement* (1679), or the anonymous *Groans from Newgate* (1683). During the eighteenth century, such first-hand complaints largely gave way to, on the one hand, more sensational accounts of the lives and imprisonment of (in)famous criminals (as collected in Alexander Smith's *A Complete History of the Lives and Robberies of the Most Notorious Highwaymen, Footpads, Shop-Lifts, and Cheats* (1713/14-19) or the numerous editions of the so-called *Newgate Calendar*) and, on the one hand, critical outside reflections on the penal system

tells only half the story, leaving the larger cultural work of the text's rhetoric unexplored. Additionally – and rather more covertly –, both the title and the just quoted passage institute a clear distinction between "the *Fault* and the *irresistible Misfortune*" (93). Not only do they contrast the cruelty of the prison with the comparative freedom of the outside world, but they also juxtapose the criminal felons – linked, without further commentary, to the jail hogs! – with the innocent debtors, who supposedly did not commit any crime but are themselves the victims of such mishap as can happen to anyone anywhere any time. Unable to serve "the Commonwealth both at Sea and at Land" ([iv]), the debtors are lodged with criminals who have lost citizens' rights and arguably "belong" to the prisons and the prisons only, i.e. to what Pitt calls "*Sanctuaries to Cheats and Villains*" ([xxvii]). More than just denoting a physically oppressive location, the place of confinement is identified as the symbolic site of a particular moral category and social behavior. By means of rhetorical associations and dissociations, Pitt's text introduces a dichotomy between the felons and the debtors. While both groups are literally housed together, Pitt represents the jail as meaningful only in reference to the villainous felons. As such, the prison becomes a textual marker. An emblematic boundary is established between those who have been 'deservedly' imprisoned for their socially disruptive activities and those who are not only innocent but even align themselves with the political and commercial endeavors of their country. Furthermore, the latter are associated with the mercantilist values of the emergent bourgeois middle class, i.e. with a life far removed from the meanings of the prison. Such rhetorical acts of demarcation infuse the carceral space with a wider collective significance: associated with moral, economic, and social deviance, this space becomes an icon for various types of cultural otherness.

This iconic use of the prison entails two further acts of delimitation. First, it places Pitt – again rhetorically – *above* the jail. His generalizing distinction between villainous felons and hapless debtors establishes a position of semiotic authority for himself, which is further underlined by his claims to truthfulness and the implication of his innocence. Unable to control his treatment within the prison, he can control the representation of its social meaning and, moreover, position himself outside of the symbolic space of cultural connotations thus delineated. While narrating his own life story, he seems curiously removed from his narrative. This allows him to dissociate himself from criminal alterity, identified with the prison, in order to (hopefully) gain the trust and compassion of readers sharing his views.

Second, for Pitt the jail is not only an icon of criminal villainy but also an emblem of national and religious otherness. As the title of his tract suggests, the treatment of insolvent debtors is supposedly without geographical or historical parallel. To emphasize this excess of cruelty Pitt evokes a series of clichés of foreign and, in particular, Catholic cruelties as possible analogies to show how this treatment is worse than the tragedies "Acted in Foreign Nations among Turks and Infidels, Papists and

---

in general, culminating in the reformatory efforts of John Howard (*The State of the Prison in England and Wales*, 1777) and Jeremy Bentham (*An Introduction to the Principles of Morals and Legislation*, 1780/89).

Idolators" ([vii]), worse even than "the Rebellion of *Ireland*, and the Tyranny and Cruelties at this time Exercis'd by that Monster of *France*, against his poor Innocent *Hugenot* [sic] Subjects" ([viii]).[5] The portrayal of the prison as an instrument of oppression and cruelty, as a place of personal hardship and suffering, then goes hand in hand with a rhetoric of demarcation. This rhetoric distinguishes not only between those who are justly suffering in prison and those who are not, but, furthermore, serves Pitt as a means to identify himself with the latter group, in opposition to an alterity seen as different on moral and national grounds.

About two hundred years later, Victorian prison autobiographies can be observed to use similar strategies. They are also based on a dissociation of the authors from the prison as a place for "real" criminals, and reproduce Pitt's figuration of the prison as an icon of cultural alterity. Here, however, the position of textual authority becomes particularly evident in the way metaphors and similes are employed to depict the supposed social and ethnic otherness of the prison inmates and, in this way, to signal the writer's difference from these associations. The account of the habitual criminal "No. 7," revealingly entitled *Twenty-Five Years in Seventeen Prisons* (1903), is a case in point. Even the individual whose criminal record is hard to ignore tries to distance himself from what the prison ought to stand for: "social outcast[s]" (1903: 21). While "No. 7" freely admits his criminal past, he insists that his criminal career was initiated solely by minor trifles and the false testimony of others (9-10; 20-21). He therefore maintains that his repeated incarcerations, unlike those of most other prisoners, do not betoken dubious character traits but are due to outward circumstances. "Real" criminal behavior, which even for "No. 7" requires punishment, is associated with others, allowing him to assume an air of Victorian respectability despite his lower middle-class background.[6] This role, in return, gives him the authority to represent the prison and its inmates from the perspective of a gentleman and, at the same time, to adopt the attitude of an (almost) outsider while, in fact, presenting his inside experiences. Like Mynshul and others, "No. 7" retains the stance of a detached observer, fashioning himself as an "explorer" who recounts "the countries through which he has passed" (201) – always on the almost documentary mission of "search[ing] after remarkable criminals" (23). By dropping the narrative position of a convicted inmate in favor of that of a public traveler who is interested in but not a part of the places he describes, he invokes a moral and social difference between his superior self and the inferior criminal world which he identifies with the prison.

---

5 Even the names of some of the jailors seem to be fabricated to underscore this. For example, the wife of the keeper of the local jail in Bury St. Edmunds, who enforces the joint lodging of felons and debtors with particular cruelty, is named Mary Patrick; the unfair under-keeper is called James King (see 62). While I have not been able to consult the local Bury St. Edmunds archives to verify (or falsify) these names, it is tempting to suspect that Pitt's tract, which was after all published only three years after 1688, is not entirely a compilation of first-hand reports of actual experiences but a carefully and purposely contrived evocation of political, denominational, and national anxieties.

6 For the social differentiations implied in the practical suggestions for the administration of prisons in late Victorian autobiographies, see also Wiener (1990: 311-12).

The ideological implications of his role as an "explorer" renders the autobiographical account of "No. 7" particularly interesting. To foreground from the outset the difference between himself and his fellow prisoners, he begins by characterizing his first cellmate with a series of debasing comparisons and metaphors. This person, who allegedly has "a more than sentimental leaning towards the ways of the African savages" (11), is associated with Nero (14) and the inferno (15) and appears to have "a taint of the salamander in his composition" (15). He is likened, in turn, to "savages," to animals, to a tyrant, and finally to the devil, and consequently can be characterized as someone who "richly deserve[s] [his] punishment" (12). Yet, such metaphorical language not only supports the writer's moral verdict but, more significantly, rhetorically exoticizes the prison and its inmates in order to institute a boundary between the assumed respectability of "No. 7" and an alterity that increasingly appears to be a cultural construct. A similar exoticizing strategy is employed in the depiction of another prisoner, "B 2, 14." He, too, is associated with a different ethnicity when he is presented as "an Ethiopian in the social sense" (49).[7] To make the difference between this prisoner and the author and the world of his readership even more explicit, "No. 7" adds the following absurd generalization:

> No one nowadays cares to undertake the task of whitewashing an Ethiopian. It is an ungrateful job, and never has been done with complete satisfaction, either to the Ethiopian or to the white-washer. (48)

Through such metaphorical associations of the prison with colonial otherness, "No. 7" joins the rhetoric of Victorian imperialism, in particular the hierarchical juxtaposition of "white" Europeanness and colonial "darkness." Similarly, "No. 7" states that for the governor of Chatham Prison – previously in charge of "the serfs on the banks of the Ganges" – running a colony or a prison makes little difference (57). Accordingly, the structure of imperial administration is easily reproduced within the prison system, and, colonial and criminal subjects can imaginatively be linked to each other as not belonging to the Victorian mainstream. In order to connect the otherness of the prison with cultural alterities, "No. 7" not only exploits the imperial playgrounds of Africa or India, but – like Pitt – instrumentalizes England's long-standing antagonism towards France. Claiming to write "in plain Anglo-Saxon" (202), he invokes a mythical sense of Anglo-Saxonness that follows the then current silencing of Norman-French roots in favor of celebrating the supposed "racial" superiority of an Anglo-Germanic ancestry.[8]

Far from merely relating their experiences of imprisonment, both Pitt and "No. 7" use them to evoke and uphold generally accepted (if bluntly nationalist, racialist, or

---

7 Another self-styled Victorian gentleman prisoner is more in tune with the imagery of his time: "One Who Has Endured It" refers to the supposedly ordinary criminal as "the wretched little street Arab" (1877: 30) to distance himself from his fellow inmates through the implication of his own Englishness.

8 For a summary of racial Anglo-Saxonism in nineteenth-century England, see Horsman (1981: 62-77).

pseudo-historical) notions of cultural hegemony. The prison, as a discursive icon of cultural communication, becomes useful in making collective classifications that place the self within the norms of bourgeois society (and, in turn, beyond the world of the prison). At the same time, this icon is used to establish important cultural boundaries. Middle-class group identity is confirmed through an insistence on moral, national, ethnic, and class identifications which are rhetorically opposed to the criminal Other, as this figure is circumscribed by the penal establishment.[9]

For prisoners of debt such as Mynshul and Pitt or for the assumed "gentleman convicts" like "No. 7" or "One Who Has Endured It," the prison emerges as a space associated with different alterities. In John Bunyan's spiritual autobiography *Grace Abounding to the Chief of Sinners* (1666), which closes with Bunyan's incarceration for his activities as a dissenter, prison is subjected to more complex semantic operations. In this text the carceral space serves as a boundary in two ways. In a first step, Bunyan, like Pitt, presents the very real miseries of imprisonment, including the exposure "to hunger, to cold, to perils, to nakedness, to enemies, and a thousand calamities" (1962: 99). He even acknowledges his dejection, his "very sad and low condition" (100), as well as his dread of "long and tedious" years ahead or, worse yet, his death (97) as well as his worries about his family (98). Hence, the prison is clearly set apart from the rest of the world in time and space. Bunyan does not, however, associate the jail with a morally or socially inferior class of person in contradistinction to whom he needs to define and affirm his own cultural identity. Instead, he elaborates on the power exerted over his body and mind during imprisonment and, by doing so, points at those who purposefully exercise this power. The prison becomes the place of High Church authority. In order to evade this immediate worldly authority, Bunyan turns towards the higher truth of the Scriptures and, ultimately, to God (see e.g. 98-99). Instead of focusing on his physical injuries and mental anxieties – and, thus, on his role as victimized object of the carceral system –, he dissociates himself from them in order to gain access to the spiritual truths of his faith. Even he, then, can rhetorically employ the prison as a boundary between those in charge of and associated with the institution and himself as part of a higher order outside and beyond the grip of the carceral sphere and the human law it represents. The prison serves to delimit an official High Church discourse from Bunyan's textualization of his own victimized Puritan self.

Yet, in a second step Bunyan gives the prison a completely different meaning. Rather than repressing his association of it with his adversaries, he now embraces his incarceration as ultimately responsible for the spiritual transcendence *offered* to him and his righteous brethren. The prison becomes the site where the Scriptures were

---

9 For a more extensive reading of late Victorian prison accounts by such "gentleman prisoners" as "No. 7," see my analysis in Lauterbach (forthcoming). I would also like to acknowledge Monika Fludernik's response to my study, in which she argues that the dissociative rhetoric in autobiographical prison accounts does not only articulate cultural categories but, furthermore, forms part of a psychological survival strategy designed to deal with the shock of entering a new, different, and essentially alien world (see Fludernik, forthcoming).

"made [...] to shine upon" him like never before and where "Jesus Christ [...] was never more real and apparent then [sic] now" (96). Only in jail can he finally receive the "conviction, instruction, and understanding" (96) he has been seeking for a long time. While his sense of the miserable reality of carceral life made him first associate it with his religious opponents, the alternative focus on his spiritual experience induces him to associate the prison with himself. Though the two strategies seem to contradict one another, they both employ the prison as a boundary between two opposite denominational (and political) convictions.[10] By reinterpreting the painful reality of imprisonment as a heightened form of religious experience (rather than denying it), the prison is made meaningful as a providential place (in the Puritan sense) which is dominated by God and, hence, fundamentally different from the religious Other.[11] Furthermore, Bunyan's association of himself with the jail takes on collective significance when he argues that his perseverance in prison can foster the steadfastness of his congregation (see e.g. 99, 100; see also 106 for a similar argument in the posthumously published *Relation of the Imprisonment of Mr. John Bunyan*).[12] As Sid Sondergard has argued in reference to Bunyan's spiritual tracts in general, *Grace Abounding* is meant "not to establish authority, but rather to compensate for prior authority displaced by his imprisonment" (1993: 223).

Both strategies – differentiating oneself from the prison as an icon of religious and political alterity and identifying with it as an emblem of one's inner convictions – are, therefore, part of a process of emphatically visualizing what for Bunyan is *the* decisive cultural rupture within the England of his time. An Anglican tradition that essentially controls the country's politics and an alternative Puritan path towards secular salvation represent the two sides of this gap for him. Thus Bunyan's errand into the carceral wilderness is both a confrontation with cultural otherness and, in typical Puritan fashion, a way to form and confirm the self and its conscience against this otherness. Yet, it is as much a textual as a politically enforced errand: what finally emerges from his autobiography is less the transparent account of inner convictions (however "authentic" they may be) than the image of the writer "John Bunyan" himself, who can

---

10 Another Puritan genre, the so-called Indian Captivity Narrative, employs the same strategy of identifying with one's own "imprisonment" to delimit religious boundaries. This leads to a conflation of Protestant and English (as opposed to native) identities. Religious and ethnic categories go hand in hand, as, for instance, in Cotton Mather's synopsis of various captivity narratives, where the indigenous tribes become "Popish Indians" (1853: 612), and their cruelties are compared to those of Catholic monks in Renaissance England (600).

11 Ironically, this providential interpretation re-establishes the power of the High Church authorities as the ultimate cause of Bunyan's religious experience – an experience made possible only by their having imprisoned him. What neither Bunyan's autobiography nor Puritan writing in general seem able to resolve is this aporia of relying on the presence of "evil" for special forms of salvation and simultaneously attempting to diminish the significance of that evil.

12 In a similar manner, *The Pilgrim's Progress* (1678) shows how Christian and Faithful embrace their imprisonment at Vanity-Fair "with much content" (1960: 92). Imprisonment reveals the presence of God – most explicitly when Faithful, upon his execution, is carried on "the nearest way to the Cœlestial Gate" (97). Here, too, imprisonment and martyrdom effect a strengthening of the believers, especially when Hopeful joins Christian (see 98).

consciously and willfully master his situation and accordingly control the representation of "his" prison's meaning(s). The very fact that he is able to employ two seemingly contradictory rhetorical strategies indicates the arbitrary nature of signification and demonstrates that Bunyan is the ultimate arbiter of semiotic representation. Bunyan, like Pitt and "No. 7," though in a different and more subtle manner, places himself at the center of his text and establishes a narrative authority outside and above the prison. Stuart Sim and David Walker have claimed that Bunyan is one of those most clearly responsible for establishing the credibility of conscience as a "recognised source of authority on religious matters" (see Sim/Walker 2000: 220). Yet it should not be forgotten that this credibility relies on the very textual authority supposedly authenticating it.

II. Theoretical Reflections

Dissimilar as the three prison autobiographies are in many respects, they all participate in the cultural work of delimiting specific collective identities. The prison is employed as an emblematic boundary to distinguish between cultural norms or groups. In this process the narrating subject is fashioned as a moral arbiter or semiotic authority for these delimitations. Depictions of imprisonment not only assign value judgments to institutional processes or the self and chart oppositions between institutions and suffering individuals but also provide interpretations of cultural experiences. These interpretations proceed by means of textual visualization. They work by turning the (seemingly) simple inside/outside (or rather prison/non-prison) dichotomy into a signifier of more complex collective classifications. Thus, either the prison or the world outside are specifically conceived as properly belonging (or not belonging) to a particular person or group that is, in turn, representative of a certain experience, type of behavior or attitude, moral value, life style, or (most fascinatingly) social, ethnic, religious, etc. group. The literary prison thus participates, however subtly, in the fashioning of *collective* subject positions.[13] Its importance is less to re-enforce (concepts of) authority or selfhood as institutional or empirical actualities – though it can, of course, do both quite forcefully – than to discover, display, organize, interpret, comment on, even generate and negotiate paradigmatically the structure of a given culture's moral and social organization.

My focus of analysis is, therefore, on imprisonment as a symbolic action rather than the materiality of the prison *per se*. I explore how the prison becomes meaningful within the webs of significance that make up culture, regardless of the depiction of its effects or functions.[14] This is not to deny either the materiality of the prison or its

---

13 Of course, the prison can also represent the individual self (as opposed to a collective self), the body (as opposed to the mind), or material reality (as opposed to the spirit of the incarcerated subject). It is worth asking to what degree these differentiations evoke such collective categories as I have outlined here.

14 This allows for an extended view of imprisonment including not only incarceration behind bars and walls in some sort of penal institution but also various forms of captivity where the physical

potential (positive or negative) penal effects, but to take into account how processes of (cultural) signification rely on material objects as visible semantic referents, as texts offering a reading of collective experiences and telling people their own story.[15] Following anthropological interpretations of the iconic (not to say totemic) significance of objects,[16] I propose an approach to literary (as well as non-literary) depictions of imprisonment that focuses on how the prison is employed as an object of collective association and is thereby rhetorically transformed into a meaningful fiber for the weaving of the cultural fabric, into an icon referring to or representing the specific group, value, or life-style identified with it. As such, it serves emblematically as a delimitatory marker, as a means for constituting a boundary in order to distinguish what is rhetorically associated with prisons from what is not (or rather what is disassociated from it).[17] This understanding of the literary prison as a delimitatory icon that does not only acquire meaning within a literary work of art but constitutes symbolic capital within the larger semiotic structure of a given culture, moves the focus of attention from the prison's function within the world of the text to the text's own semantic operations (as they refer to the penal system).[18]

As such, the suggested analysis of imprisonment is part of a wider investigation into the ways inner-cultural or intercultural relationships are conceived. Every group has to address the presence of otherness (inside or outside itself) and relate to this alterity in some particular manner. At the same time, this process of relating to something else causes one's own collective identity to be articulated as well. The construction of self and other is the result of their interrelation. If literary imprisonment can be seen as a delimitatory marker, then this analysis can help us

---

markers of enclosure are less immediately perceptible. (See, for example, my brief reference to the "Indian Captivity Narrative" above.)

15 I am adapting here, in fact paraphrasing, Clifford Geertz's seminal analysis of the function of the Balinese cockfight (1973: 448 and ff.).

16 For the presence and function of totems within the contemporary pensée bourgeoise of Western societies, see Sahlins, who argues that because objects stand as "human concept[s] outside [themselves], as man speaking to man through the medium of things" (1976: 178), they can obtain "the power of making even the demarcation of their individual owners a procedure of social classification" (176). See also Lauterbach (forthcoming) for a more detailed view of the prison as "bourgeois totem."

17 In this respect, my argument resembles Gerlinda Smaus's contention that criminal law is one of those institutions which structures the social system (1998: 12) and reproduces social differentiations (11: "[Das Strafrecht] wird als eine derjenigen Institutionen verstanden, die insgesamt auf eine spezifische Weise die gesellschaftliche Differenzierung reproduzieren.") Unlike Smaus, I am, however, not concerned with the normative expectations expressed in the rules of criminal law, but with the imaginative representation of imprisonment and the discursive re-fashioning of the penal experience in literary works.

18 In a somewhat similar analytical move, Laura Struve (2000) argues that by challenging the legal court's authority and questioning its ability to represent events and individuals accurately, Victorian literature celebrates its own superior means for pronouncing judgments. As an alternative public sphere it becomes what she calls a "shadow courtroom" that proceeds on the interpretative level of society rather than the interpreting level of the literary world.

understand the different forms of defining and connecting selfhood and otherness. And if the literary depiction of the prison is, indeed, a textual errand into a carceral wilderness, then an analysis of just how "wild" this wilderness is for those who perceive and represent it as such enables us to describe a given culture's discursive treatment of difference.

This is not to imply that prison writings cannot be read as either a celebration of the jailed subject's individuality or as a form of social criticism, which is effectively involved in the improvement of prison conditions and the alleviation of the failures and injustices of the legal system at large.[19] In fact, we owe to such texts our insights into the often heart-breaking realities of incarceration and their destructive power over inmates. As the example of Pitt has shown, the passionate attack on these realities can even serve as a vehicle for drawing cultural boundaries. Nevertheless, I want to argue for the need to move beyond an analysis that focuses on the prison's role as a legal instrument or its function for the prisoner's subjectivity. As the autobiographical examples have indicated, it is not sufficient to look at the *effect* of the penal institution on its inmates – whether this effect is cruel or reformatory, maddening or liberating, disciplining or enhancing. So far, most criticism has focused on one of these two parameters, the prison's institutional effect or the centrality of the incarcerated individual, by either emphasizing the repressive nature of penal institutions or by celebrating the liberating effect of imprisonment on the self in spite of adverse circumstances. For example, in what is arguably the most comprehensive comparative study of literary imprisonment, Maria José de Queiroz' *A literatura encarcerada*, the author concentrates on the idea of oppression, on "the demoralizing influence of the prison" (1980: 21: "a influência desmoralizadora da prisão"), which is embedded in "the universal history of offense" (19: "a história universal da injúria") as depicted (and resisted) by incarcerated writers through the ages. Likewise, Bruce Franklin, in his analysis of the function of the United States penal system, sees a particular form of oppression at work when he argues that a state-sanctioned racism underlies the incarceration of minorities in the States (1989: xiii-xv). And John Bender (1987: 11 et passim) considers the organizational structures of the modern penitentiary to have been anticipated in the very form of early novelistic discourses of representation.

Whereas these three critics view the individual as being subjected by the prison's repressive effects (or by narrative mechanisms supposedly similar to those of the prison), a large number of scholars have focused on the frequency with which prison literature has celebrated the "victory of mind over matter, spirit over body" (Fludernik 1999: 63). Such attempts to causally link imprisonment to forms of transcendence,

19 As Monika Fludernik (forthcoming) has pointed out, the very construction of social boundaries in prison memoirs can actually support the movement towards penal reform, since the writers of autobiographical prison narratives establish a feeling of communality with the reader by setting themselves apart from convicts. Thus they induce sympathy and understanding for their own plight and demands.

imagination, or inner freedom emphasize its opportunities for the individual subject.[20] Here, the prison becomes "a centre of intellectual activity" or "a school for writers" (Davies 1990: 3), a "place of protection, of reverie, of freedom" (Brombert 1975: 13: "lieu de protection, de rêverie, de liberté"), or a space "which promises autonomy and freedom within bondage" (Weigel 1982: 98: "ein [...] Raum [...], der Autonomie und Freiheit in der Fesselung verspricht").[21]

Yet, exactly what *cultural* significance this "freedom" of the individual has or what discursive mechanisms underlie the oppressive system he or she has to defend against, remains open in such claims. To find a position within or without a particular prison discourse, the self has to identify with specific values, meanings, or cultural categories associated with either the inside or the outside of the penal institution, which, in turn, constitutes the boundary between different sets of values, meanings, or categories.[22] This cultural work of employing the prison as a boundary seems to have developed as a dominant strategy of prison literature throughout the eighteenth and nineteenth centuries (see the Victorian prison accounts) after having emerged in the seventeenth century as a structure of feeling (rather than an ideology) in autobiographies by writers such as Mynshul, Pitt, or Bunyan. There are, however, other possible ways of conceiving of the prison. Thus I conclude with a comparative glance at two non-autobiographical works: St. Thomas More's *A Dialogue of Comfort against Tribulation* (1534), an early text in which the prison does not yet function as a

---

20 This can be compared to Michel Foucault's classic claim that penal "[d]iscipline 'makes' individuals" (1979: 170; cf. Foucault 1975: 172: "La discipline 'fabrique' des individus; elle est la technique spécifique d'un pouvoir qui se donne les individus à la fois pour objets et pour instruments de son exercice.") – a view that finds its precursor in Max Horkheimer's and Theodor W. Adorno's contention that the modern penitentiary is informed by the self-centered individuality of bourgeois "monadism" in the sense of Leibniz's *La Monadologie* (Horkheimer/Adorno 1969: 202). However, Jeremy Bentham's Panopticon, the most famous penitentiary project, is supposed to serve as a model for how to treat all kinds of prisoners alike, "[n]o matter how different, or even opposite the purpose" (1838: 40). While the architectural set-up of Bentham's model prison includes partitions to "cut off from each prisoner the view of every other" (41), the uniform management of every inmate contradicts this feature's possible effect of individualizing an incarcerated person. Instead, the separation of the inmates into individual cells operates on the assumption that there are other prisoners from whom the self is to be separated and, more importantly, that all of these are treated in a similar fashion. Thus, it creates an awareness among the convicts of being part of a group – even at the moment of complete physical separation from that group.

21 See also Carnochan (1977) and Karpenstein-Eßbach (1985) on the paradoxical dialectic between confinement and mental flight or between physical incarceration and imaginative liberties.

22 I follow Monika Fludernik's re-evaluation of the simplistic dichotomy between institution and individual; she concentrates on "the experience of imprisonment as figured in symbolic terms in the spatiality of the prison cell" (1999: 46). In contrast to the two general critical positions I have outlined above, Fludernik relates the concrete manifestations of "carceral topography," of the actual place of confinement, to the prisoner's prior subject position. While I adopt the dialectical dynamics of her approach, I am less concerned with the personal experience of prisoners than with the cultural meaning that their imprisonment takes on.

boundary, and Thomas Pynchon's *The Crying of Lot 49* (1965), a postmodernist novel in which such a function is already residual.[23]

More – in contrast to Bunyan – refuses to admit any discomfort regarding imprisonment. Claiming that it is our "fantasy" which "frameth vs a false opynion, by which we deceyve our selfe and take yt for sorer than yt is" (1976: 276), he avoids considering the prison's purpose and carceral reality. Instead, he reflects on the *conditio humana* in general. His alter ego Antonye argues that "euery man vniuersally ys a very prisoner in very prison playnly" (263) and, thus, uses the traditional image of human existence *per se* as a prison, with God as "the chiefe gaylour ouer this whole brode prison / the world" (271). Hence, the "real" prison (in our understanding of the word) is only one of the many places that constitute the all-embracing confinement of humans in this world. It is no different from any other place. Prison serves as a metonymy for human existence at large; exaggerated and realistic notions of the prison are (and ought to be) indistinguishable. Consequently, for Antonye/More the prison does *not* establish a boundary between different spheres of existence. Since it is void of any particularity, it can neither be associated with specific forms of identity nor serve as a delimitatory marker. The prison becomes, in Stephen Greenblatt's words, a "mirage, compelling, tenacious, and utterly unreal" (1980: 13).

In a very different manner, the prison has ceased to mark any delimitations in Pynchon's novel. Its heroine Oedipa Maas recalls the painting "Bordando el Manto Terrestre" ("Embroidering the Cloak of the Earth") by Remedios Varo, which depicts a number of frail girls imprisoned in a tower – an image evoking medieval forms of incarceration. In the words of the novel, these figures are "embroidering a kind of tapestry which spilled out the slit windows and into a void, seeking hopelessly to fill the void: for all the other buildings and creatures, all the waves, ships and forests of the earth were contained in this tapestry, and the tapestry was the world" (1965: 21).[24] While the imprisonment of the girls, at first, seems to follow the conventional set-up of an inside/outside dichotomy, the tapestry (or cloak) they are embroidering shows that there is no outside apart from them. The prison/tower is surrounded by a void. The world one imagines surrounding it exists only in the tapestry, which, in turn, exists only as the handicraft of the girls, who are themselves then only another element of their own production.[25] The inside is the outside, the tapestry is its own world, and the prison is the world – or the world is the prison.[26] As the dividing line between inside

23 While this is not the place to develop a historical outline of prison literature, my use of Raymond Williams's terminology is meant to suggest a possible framework for theorizing such an outline (see esp. Williams 1977: 121-35).

24 Varo's oil painting from 1961 is in the Colección Particular in México City. While the description in *The Crying of Lot 49* neglects the Catholic context of the tapestry's production, it exaggerates some of the embroidered images and, more significantly, the emptiness of the supposed "void."

25 In fact, the title's gerund "bordando" ("embroidering") can easily be misread homonymically as "borrando" ("erasing"), which would mean that the world, as created, does not exist at all.

26 This is not the same as the topical claim that the world is like a prison. "Bordando el Manto Terrestre" visualizes the more radical idea that there is nothing outside of textuality, as

and outside is blurred, the act of associating anything with either the inside or the outside of the prison becomes obsolete. The prison no longer marks material or semiotic boundaries.[27]

By not employing the prison to further cultural delimitation, both *A Dialogue of Comfort against Tribulation* and *The Crying of Lot 49* suggest, in very different ways, that sign systems operate autonomously without being purposely controlled or even manipulated by a representing agent outside of themselves. As such, they "spill" over those boundaries that many autobiographical texts are eager to construct in order to dissociate the narrating self from the jail. This construction lies at the center of perceptions of the prison as something like a carceral wilderness which must be subordinated hegemonially through the textual errand of narrative representation.

Works Cited

Bender, John (1987) *Imagining the Penitentiary: Fiction and the Architecture of Mind in Eighteenth-Century England.* Chicago, IL: Univ. of Chicago Press.

Bentham, Jeremy (1838) *The Works of Jeremy Bentham, Now First Collected.* Ed. John Bowring. Vol. 3. Edinburgh: William Tait.

---

understood as a system of signs which are represented by the tapestry. The painting is part of the postmodernist (or post-structuralist) project most famously summed up in Derrida's dictum "Il n'y a pas de hors-texte" (1967: 227), indicating that "there have never been anything but [...] substitutive significations [...], the 'real' [...] being added only while taking on meaning from a trace." (1976: 159; see 1967: 228: "[I]l n'y a jamais eu que des suppléments, des significations substitutives qui n'ont pu surgir que dans une chaîne de renvois différentiels, le 'réel' ne survenant, ne s'ajoutant qu'en prenant sens à partir d'une trace et d'un appel de supplément, etc.") As a consequence, "[w]hat has happened [...] is a sort of overrun [débordement] that spoils" all those "boundaries that form the running border of what used to be called a text, of what we once thought this word could identify, i.e., the supposed end and beginning of a work" (Derrida 1979: 83). Likewise, the girls' tapestry "overruns" the boundaries of what we are accustomed to perceiving as the enclosed space of the prison in a manner that questions the end of that prison – or the end of their work of art – or the beginning of the world – or ...

27 In addition, the contextualization of the painting within the novel blurs various other types of distinctions. Wanting to preserve the impression of the painting through her tears (see 21) – itself a metaphor for blurring rather than focusing –, Oedipa fancies overcoming both the difference between the observer and the observed and perception and recollection. Furthermore, the description of Remedios Varo (whom Oedipa does not otherwise seem to know) as "beautiful" (20-21), embedded in Oedipa's free indirect discourse, makes little sense apart from a synecdochic extension that questions the distinction between painter and painting. Finally, her looking at the work of a Spanish exile in a museum in México City, places the episode in both a transatlantic and a trans-American context (as does, by the way, the [incorrect] use of English capitalization rules for the Spanish title).

Brombert, Victor (1975) *La prison romantique: Essai sur l'imaginaire*. Paris: José Corti.

Bunyan, John (1960 [1678]) *The Pilgrim's Progress from This World to That Which is to Come*. Ed. James Blanton Wharey. 2nd rev. ed. by Roger Sharrock. Oxford: Clarendon.

Bunyan, John (1962 [1666]) *Grace Abounding to the Chief of Sinners*. Ed. Roger Sharrock. Oxford: Clarendon.

Carnochan, W. B. (1977) *Confinement and Flight: An Essay on English Literature of the Eighteenth Century*. Berkeley: Univ. of California Press.

Davies, Ioan (1990) *Writers in Prison*. Oxford: Basil Blackwell.

Derrida, Jacques (1967) *De la grammatologie*. Collection critique. Paris: Éditions de Minuit.

Derrida, Jacques (1976) *Of Grammatology*. Trans. Gayatri Chakravorty Spivak. Baltimore, MD: Johns Hopkins Univ. Press.

Derrida, Jacques (1979) "Living On / Border Lines." Trans. James Hulbert. *Deconstruction and Criticism*. Ed. Geoffrey Hartman. London: Routledge & Kegan Paul. 75-176.

Fennor, William (1930 [1617]) *The Counter's Commonwealth: Or, A Voyage Made to an Infernal Island, Discovered by Many Captains, Seafaring Men, Gentlemen, Merchants, and Other Tradesmen* [...]. *The Elizabethan Underworld*. Ed. A. V. Judges. London: George Routledge. 425-87, 517-20.

Fludernik, Monika (1999) "Carceral Topography: Spatiality, Liminality and Corparality in the Literary Prison." *Textual Practice* 13.1: 43-77.

Fludernik, Monika (forthcoming) "'Stone Walls Do (Not) a Prison Make': Fact and Fiction in Nineteenth-Century Literary and Non-Literary Representations of Imprisonment." *Captivating Subjects: Writing Confinement, Citizenship and Nationhood in the Nineteenth Century*. Ed. Jason Haslam and Julia Wright. Toronto: University of Toronto Press (2004).

Foucault, Michel (1975) *Surveiller et punir: Naissance de la prison*. Bibliotèque des histoires. Paris: Éditions Gallimard.

Foucault, Michel (1979) *Discipline and Punish: The Birth of the Prison*. Trans. Alan Sheridan. New York: Vintage.

Franklin, H[oward] Bruce (1989 [1978]) *Prison Literature in America: The Victim as Criminal and Artist*. Expanded ed. New York: Oxford University Press.

Geertz, Clifford (1973) *The Interpretation of Cultures: Selected Essays*. New York: Basic Books.

Greenblatt, Stephen (1980) *Renaissance Self-Fashioning: From More to Shakespeare*. Chicago, IL: Univ. of Chicago Press.

Greene, Roland (1999) *Unrequited Conquests: Love and Empire in the Colonial Americas*. Chicago, IL: Univ. of Chicago Press.

Horkheimer, Max, and Theodor W. Adorno (1969 [1944]) *Dialektik der Aufklärung: Philosophische Fragmente*. Frankfurt/Main: S. Fischer.

Horsman, Reginald (1981) *Race and Manifest Destiny: The Origins of American Racial Anglo-Saxonism*. Cambridge, MA: Harvard Univ. Press.

Karpenstein-Eßbach, Christa (1985) *Einschluß und Imagination: Über den literarischen Umgang mit Gefangenen*. Tübingen: Edition Diskord.

Lauterbach, Frank (2003) "Entre poesía, amor e imperio: Juan Boscán y la importación del endecasílabo a España como práctica social." *Texto social: Estudios pragmáticos sobre literatura y cine: Homenaje a Manfred Engelbert / Festschrift für Manfred Engelbert*. Ed. Annette Paatz and Burkhard Pohl. Berlin: Edition Tranvía. 31-47.

Lauterbach, Frank (forthcoming) "'From the slums to the slums': The Delimitation of Social Identity in Late Victorian Prison Narratives." *Captivating Subjects: Writing Confinement, Citizenship and Nationhood in the Nineteenth Century*. Ed. Jason Haslam and Julia Wright. Toronto: Univ. of Toronto Press (2004).

Mather, Cotton (1853 [1702]) *Magnalia Christi Americana: Or, The Ecclesiastical History of New-England, from Its First Planting, in the Year 1620, unto the Year of Our Lord 1698*. Vol. 2. Hartford, CT: Silas Andrus.

Miller, Perry (1956) *Errand into the Wilderness*. Cambridge, MA: Belknap Press.

More, Thomas (1976 [1534]) *A Dialogue of Comfort against Tribulation*. Ed. Louis L. Martz and Frank Manley. *The Complete Works of St. Thomas More* 12. New Haven, CT: Yale Univ. Press.

Mynshul, Geffray (1821 [1618]) *Essayes and Characters of a Prison and Prisoners*. Edinburgh: James Ballantyne.

"No. 7" (1903) *Twenty-Five Years in Seventeen Prisons: The Life-Story of an Ex-Convict: With His Impressions of Our Prison System: By 'No. 7'*. London: F. E. Robinson.

"One Who Has Endured It" (1877) *Five Years' Penal Servitude: By One Who Has Endured It*. London: Richard Bentley & Son.

Overbury, Thomas (1936 [1614]) *The Overburian Characters, to Which Is Added A Wife*. Ed. W. J. Paylor. Percy Reprints 13. Oxford: Basil Blackwell.

Pitt, Moses (1691) *The Cry of the Oppressed: Being a True and Tragical Account of the Unparallel'd Sufferings of Multitudes of Poor Imprisoned Debtors, in most of the Gaols in England* [...]. London: Moses Pitt.

Pynchon, Thomas (1965) *The Crying of Lot 49*. Philadelphia, PA: J. B. Lippincott.

Queiroz, Maria José de (1980) *A literatura encarcerada: Ensaio*. Rio de Janeiro: Civilização Brasileira.

Sahlins, Marshall (1976) *Culture and Practical Reason*. Chicago, IL: Univ. of Chicago Press.

Sim, Stuart, and David Walker (2000) *Bunyan and Authority: The Rhetoric of Dissent and the Legitimation Crisis in Seventeenth-Century England*. Religions and Discourse 6. Bern: Peter Lang.

Smaus, Gerlinda (1998) *Das Strafrecht und die gesellschaftliche Differenzierung*. Baden-Baden: Nomos.

Sondergard, Sid (1993) "'This Giant Has Wounded Me as Well as Thee': Reading Bunyan's Violence and/as Authority." *The Witness of Times: Manifestations of Ideology in Seventeenth Century England*. Ed. Katherine Z. Keller and Gerald J.

Schiffhorst. Duquesne Studies: Language and Literature Series 15. Pittsburgh, PA: Duquesne Univ. Press. 218-37, 288-91.

Struve, Laura Christine (2000) "The Shadow Courtroom: Literature, Law, and Narrative Authority in Victorian England." Diss. Princeton University. Ann Arbor: UMI, 9957371.

Weigel, Sigrid (1982) *"Und selbst im Kerker frei...!": Schreiben im Gefängnis: Zur Theorie und Gattungsgeschichte der Gefängnisliteratur (1750-1933).* Marburg/Lahn: Guttandin und Hoppe.

Wiener, Martin J. (1990) *Reconstructing the Criminal: Culture, Law, and Policy in England, 1830-1914.* Cambridge: Cambridge Univ. Press.

Williams, Raymond (1977) *Marxism and Literature. Marxist Introductions.* Oxford: Oxford Univ. Press.

Prison Metaphors – The Carceral Imaginary?

Monika Fludernik

1. Carceral Imagery

Much work has already been done to elucidate the images of carcerality as they are displayed in the fictional representation of prison settings. From the sentimentalist prison scenes (e. g. in Sterne's *A Sentimental Journey* or Richardson's *Clarissa*), and the sensational depiction of prisons and dungeons in the Gothic novel, and on to the Romantic conceptions of imprisonment as oppression by tyranny in Byron or Shelley, and finally to the portraits of benign confinement allowing for meditation and artistic creativity (in Stendhal and others, see Brombert 1978), literary prose and poetry have played with a range of contradictory emotions and utilized heterogeneous contexts in their representations of prison locations and the experience of confinement. On the whole, these scenarios of carceral space (with the exception of the 'happy prison') tend to depict the site of imprisonment as a dark and cruel dungeon in which inmates languish in chains. Such Gothic visions concentrate on political imprisonment or the victimization of innocent protagonists; they invoke potent images of despotism and cruelty, of despondency, anguish and abjection.

Another line of associations is linked to the experience of imprisonment for debt and to criminal (auto)biographies. Here one can point to Hogarthian scenes from *The Rake's Progress* and *Industry and Idleness*, to the works of Fielding and Dickens (especially the *Pickwick Papers* and *Little Dorrit*). This type of prison setting lends itself to generalizations about society at large. The prison population represents a cross-section of society and has its contingent of every rank and class of society. The emphasis in texts concentrating on the typical eighteenth-century prison usually lies on satire, on an analysis of people's manners and morality which are argued to be the same inside and outside prison. Leading characteristics of debtors' prison are the promiscuous mixture of different types of inmates (whole families and trades move into the house), their sociability (the free association among inmates including their indulgence in gambling, drinking and prostitution), and their openness to entry from outside.

Finally, the penitentiary and its successor, the modern prison, constitute a third recurring setting. Texts representing Victorian or twentieth-century penal institutions focus on real-life developments in penal practice and on changes in the circumstances of modern-day imprisonment. Most prominently, these settings are nowadays influenced by images from the American prison movie. Thus, the recurring images of cells with bars rather than doors, and the emphasis on slop pails, plank beds, mattresses or blankets. However, whereas the Victorian penitentiaries are depicted as places of silence, solitude and hard labor, the late twentieth-century scenario emphasizes boredom and inmate violence. Owing to their proliferation in popular prison movies, these images are now extremely common in literary prison settings depicting modern penal institutions.

All three types of prison settings compete as focus for readers' conceptions of imprisonment and provide sources for literary and non-literary prison imagery. Metaphors and similes comparing two areas of human experience, one of which is the prison, depend on current notions of what constitutes a prison and what is prototypical of the experience of imprisonment. These representative features are clearly very different in the three scenarios that I have just outlined. Whereas the dungeon setting invokes physical constraint, darkness, and the feeling of being buried alive,[1] the debtor's prison foregrounds promiscuity, sociability, crowding and criminality. Finally, the penitentiary and its successors feature visual images of cells, bars and infinite boredom.[2] As a consequence, prison metaphors focus on a large variety of quite disparate associations.

In this paper I want to concentrate on literary prison imagery, i.e. on the use of the prison or related lexemes as *vehicle* (source domain) for a metaphor, or as point of comparison in a simile. Once or twice I will also consider passages describing the prison (experience) by means of a metaphor taken from a different word field. In such cases the prison is the *tenor* (target domain) of the metaphor. My intention is to provide a rough preliminary list of associations or connotations of the carceral institution and experience in literary texts. This will eventually allow me to demonstrate which features are foregrounded in literary texts, and which aspects of imprisonment treated in the criminological literature or in autobiographical texts *fail* to show up in the literary prison imagery.

In this essay, metaphors and similes are treated as roughly equivalent since my major concern is with the *ground* of the (implicit) comparison between vehicle and tenor or with the results of blending source and target domains.[3] I will use the terminology of I. A. Richards and the cognitivists (Lakoff, Turner, Johnson) concurrently since my major aim at this point is to collect some basic material about how prison imagery works. This descriptive approach will be supplemented later by a reconsideration of the theoretical issues of metaphor study. Suffice it to say for the moment that cognitivist metaphor theory supplies two basic frames to characterize imprisonment: the container metaphor (PUT IN or TAKE OUT)[4] and the bondage

---

1 Compare my article on the symbolization of prison space (Fludernik 1999) for some of these key features.

2 Obviously, this list is too short, but see Jan Alber's paper in this volume. Compare also the superb study by Simone Buffard on the 'penitentiary iciness' (*Le froid pénitentiare*, 1973) for a more extensive list.

3 For an introduction to blending, see Fludernik et al. (1999) and Turner/Fauconnier in the same special issue.

4 See Lakoff/Johnson (1980: 29-32) and Lakoff (1990: 271-73).

metaphor (LIFE IS BONDAGE).[5] The second frame clearly corrresponds with the medieval and early modern image of the soul's imprisonment in the body, a religious characterization of our secular life as a temporary period of physical suffering prior to liberation and glorification in life after death.[6] Since most of the example passages that I will be looking at in this essay come from nineteenth- and twentieth-century fiction, this particular frame does not figure prominently in my corpus. As for the container metaphor, I would like to leave its usefulness open at this point in order to judge it on the merits of the inductive analysis in section 2 of this paper. I will return to the issue in my conclusions.

The article is divided into five sections. Sections 2 and 3 present and inductively analyze a number of prison metaphors. Section 4 discusses some passages from Victor Hugo's *Les Misérables* to demonstrate the larger textual ramifications of prison imagery. Section 5 presents preliminary conclusions on the subject.

2. Metaphors at Work

As one would expect, prisons are primarily associated with restraint, confinement, the feeling of being locked in and unable to freely decide on one's actions. This basic connotation of confinement comes out very well, for instance, in a passage early in John Edgar Wideman's novel *Philadelphia Fire* (1990). In this first section of the novel, the Greek fisherman Cudjoe cannot go out to sea; rough tides keep him 'imprisoned' on the island:[7]

> The island exiled today. ***Jailed by its necklace of churning sea***. No one could reach Mykonos. No one could leave. [...] Cudjoe's flight home disappearing like the patches of blue sky. Sea pitches and shivers and bellows in its ***chains***. Green and dying. [...] Gray clouds thicken. White clouds pull apart, bleed into the green sea. A seamless curtain of water and sky ***draws tighter and tighter***. The island is sinking. Sea and wind wash over its shadow, close the ***wound***. (1990: 5)

Cudjoe is exiled on the island and feels its "necklace," the sea, suffocating him, threatening death. The metaphor at first seems far-fetched, but one has to remember that this novel, like all of Wideman's novels, centrally deals with imprisonment, even autobiographically so (both Wideman's brother and his son eke out life sentences in American prisons). After the initial image of the sea operating like an iron collar on the island of Mykonos and on Cudjoe, who wants to depart and is stuck, the passage, interestingly, shifts the prison metaphor to the sea itself that wants to flood the island and sink it, chafes against its "chains" as it rocks the 'boat' of the island, threatening its moorings. The penal collar is effaced by the water of rain and flooding which closes (and heals?) the wound created by the impatient charging of tide on cliff, of collar on neck skin. A fairly simple metaphor within a few lines has become extremely complex and starts to resonate with the themes of racial violence, legal injustice, despair and

5 See Lakoff/Turner (1988: 23-25).

6 See the discussion of this in Fludernik (2003).

7 All bold italics in this paper are my emphasis.

death which are so prominent in the novel. In particular, the notion of constraint is applied to both sides of the interaction between island and sea – Cudjoe confined to the island, whose necklace threatens to garrot him as it grows "tighter and tighter"; on the other hand, there is the sea, fighting for its liberation from constraint, "churning" in its "chains," swallowing up the island which is a wound on its surface. The sea turns into the ship that it rocks on its waves (pitching, shivering and bellowing are lexemes typically associated with vessels threatened by storms); the experience of constriction and death is transferred on the power that exerts this threat – the victimized turns victim. At the same time the empathy shifts from Cudjoe to the island and then to the chained giant of the sea itself. We may also note that the prison imagery, first introduced by the verb "jailed," immediately starts to proliferate by a series of metonyms – "necklace" (for iron collar), "chains" and "drawing tighter and tighter" (again the collar, and garroting). The sea, like a ship struggling to escape its moorings, and the island both exemplify the experience of bondage, and they figure this restraint in the traditional metonym of carceral chaining.

Similarly, in a key passage from Mary Wollstonecraft's novel *Maria; or, The Wrongs of Woman* (1798 posth.), the prison metaphor has immediate relevance to the main themes of the novel. Maria tells the story of her life to Darnford while they are both imprisoned in a lunatic asylum, and says:

> Marriage had ***bastilled*** me for life. I discovered in myself a capacity for the enjoyment of the various pleasures existence affords; yet, ***fettered*** by the partial laws of society, this fair globe was to me an universal blank. (1994: 87)

Here it is the institution of marriage which is compared to the Bastille, and the legal provisions of patriarchy are compared to fetters. As in Wideman's text, confinement is figured as metonymic chaining by association with the dungeon scenario. The passage moreover describes the results of this metaphoric imprisonment as despondency and the loss of joy in life. Although the metaphor, taken out of context, appears to be rather extreme, in the novel it is fully appropriate to the situation of Maria and her new friend Jemima. Both women have suffered from the British marriage laws and legitimately feel deprived of their liberty on their account.

The image of the law as a chain is also employed by Victor Hugo in his important novel of social criticism, *Les Misérables* (1862). At one point, the hero of this novel, Jean Valjean, a former convict, muses on the power of the law that keeps even those imprisoned who have escaped from their term of confinement in the penitentiary:

> He was a man who had endured all the forms of suffering and was still bleeding from the wounds inflicted upon him by life. He had been almost a villain and had become almost a saint; and after being ***chained with prison*** irons he was still ***fettered with a chain*** that was scarcely less onerous although invisible, that of his prison record. The law had never lost its claim on him. It might at any moment lay hands on him and drag him out of his honourable obscurity into the glare of public infamy. (Part IV/Book III, v; 1998: 770)[8]

8 "Cet homme qui avait passé par toutes les détresses, qui était encore tout saignant des meurtrissures de sa destinée, qui avait éte presque méchant et qui était devenu presque saint, qui,

Here Jean Valjean's prison record is described as an invisible chain that keeps him shackled to a legal system that has 'bastilled' him 'for life' and that, when discovering his whereabouts, could recapture and reincarcerate him at will. Again, a situation of a perceived lack of freedom is figured as metaphoric restraint in the image of fettering, a metonym of the prison experience – though this time in reference to contemporary French practices of chaining convicts. The secret chains of the metaphor fetter Valjean to dishonor and force him, in a neat inversion of the normal ways of life, to seek honor in obscurity, since the appropriate place for honor, the glare of public life, would result in the discovery of his criminal record and, thus, ignominy.

The metaphor of confinement and physical constraint can be applied to a variety of situations. In *A Bend in the River* (1979), V.S. Naipaul uses the prison image to characterize the colonial situation. Indar describes his visit to England and his realization of being constrained by his colonial ancestry – he feels forced into the category of those who cannot win. Indar had gone to study in England after his family lost all their possessions to African nationalization policies:

> I thought when I went to England I would put all that behind me. I had no plans beyond that. The word "university" dazzled me, and I was innocent enough to believe that after my time in the university some wonderful life would be waiting for me. At that age three years seems a long time – you feel that anything can happen. But I hadn't understood to what extent our civilization had also been our ***prison***. I hadn't understood either to what extent we had been made by the place where we had grown up, made by Africa and the simple life of the coast, and how incapable we had become of understanding the outside world. [...] (1980: 148)

> For the first time in my life I was filled with a colonial rage. And this wasn't only a rage with London or England, it was also a rage with the people who had allowed themselves to be ***corralled*** into a foreign fantasy. My rage didn't die down when I went inside [India House]. There again were the oriental motifs. (152)

Indar realizes that, as an Indian, he is imprisoned within an orientalist discourse of clichés, a stereotyping of India most prominently displayed at India House.[9] Not only

après avoir traîné la chaîne invisible, mais pesante, de l'infamie indéfinie, cet homme que la loi n'avait pas lâché et qui pouvait être à chaque instant ressaisi et ramené de l'obscurité de sa vertu au grand jour de l'opprobre public" (Hugo 1951: 912).

9 India House: "The first High Commissioner of India, Sir William S. Meyer, was appointed on 1 October 1920. At that time four buildings were rented at Grosvenor Gardens in Victoria to accommodate the office of the High Commission. Sir Atul Chatterjee, who became the High Commissioner in 1925, proposed a plan to build a House for the High Commission to the Governor General Lord Reading and the proposal was subsequently approved by the Governor General Lord Irwin. A plot measuring 12,400 square feet was found between Marconi House (now Citibank) and Bush House in Aldwych and a 999 years' lease was granted by the London County Council for construction of the building. Sir Herbert Baker who built the Secretariat Buildings and Parliament House in New Delhi was appointed the Chief Architect. The building was completed in 1930 and, in a very impressive ceremony, King Emperor George V opened the main gate of India House on 8 July 1930 with a solid gold key. The total cost for the building, including furniture and fixtures, was £324,000." (<www.hcilondon.net/ aboutus/history-indiahouse.html>, 15 October 2003)

does he feel caged in native ways of thinking which are no longer appropriate to the real world; he is also angry at the complicity of his countrymen who allow themselves to be "corralled" into orientalist categories like cattle ready to be slaughtered. Confinement and oppression again converge, laced with threats of extinction (slaughter of cattle). At the same time, the prison metaphor is expanded by metonyms, not chains in this case but the physical borders (the fences) of the imaginary prison of colonialism.

The two passages from Naipaul's novel also document how the association of restriction and confinement can be extended to other types of locking in, such as that of cattle in their pens. One is reminded of the fact that modern American prison cells resemble cages, and that the situation of prisoners evokes that of caged animals. Ondaatje, in *In the Skin of a Lion* (1987) makes this quite explicit. The protagonist Patrick Lewis has just been released from prison in Canada. In Toronto's Union Station he observes dogs in cages:

> A group of redcaps were standing with three large cages full of dogs, all of whom were barking like aristocrats claiming to be wrongly imprisoned. He went up to the cages. They were anxious with noise. He had come from a place where a tin cup against a cell wall was the sole form of protest. He got closer to the cages, looked into the eyes which saw nothing, the way his own face in prison had looked in a metal mirror. (1987: 210)

This image takes confinement for granted and foregrounds protest and resistance, and the loss of hope and lack of response induced by the futility of protest. The cage metaphor is literalized in another key text of political imprisonment, Breyten Breytenbach's *Mouroir* (1984). The section entitled "The Break" depicts the dystopia of a detention camp for those condemned to death, appropriately called the "Terminus." The camp consists of a "tent of enormous proportions":

> The inside space is entirely occupied by cages made of steel bars in which the prisoners are held, two storeys high but without solid floors (everywhere the grid only) so that people can spy on one another from every angle. Between the stacked cages, every stack consists of a block covering nearly 100 x 100 metres, there are streets wide enough for lorries to pass. The streets are slushy with pools of water. (Breytenbach 1984: 112)

Later, when "the lorries come to remove those condemned to die," the "prisoners remaining behind swing like apes from their own bars to shout goodbyes" (112-13). The indignity, rage and despair associated with imprisonment are here figured in the humiliation of caging, of being treated like a dog or monkey. One could compare the scene to Eugene O'Neill's famous expressionist play *The Hairy Ape* (1922), in which the imprisonment of the ape metaphorically correlates with Yank's subjection to exploitation by the class system.

The depth of despair typically induced by imprisonment is figured by Victor Hugo in a very subtle simile that – by the very inconspicuousness of the token triggering the effect – implies the depths of hunger and suffering of prisoners:

> The wonders conjured up by love! The fantasies! That intervention of angels, that celestial chance, was like the hunk of bread tossed from one inmate to another, from one courtyard to another, over the walls of the prison of La Force. (Part IV/Book V, v; 1998: 808)[10]

The situation of prisoners, their hunger and despair, provide the background for the significance of a chunk of bread relieving and reviving a starved fellow inmate. This comparison figures prisoners' solidarity and care for one another – a major life line – as emotional food for the starving Cosette. The passage refers to Cosette's discovery of love, after she has found Marius's love letter in the garden. It is the prison experience that is the vehicle in this metaphor: Cosette discovers the "celestial" nature of love, and the narrator likens it to the blessings of food shared between prisoners. This comparison – inappropriate though it may seem out of context – literalizes Cosette's situation, identifying it as a type of imprisonment which the advent of Marius is going to alleviate. In fact Cosette has been confined in the convent where she was raised and later watched over like a prisoner by Jean Valjean and by the housekeeper at their house.[11] Besides, her emotions have been stunted by her religious training. Marius wakens her from indifference and live burial: "The manuscript [...] affected her like the opening of a closed door" (IV/V, v; 806). Doors of course figure prominently in representations of the prison experience – the opening of a door may symbolize the return to freedom (Fludernik 1999). The passage, therefore, heightens the significance of Cosette's experience by hinting at the oppression to which she has been subject and by characterizing the gift of love in terms of angelic charity dispensed, tellingly, from one thief ("voleur" in the original) to the other. Both Cosette and Marius are protagonists deserving the reader's pity, so their comparison with convicts is not as far-fetched as it might seem; the simile moreover has strong Christian resonances of Christ associating with thieves and the saving of one thief on Calvary.

Hugo's image of the closed door ties in with a whole series of traditional associations of prisons with dark, airless dungeons and tomb-like cells. Many connotations of imprisonment are therefore geared towards a stifling atmosphere or the feeling of being buried alive. In Sarah Waters's prison novel *Affinity* (1999), Margaret Price, the prison visitor, hears of the death of a woman prisoner who had not received sufficient medical attention and of a matron's punishment for having acted charitably by giving the prisoner some additional clothing to keep her warm: "All about me Millbank reared, bleak as a ***tomb***, and silent, yet filled with wretched men and women. I had never, in all my visits, felt the weight of their combined despair as I

---

10 In the original: "Ô transfigurations de l'amour! ô rêves! ce hasard céleste, cette intervention des anges, c'était cette boulette de pain lancée par un voleur à un autre voleur, de la cour Charlemagne à la Fosse-aux-Lions, par-dessus les toits de la Force" (Hugo 1951: 957).

11 The housekeeper, Toussaint, assures Cosette that they are safe in their "lonely spot" and that "the shutters are properly ***barred***" and ends with: "I lock the place up as though it were a ***prison***" (Part IV/ Book V, iii; 802). The imprisoning of Cosette serves to keep out murderers who could enter and cut one's throat – a parallel to Jean Valjean's earlier behavior when he stole the silver and nearly murdered the bishop Myriel (I/I, i).

felt it press upon me now" (2000: 278).[12] This utilizes the familiar tomb imagery, as does the following passage from Anthony Trollope's *Can You Forgive Her?* (1864-65) in which Mr. John Vavasor's office is described in terms of a dungeon:

> It was certainly a melancholy place, that signing-office, in which Mr. John Vavasor was ***doomed*** to spend twelve hours a week, during every term time, of his existence. Whether any man could really pass an existence of work in such a workshop, and not have gone mad, – could have endured to work there for seven hours a day, every week-day of his life, I am not prepared to say. I doubt much whether any ***victims*** are so ***doomed*** [...]. (1991: II 213)

> [...] this hall, though open at both ends, was as dark as *Erebus*; and any who lingered in it would soon find themselves to be growing damp, and would smell mildew, and would become naturally affected by the exhalations arising from those Chancery records beneath their feet.
>
> Up the stone stairs, from this hall, John Grey passed to Mr. Vavasor's signing room. The stairs were broad, and almost of noble proportions, but the ***darkness*** and ***gloom*** which hung about the hall, hung also about them, – a melancholy set of stairs, up and down which no man can walk with cheerful feet. [...] Pausing for a moment, that he might look round about him and realize the ***deathlike stillness*** of the whole, John Grey could just distinguish the heavy breathing of a man, thereby learning that there was a ***captive*** in, at any rate, one of those ***prisons*** on each side of him. As he drew near to the door of Mr. Vavasor's chamber he knew that the breathing came from thence. (II 214-15)

The building of the Inns of Law is here described in suitably Gothic fashion. Mr. Grey has to descend into prison-like tombs in order to see Alice's father. It is less obvious, however, what might be the function of the passage in Trollope's novel. Although *Can You Forgive Her?* clearly criticizes the political system of parliamentary democracy, the law itself does not constitute one of the main targets of Trollope's satire. The dungeon-like setting of Mr. Vavasor's work place, therefore, cannot be intended to cast ridicule on English institutions for their despotism and cruelty. If anything, the passage seems to use the extended metaphor to characterize Vavasor's feelings of imprisonment by his job for which he has no liking at all. It is Vavasor who feels that his occupation suffocates him and constitutes a cruel sentence of confinement in a bureaucratic hell ("Erebus") as part of a kind of forced labor. (Note the allusions to work in a workshop on seven days a week, invoking prison discipline and slavery.) Vavasor *feels* that the tyranny of societal expectations (he needs to work in order to feed his family) has victimized him.

In contrast to such conventional prison metaphors of darkness, dampness and underground obscurity, more up-to-date prison images instead focus on barrenness, deprivation and a lack of human contact. Thus, in Anita Desai's short story "The Rooftop Dwellers," an otherwise hilarious account of the housing problems of unmarried women in India, the protagonist Moyna finds herself in a hostel for single women which at first appears to be like a prison:

---

12 Note that we are here dealing with a metaphor in which Millbank Prison is the tenor (the target domain) and entombment serves as the vehicle (source domain).

> There was nothing in [the hostel] except what was absolutely essential [...] upstairs the rows of rooms, eight feet by ten, each equipped with a wooden bedframe, and a shelf nailed to the wall. She had had to purchase a plastic bucket to take to the bathroom [...] The minimalism of these living arrangements was both a novelty and a shock to her. [...] So for the first two weeks she felt she was ***trapped*** in a ***cell***; whenever she shut the door, she was swallowed by the ***cell***, its ***prisoner***. (2000: 160)

It is only when Moyna acquires a kitten that the situation changes: "It was curious how instantly the room ceased to be a prison" (162). The bareness of the room invokes the depressing sensory deprivation of prison cells which in turn symbolizes Moyna's loneliness and depression. As soon as she has the cat, she is happy, and the architecture no longer bothers her.

Besides these architectural associations with prisons and imprisonment, we have already noted in Hugo that shame ("ignominy") functions as another connotation of the status of a prisoner. Elizabeth Gaskell, in a very interesting passage in *North and South* (1855), describes Margaret's shame at having interfered between Thornton and the workers during the strike in an image that likens her to a prisoner too proud to justify herself:

> She stood by the table, not offering to sit down. Her eyelids were dropped half over her eyes; her teeth were shut, not compressed; her lips were just parted over them, allowing the white line to be seen between their curve. Her slow deep breathings dilated her thin and beautiful nostrils; it was the only motion visible on her countenance. The fine-grained skin, the oval cheek, the rich outline of her mouth, its corners deep set in dimples, – were all wan and pale to-day; the loss of their usual natural healthy colour being made more evident by the heavy shadow of the dark hair, brought down upon the temples, to hide all sign of the blow she had received. Her head, for all its drooping eyes, was thrown a little back, in the old proud attitude. Her long arms hung motionless by her sides. Altogether she looked like some ***prisoner***, falsely accused of a crime that she had loathed and despised, and from which she was too indignant to justify herself. (1986: 251-52)

The prisoner metaphor may seem far-fetched, but is deliberate on Gaskell's part. The chapter describes the first meeting between Thornton and Margaret after she embraced him to ward off the workers' violence during the strike. The passage represents Thornton's impressions of Margaret, so the prison image and the associations of her behavior with pride and shame are his. Margaret will in fact come under a terrible suspicion of inchastity later when she has to hide the fact that she accompanied her brother to the train station. (The brother is liable to arrest in England.) The passage, therefore, anticipates Margaret's later predicament of false accusation and of pride struggling with shame. The scene quoted here moreover marks the point in the narrative when Thornton realizes he is in love with Margaret but she has not yet come to understand her feelings for him. Chapter 24, from which the passage is taken, appropriately starts with an epigraph of a love poem by William Fowler which employs the 'love is imprisonment' topos (*la prison amoureuse*)[13]:

---

13 See Göller (1990) for the history of this common late medieval topos which was prominent until the middle of the seventeenth century. The love-as-imprisonment topos describes a love relationship as one in which the (usually male) lover is imprisoned by his lady, in voluntary

'Your beauty was the first that won the place,
And seal'd the walls of my undaunted heart,
Which, ***captive*** now, pines in a caitive case,
Unkindly met with rigour for desert: –
Yet not the less your servant shall abide,
In spite of rude repulse or silent pride'. (250)

Gaskell's *North and South* is a rewriting of *Pride and Prejudice*; the chapter epigraph and the metaphor I have quoted underline that Thornton is the prisoner of love; but he would also like to have Margaret in his keeping, have her as his prisoner. The epigraph moreover suggests that Margaret is really imprisoned by her pride. Imprisonment does not only connote shame and love; in fact, the novel in a second passage reiterates the image of personal honor despite the dishonorable status of a prisoner. When Mr. Thornton defends his views of what is a "man" (against Margaret's praise of the "gentleman"), he says: "A castaway, lonely as Robinson Crusoe – a ***prisoner*** immured in a dungeon for life – nay, even a saint in Patmos, has his endurance, his strength, his faith, best described by being spoken of as 'a man'" (218). The image fits Thornton's constitutive independence and loneliness, but it also shows his craving for being released from it through his love for Margaret. In Margaret's original prejudice, gentlemanly behavior was not compatible with work. Thornton argues that personal worth is constituted outside society (even outside work) and relates to inherent moral dignity. Gentlemanliness, from Thornton's perspective, merely touches on polite behavior in society. Thornton's ultimate proof of his own worthiness comes when his factory collapses and he gives up everything, making sure the workers and his debtors are served before his own interests and comforts are considered. These dealings certainly earn him a place alongside the lonely castaway, prisoner and hermit in his fable of manly virtue and honor. In fact, it is dignity in suffering and endurance, thus very Christian virtues, that Thornton illustrates by his three scenarios; being a fine gentleman when you have money and can make a figure in the world, he seems to imply, does not count. It is therefore Margaret's pride, her conviction of her own innocence despite apparently shameful actions, that stimulate Thornton's love for her – they ultimately share similar conditions of embattled loneliness in which arrogance, pride and uncompromising notions of honor contend with their love. They are both, implicitly, prisoners of their moral outlook on life.

Imprisonment often correlates with a variety of emotions and psychological states: guilt, shame, hopelessness, despondency, despair, rage. A good example of this is the following passage from Derek Walcott's poem *Omeros* (1990) which I owe to an essay by Ramazani (1997):

His knee was radiant with iron,
his chest was a sack of ice, and behind the bars

---

bondage to his love. Famous examples of the *prison amoureuse* are the poems of Charles D'Orléans (fifteenth century) or Sir Richard Lovelace's "To Althea: From Prison."

of his rusted teeth, like a mongoose in a cage,
a scream was mad to come out; his tongue tickled its claws
on the roof of his mouth, rattling its bars in rage. (Walcott 1990: 21, qtd. Ramazani 406)

The passage describes Philoctete, who suffers from arthritis and the pains of old age, tending his yam beds. In these lines the scream of pain is figured as a caged animal, with Philoctete's mouth and teeth representing the bars of its cage. The metaphor combines the target domain of the scream with the blend of dangerous animals, prison bars, gnashing teeth, madness and rage at imprisonment, thus engendering a multiplicity of associations and applications of the imagery.

One could go on with many more examples. Instead, I would now like to turn to the historical aspects of imprisonment and how they affect prison metaphors.

3. Historical Differentiations

As we have seen in the above representative selection of prison metaphors from nineteenth- and twentieth-century texts, the associations of physical constraint and the dungeon scenario are overwhelmingly present. The metaphors deploy both a number of literal referents to imprisonment such as the lexemes *prison(er)* or *imprisoned*, *captivity*, etc. and a selection of metonymical equivalents of carceral architecture and other prominent aspects of imprisonment: *bars*, *chains*, *vaults*, *cell*. Moreover some of the experiential correlates of imprisonment (despair, rage, guilt) serve as the ground of the prison metaphors supplementing mere confinement, entrapment or violent oppression. Sometimes the emotions associated with imprisonment are implied through their opposite, the liberating or healing effects of love.

Invocations of modern prison settings (bars etc.) are much less frequent in my corpus of nineteenth- and twentieth-century texts, though they do represent a large portion of the prison metaphors. I have so far not found any metaphors specifically relating to the eighteenth-century debtors' prison. Basically, confinement is a constitutive feature of all types of imprisonment; the features exclusively relevant to debtors' prison do not *per se* evoke an image of confinement – after all, they mostly relate to sociability, promiscuity and corruption – all aspects of many other areas of life. It is therefore one first result of the analysis of prison imagery that it concentrates first and foremost on physical restraint and secondarily on the architectural specifics of the dungeon and the modern prison cell. As we have seen, these details metonymically serve to invoke prison settings within both pars-pro-toto and contiguity frameworks (fetters or bars as *part of* the place of confinement; guilt, shame, moldy food as *correlating with* the prison experience). One main reason why the prototypical eighteenth-century prison fails to appear in prison metaphors may relate to the similarity with early modern types of imprisonment. In fact, the differences between the dungeon scenario and the eighteenth-century jail are a matter of degree rather than quality. Thus, in the dungeon scenario prisoners tend to suffer from even more insanitary conditions and a more extensive use of chains and fetters. Since prisoners with money could rent a cell to themselves in the eighteenth century, shared cells were apparently not perceived as a feature worthy of deployment in metaphoric discourse. Therefore, the typical image of the lone prisoner in a dungeon vault differs from an eighteenth-century prisoner in solitary confinement only to the extent that the dungeon has an underground location. But even this difference disappears when the prisoner is a dangerous criminal of the Jack Shepard type who will be thrown in the hole and loaded with chains.

There are, infrequently, some metaphors that specifically relate to the Victorian penitentiary and the institution of penal servitude. One of the most common tasks set for prisoners constrained to hard labor was oakum picking (cp. Mayhew/Binny 1971: 310-13) Thus, when Beckett's narrator describes Celia in the following terms, he is specifically alluding to Victorian prison conditions:

> Celia unpacked her bag, but not Murphy's. [...] She closed her eyes and was in her mind with Murphy, Mr. Kelly, clients, her parents, others, herself a girl, a child, an infant. In the ***cell of her mind, teasing her oakum*** of her history. Then it was finished, the days and places and things and people were untwisted and scattered, she was lying down, she had no history. (Beckett 1957: 148-49)

Celia's mind is described as the 'happy prison' of a convict teasing the tar from the ropes, untwisting her past into its basic structures, scattering the "days and places and things and people" which had cluttered her life, constituting her history. Arrived at the bare bones of her unencumbered self, she feels released, like the prisoner who, by performing his tasks well and diligently, arrives at moral improvement (at least as far as the theory goes).

Whereas hard labor in this passage from Beckett's *Murphy* appears in a rather sentimentalized form, Dickens's use of hard labor in his prison imagery brings out the cruelty and painfulness of the Victorian regimen of penal servitude. In *Martin Chuzzlewit* (1843-44), the settlers in swampy "Eden" are trying to survive under gruelling circumstances.

> In the meantime they [Martin and Mark] devoted such strength as they had to the attempted improvement of their land; to clearing some of it, and preparing it for useful purposes. Monstrously defective as their farming was, still it was better than their neighbours'; for Mark had some practical knowledge of such matters, and Martin learned of him; whereas the other settlers who remained upon the putrid swamp (a mere handful, and those withered by disease), appeared to have wandered there with the idea that husbandry was the natural gift of all mankind. They helped each other after their own manner in these struggles, and in all others; but ***they worked as hopelessly and sadly as a gang of convicts in a penal settlement***. (ch. xxxiii; 1968: 599-600)

Compare also, in *Nicholas Nickleby* (1838-39):

> [...] it will be readily imagined that that young lady's daily life was none of the most cheerful or enviable kind. She hailed the arrival of Saturday night, as a ***prisoner*** would a few delicious hours' respite from slow and wearing [sic] torture, and felt, that the poor pittance for her first week's labour would have been dearly and hardly earned, had its amount been trebled. (ch. xix; 1982: 229)

Kate, who is forced to support her mother and herself, finds her employment as a companion of an abusive old woman as tedious as hard labor. In both passages unbearable situations are described as similar to convict work, and they implicitly suggest that Kate and Martin are 'imprisoned' in a hopeless predicament.

By contrast, metaphors that relate to the architecture and regime of modern prisons focus on anonymity or boredom. Compare, for instance, George Eliot's emphasis on darkness in *Silas Marner* (1861), "the grim walls of the jail":

> 'O, what a dark, ugly place!' said Eppie. 'How it hides the sky! It's worse than the workhouse. [...] (1985: 239)

with the following passage from Joseph Conrad's *Almayer's Folly* (1895):

> Those few who saw Almayer during the short period of his remaining days were always impressed by the sight of that face that seemed to know nothing of what went on within: like the ***blank wall of a prison*** enclosing sin, regrets, and pain, and wasted life, in the cold indifference of mortar and stones. (Conrad 1976: 154)

Already on the first page of the text, Almayer had been described as a "prisoner" (7)[14] hoping to be rescued from his disappointments by the success of his daughter. When he loses her, his life ceases to have any meaning. Like a prison wall of cold stone, his expressionless face hides the tragedy of his life – he is lost to the world, a predicament that resembles imprisonment in the modern penitentiary of bare walls and lonely cells.

Old and new types of prisons can also be juxtaposed in terms of their association with tyranny on the one hand and disciplining on the other. Thus, in *Nicholas Nickleby*, the narrator characterizes Mr. Lenville as a petty tyrant who incarcerates those not to his liking:

> Thus speaking, Mr. Lenville folded his arms, and treated Nicholas to that expression of face with which, in melodramatic performances, he was in the habit of regarding the tyrannical kings when they said, 'Away with him to the deepest dungeon beneath the castle moat'; and which, accompanied with a little jingling of fetters, had been known to produce great effects in its time. (xxix; Dickens 1982: 380)

By contrast, in Jhabvala's *Heat and Dust* (1975), the situation of young women in India is figured as that of prisoners under guard:

> They gossip and joke and giggle like school-girls: very different from their daughters-in-law who are sometimes seen shuffling behind them, heavily veiled and silent and with the downcast eyes of prisoners under guard. (Jhabvala 1991: 54)

---

14 "Witnessing her triumphs he would grow young again, he would forget the twenty-five years of heartbreaking struggle on this coast where he felt like a ***prisoner***" (7).

These examples demonstrate that prison metaphors do sometimes refer to specific historical types of imprisonment. However, for this historical aspect to become salient, the metaphors need to choose a feature of the prison setting or prison regime that is specific to a particular period or type of imprisonment. As we have seen, most prison metaphors do not focus on historically specific situations but on a general situation of confinement, restraint and oppression, and they choose a variety of metonyms for the purpose that do not need to be historically consistent or accurate. Hence the common use of fetters and chains even in late twentieth-century texts. Images and conceptualizations of imprisonment thus can be figured as a pool of tropes from which writers draw in rather indiscriminate fashion.

So far we have looked at metaphors more or less in isolation. In the final section of this article I want to discuss how metaphors, besides the very local effects already outlined, additionally have larger significance in individual texts, particularly texts that are also thematically concerned with prisons and imprisonment. Primary candidates for such an analysis would be Samuel Richardson's *Clarissa* (1747-48), William Godwin's *Caleb Williams* (1794), Charles Dickens's *Little Dorrit* (1855-57), Victor Hugo's *Les Misérables* (1862), or John Edgar Wideman's *Brothers and Keepers* (1984).[15] I have chosen Hugo because the novel is a representation of nineteenth-century penal practice and because I have analyzed most of the other texts elsewhere.

4. Image and setting in Hugo's *Les Misérables*

In this section I would like to return to *Les Misérables*, briefly quoted above, and discuss some longer passages which I take to be highly significant of the novel as a whole and which therefore deserve a much more thorough analysis.

The first such passage compares the convent in which Jean Valjean and Cosette shelter from the police to Valjean's life as a convict. It is narrated from Valjean's perspective and details how he compares the severities of convict existence (long hours of hard labor; cold; discomfort; flogging; rule of silence – all the 'blessings' of the penitentiary model) with the self-imposed severities undergone by the nuns who conceive of their voluntary suffering as a sacrifice of love. I quote the passage in several sections.

> The convent had put a stop to this. It was his second place of ***confinement*** ["lieu de captivité" – 1951: 586]. In his youth, at what for him had been the beginning of life, and later, all too recently, he had known another, an ugly, a terrible place whose harshness seemed to him an iniquitous distortion of justice, a crime on the part of the law. After prison, a convent:[16] from being an inmate of the one he had become an observer of the other, and he scrupulously compared them in his mind.
>
> At times, leaning on his spade, he would let his thoughts drift in meditation. He would recall the wretchedness of his former companions. They rose at dawn and worked till dark, such sleep as they were allowed being on plank-beds with the thinnest of mattresses in rooms warmed only

15 See my discussion of the 'world as prison' topos in Fludernik (2003).

16 "Aujourd'hui après le bagne il voyait le cloître" (1951: 586).

during the harshest winter months. They wore hideous red caps and, as a concession, cotton trousers in the hot season and a woollen cloak in the cold. They drank no wine and were allowed meat only when on hard labour. They lived without names, were known only by numbers and to some extent turned into numbers themselves, eyes and voices lowered, hair cropped, subject to the lash and to constant humiliation.

Then his thoughts would turn to this other community. These women, too, had cropped hair, eyes and voices lowered, not in humiliation but under the mockery of the world, and their shoulders bore the marks not of the lash but of the scourging of their self-inflicted discipline. They too had discarded their worldly names, but in favour of others more austere. Never did they eat meat or drink wine, and they often went without food until evening. They were clad, not in red but in black woollen robes like shrouds, oppressive in summer and insufficient in winter, nothing added or subtracted according to the season, no comfort of linen in summer or wool in winter; and for six months in the year they wore hairshirts which induced fever. They lived in unrelieved cold, in cells where no fire was ever lighted, and they slept, not on mattresses but on straw. Nor were they allowed to sleep in peace after the day's work but must rise out of the first warmth of slumber to pray in the ice-cold, gloomy chapel, kneeling on its stones. And each must take her share in the ritual of atonement,[17] kneeling for twelve hours on end, or prostrate with her head on her crossed arms.

Those others had been men, these were women. The men had been criminals – thieves and murderers, bandits, fire-raisers, patricides. And what crime had these women committed? They had committed none.

On the one side, outrage, sacrilege, violence, all the forms that evil can take; on the other hand perfect innocence [...]. (Part II/Book VIII, ix, 488-9)

The comparison suggests that the nuns, who are women, endure greater severities than the convicts since they do not even allow themselves sufficient sleep, do not even have mattresses, and wear the same habits in winter and summer, and additionally chastise themselves with their hairshirts. Moreover – and this is a particularly un-Christian way of putting it – the convicts, according to Valjean, have the advantage of knowing there will be an endpoint to their suffering, whereas the nuns are to be released only by death:

Two places of ***slavery***, but in the first a possible end, the legal limit of the sentence, the hope of escape; in the second perpetuity, with no other aspiration than, in the distant future, that light of liberty that men call death. In the first, only ***chains*** of metal, in the second the ***chains of faith***.

And what comes out of these places? From the first a vast malediction, a gnashing of teeth, in hatred, the evil of despair, a rage against all human kind, and a mockery of Heaven; from the second, blessedness and love. Yet in both places, so alike and so unlike, two sets of utterly different beings were accomplishing the same task, a work of expiation.[18] (489-90)

---

17 "Atonement" not in original: "A de certains jours, il fallait que chacun de ces êtres, à tour de rôle, restât douze heures de suite agenouillé sur la dalle ou prosterné la face contre terre et les bras en croix" (1951: 587).

18 "Deux lieux d'esclavage; mais dans le premier la délivrance possible, une limite légale toujours entrevue, et puis l'évasion. Dans le second, la perpétuité; pour toute espérance, a l'extrémité lointaine de l'avenir, cette lueur de liberté que les hommes appellent la mort. Dans le premier, on n'était enchaîné que par des chaines, dans l'autre, on était enchaîné par sa foi.

Que se dégageait-il du premier? Une immense malédiction, le grincement de dents, la haine, la méchanceté désespérée, un cri de rage contre l'association humaine, un sarcasme au ciel. Que

This passage also again contrasts the moral turpitude of the convicts with the saintly nuns. Both are working in "slavery" and both perform a work of "expiation." The narrator at this point explicity steps in to say that these were the thoughts of Jean Valjean ("there we refrain from all personal reflections. We are simply the narrator [...]" – 490) and that Valjean remembers as a convict he "had dared to pity himself" and had "shaken his fist at God" (490). Valjean – unlike the narrator and, presumably, the reader – in fact falls for the contemporary justifications of the rigors of the convict system: the penitentiary was instituted to convert criminals into quasi-saints. The same type of slavery designed as a practice of expiation works as voluntary self-punishment but fails as a penal system of retribution.

At this point in the narrative, these reflections of Valjean's serve to impress on the reader that he is a changed person, a saint, somebody who – like the bishop Myriel – acquired superhuman moral strength and is performing the work of real penitence. Read in contrast with the monastic institution, the convict prison does indeed appear a well-deserved place of punishment whose severities are not unduly exaggerated. The novel, however, has been suggesting quite a different lesson. In terms of the plot, *Les Misérables* has made it quite clear that monastic slavery produces saintliness only in those who enter it with a saintly frame of mind; those forced into slavery against their will and chained to associates of evil character become more evil still since they lack the acknowledgement of their own sins and the wish for expiation. The novel's first accusation of the prison system is therefore its uselessness except as a measure of cruel punishment; the second indictment concerns the disproportionate sentencing practice in relation to the insignificance of the crimes. Valjean's nineteen-year imprisonment for stealing bread for his family because they were starving in no way tends to support the justice of the legal and penal system.

Nevertheless, Hugo's narrative presents us with Valjean's comparison of convent and prison as a way of defining the difficulties of the truly narrow path of saintliness which he associates with the "mystery of the Sublime" (491) – a saintliness that even Valjean never emulates. In this comparison, the prison is seen as the site of austerity, hard work, hunger, cold and discomfort. This conception clearly fits the penitentiary model. However, in the continuation of the passage we have been analyzing, Valjean also recurs to more traditional associations of imprisonment like enclosure by walls and the caging of animals:

> This house, too, was a ***prison***, dismally resembling the one from which he had escaped, though it had been conceived with no such thought in mind. He was again confronted by ***locks*** and ***bars***, but these protected angels. The high walls he had seen ***caging*** tigers here enclosed lambs.[19] This was a place of expiation, but not of chastisement; yet it was more austere, more sombre and relentless than the other. These virgins were more harshly subdued than the convicts. A cold,

sortait-il du second? La bénédiction et l'amour. Et dans ces deux espèces d'êtres si différents accomplissaient la même œuvre, l'expiation" (588).

19 In the original: "Il revoyait des grilles, des verrous, des barreaux de fer, pour garder qui? Des anges. Ces hautes murailles qu'il avait vues autour des tigres, il les revoyait autour des brebis" (589).

rough wind, the wind that had frozen his youth, had blown through the nest of vultures; but the wind blowing through this dovecote was keener and more piercing still. (490)

The high walls, locks and bars, and the wind of austerity are meant to keep the "lambs" ("brebis") and 'doves' ("dovecote"; "la cage des colombes") secure from the outside world, not to cage "tigers" and "vultures." Valjean had turned into a vulture in the prison and nearly became a murderer, but he is expiating his sins in actively helping others, just as Marius is trying to do good politically by joining the revolutionaries. The penal system is one aspect of the status quo that has to be reformed, destroyed and reconceived. Nevertheless, Valjean has only learnt expiation and humanity through love (Myriel's and later Cosette's). The convict system fails to work in the absence of penitence which alone would convert punishment into expiation. It signally lacks both charity and human affection, the love of God and the love of man.

Society as an obsolete institution in need of transformation is also depicted strikingly in the description of Thénardier's tavern at the beginning of Part I/Book IV. The vehicle placed outside Thénardier's inn, the "Sergeant of Waterloo," is landlocked by rust, "and from the axle there hung in loops a great ***chain*** that could have served to secure a criminal Goliath. It might have been designed for the harnessing of mastodons rather than the transport of timber; and it had a look of ***prison*** about it, superhuman ***fetters*** that could have been struck off the limbs of some monster" (144).[20] The significance of this chain is symbolic of the institution of convict prisons, their exaggerated practice of inordinate punishment, and of the obsolescence of this system: "What was it [the cart?] doing there? It served no purpose except to block the street until it mouldered into dust. Our ancient social order is filled with similar encumbrances, surviving for no other reason" (144). The irony of the passage consists in the fact that Thénardier, a villain of major proportions, has the law moulder away in his front garden, believing he will escape from justice. The prison, like other monsters of state institutional order, is doomed. They are crumbling, decomposing with age (usually regarded as their prime asset since age signifies traditional sanctity), and dissolving in the light of reason or through the force of humanity.

In sections 2 and 3 we had observed that prison metaphors frequently combine with metonymy at almost every point since spatial contiguity and semantic associations feed into the choice of lexemes (bars, chains, etc.) as well as into the correlates of imprisonment (despair, rage, etc.). In addition, we can now observe that prison metaphors often *denote* imprisonment or sites of incarceration (as the *tenor* or *ground* of the metaphor) and figure the prison as hell, as entombment, as death or as slavery. As we saw earlier in the long passage from Trollope's *Can You Forgive Her?*, Vavasor's entrapment in his job was figured in terms of imprisonment and described by a series of lexemes contiguous with a dungeon environment. At the same time, the

20 In the original: "Sous l'essieu pendait en draperie une grosse ***chaîne*** digne de Goliath forçat. Cette chaîne faisait songer, non aux poutres qu'elle avait fonction de transporter, maix aux mastodontes et aux mammons qu'elle eût pu atteler; elle avait un air de ***bagne***, mais de bagne cyclopéen et surhumain, et elle semblait détachée de quelque monstre" (153).

use of "Erebus," "doomed" and "death-like stillness" in turn figured imprisonment as death or being buried alive. I do not think that one can pull these two metaphoric strands apart – the metaphoric use of prisons to denote entrapment, and the metaphoric use of death to figure imprisonment. In fact, this is another advantage of the blending theory: source and target domains produce a pool of associations whether by contiguity or similarity and create an intricate web of metaphoric and metonymic connections that combine diverse aspects into a mosaic of images.

The same processes could be observed in the extracts from Victor Hugo's masterpiece. On the one hand, the passages describe the convent as a prison – the convent serves as the target domain, the prison as the source domain. Yet not only does this comparison involve a chain of metonymic associations in both areas, the passages in fact end up inverting the direction of the metaphoric transfer by imaging the prison as a convent of vultures and tigers, an institution of penance without religion or love. In short, the prison becomes a perverted monastery, a corruption of its originally religious purpose of reformation, healing and atonement.

The passage starts out with a characterization of the convent as a place of confinement and then in extension a type of prison. It then, using another source metaphor, metonymically related to the hard labor prison regime, describes the convent as a place of slavery in which the chains of iron are transformed into chains of faith and duty. In the subsequent passage the prison metaphor recurs and is now again metonymically elaborated in terms of enclosure (locks, bars, walls). From enclosure we then move to the cage metaphor of tigers vs. lambs and doves, a metaphor that illogically moves from the walls of the convent to the cage image. In other words, from focussing on enclosure, the passage metaphorically characterizes the inmates as tigers, and this evokes the verb "caging."[21] Once the cage metaphor is in place, the rough wind can enter into the home ("nest") of vultures and into the dovecote. Because the entire novel is ultimately about imprisonment, these moves from the syntagmatic axis (prison → bars, chains, walls, hard labor) to the paradigmatic axis (confinement → prison, cage) and back again to the syntagmatic axis (cage → animals, wind) support the major comparison of convent and prison and end up equating them in their secular alignment with slavery while symbolically opposing them in sequences of binary oppositions which structure the text. These binary opposites are both metaphorical (tigers/vultures vs. lambs/doves) and symbolic (crime/innocence; ignominy/sanctity). Yet, as we observed earlier, the oppositions end up as equivalents; neat moral distinctions in the novel are undermined by Valjean's career of criminal to saint and the inverse movement of Thénardier from the supposed savior of Marius's father to his exposure as the villain of the narrative. In short, the novel operates most forcefully in deconstructing the apparently irreconcilable moral attributions with which the text is cluttered.

The explicit meanings of the metaphors in this novel are therefore not to be taken at face value. Returning to Thénardier's vehicle with its giant chains, one can now note that what merely seemed a symbol of an antiquated legal system at the same time serves to mark Thénardier's iniquity metonymically (by being stationed outside his

21 Note that this creative metaphor occurs only in the translation of N. Denny.

inn) and metaphorically by suggesting the grossness of his crimes in the huge proportions of the vehicle and chains. Finally, the metaphors of imprisonment in the novel do not allow for simple explanations. They clearly underline the inhumanity of the French penal system in Hugo's time, yet they additionally remind us of the existence of more positive types of confinement and of the ambivalence of such refuges from life. After all, Cosette and Valjean may be safe in the convent, but their liberation, even if possibly dangerous, remains a welcome release.

5. Fiction or Reality: Images, Sources and Influences

In section 2 I have discussed a number of common prison metaphors. As was to be expected, these focussed on the notion of confinement as a basic connotation, but then diversified to embrace more specifically historical contexts. The 'old prison' system, with its images of dark dungeons and chains, persists in a number of metaphors that emphasize entombment and enclosure. The penitentiary, on the other hand, is clearly responsible for associations of austerity, deprivation, bareness and the inhumanity of carceral regimes. A third major line of connotations refers to the humiliation and shame of criminality, metonymically attaching to all arrest and imprisonment, but as we have seen, this attribution is also contested, allowing for the honor of those innocently accused or the virtue of men or women that voluntarily undergo imprisonment or repent of their crimes.

If one looks at the descriptions of prisons in modern literature and the factual accounts of imprisonment by a variety of authors, many other features of the carceral reality are salient but less frequently constitute the source of prison metaphors. For instance, the persistent sound of locks and gates being opened and shut – a prime focus in many fictional and nonfictional accounts and prominent in prominent prison films – rarely shows up in metaphoric shape, although I have come across a passage in which the protagonist's hopes disappear as when prison doors clang shut on an inmate.[22] The indifference and unpredictability if not downright cruelty of jailors and prison personnel, an aspect noted invariably in texts from the sixteenth to the nineteenth centuries, does not feature in prison imagery ('cruel as a jailor'). Nor have I so far encountered formulae that rely on the absurdity of prison regulations (to invent a possible image: 'The absurdity of the situation struck her. Her work seemed to be ruled by prison regulations, maximizing cruel indifference and illogicality.'). Bureaucratic idiocy and indifference, after all, are not peculiar to prisons but apply to all kinds of institutions, and presumably are resented equally in the army, in schools or anywhere else. Again, although cruel indifference to the needs of prisoners and the inhumanity of present-day American conditions of incarceration are prominent in fictional and nonfictional texts about prisoners, these features have not yet acquired prototypical status and therefore do not (yet) yield sources for metaphorical expressions, although they show up as the ground of some prison metaphors. Thus, in our example passage from *Almayer's Folly* in which Almayer's face is compared to a

22 "Urquhart felt the cell door slam shut" (Dobbs 1993: 53).

"blank prison wall," the anonymity of modern-day prisons may well be one of the aspects of the source domain that resonate in the passage for the reader, even though Conrad goes on to focus on the turmoil of emotions hidden behind the anodyne façade.

On the other hand, references to insanitary conditions and prisoners' experience of deprivation are standard even on a metaphorical level for the older literature, but have been phased out in the wake of the penitentiary reforms. It is assumed these days that prisons, like hospitals, are extremely clean and hygienic places and that prisoners do not suffer from a lack of basic-level facilities. However, these assumptions – as factual accounts demonstrate – have to be revised in the light of increasingly insanitary conditions and soaring levels of elementary deprivation in American institutions (lack of safety from rape and violent attack; lack of safety from infection with AIDS; refusal to provide necessary medicine and medical aid; insufficient access to fresh air, exercise, showers, fresh laundry, or books and legal literature, etc.), to the extent that third-world conditions of imprisonment have reentered the so-called civilized world. Other salient elements of the prison experience such as fear, boredom, loneliness, loss of communicative and emotional competence, etc. as yet rarely occur in prison metaphors. In the wake of the current prisonization of American society, however, these experiences may become more common knowledge and acquire the necessary prototypical status that might render them productive of metaphorical use.

We can now summarize the results of this paper in the following terms. The use of prison settings and prison metaphors in literature relates to the institution of prison and of the carceral experience in society. To the extent that crime and punishment are prominent social and literary topics, the prison is a place metonymically related to this recurrent narrative. Interestingly, the 'prison of love' topos which focusses on love as voluntary bondage anticipates the carceral reality of the Elizabethan bridewells that first instituted hard labor servitude for the traditional spectacle of punishment.

As with the topic of crime, many different motivations exist to depict the institution or experience of prison or to refer to it metaphorically. As the most common patterns of use, one can distinguish two basic tropes: the comparison and assumed homological structure between world and prison, a parallel that is usually drawn in order to criticize society; and the presentation of the prison as a counter-world for exotic, moral or psychological purposes (Fludernik 2003).

Prison metaphors, like all metaphors, require an easily recognized, prototypical set of associations that can be used as a source domain for the imagery and which allows transfers into a blend highlighting analogies between source and target domains. In this area, literary constraints operate even more forcefully, and the metaphors significantly lag behind realities. Although I have not addressed this issue in sections 2 to 4, it will have become obvious that none of the examples discussed are easily alignable with the structures of the container metaphor or the LIFE IS BONDAGE metaphor as presented by cognitive metaphor theory. Some of the recurrent metonyms can be integrated into the cognitive paradigm by arguing for structures like IMPRISONMENT IS CONSTRAINT or IMPRISONMENT IS BONDAGE as underlying the prison metaphors. Note, however, that the texts use such equations to create the ground or blend of the metaphor. Metaphors that target imprisonment do not usually employ abstract notions like constraint or bondage (or their metonymic specifics like chains or bars) as source domains but heterotypical concepts like hell or entombment. It may be that a trained cognitive metaphor scholar is more ingenious in fitting this material into the theory. For my part, I have found that the concept of mental spaces and of the blend is of more use to my analyses which are, after all, geared towards interpretation and semantic significance of the prison metaphor.

As I have tried to show in the analysis of several passages, the use of a prison metaphor is often not a spontaneous gesture but a deliberate stylistic strategy that helps to highlight connections to different parts of a narrative and to different levels of analysis (irony). Prison metaphors, although they often can be found in texts that have no legal or penal preoccupations (our examples above from Gaskell, Trollope and Desai), more frequently are employed in novels that already have a strong thematic interest in prisons and in which the metaphors therefore serve to corroborate, complement, or counterpoint the main arguments of the text. This could be demonstrated most extensively in the case of *Les Misérables*.

Preliminary results such as these need to be significantly modified in the light of a more extensive corpus of texts. Nevertheless, one can note at this early stage that the metaphoric use of the prison tends to focus on the spatial and psychological coordinates of imprisonment and therefore provides an internal, experiential, perspective on incarceration. Although the prison serves as the most typical site of otherness in modern society, this otherness (whether a heterotopical, racial or gendered alterity) is rarely figured in the metaphors taking carceral institutions as their source domains: race or homosexuality are not often described as situations of imprisonment. Conversely, prison when described metaphorically is figured largely by means of metaphoric vehicles that relate to counterworlds and otherness: hell, animality, monstrosity.[23] Thus prison metaphors (using prison-linked concepts to describe loneliness, suffering, etc.) do not foreground the otherness of prisons but their victimizing effect and anonymity, whereas metaphors describing prisons by recourse to images meant to characterize the carceral experience do indeed prominently emphasize the prison's heterotopical features.[24] This could suggest that prison does not convey a strong idea of punishment, since metaphorical references to punishment continue to be figured in terms of corporal punishment and the death penalty. On the other hand, present developments in incarceration rates could come to reinterpret both the social significance and the conceptualizations of penal institutions

---

23 An interesting exception to this is Dickens's chararacterization of Newgate as a garden in which Wemmick tends his flowers (prisoners) in *Great Expectations* (ch. 32; Dickens 1996: 246). Even this garden, though, is a counterworld since the prisoners (flowers) are on the point of breaking into bloom (getting executed). Death is therefore figured as fulfilment, hell as paradise, in a neat inversion of traditional imaging.

24 Nevertheless, one could argue that alterity creeps in by the back door, if only implicitly, when one considers key features of the carceral iciness described by Buffard (1973) to relate to prison as the opposite of 'home' (love, warmth, happiness, etc.). Moreover, the greyness and artificiality of correctional institutions could be contrasted not with normal (city) life but with nature (figured in its metonyms of light, sky, meadows, trees, etc.). Prisoners are completely deprived of nature, their counterworld is therefore an artificial no-man's land.

and the prison experience to such an extent that literary prototypes may change in their wake. Already the theme has become more and more common in recent publications.[25] It seems in fact as if a resuscitation of the literature of social criticism is in store which will focus on the injustices of carceral policy. In this context, Victor Hugo's *Les Misérables*, although a text justly denigrated for its sentimentalism and suspect on account of its religious message, may perhaps be of considerable topical relevance to this turn of the century.

Works Cited

Abbott, Jack Henry (1982 [1981]) *In the Belly of the Beast: Letters from Prison.* Intr. Norman Mailer. New York: Random House.

Beckett, Samuel (1957) *Murphy*. New York: Grove Press.

Breytenbach, Breyten (1984) *Mouroir: Mirrornotes of a Novel.* New York: Farrar Straus Giroux.

Brombert, Victor (1978) *The Romantic Prison. The French Tradition* [*La prison romantique. Essai sur l'imaginaire.* 1975]. Baltimore: Johns Hopkins Univ. Press.

Buffard, Simone (1973) *Le froid pénitentiaire. L'impossible réforme des prisons.* Paris: Seuil.

Conrad, Joseph (1976 [1895]) *Almayer's Folly*. London: Penguin.

Desai, Anita (2000) "The Rooftop Dwellers." *Diamond Dust.* Boston: Houghton Mifflin. 158-207.

Dickens, Charles (1986 [1843-44]) *Martin Chuzzlewit*. London: Penguin.

Dickens, Charles (1982 [1838-39]) *Nicholas Nickleby*. Oxford: Oxford Univ. Press.

Dickens, Charles (1996 [1860-61]) *Great Expectations*. Ed. Janice Carlisle. Boston/New York: St. Martin's Press.

Dobbs, Michael (1993 [1990]) *House of Cards*. London: HarperCollins.

Eliot, George (1985 [1861]) *Silas Marner. The Weaver of Raveloe*. London: Penguin.

Fludernik, Monika (1999) "Carceral Topography: Spatiality and Liminality in the Literary Prison." *Textual Practice* 13.1: 43-77.

Fludernik, Monika (2003) "The Prison as World – The World as Prison: Theoretical and Historical Aspects of Two Recurrent Topoi." *Symbolism* 3: 145-89.

Fludernik, Monika (forthcoming) "'Stone Walls Do Not a Prison Make': Fact and Fiction in Nineteenth-Century Literature on Incarceration." Ed. Julia Wright and Jason Haslam. *Captivating Subjects: Writing Confinement, Citizenship and Nationhood in the Nineteenth Century*. Toronto: Univ. of Toronto Press, 2004.

Fludernik, Monika, Donald C. Freeman and Margaret H. Freeman (1999) "Metaphor and Beyond: An Introduction." *Poetics Today* 20.3: 383-96.

25 Between 2000 and 2002 alone, the MLA Bibliography cites 93 entries on the subject.

Foucault, Michel (1979 [1975]) *Discipline and Punish. The Birth of the Prison.* New York: Vintage.
Gaskell, Elizabeth (1986 [1855]), *North and South.* Harmondsworth: Penguin.
Jhabvala, Ruth Prawer (1975) *Heat and Dust.* New York: Simon & Schuster.
Hugo, Victor (1951 [1862]) *Les Misérables.* Paris: Bibliothèque de la Pléiade.
Hugo, Victor (1998) *Les Misérables.* Trans. N. Denny. London: Penguin.
Lakoff, George (1987) *Women, Fire, and Dangerous Things: What Categories Reveal About the Mind.* Chicago: Univ. of Chicago Press.
Lakoff, George, and Mark Johnson (1980) *Metaphors We Live By.* Chicago: Univ. of Chicago Press.
Lakoff, George, and Mark Turner (1989) *More Than Cool Reason: A Field Guide to Poetic Metaphor.* Chicago: Univ. of Chicago Press.
Lauterbach, Frank (forthcoming) "'From the slums *to* the slums': The Delimitation of Social Identity in Late Victorian Prison Narratives." Ed. Julia Wright and Jason Haslam. *Captivating Subjects: Writing Confinement, Citizenship and Nationhood in the Nineteenth Century.* Toronto: Univ. of Toronto Press, 2004.
Mayhew, Henry and John Binny (1971 [1862]) *The Criminal Prisons of London and Scenes of Prison Life.* London: Cass.
Naipaul, Vidiadhar S. (1980) *A Bend in the River*, London: Penguin.
O'Neill, Eugene (1988 [1922]) "The Hairy Ape". Eugene O'Neill. *Complete Plays 1920–1931.* Ed. Travis Bogard. New York: The Library of America. 119-63.
Ondaatje, Michael (1987) *In the Skin of a Lion*, London: Picador.
Ramazani, Jahan (1997) "The Wound of History: Walcott's *Omeros* and the Postcolonial Poetics of Affliction." *PMLA* 112.3: 405-17.
Trollope, Anthony (1991 [1865]) *Can You Forgive Her?.* Oxford: Oxford Univ. Press.
Turner, Mark and Gilles Fauconnier (1999) "A Mechanism of Creativity." *Poetics Today* 20.3: 397-418.
Walcott, Derek (1990) *Omeros.* New York: Farrar Straus Giroux.
Waters, Sarah (2000 [1999]) *Affinity.* New York: Riverhead.
Wideman, John Edgar (1991 [1990]) *Philadelphia Fire.* New York: Vintage.
Wideman, John Edgar (1995 [1984]) *Brothers and Keepers.* New York: Vintage.
Wollstonecraft, Mary (1994 [1798]) *Maria; or, the Wrongs of Woman.* Intr. Anne K. Mellor. New York: Norton.

Realities of the Prison: Dickens, Scott, and the Secularization of their Eighteenth-Century Inheritance

Harry E. Shaw

I.

Few novels are as thoroughly imprisoned as *Little Dorrit*. Shades of the prison house fall throughout the novel.[1] Its opening scenes play the confinement of quarantine against an actual French prison in Marseilles, the latter painted in such dark colors as to make it seem as if the Bastille had never fallen. Images of imprisonment, actual and metaphorical, physical and mental, individual and societal, proliferate as the novel proceeds, so by its end we are more than half persuaded that the world itself is a prison. What other conclusion can we draw from a novel in which the heroine's father, after passing from a debtor's prison to extreme wealth, sits at the head of an opulent dinner party in Rome and rises to give a speech to his guests, only to come out with the words, "Welcome to the Marshalsea!"

An equally remarkable scene occurs in the prison to which Mr. Dorrit welcomes his guests and readers. When Arthur Clennam's financial ruin sends him to the Marshalsea, he enters a physical, emotional, and spiritual decline, into which an unexpected vision breaks:

> With an aching head and a weary heart, Clennam had watched the miserable night out, listening to the fall of rain on the yard pavement, thinking of its softer fall upon the country earth. [...] Light of head with want of sleep and want of food (his appetite, and even his sense of taste, having forsaken him), he had been two or three times conscious, in the night, of going astray. He had heard fragments of tunes and songs, in the warm wind, which he knew had no existence. Now that he began to doze in exhaustion, he heard them again; and voices seemed to address him, and he answered, and started.
>
> Dozing and dreaming, without the power of reckoning time, so that a minute might have been an hour and an hour a minute, some abiding impression of a garden stole over him – a garden of flowers, with a damp warm wind gently stirring their scents. It required such a painful effort to lift his head for the purpose of enquiring into this, or enquiring into anything, that the impression appeared to have become quite an old and importunate one when he looked round. Beside the tea-cup on his table he saw, then, a blooming nosegay: a wonderful handful of the choicest and most lovely flowers.

---

1 Collins (1980) reminds us that for over eighty years, critics seemed oblivious to the presence of the prison in the novel, though its pervasiveness has more recently become a critical cliché.

> Nothing had ever appeared so beautiful in his sight. He took them up and inhaled their fragrance, and he lifted them to his hot head, and he put them down and opened his parched hands to them, as cold hands are opened to receive the cheering of a fire. It was not until he had delighted in them for some time, that he wondered who had sent them; and opened his door to ask the woman who must have put them there, how they had come into her hands. But, she was gone, and seemed to have been long gone; for the tea she had left for him on the table was cold. He tried to drink some, but could not bear the odor of it; so he crept back to his chair by the open window, and put the flowers on the little round table of old.
>
> When the first faintness consequent on having moved about had left him, he subsided into his former state. One of the night-tunes was playing in the wind, when the door of his room seemed to open to a light touch, and, after a moment's pause, a quiet figure seemed to stand there, with a black mantle on it. It seemed to draw the mantle off and drop it on the ground, and then it seemed to be his Little Dorrit in her old, worn dress. It seemed to tremble, and to clasp its hands, and to smile, and to burst into tears. (Dickens 1982: 630-31)

But the figure is no illusion, no night-tune; it is instead the novel's heroine, whom Clennam's stay in prison has taught him he loves. The pathos here may not be to everyone's taste, but it would be folly to deny that Dickens has accomplished what he set out to do. The evocation of Clennam's weakened state is deft and understated; the affecting details about his "thinking of [the rain's] softer fall upon the country earth" and hearing hallucinatory night-tunes introduce the glimmerings of subjective and seemingly delusional desire, which magically blossom into real flowers and, finally, into Little Dorrit herself. The management of narrative focus here inveigles us as readers into sharing Clennam's weakness, his desire, and his sense of astonishment at the beauty of the flowers, while maintaining just enough distance from Clennam to allow us the pleasure of anticipating his discovery that the figure at the door is anything but a dream.

Even the most lively appreciation of Dickens's rhetorical skill, however, seems insufficient to explain the power of this scene as part of the experience of reading *Little Dorrit* as a whole. Of course, part of its impact must derive from its reference to some of the deep commonplaces of human life, above all to memories of the curative touch of simple beauty in illness and convalescence. I shall argue that another source of its power is the way in which Clennam's sojourn in the Marshalsea draws on views of the prison that had informed British fiction since the time of Richardson and Fielding. The scene is a brilliantly condensed echo of two modes of imagining the prison and its relation to everyday life outside the prison that pre-date Dickens and persist beyond him. In what follows, I shall use works by Richardson and Fielding to define these modes. When we return to see what Dickens makes of them, it will come as no surprise that his great prison novel is named for a woman.

II.

When Tom Jones and Clarissa find themselves in prison, they set the tone for depictions of incarceration in the British novel for at least a century. For the British realist novel, the prison means many things, but the chief of these is a heightened access to reality. In prisons, psychic and social realities of different kinds emerge: characters and societies find out about themselves and their desires. (Just what emerges in a given novel has much to tell us about the author's conception of what is real.) There would seem to be no logical necessity for reality to inhabit prison cells and yards. Perhaps its emergence can be explained by the way in which the prison focuses issues of judgment: perhaps it's simply that the prison, like the gallows, wonderfully concentrates the mind. Then too, the realist novel explores both the depths of the human psyche and the web of social relationship that informs human societies, and it is hard to forage in either area without encountering guilt. And the prison is a place of guilt.

For Tom Jones, a trip to Newgate affords the opportunity to learn the true implications of actions he has been unreflectively performing. Sleeping with Mrs. Waters might have meant sleeping with his own mother; a swordfight could mean murder, and lead to his own execution. Time, always of interest to Fielding, is central here. The prison provides time and space for reflection; it makes room for the possible implications of actions to precipitate and clarify. Prison gives Fielding's celebrated plot in *Tom Jones* the chance to pause and come to a point. When Tom emerges from prison, the pace picks up again, and though Sophia sagely announces that she cannot marry him any time soon, because only time will tell whether he has truly reformed, the novel and its plot won't wait, and she finds herself promised to him in the next breath, on the next page.[2] Fielding's final novel, *Amelia*, over which the prison looms as insistently as it does over *Little Dorrit*, rings some amusing changes on this notion of the prison as a space where time slows down or is suspended. In *Amelia*, the protagonist's final incarceration gives him the time to read a book of sermons he finds there (and why not? – this is the sort of random thing that happens in ordinary life, Fielding's chosen element) and as a result, he regains his Christian faith. An earlier incarceration made time for less elevating results. Taken out of the stream of his normal existence, Booth slips into an affair with a woman from his past, even though he is still deeply in love with a better woman, his own wife. This has a Borgesian ring: by cutting him off from his normal life in the present, Booth's imprisonment seems to project him into an alternative time-stream, propelling him down a path he had neglected in the past. However that may be, the truth the prison reveals in Fielding's novels is always an extension, and usually a concentration, of the truths that underlie normal life.[3] For Tom Jones and for Booth, what they learn in prison fits them for the outside world. Being in prison makes a difference, but along the same axis of reality that Fielding's characters normally inhabit. Such a view of the prison might lead, easily enough, to the conclusion that the world in general is really only a larger prison. But the central point for our purposes is that, in this view of the prison, the stress falls on the continuities between the world of the prison and the world outside its walls. To put it a different way, when Fielding thinks of the prison and the realm beyond it, he

---

2 I owe the insight and the example to Murray Cohen.

3 This characteristic of Fielding's view of the prison may help to make his writings prime exhibits in the Foucauldian interpretation offered by Bender (1987).

imagines a single, everyday world divided into two compartments; he does not imagine two worlds existing on different planes of reality.

The vision of the structure of reality that arises from Clarissa's incarceration is different. Here, experience of the prison leads to the emergence of levels of reality that elude the grasp of the quotidian, whether by rising above it in religious transcendence, or sinking beneath it into the realm of the individual psyche. Clarissa takes both routes, more or less simultaneously. When, arrested for a debt she does not owe, she enters that prelude to formal incarceration known as the "sponging-house," she hits bottom in ways that are both positive and (mainly) negative.[4] In the sponging-house, she is delivered from illusion; henceforth she will allow herself to be known only by her own, true name, and not as Lovelace's wife. At the same time, the threat the sponging-house poses to her class identity is absolute; the stigma she feels seems somehow to include and even to exceed that of her rape. Such issues involve the normal, everyday world, but they soon give way to other dimensions. Entering the sponging-house is not for Clarissa (as it is for Tom Jones) merely the occasion for a certain clarifying hiatus, it signals the eruption into normal quotidian existence of divergent planes of reality, as the physical prison is transformed into a powerful symbol both of Clarissa's individual mental state and also of hidden spiritual realities that exceed her, though they involve the core of her being. With the sponging-house scene, Clarissa begins to leave the realm of the world and the body behind, in preparation for her ascent to heaven. At the same time, our sense of her psychic life deepens, suggesting another avenue of escape from the oppressions of her daily life. What matters about Clarissa's experience of prison thus involves not a continuity between the prison and normal life, but a dramatic (in one of its two guises, a cosmic) difference. Richardson imagines this difference in terms of soul-searching on the one hand, and an ascent to eternity on the other.

The novels of Richardson and Fielding, then, evoke two different axes along which representations of the prison in subsequent British realist novels explore reality.[5] One, which we may call the "guilt/everyday life" axis, views the prison as a space that, despite some obvious differences, extends the conditions of everyday social life. This is the vision of the prison we find in Fielding. The other, which we may call the "guilt/transcendence" axis, finds in the prison an opening to realities occluded by everyday existence, whether those realities involve religious transcendence or the depths of the individual psyche. This is the vision of the prison we find in Richardson. The difference we have been charting between Richardson's

---

4 For an excellent discussion of prison images and iconography in *Clarissa*, see Doody (1974: 206-15).

5 The two modes I have identified are, of course, one way of dividing a large and important discursive territory. The mode I identify with Richardson has, until recently, been the more familiar of the two; it was expertly canvassed by Brombert, who remarks that in the broad tract of literature he considers, "the link between enclosure and spirituality is unmistakable" (1978: 4). The notion that the quotidian world is in reality continuous with the prison has become familiar under the influence of Foucault. Conger (1997) offers a study of prisons in the fiction of Wollstonecraft and Shelley, which demonstrates that the notion that society is simply a larger prison can be particularly resonant for female writers.

view of the prison and Fielding's is registered in the reader's relation to their fiction. Fielding invites us to maintain the stance of spectators when Jones and Booth enter prison: we are concerned, but we stay in our places and they stay in theirs. We continue to view these characters as actors in a quotidian world. Richardson, by contrast, drags us into the picture, using the energy created by our intense involvement to fuel us for a leap into dimensions that escape the world we normally observe.

If we look for a moment beyond the novel, we can find expressions of the two views of the prison I have been outlining. Beethoven's *Fidelio* exemplifies the this-worldly view we find in Fielding, while works of art by Raphael on the one hand and Piranesi on the other exemplify the two varieties of transcendence we have traced in Richardson. *Fidelio* reminds us that enormous human grandeur and nobility can arise from the "real-world" orientation I have associated with Fielding. The triumphs depicted in Beethoven's opera begin with the heroine's magnificent "martial devotion" to her imprisoned husband; by the finale, they have come to include "the liberation of an entire prison, to say nothing of the whole of humanity" (Robinson 1996: 70). None of this, however, involves either the spiritual transcendence or the personal inwardness that allow Clarissa to escape the world around her. For an analogue to the spiritually transcendent side of Clarissa's prison experience, we may turn to the central section of Raphael's painting, *The Liberation of St. Peter from Prison*, in which the angel who has come to free St. Peter radiates brilliant light in the otherwise monochromatic prison setting. (Many other paintings of this subject exist.) For the side of Clarissa's prison experience that escapes from quotidian social life by descending into the depths of her own personal consciousness, we may turn to Piranesi's *Carceri* drawings, with their quite different sublimity. As our eyes travel up and down the endless staircases Piranesi depicts, and we contemplate the terrible, unreadable machines that punctuate them, we enter a realm of dreams and nightmares. One hopes (though human ingenuity has sometimes thwarted that hope) that this realm belongs to the individual psyche alone and is therefore as far removed from the world of the quotidian as is the realm of religious transcendence that Clarissa's prison experience also evokes.

Before we examine the use Dickens makes of these modes of imagining the prison, we need to consider a component that both Richardson's and Fielding's depictions share, despite the basic difference of orientation I have been insisting on. In both authors, the prison is shadowed by images of female debasement. (These images come in a wide variety of forms, and the women whose imprint they bear are sometimes merely associated with criminality and prisons, instead of being actual prisoners themselves.) As we have seen, part of the poignancy of Clarissa's situation in the sponging-house is that such a setting identifies her as both transcendent and debased at once.[6] What kind of woman *goes* to prison? To underline the darker possibility, Richardson has her visited by two prostitutes. The unkindest cut comes

6 Half a century later, Madame Roland, placed in a female prison by the French Revolution, "was offended by her imprisonment 'in the midst of murderers and women of the town' [...] she voluntarily spent her days confined within her cell rather than mix with these women in the common room where they led their dissolute lives" (Scheffler 1988: 100).

when Sally Martin (whom Lovelace had seduced and abandoned to the brothel long before he raped Clarissa) equates Clarissa with herself, by averring of Lovelace that "'bating [setting aside the fact] that he will take his advantage where he can of *us* silly credulous girls, he is a man of honour" (Richardson 1985: 1062; Richardson's italics). A few pages later, Clarissa herself underlines both her "ruin" and her divine capacity to forgive, when she says of Lovelace: "Give him, good God! repentance and amendment; that I may be the last poor creature who shall be ruined by him! – and, in thy own good time, receive to *thy* mercy, the poor wretch who had *none* on me!" (Richardson 1985:1071; Richardson's italics).

In keeping with his this-worldly orientation, Fielding never creates anything approaching this symbolic concentration and superimposition of polar female images. Equivocal females do, however, form an insistent part of his vision of the prison. To be sure, Tom Jones is visited in prison by his faithful supporter, the virtuous Mrs. Miller, and Booth in *Amelia* is succored by his paragon of a wife. But Tom Jones also entertains in prison Mrs. Waters, with whom he had what subsequently (though wrongly) appears to have been an incestuous affair, as well as Mrs. Fitzpatrick, who during her visit does her best to set in motion an affair with him. And one of the first persons Booth encounters when he enters the prison is a "very pretty Girl" in whose "Countenance" he thinks he sees "great Innocence." She turns out to be a "common Street-walker," who "discharge[s] a Volley of Words, every one of which was too indecent to be repeated" (Fielding 1983: 33). The woman Booth has an affair with during his stay in prison is, in a similar but more complex way, a mixture of contraries that include a languishing sensibility, a literally murderous ferocity, an icy disdain for some men, and a powerful urge to seduce others. Equivocal female figures become a staple of subsequent prison fiction, bringing with them a heated voyeurism that informs scenes of imprisonment in the Gothic novels of Lewis and Maturin. That prison scenes should be limned by sexually compromised female figures should come as no surprise. The prison is a place of guilt, and women often serve in Western literature as crystallizations of guilt, actual or imputed.

III.

If we return to the scene from *Little Dorrit* with which we began, keeping in mind the two modes of imagining the prison I have outlined, we realize that one source of its power is that it consolidates a remarkable balance. In that scene, as in the novel as a whole, Dickens is at pains to keep alive both modes, without allowing either to cancel out the other. He invites us as readers to experience what I have called the guilt/everyday life axis at the same time and with the same intensity as we experience the guilt/transcendence axis. I will content myself with a few examples of the different ways in which this is accomplished, beginning with a paragraph describing Clennam's thoughts immediately after he has entered the Marshalsea:

> In the unnatural peace of having gone through the dreaded arrest, and got there, – the first change of feeling which the prison most commonly induced, and from which dangerous resting-place so many men had slipped down to the depths of degradation and disgrace, by so many ways, – he

> could think of some passages in his life, almost as if he were removed from them into another state of existence. Taking into account where he was, the interest that had first brought him there when he had been free to keep away [that is, his interest in Little Dorrit and her possible connection with his family], and the gentle presence that was equally inseparable from the walls and bars about him and from the impalpable remembrances of his later life which no walls nor bars could imprison, it was not remarkable that everything his memory turned upon should bring him round again to Little Dorrit. Yet it was remarkable to him; not because of the fact itself; but because of the reminder it brought with it, how much the dear little creature had influenced his better resolutions.
>
> None of us clearly know to whom or to what we are indebted in this wise, until some marked stop in the whirling wheel of life brings the right perception with it. (Dickens 1982: 602)

When, in the opening sentence, we are told that it was "almost as if [Clennam] were removed [...] into another state of existence," we seem ready to enter the guilt/transcendence axis: Clennam's exhaustion and suffering promise an escape from his present mundane state. Yet by the end of the passage, we are back in the world of Fielding's prisons, in which a bracketing of our normal temporality (or as Dickens puts it, a "marked stop in the whirling wheel of life") brings into focus the implications of our past actions, producing the "right perception" of the meaning of our lives in the world outside the prison. This balance between the two visions of the prison is echoed in the assertion that the "gentle presence" of Little Dorrit permeates not only the "walls" and "bars" that surround Clennam, but also the "impalpable remembrances" those walls and bars cannot contain.

I turn now from a single passage to the symbolic networks that, as so many critics have noted, pervade *Little Dorrit* as a whole. Clennam's vision of the flowers and his yearning for the rain's "softer fall upon the country earth" draws on one of these. That flowers can signal a pastoral world offering a fleeting transcendence of the prison has been established early in the novel. In the second Number, Little Dorrit sits as a child with the Marshalsea turnkey, who has befriended her, "looking up at the sky through the barred window, until bars of light would arise, when she turned her eyes away, between her and her friend, and she would see him through a grating, too." Noting her abstraction, the turnkey suggests that she must be "thinking of the fields." But she has never seen the fields, and so he decides to make regular trips with her to the "meadows" and "green lanes," which he tells her are "[l]ovely. Full of flowers" (Dickens 1982: 57-58). The two of them, however, always return to the prison after their excursions, which fail to erase the grating through which Little Dorrit views him, and not only him.[7]

Such pastoral longings are, to be sure, subjected to a gentle and amused irony later in the novel, when they take the form of the Plornishes' vine and flower covered "Happy Cottage" – a non-deceiving trompe l'oeil on the wall of their London shop. Yet though pastoral transcendence in *Little Dorrit* is partial, it never loses a certain potency. In a pivotal scene, Clennam sums up his life as a failed pastoral, only to have his sad musings capped by the promise that Little Dorrit may redeem his decline:

---

7 For a thorough study of pastoral elements in *Little Dorrit*, see Petch (1981-82).

> To review his life, was like descending a green tree in fruit and flower, and seeing all the branches wither and drop off one by one, as he came down towards them.
>
> "From the unhappy suppression of my youngest days, through the rigid and unloving home that followed them, through my departure, my long exile, my return, my mother's welcome, my intercourse with her since, down to the afternoon of this day with poor Flora," said Arthur Clennam, "what have I found!"
>
> His door was softly opened, and these spoken words startled him, and came as if they were an answer:
>
> "Little Dorrit." (Dickens 1982: 140)

The transcendent promise of Little Dorrit's magical appearance, proleptic of the appearance of the flowers in Clennam's Marshalsea cell, cannot at this point in the novel be allowed to persist for too long. It must be displaced by reminders of the power of the quotidian, if Dickens is to maintain the remarkable balance between the "guilt /transcendence" axis and the "guilt/everyday life" axis we have claimed as his special achievement in *Little Dorrit.* To bring Little Dorrit back to earth, Dickens calls on the figure of the debased woman that so often shadows novelistic depictions of the prison, in a way that is sufficiently complex to require extended commentary.

When Little Dorrit appears at Clennam's door, her purpose is to thank him for real-world benefits and to beg him not to encourage her father's cadging for small change. Her gesture has the this-worldly consequence of leaving her and her companion Maggie locked out the Marshalsea, which means that the two of them must wander the London streets until the gates reopen the next morning, a fact she carefully hides from Clennam.

During the wanderings of Little Dorrit and Maggie occurs a scene only Dickens's melodramatic genius could have produced. Throughout the night, Dickens has made much of how Maggie and Little Dorrit change places in the eyes of those who see them. Though Maggie is mentally a child who habitually refers to Little Dorrit as "Little Mother," she is so much taller than Little Dorrit that she is taken to be her mother, and Little Dorrit is so small that she is taken to be Maggie's child. This reversal protects Little Dorrit from unwelcome male advances. But then a young prostitute demands to know what Maggie is doing out in the streets with a child at this time of night:

> "Poor thing!" said the woman. "Have you no feeling, that you keep her out in the cruel streets at such a time as this? Have you no eyes, that you don't see how delicate and slender she is? Have you no sense (you don't look as if you had much) that you don't take more pity on this cold and trembling little hand?"
>
> She had stepped across to that side, and held the hand between her own two, chafing it. "Kiss a poor lost creature, dear," she said, bending her face, "and tell me where she's taking you."
>
> Little Dorrit turned toward her.
>
> "Why, my God!" she said, recoiling, "you're a woman!"
>
> "Don't mind that!" said Little Dorrit, clasping one of the hands that had suddenly released hers. "I am not afraid of you."
>
> "Then you had better be," she answered. "Have you no mother?"
>
> "No."
>
> "No father?"
>
> "Yes, a very dear one."

"Go home to him, and be afraid of me. Let me go. Good night!"

"I must thank you first; let me speak to you as if I really was a child."

"You can't do it," said the woman. "You are kind and innocent; but you can't look at me out of a child's eyes. I never should have touched you, but that I thought you were a child." And with a strange, wild cry, she went away. (Dickens 1982: 148-49)

Amy Dorrit can absolve Mrs. Clennam, she can absolve the Marshalsea itself, but her attempt to reach out to the prostitute becomes a condemnation that is all the more definitive because it is inadvertent.[8] Why does this happen? The answer lies in the most striking element of the scene, the glance the two women finally manage to share. That glance is so powerfully charged as to suggest a momentary merger, even an exchange, of identities. When things come to such a pass, the line between the two women must be redrawn, and quickly. But redrawing a boundary emphasizes that it has been breached. Amy Dorrit is thus shown to be part of the world after all: she is not quite cut off from our fallen existence. Transcendent beings are not vulnerable to pollution, but she is.[9] Her place in the everyday world is, definitively if paradoxically, ensured by the strength of the narrative's desire to defend her against the sexual pollution of a fallen sister. Contact with the prostitute draws her back into the real world; at the same time, the prostitute's recoil prevents Amy from being pulled too far in the direction of the mundane, and thus preserves Amy's ability to hover between that world and transcendence.

To be sure, the possibility of a paradoxical coexistence of guilt and innocence in Little Dorrit herself is one that Dickens has built into her depiction all along, though in less glaring colors.[10] From the outset, he makes the embodiment of transcendence in the novel a child of the prison in as literal a way as he can. He delights in this paradox, at one point trumping up a single prison "taint" that Little Dorrit is accused of harboring (and then immediately forgiven for harboring) – the feeling that her father, having paid for his supposed financial derelictions with so many years of his life, should not also be required to pay back his creditors in cash when he suddenly inherits a fortune (Dickens 1982: 353-54).

For all of that, Little Dorrit does more than any other figure in the novel to keep alive its powerful suggestions that life in the prison can promote a transcendence hardly to be discovered outside its walls. Given her centrality, it is important not to

---

8 The scene with the prostitute has been much commented on, often in a way that treats Amy Dorrit with considerable suspicion. Ingham, who suggests that Amy is "simultaneously perfect and corrupt" (1992: 123), is alive to the potential confusions of identity the scene promotes: she believes that the prostitute's recoil leads readers to recoil from Little Dorrit as well. Wolf suggests that Little Dorrit's function is to inveigle such persons as the prostitute to identify with her, so that they will feel "all the more guilty" (2000: 235) when her difference from them manifests itself.

9 The scene thus instantiates what Anderson describes as the "move to define oneself against the fallen [woman], socially and formally" (1993: 94, n. 49).

10 Clayton (1987:128) suggests that Little Dorrit is a "liminal" figure; this would place her by definition at the intersection of the axes we have defined. His discussion provides a useful summary of analyses of the novel that attempt to confine her to either the everyday or the transcendent.

lose sight of how relentlessly other aspects of the novel drive home the vision of the entire world as a prison on all of its levels, from the psychological fetters that bind Miss Wade and so many other characters, to the economic and political mechanisms that dominate society as a whole. Disease provides a convenient metaphor for asserting the intimate connection between the personal and social dimensions of this imprisonment. In the following passage, Dickens is describing the spread of a universal infatuation with Merdle's "wonderful bank":

> That it is at least as difficult to stay a moral infection as a physical one; that such a disease will spread with the malignity and rapidity of the Plague; that the contagion, when it has once made head, will spare no pursuit or condition, but will lay hold on people in the soundest health, and become developed in the most unlikely constitutions; is a fact as firmly established by experience as that we human creatures breathe an atmosphere. A blessing beyond appreciation would be conferred upon mankind, if the tainted, in whose weakness or wickedness these virulent disorders are bred, could be instantly seized and placed in close confinement (not to say summarily smothered) before the poison is communicable. (Dickens 1982: 476)

At the end of the passage, we seem to have returned to a very simple notion of the prison indeed, as a place cordoned off from the rest of life, a container in which the dangerous can be safely isolated. If such a plan had any chance of success, the forces that make the world a prison might conceivably be countered. But the over-the-top suggestion that the "tainted" should be "smothered" (a word with mordantly comic associations in this novel; one recalls Affery Flintwinch's reference to her marriage as a "smothering") reveals the futility of any such hope.

Dickens's attention to the economic and political dimensions of the larger prison that is the world would seem to indicate that one area in which he has moved beyond his eighteenth-century predecessors is to give his vision of the prison a substantial, concrete historicity.[11] This is an issue of some interest for the present discussion. The two axes I have been exploring divide reality into the mundane and the transcendent. But as the European novel moves from the eighteenth to the nineteenth century, its ability grows to incorporate a sense of substantial historicity into its depiction of the mundane.[12] We might therefore expect the axis of the mundane to grow at the expense of the transcendent, the more so given the growing secularization characteristic of the period. No doubt some movement in this direction does occur in *Little Dorrit*. Turning to a prison novel by another, earlier author, however, suggests limits to how fully society is embedded in history in *Little Dorrit*. It also provides an example of a different way in which the two axes we have been following may be deployed.

---

11 For the view that *Little Dorrit* contains an everyday historicity focused on individuals, not public events, see Easson (1991).

12 For explorations of the issues here, see Shaw (1983 and1999); both stress the centrality of historicism to Scott's achievement as a novelist, and the importance of his depiction of history to the development of the fiction that followed him.

IV.

Though *The Fortunes of Nigel* has some claim to be considered Scott's premiere prison novel, that honor must go to *The Heart of Mid-Lothian*, which also (and not coincidentally) contains Scott's most celebrated female characters. *The Heart of Mid-Lothian* opens with an actual historical incident, the storming of Edinburgh's jail by a mob that extracts and hangs a man whose execution had been, in its view, unjustly delayed. When the jail's door falls in fiery brands, all but two of the other prisoners escape. Before we consider their place in the pattern we have been tracing, it's worth pausing to note that the storming of the prison itself contains an element lacking in depictions of the prison by both Richardson and Fielding, but strongly present in Dickens – an explosive and sometimes efficacious rage at prison walls. Images of the fall of the Bastille must lie behind such scenes. In Dickens, we find something of a replay of that fall in *Barnaby Rudge* and a direct replay in *A Tale of Two Cities*. In *Little Dorrit*, the echo is less direct, occurring when the physical house of Clennam (associated with the fiercely repressive puritanism of Clennam's mother and the financial chicanery epitomized by Merdle) implodes. Scott lacks Dickens's capacity for fury and his fascination with violence. His single depiction of violent prison destruction is the scene we have just mentioned. The presence of such material in any of his novels seems the more remarkable considering that, when he wrote the history of the French Revolution in his *Life of Napoleon*, he declined to describe the fall of the Bastille ("We are not tracing minutely the events of the Revolution, but only attempting to describe their spirit and tendency," he blandly announces, after mentioning the Bastille's fall in one clause of the preceding sentence [Scott 1843: 76].) A few pages later he does, however, give a detailed account of the march of the Parisian women on Versailles, in what, given his evident wish that the French Revolution had never occurred, seems yet another example of the use of woman as scapegoat – and of the way in which "debased" women shadow the prison.

When in *The Heart of Mid-Lothian* the Edinburgh prison loses its door, a male and a female prisoner refuse the chance to escape. Their motivations differ. The male, a noted criminal and proficient jail-breaker named Ratcliffe, decides to avail himself of this opportunity to cross the line from jailed to jailor. He reckons that the astonished authorities will take his decision to remain in his cell as a sign of the seriousness of his plan to reform. He also supposes that the success of the jail break will alert them to the need for better security. Who could provide it more effectively than the best jail-breaker in Scotland? In the event, his surmises prove true: he's pardoned, and he gets the job. The ease with which he crosses the boundary from thief to thief-keeper suggests that it is readily permeable, a feeling Scott dramatizes in a number of ways, including a description of how Ratcliffe and Edinburgh's public prosecutor prepare to spar with one another on the issue of whether the former will be hanged or hired: "They sate for five minutes silent, on opposite sides of a small table, and looked fixedly at each other, with a sharp, knowing, and alert cast of countenance, not unmingled with an inclination to laugh, and resembled, more than any thing else, two dogs, who, preparing for a game at romps, are seen to couch down, and remain in that posture for a little time, watching each other's movements, and waiting which shall begin the game" (Scott 1994: 165).[13] No definitive line between the prison and its overseers separates *these* two.

If we considered the case of Ratcliffe alone, we would conclude that Scott's vision of the prison rests along the guilt/everyday life axis, in which prison life lies on a continuum with that of the larger society. But Effie Deans, the female prisoner who remains behind, does so for very different reasons. By this-worldly, quotidian standards, she has every reason to escape, since she has been condemned to death for an action she didn't perform, namely murdering her recently-born illegitimate child. But she refuses the opportunity to flee, even though she is urged to do so by the father of her child (who as it happens is disguised as a woman): "faintly muttering, 'Better tyne [lose] life, since tint [lost] is gude fame,' she sunk her head upon her hand, and remained, seemingly, unconscious as a statue of the noise and tumult which passed around her" (Scott 1994: 69). Both her answer and her physical attitude place her beyond the realm of practical, purposeful everyday life. As with Clarissa, her elevation above quotidian concerns finds a grounding in religion. Though the religious aura here is less powerful than in Richardson, it is broader in its sources and associations. Effie's value for "gude fame" is, in the first instance, mediated by her Calvinist upbringing. Her connection with Scottish folk culture suggests a further, hazier set of possibilities for transcending rational, this-wordly calculation. Ballad heroes and heroines are as likely to find themselves in Fairy Land as in Heaven.

Effie Deans's refusal to leave the prison, then, evokes the guilt/transcendence axis, which here as in *Little Dorrit* is bound up with issues of female purity and transgression. Unlike *Little Dorrit*, however, *The Heart of Mid-Lothian* does not sustain a balance between the opposed visions of the prison embodied by the two figures who decide to remain within its walls. Instead, history enters the picture. Scott historicizes Effie in a way that places the guilt/transcendence axis firmly in the past (or at best, on the backward-looking, pastoral margins of present-day society), so that among other things, *The Heart of Mid-Lothian* becomes a history of the inevitability of secularization and the triumph of a certain kind of modernity. Secularization leaves its marks on *Little Dorrit*, but on a different level. Lionel Trilling's claim that Amy Dorrit is "the Paraclete in female form" (Trilling 1979: 57) rings true, but that is because the religious aura with which the novel surrounds her is nebulous. Such a claim would never pass muster with Richardson. For all her sanctity, we are never allowed to imagine that Clarissa has somehow merged with the Holy Spirit, because such beings have substantial, well-defined places in the system of religious values that underlies the world Richardson imagines. This is no longer the case with Dickens. *Little Dorrit* thus reflects and participates in the history of secularization; unlike *The Heart of Mid-Lothian*, however, it does not give secularization a history by thematizing it and presenting it as a historical phenomenon.

How does Scott identify the guilt/transcendence axis with a receding past? Though a full answer would necessitate an extended consideration of the novel as a whole, we

---

13 In what remains an invaluable brief introduction to *The Heart of Mid-Lothian*, Raleigh (1966) comments on the symbiotic relationship between Ratcliffe and the public prosecutor; he also has valuable things to say about the novel's folk and pagan elements.

may obtain a glimpse of what such an analysis would produce by concentrating on Effie Deans herself. When Effie gives her reason for remaining in prison, her language is the language of the Scottish folk, and she draws on a proverb. This is not her only connection with a peasant Scottish tradition extending into the distant past. Before her imprisonment, she seems a figure from a ballad. We see her in the twilight returning from a tryst with her lover, singing old songs and fending off her sister's remonstrances by making irreverent use of folk sayings ("I'm sure, if ye'll ask nae questions, I'll tell ye nae lees" [Scott 1994: 101]). Such associations are thickened by the existence of a double for Effie, a madwoman called Madge Wildfire. Madge is a habitué of prisons. She was seduced and abandoned by the same man who seduced Effie, and she is even more closely identified than Effie is with folk tradition and folk music. (Among many other things, on her deathbed she sings the greatest ballad imitation in Scots, "Proud Maisie," written by Scott for the occasion.) It is unsurprising that Madge cannot survive in the modern world and entirely fitting that she is killed by a city mob.[14]

Effie Deans cannot survive either, at least as a traditional figure, but she is not called upon to die in the course of the novel. Her fate is more interesting. *The Heart of Mid-Lothian* is, like all of Scott's great novels, an extended meditation on the coming of modernity, and Effie's role in furthering this meditation is its most brilliant part. What happens to Effie is that she herself modernizes, abandoning her place on the heroic guilt/transcendence axis and entering the axis of ordinary, modern everyday life.[15]

For a time, it seems that she will remain a folk heroine of a familiar kind, that she will continue to be the sort of vibrant figure from the past who can participate in the guilt/transcendence axis as Scott imagines it. After she escapes death for the child-murder she didn't commit, she runs off with her seemingly disreputable lover. He, like many a ballad hero, turns out to be an aristocrat in disguise.[16] After marrying her, he resumes his proper place in society and expects her to assume the role of an aristocratic Scotswoman. A quick learner, she does not disappoint him. Indeed, she learns so well that no less than the Duke of Argyll finds her a charming example of refined Scottish aristocratic femininity. (She is in fact the daughter of a cow-feeder.) In the process, however, she develops in ways foreign to the ballad pattern, and the world of the ballads. One sign of this is that she becomes an ardent and genuine connoisseur of nature. In her earlier incarnation, we see her as part of the Scottish countryside (in a way that recalls, to be sure with an added sexual dimension, Wordsworth's "solitary Highland Lass"). Now, she herself makes excursions to admire Highland scenery. In Schiller's terms, she has passed from the "naïve" to the

14 Wilt (1985:129-42) finds crucial similarities among all the women in the novel.

15 In viewing the two carceral axes in the light of a general modernization and secularization, I seek to supplement the familiar and more specific Foucauldian schema that traces how the "new" prison replaces the "old" prison during this period. For a treatment based on the latter schema, covering a longer historical period than I do, see Fludernik (2003).

16 In "Glasgow Peggy" (Child 228), for instance, the Lowland heroine runs off with a wild and seemingly impecunious Highlandman, only to discover that he is the Lord of Skye.

"sentimental," from having a place to admiring places. She has become one of us, a tourist, the sort of person who collects ballads (as Scott did) instead of singing them (or appearing in them). In a conversation with her upright sister, she attributes her successful transformation to the same ability to lie that led to her original downfall. Those who grasp the significance of her development in the novel will recognize that the "lying" to which she refers involves the modern ability to inhabit multiple, inauthentic roles, instead of the fixed, single role characteristic of traditional society. Her reference to herself as a liar rings with an amused self-irony that suggests that she has come to think of lying, not as the breaking of one of God's commandments, but simply as a condition of her new social being.

Effie Deans does not, however, leave guilt and transcendence behind forever. Far from it. She is cursed with barrenness, she cannot discover what has become of her illegitimate son, and she must endure a marriage embittered by a lack of further offspring, as well as by her husband's moody pangs of conscience and general discontent at the civilized role to which he clings so fiercely. Finally, when her missing son surfaces for long enough to kill a man he doesn't realize is his father, Effie reclaims her place on the guilt/transcendence axis by retiring to a nunnery, for despite the Presbyterian upbringing that was part of her folk heritage, she has converted to Catholicism under her husband's influence. Her retreat to a locale from the Gothic novel underlines how irretrievable, save on the plane of fantasy, is the loss of transcendence for those who have entered a secularized modernity.

V.

The claims of Dickens to a full historicity in his treatment of the prison in *Little Dorrit* pale beside the accomplishment of Scott in *The Heart of Mid-Lothian*. The contrast reveals an element of the timeless in Dickens's depiction of the prison, even at its most socially embedded. At the end of *Little Dorrit*, Arthur and Amy, having escaped the Marshalsea, enter the streets of that larger prison, London. When the narrator depicts them as encountering, and through their love for one another transcending, the "usual uproar" that confronts them there, we take the usualness of the uproar to be part of an eternal truth about the human condition, not the result of historically specific processes. Whether one considers this a strength, or a weakness, or both at once, will depend upon judgments that transcend the literary. We can, however, say that this aura of timelessness contributes to the visionary power of the moment when Arthur Clennam wakes in the Marshalsea prison to see a bowl of flowers, during an incarceration that reminds us of the prison's power to reveal the truth about the everyday world, while at the same time gesturing toward an altogether different order of reality.

In their differing ways, the depictions of the prison in *The Heart of Mid-Lothian* and *Little Dorrit* are part of the story of a growing secularization. Just as Scott's novel seeks an acceptable way of bidding farewell to what we lose as we float down the stream of history, so the timeless aspect of *Little Dorrit* seeks an antidote to certain consequences of that development. Arthur Clennam's vision of the flowers may gain its deepest poignancy from its echo of a fantasy evoked by Coleridge in one of his notebooks: "If a man could pass thro' Paradise in a Dream, & have a flower presented to him as a pledge that his Soul had really been there, & found that flower in his hand when he awoke – Ay! And what then?" (Coleridge 1974: entry 4287). What the melancholy Clennam, an authentic inhabitant of a desacralized modernity, most needs, however, is not a token that his soul has visited Paradise, a destination that in the world of *Little Dorrit* is in any case out of the reach of anyone save its heroine. What Arthur Clennam needs is reassurance that such things as souls might exist, that he might turn out to have one, and that another human being might help him find it, despite the walls that surround him in and out of prison. This the scene with the flowers offers him, and us.

Works Cited

Anderson, Amanda (1993) *Tainted Souls and Painted Faces: The Rhetoric of Fallenness in Victorian Culture*. Ithaca: Cornell Univ. Press.

Bender, John (1987) *Imagining the Penitentiary: Fiction and the Architecture of Mind in Eighteenth-Century England*. Chicago: Univ. of Chicago Press.

Brombert, Victor (1978) *The Romantic Prison: The French Tradition*. Princeton: Princeton Univ. Press.

Child, Francis James, ed. (1883-98) *The English and Scottish Popular Ballads*. 5 vols. Boston: Houghton Mifflin.

Clayton, Jay (1987) *Romantic Vision and the Novel*. Cambridge: Cambridge Univ. Press.

Collins, Philip (1980) "Little Dorrit: The Prison and the Critics." *TLS* 18 April 1980: 445-46.

Coleridge, Samuel (1974 [1815-16]) *The Notebooks of Samuel Taylor Coleridge: Volume 3, 1808-1819*. Ed. Kathleen Coburn. Princeton: Princeton Univ. Press.

Conger, Syndy McMillen (1997) "Mary Shelley's Women in Prison." *Iconoclastic Departures: Mary Shelley after Frankenstein*. Ed. Syndy M. Conger, Frederick S. Frank, and Gregory O'Dea. Madison: Fairleigh Dickinson Univ. Press.

Dickens, Charles (1982 [1855-57]) *Little Dorrit*. World's Classics. Oxford: Oxford Univ. Press.

Doody, Margaret Anne (1974) *A Natural Passion: A Study of the Novels of Samuel Richardson*. Oxford: Clarendon Press.

Easson, Angus (1991) "A Novel Scarcely Historical? Time and History in Dickens's Little Dorrit." *Essays and Studies* 44: 27-40.

Fielding, Henry (1983 [1751]) *Amelia*. Ed. Martin C. Battestin. Middletown: Wesleyan Univ. Press.

Fludernik, Monika (2003) "The Prison as World – The World as Prison: Theoretical and Historical Aspects of Two Recurrent Topoi." *Symbolism: An International*

Annual of Critical Aesthetics 3. Ed. Rüdiger Ahrens. New York: AMS Press. 145-90.

Ingham, Patricia (1992) *Dickens, Women and Language*. Toronto: Univ. of Toronto Press.

Petch, Simon (1981-82) "Little Dorrit: Some Visions of Pastoral." *Sydney Studies in English* 7: 102-114.

Raleigh, John Henry (1966) *Introduction. The Heart of Mid-Lothian.* By Sir Walter Scott. Boston: Houghton Mifflin.

Richardson, Samuel (1985 [1747-48]) *Clarissa*. Ed. Angus Ross. London: Penguin.

Robinson, Paul (1996) *Ludwig van Beethoven: Fidelio*. Cambridge: Cambridge Univ. Press.

Scott, Sir Walter (1994 [1818]) *The Heart of Mid-Lothian*. Ed. Tony Inglis. London: Penguin.

Scott, Sir Walter (1843 [1827]) *The Life of Napoleon Buonaparte, with a Preliminary View of the French Revolution.* 5 vols. Edinburgh: Cadell.

Shaw, Harry E. (1983) *The Forms of Historical Fiction: Scott and his Successors*. Ithaca: Cornell Univ. Press.

Shaw, Harry E. (1999) *Narrating Reality: Austen, Scott, Eliot*. Ithaca: Cornell Univ. Press.

Scheffler, Judith (1988) "Romantic Women Writing on Imprisonment and Prison Reform." *The Wordsworth Circle* 19: 99-103.

Trilling, Lionel (1979 [1953]) "Little Dorrit." *The Opposing Self.* The Works of Lionel Trilling: Uniform Ed. New York: Harcourt Brace Jovanovich. 44-57.

Wilt, Judith (1985) *Secret Leaves: The Novels of Walter Scott*. Chicago: Univ. of Chicago Press.

Wolf, Sherri (2000) "The Enormous Power of No Body: Little Dorrit and the Logic of Expansion." *Texas Studies in Language and Literature* 42: 223-54.

The Innocent Convict: Character, Reader Sympathy, and the Nineteenth-Century Prison in *Little Dorrit*

Carol Colatrella

Presenting a panorama of inequity in the criminal justice system, in other government bureaucracies, and in society at large, Charles Dickens's *Little Dorrit* (1855-57) sketches the figure of the innocent convict as a means of understanding criminality, particularly representing cultural anxieties about who ought to be judged criminal and how criminals ought to be punished. The novel depicts characters whose fates illustrate the injustices meted out to innocent convicts, and it examines how difficult it is to assess legal and ethical wrongdoing by appearances. In doing so, *Little Dorrit* criticizes how the criminal justice system and social conventions conspire against the poor and innocent and illustrates how individuals can be unjustly convicted and/or maligned despite their virtues.

In the nineteenth century, the United States, Britain, and France were homes to active reform campaigns to improve criminal justice systems, including the detection, trial, and punishment of offenders. Many reformers recognized that innocent persons could be falsely convicted, that the imprisoned might be brutalized by prison conditions, and that both erroneous and extreme punishments incurred psychological costs for those incarcerated. An 1845 story in *The United States Magazine and Democratic Review*, "The Innocent Convict," recounts how a poor collegian is framed by a classmate for a theft, an error that contributes to his becoming a bitter, fearful man.[1] After being released from prison, he writes: "I live in daily fear of arrest, and whenever a murder or a theft is committed, I tremble lest I be taken for a perpetrator" (22). Both the mistakenly convicted and those cruelly punished suffered from errors of judgment concerning due process and/or extreme punishment. Dickens in *American Notes* (1842) argues against inhumane punishment, noting that the mechanism of

---

1 See Briggs (1845). Expelled for the theft, the innocent young man suffers the contempt of his former friends before he is enlisted against his will into the army. After seeking release from military service by writing to the Secretary of War, he is confined for breaking army regulations forbidding such action without permission of one's commanding officer but is eventually acquitted. Another episode concerns how he was fooled into becoming an unwitting accessory to a burglary, a crime that landed him in the penitentiary despite his innocence. After the innocent man completes his prison term, the old classmate finally confesses to the original theft. When the old classmate is found dead, the former convict is charged. By this time in possession of funds, he finds a lawyer to represent him and is acquitted of the murder charge.

solitary imprisonment, which was intended to prevent criminal contagion and to encourage inmates to repent for their crimes, damaged individuals whether they were innocent or guilty.[2]

Little Dorrit claims that those judged as criminals are often no more or less guilty than others and that even the innocent transgress against laws or social norms (cf. Clayton 1991). Within a frame of action describing the villain Rigaud's plot to blackmail the wealthy Mrs. Clennam for concealing a relative's bequest to Frederick Dorrit's niece Amy, the novel recounts the incarceration, release, and demise of Amy's father William Dorrit and the imprisonment and release of Arthur Clennam. Both William Dorrit and Arthur, Mrs. Clennam's son, serve sentences as debtors in the Marshalsea, the prison where Dickens's father served time as an insolvent debtor.[3] Showing how prisons might become comfortable homes for inmates while even aristocratic homes may be prison-like, the novel explores how social status, money, family connections, and gentility are transient states rather than reliable indicators of innocence or criminality.

Material circumstances do not protect other individuals from exhibiting criminal propensities or extreme punishments, nor does a stint in prison remain convincing proof of an individual's guilt. *Little Dorrit* unpacks Amy's innocence while detailing how prison and social success reveal nothing about morality. Dickens's novel demonstrates that innocence and guilt are moral terms applicable only to an individual's specific actions or thoughts and cannot provide a total summary of one's moral character. The fiction suggests no individual could be completely innocent in deed and word and that most individuals betray good and bad intentions and actions.

As various subplots in *Little Dorrit* reveal, it is possible for the incarcerated debtor Dorrit and the greedy landlord Casby to be celebrated as beneficent patriarchs, the devious fraud Merdle to masquerade as a powerful speculator, the dangerous murderer Rigaud to elude capture by acting as a society gentleman, and the hard-hearted Mrs. Clennam to appear a concerned mother. The novel also portrays the inverse in showing how the saint-like Amy Dorrit and generous Arthur Clennam are sometimes judged as transgressors against propriety. Like Mrs. Plornish's Happy Cottage mural, which represents a country scene in the grimy urban patch of Bleeding Heart Yard (Dickens 1975: 630), paradoxes associated with individual characters abound in a novel where plot and setting aid characterization to show how minor offences can be cruelly punished, while more serious crimes elude detection and punishment.

Suggesting that relying on a pleasant fiction is suspect, *Little Dorrit* acknowledges the difficulties many characters have in processing the social world and finding their pathways through it. Social conventions concerning criminality and poverty are faulty, the novel shows, because they do not explain social inequalities. According to the unemployed plasterer Plornish, a former resident of the Marshalsea, the impoverished inhabitants of Bleeding Heart Yard struggle without knowing why circumstances are

---

2 For an extended analysis of Dickens's ideas about crime, see Collins (1962).

3 For historical information about the Marshalsea, see Philpotts (1991), Easson (1974), and Hennelly (1997).

such as they are or how to change them. The narrator interrupts Plornish's rant and corrects his word choice, which intensifies the critique by suggesting that upstanding, respectable people (manufacturers) can be criminals:

> There were old people, after working all their lives, going and being shut up in the workhouse, much worse fed and lodged and treated altogether, than – Mr. Plornish said manufacturers, but appeared to mean malefactors. Why, a man didn't know where to turn himself for a crumb of comfort. As to who was to blame for it, Mr. Plornish didn't know who was to blame for it. He could tell you who suffered, but he couldn't tell you whose fault it was. It wasn't *his* place to find out, and who'd mind what he said, if he did find out? He only know'd that it wasn't put right by them what undertook that line of business, and that it didn't come right of itself. And, in brief, his illogical opinion was, that if you couldn't do nothing for him, you had better take nothing from him for doing of it; so far as he could make out, that was about what it come to. Thus, in a prolix, gently-growling, foolish way, did Plornish turn the tangled skein of his estate about and about, like a blind man who was trying to find some beginning or end to it; until they reached the prison gate. (184)

Given that Dickens's original title was *Nobody's Fault*, it is not surprising that Mr. Plornish reaches his logical and logistical conclusions: no one is to blame, but it all ends at the prison gate. Connecting the prison with society in England and abroad, the novel sketches a spectrum of crimes – ranging from unethical actions and those offending social taste to deliberate fraud, murder, and theft – and describes how the most innocent actions receive the harshest punishments.

Little Dorrit blends characterizations of debtors and criminals, descriptions of jail and other prison-like settings, and thematic references to the government's favoring the elite as part of elucidating Amy's character as an innocent in a world full of deceit, hypocrisy, and wrongdoing. Every chapter describes a prison, a setting like a prison, a prisoner, a person acting as a prisoner, and/or the inexorably tedious interactions with bureaucracy that make the patriotic, genial citizen ready to riot against government. The relentless presentation of individuals (whether virtuous or vicious) in captive situations produces a social critique directed against legal fraud, social hypocrisy, false gentility, and the ambiguous results of fiction-making.[4] Recognizing a human propensity to transgress, Dickens's novel serves as an advocate for its dispossessed populations by encouraging readers to sympathize with prisoners such as debtors whose punishments far exceed the magnitude of their crimes, a more progressive view of criminality than represented in many other narratives of the period.[5]

A number of realist fictions contemporary with Dickens's novel describe the mistaken incarceration of an innocent, amiable person who is blamed for a crime committed by another, or an individual who commits a crime to survive or to save

---

4 See Carlisle (1975) 199: "Dickens continually emphasizes the role that the creation of fictions plays in the world of *Little Dorrit* [...]. One need only realize the extent to which Little Dorrit herself is intimately involved in analogous acts of fictionalization, of deception and lying, to recognize the complexity and subtlety with which Dickens formulates this problem." See also Rotkin (1989).

5 Sen (1998) connects Dickens's novels with radical ideologies.

others. In Catharine Sedgwick's *Married or Single?* (1857), heroine Alice Clifford visits her brother Max in the Tombs. Max has been falsely indicted for forgery. Alice spends a night in a jail cell adjacent to his. Max is released because several individuals help Alice prove his innocence at a hearing. Elizabeth Gaskell's *Mary Barton* (1847) describes how the heroine's lover Jem Wilson is mistakenly incarcerated for a crime her father has committed. Often a character's likability is a significant factor in gaining reader sympathy. David Reynolds describes Herman Melville's character Bartleby the scrivener as follows: "A social outcast finally imprisoned in the Tombs, he falls in a long line of American criminals who could not summarily be dismissed as wicked but were regarded as an ambiguous mixture of good and evil, normal and abnormal qualities" (Reynolds 1989: 296). According to Reynolds, portraits of sympathetic criminals appear in other works by Melville but reach a culmination in Billy Budd, who is "lovable" (306). Indeed, few critics suggest that Billy is guilty of anything because he appears charmingly naive when compared with those who entrap, sentence, and execute him.[6] Sympathy also occurs when a punishment is out of proportion to the crime. Victor Hugo's *Les Misérables* (1862) presents Jean Valjean, a man who begins a life of crime by stealing bread to feed his family. As Valjean flees and the police pursue him, readers sympathize with an essentially good man who avoids prison and protects his family. In *Laboring Classes and Dangerous Classes* (1973), Louis Chevalier argues that such sympathies are class-based, noting that Hugo criticizes elites who fear lower-class social mobility as transgressive.

Whereas Hugo stresses Valjean's fundamental moral integrity, what we might think of as likability under extreme circumstances, making him exceptional as a criminal and as a man, Dickens illustrates the ambiguous moral qualities of all the characters in *Little Dorrit*, even those who do not engage in criminal or unethical behaviors and who are generally considered as innocent. The novel uses oppositions, inversions, and doubles to connect moral integrity and criminality. To take a phrase as an example: the title and nickname *Little Dorrit* simultaneously allude to Amy's slight build and her father's great pretensions to gentility; yet the phrase reinvests the adjective "little" with positive connotations that reference Amy's hard work and great heart, while diminishing positive values one might associate with Dorrit, a name suggestive of "Doric," the plainest of the three classical orders of architecture, and of the Dorian mode in music, which is characterized by simplicity. The original title page of Dicken's novel emphasizes this contradictory mix of high/low and noble/humble associated with the title in using an unadorned font for both words but wrapping the name Dorrit in chains.[7]

Of all families noted in the novel, the Dorrits are most closely associated with the prison, for residence in the Marshalsea develops their moral characters, connects them

---

6 See Colatrella (2002: 227-245) for an analysis of the mixed messages in Melville's novella.

7 The original title page from the 1857 Bradbury and Evans edition of *Little Dorrit* is reproduced in John Holloway's Penguin edition (1967, reprinted 1975). *The Compact Edition of the Oxford English Dictionary* (607) also notes the obscure word "dort," indicating sulkiness or ill-humor, which is a predominating emotion for William, Fanny, and Edward Dorrit.

as family members, and encourages their interactions with others. As Dickens knew, nineteenth-century American and European prison reformers worried about convicts teaching their trade to fellow prisoners and promoted silent and separate systems of incarceration to prevent the spread of criminality. Representing prison as a source of contagion in that incarceration demoralizes all prisoners, Dickens's fictional rendering of the Marshalsea stresses its close conditions and poor sanitation.[8] The Dorrits' jail taint is identified as a moral quality, derived from imprisonment or associating with those in prison and causing degeneration of the will to work honestly. The taint is an infection that manifests different symptoms in each individual: it causes William Dorrit to lapse into narcissism and false gentility, his son Tip to eschew any honest profession, and his daughter Fanny to seek the highest possible social status at the cost of her own happiness and well-being.

The family's condition has the opposite effect on daughter Amy, who is "inspired" "to be that something, different and laborious, for the sake of the rest" (Dickens 1975: 111). Amy's inspiration and her diligence are linked to her innocence. Despite "drinking from infancy of a well whose waters had their own peculiar stain," she refuses to fall prey to manipulation to improve her situation and instead frequently cautions her siblings against such impulses (111). Presenting the family as a case study of how punishing poverty encourages criminality in most subjects, *Little Dorrit* indicts society for hypocritical gentility and fraud. The novel describes how all individuals and institutions are subject to corruption in familial, romantic, and social relations; philanthropy; investment practices; medical care; legal disputes, and government bureaucracy.

Characterization and Reader Sympathy

While society is more interested in appearances rather than humanity, Amy and other individuals on its margins are rendered as generous and good. *Little Dorrit* is focalized by a narrator sympathetic to Amy and Arthur Clennam, whose attitudes and actions bespeak moral innocence and assistance to others. Invoked frequently as the child of the Marshalsea, who was born and grew up within its walls, Amy is the character most often described as innocent, particularly with regard to her childhood spent in the debtors' prison, her continuing care for her incarcerated father and others, and her quiet love for Arthur Clennam.[9] Amy stands as a beacon of common sense and affection, serving her family, friends, and others without requiring anything of them, whether they are in the Marshalsea or installed in a huge Venetian palace, which goes to show that debtors' prison and high society do not much differ. Her steady kindness and hardworking generosity do not prevent her from finding fault with social conventions and institutional policies, nor do they blind her to how society too harshly

---

8 Philpotts (1998: 138) notes "the foulness of the drinking water" and Dickens calling it that "peculiar stain."

9 Some references to Amy's childlike innocence appear in Book the First, Chapters 1, 7, 9, 14, and 19, and in Book the Second, Chapters 5, 6, 8, 22, 27, 29, and 30, among other places.

punishes debtors such as her father and her lover. Her care is explicitly qualified as innocent in Book I, Chapter 19 (274: "comforting her father's wasted heart upon her innocent breast") and in Book II, Chapter 29 (825: "nursed him as lovingly, and god knows as innocently, as she had nursed her father").

In keeping with Mr. Plornish's murky understanding of responsibility, even the most virtuous characters in the novel are blamed, sometimes for virtuous behaviors. Amy and Arthur are separately described as guilty of caring too much for others: her overweening love for her father and his speculation with their partnership company's money to benefit Doyce are noted in the text as adversely affecting their otherwise pure moral characters. A novel featuring a number of characters who appear as twins or doubles, *Little Dorrit* suggests Arthur and Amy are male and female doubles, for Amy's innocent imprisonment is succeeded in the plot by Arthur's entering the same prison for nonpayment of debt when his well-intentioned speculations in the Merdle concern on behalf of Doyce and Clennam come to ruin. Further crimes of debt and fraud cause Amy's father William Dorrit and Arthur's mother Mrs. Clennam, who is also represented as acting out of strong emotions with a conviction of her own rectitude, to incur the lifelong punishment of self-imprisonment. Amy and Arthur act righteously, but both are incarcerated while mean, malicious individuals escape punishment.[10]

Contrasting Amy's and Arthur's intentions to do good with the selfish impulses of many greedy, snobbish characters, Dickens notes that obsessions come in all types and that narcissistic desires nourish oppressive social conventions. The list linking monomaniacal or self-deluded characters with their pet projects with diminished outcomes is long: Bob the turnkey desires to leave money to Amy that might not be given to her family (110), Mrs. Merdle wishes to dominate society, Fanny revenges herself on Mrs. Merdle, Gowan and Mrs. Gowan vaunt their social status over the Meagles, the Meagles enshrine Pet and her dead twin sister, Mrs. Plornish believes she speaks Italian. Ameliorating conflict and avoiding self-deception, Arthur and Amy (with the occasional assistance of Plornish, Pancks, and Mr. Meagles) act as communicators, mediators whose actions link various individuals to each other, stitching together pieces of narrative into a pattern that suggests innocence is often trumped by selfishness.

Amy's and Arthur's mediations reflect their shared sense of responsibility toward friends, family, and acquaintances, an ethical virtue that becomes a social vice when the objects of their philanthropy abuse them. Amy manages to get jobs for her sister and brother that provide her incarcerated father with resources that keep him fed and clothed. She connects the Plornishes with the Clennams as well as later transmitting messages between Pet Meagles and Arthur. Arthur is also a go-between for various households, including his mother's, the Dorrits', Mr. Casby's, and the Meagles'. Arthur considers what might be best for his friends more than he acknowledges his own feelings, as demonstrated by his unwillingness to allow himself to admit liking Pet

10 Miller (1958) notes how the characters of *Little Dorrit* such as William Dorrit and Mrs. Clennam embody self-imprisonment and how others reveal incapacitating dysfunctional qualities.

Meagles, much less to actively court her. Amy also resists imposing her needs on others, similarly avoiding professions of love to Arthur.

Desiring "to make up for a bad past," Arthur and Amy work toward improving individual situations, and they struggle against difficult circumstances, including coping with the indolence and selfishness of their family members.[11] Arthur attempts to assist Doyce, to protect Amy's brother Tip, and to advance all the Dorrits by having Mr. Dorrit released from the Marshalsea. But Arthur's kind intentions are not enough to protect himself: he winds up speculating with his company's funds to promote his partner Doyce's interests. Like Amy, Arthur fails to save Tip. Even William Dorrit's release from the Marshalsea, as effected at Arthur's urging and Pancks's intervention, becomes a matter of appearances in that the released prisoner remains circumscribed by surrounding forces, although he becomes a rich man in society.

Judgments of characters' innocence and guilt in the novel are relative and contingent, based on studying their intentions and behavior toward others. Characterization and setting support the theme of innocence under siege apparent in Amy's history, for Dickens links moral temperaments to environment, exemplifying acceptance or resistance to general corruption (cf. Smith 2000). After first seeing Amy at his mother's, Arthur follows the girl into the Marshalsea to learn what brings her there. He meets her father, learning of William Dorrit's peculiar status as the senior resident of the prison. Arthur's compulsion to find out whether Amy's father is imprisoned as a consequence of Mrs. Clennam's wrongdoing keeps him within the prison wall too long, and he is locked up for the night. The next morning, after waiting for Amy at her uncle's and sister's rooms near the prison, Arthur accompanies her through the neighborhood:

> They walked back through the miserable muddy streets and among the poor, mean shops, and were jostled by the crowds of dirty hucksters usual to a poor neighbourhood. There was nothing, by that short way, that was pleasant to any of the five senses. Yet it was not a common passage through common rain, and mire, and noise, to Clennam, having this little, slender, careful creature on his arm. How young she seemed to him, or how old he to her; or what a secret either to the other, in that beginning of the destined interweaving of their stories, matters not here. He thought of her having been born and bred among these scenes, and shrinking through them now, familiar yet misplaced; he thought of her long acquaintance with the squalid needs of life, and of her innocence; of her solicitude for others, and her few years, and her childish aspect. (140)

Arthur's assumption of responsibility for resolving the Dorrits' problems leads him to the Circumlocution Office, where he only finds the Barnacles in confusion, instead of a solution for William Dorrit. He reencounters his traveling acquaintance Mr. Meagles, on an errand to assist Daniel Doyce; Meagles blurts out his own exasperation with the official process that refuses to recognize Doyce's invention. The encounter demonstrates that English society and government are stolidly intractable, resisting

11 Rainsford (1995: 12) remarks of Dickens's late works: "A constant desire is manifest in the novels for a bad past – for which the protagonist may be to blame, or for which he or she, like Esther Summerson may simply be persuaded they are to blame."

efforts at improvement and efficiency that could save the Dorrits and Doyce in the interest of protecting the Barnacles' sinecures.

Varieties of Prisons and Forms of Imprisonment

Many settings in Dickens's novel are literally prisons or other places of confinement depicted as close, constraining environments inhibiting one's prospects, while almost every domestic scene is set in a home where unhappy family members turn on each other. The individual prison and prison-like settings of the novel connect inextricably to complex webs of political, social, and criminal networks across London and Europe. Consequently, all of society appears as a prison, with each character suffering physical or mental captivity.[12] Forms of incarceration, confinement, and constraint represented in the novel are diverse: prisons for criminals and debtors (respectively the Marseilles prison for Rigaud and Cavalleto and the Marshalsea for William and Edward Dorrit and Arthur Clennam) and a remote mountain retreat (St. Bernard's monastery) where the monks unknowingly shelter escaped criminals.

But many prisons do not assure rehabilitation for the many criminals noted in the novel. Although only one unregenerate criminal appears (Rigaud), a number of characters in *Little Dorrit* are excessively punished (on stage or off) for transgressions in jails or similar situations (Dorrit, Clennam, Clennam's birth mother). Some characters are imprisoned by being physically constrained or in expressing compulsions: Mrs. Clennam confines herself to a wheelchair throughout most of the narrative, the celebrated banker Mr. Merdle continually cuffs himself, and Jeremiah Flintwich wears his tie under his ear as if hanging himself. Mrs. Merdle and Amy's sister Fanny scheme, the former for social dominance and the latter against her mother-in-law; their reciprocal obsessions create existential prisons in that their lives are consumed by hatred, a situation resembling that of the sinners eternally punished in Dante's *Inferno*. The "fascination" the narrator finds in Tip, who is constitutionally unable to stay in any job Amy finds for him, compels other characters as well and is linked to the novel's thematic of imprisonment: "Wherever he went, this foredoomed Tip appeared to take the prison walls with him and to set them up in such trade or calling; and to prowl about within their narrow limits in the old slip-shod, purposeless, down-at-heel way; until the real immovable Marshalsea walls asserted their fascination over him, and brought him back" (116).

Although it is the Dorrits who are linked most closely with the prison, even individuals with more money and social status reveal criminal and ethical lapses. For all his wealth and fame, Mr. Merdle has difficulties figuring out how to navigate society, remaining a wallflower during parties in his home (293) and an enigma suffering from a mysterious illness even as he is celebrated as a successful speculator

---

12 Regarding the central symbol of the prison, Trilling (1967: 148) argues that as the historical "particulars seem less immediate [...] the general force of the novel becomes greater."

whose investments attract money from others.[13] These facts become clues after his crime is discovered, although Merdle was always subject to his wife's scrutiny regarding his social behaviors. When Mrs. Merdle tells him that he carries his business into society, he responds "You supply manner, and I supply money" (447). She complains that is not enough, for he does not live up to her expectations and those of society that he should "seem to care about nothing" (447). Demurring, he questions "Did I ever say I care about anything?" only to be subjected to Mrs. Merdle's prodding her son Sparkler to state the common view of Merdle: "Fellers [...] occasionally compliment my Governor in a very handsome way on being immensely rich and knowing [...] but say [...] he carried the Shop about, on his back rather – like a Jew clothesman with too much business" (449). No one criticizes Merdle for making money, only for his manners (looking like he is always doing business), which could make people suspicious that he might be doing something unethical or illegal. Instead, his silence, constant work, and social awkwardness incur aesthetic (and racist) judgments until his conundrum (how to make money without seeming to do so) ultimately outs him in revealing his secret: he is rich as a result of fraudulently stealing others' investments. But he manages to conceal these crimes for a long time because everyone lauds him for his financial skill. The society that promotes Merdle as the brilliant speculator collaborates in his crimes by providing him a means of committing them: many people "know" of his business acumen, even the cynical Pancks and the cautious Arthur. The repetition and congruence of such information about Merdle's skills creates a 'truth' that even the skeptical eventually accept.

In tying the stories of the Dorrit and Clennam families together with those of the Meagles, Merdles, Plornishes – and even the villainous Rigaud and numerous Barnacles in public service – *Little Dorrit* episodically accounts for rapid movements from prison to affluence that seem easily reversible. William Dorrit is imprisoned for twenty-five years in the Marshalsea before he is released into society, where he lives in fear of discovery until becoming unhinged and revealing all at the most formal of dinner parties before finally collapsing. His last public speech memorializes the prison he can never leave, poignantly invoking his moment of degradation while celebrating what appears to be his greatest achievement, acting as the Father of the Marshalsea welcoming new prisoners (708). The overturning of financial expectations also provokes sympathy for Pancks and Clennam, who are caught short by the swings in the Merdle market after they enter into speculation.

Little Dorrit's original title *Nobody's Fault* appears an ironic claim, for the social problems examined – the punishments meted out to debtors, the philosophy of How Not to Do It emulated at the Circumlocution Office, the acceptance of shady business practices as brilliant financing, and the way self-interest assails innocence at every turn – are everyone's fault. The question of guilt in the novel remains unresolved. To be associated with a prisoner or even to be in jail is not a clear indication of moral failing, nor is avoiding arrest any protection from having criminal qualities or from being

13 For the mystery of Merdle, see Hobsbaum (1973).

punished. All too often, the innocent are subject to malicious parties who veil their insidious desires and actions.

Webs of Deceit

A shared thematic regarding selfishness and imprisonment as issues affecting character and environment connects various subplots of the novel. One thread of narrative concerning selfishness involves the host of excuses provided by dangerously obsessed, static characters. Rigaud's rationalization of how his wife forced him to murder her (49), Mrs. Clennam's account of stealing the child of her husband's lover (846), and Casby's continuing insistence that his employee Pancks squeeze the impoverished inhabitants of Bleeding Heart Yard demonstrate the ubiquity of criminality. Henry Gowan's willingness to see all fellows as "splendid," and his friend Sparkler's tendency to regard all women as "damned fine" reveal the speakers' intellectual and moral impoverishment, a common condition among those who treasure social standing and material acquisitions. These less criminally motivated characters let their self-interested obsessions limit their understanding of the world; in doing so, they demonstrate a tipping point for criminal behaviors that helps to shelter those who commit crimes, notably Merdle and Rigaud.

Excessive behaviors of certain individuals attract the attention of other characters and readers, but a close inspection of the narrative shows that sometimes the guilty are eventually punished. Most notably, Rigaud dies in the collapse of the Clennam house, and the crimes committed by Mr. Merdle come to light, prompting his suicide. Mrs. Clennam eventually confesses to Amy Dorrit about the codicil she hid to protect the Clennam family's shameful secret, that Arthur's true mother was a singer loved by Mr. Clennam. Other characters are also transformed in unexpected ways: Casby is made ridiculous when Pancks cuts his employer's hair, and Tattycoram suddenly returns to the Meagles.[14] But some, notably the Barnacles who perpetrate the policies and procedures of the Circumlocution Office, never acknowledge that their success requires the sacrifices of others. In representing such interrelations, the novel blames social pretensions, excessive religious zeal, and the conservative nature of social institutions in allowing and abetting crimes that too often imprison innocence.

Connections between characterization and setting enforce the thematic of imprisonment, as the ambiguous moral understanding of each character reflects the imprisoning aspects of his/her environment. Narrative theorist Shlomith Rimmon-Kenan (1983) outlines various modes of the direct and indirect presentation of character, the latter form including references to action, speech, external appearance, and environment. She notes that characterization is sometimes reinforced by analogies, particularly referring to name, landscape, and comparisons with other characters.[15] *Little Dorrit* makes use of all of these modes of characterization in that different minor

---

14 Young (1999: 75) comments on the class issues associated with this action.

15 See also Sipe (1975).

characters are developed via one mode or another, and primary and other major characters are developed via more than one mode. The novel appears a rich texture of characterizations enlivening dreary settings and reinforcing the thematic of innocence under siege in a world of ambiguous morality.

While the stylistics of diverse characterizations differ, they develop themes of imprisonment, social inequity, and struggling innocence, continuing the realist tradition of incorporating loosely scientific ideas about physiognomy and environment to connect moral character to appearance and landscape.[16] Dickens's characters compel the reader's attentions whether one accepts them as mimetic, thematic, or synthetic constructs.[17] Linking qualities of individual characters and various settings, *Little Dorrit* classifies each individual within the larger social system. Every character in the novel appears an ethical specimen demonstrating the Dickensian principle that to be human is to have some predisposition toward guilty thoughts and/or conduct.[18] Consequently, society inclines toward degeneration and corruption even though a few individuals are upstanding citizens and generous toward humanity.

Every character represents a mix of good and bad impulses, based on instincts and behaviors that cannot be easily mapped on a spreadsheet. In keeping with the murky plot and somewhat indistinct setting of the city of London, the moral calculus of the novel shifts according to ongoing interactions among characters. The difficulty of comparing variant forms of falseness, cheating, and ingratitude based on particular situations and circumstances challenges the imagination. Dickens's novel acknowledges that all (even the sympathetic Arthur and Amy) are at fault and suffer for it; however, the narrative suggests that redemption is possible, even if it is rare and incomplete. That Mrs. Clennam is capable of regretting the consequences of her behavior and apologizing to Amy for the long standing crime of hiding the legacy due the latter redeems what appears to be an unregenerate character who is defined by vindictiveness. Yet no amount of rehabilitation could save the assassin Rigaud, or Edward, or Fanny Dorrit, who are doomed by their worst behaviors and attitudes even when they become heirs to a fortune that saves them from penury, if not perversity.

As everyone in *Little Dorrit* is guilty of some crime or moral error, even excessive love and generosity are depicted as problems. Amy, who never commits a crime and who devotes herself to protecting her family and many others, also appears subject to the jail's corrupting influence. Learning her father can be released but still must pay his debts, she asks Arthur, "You are glad that he should do so?" After Arthur affirms

---

16 A number of essays focus on relatively minor characters to open up the novel, including Wilde (1964) and Bell (1965).

17 See Phelan (1989: 9): "The distinction between dimensions and functions is based on the principle that the fundamental unit of character is neither the trait nor the idea, neither the role nor the word, but rather what I will call the *attribute*, something that participates at least in potential form in the mimetic, thematic, and synthetic spheres of meaning simultaneously. Thus, the rhetorical theorist need not stipulate in advance that the characters in a given work will be represented people, or themes with legs, or obvious artificial constructs."

18 Gold (1972) and Reed (1998) offer extended analyses of ethics in Dickens's novels.

he is "most heartily glad!", Amy tries to believe the same; yet she cannot help but say of her father "It seems to me hard [...] that he should have lost so many years and suffered so much, and at last pay all the debts as well. It seems to me hard that he should pay in life and money both" (472). The narrator notes,

> The prison, which could spoil so many things, had tainted Little Dorrit's mind no more than this. Engendered as the confusion was, in compassion for the poor prisoner, her father, it was the first speck Clennam had ever seen, it was the last speck Clennam ever saw, of the prison atmosphere upon her. (472)

The narrator suggests obliquely that perhaps Amy is right: her father has paid too heavy a price, in both years and money. Clennam regards such a thought as deviant in believing that some debts require an overpayment of money and time, an idea his own imprisonment enacts.

Amy regards her father's sentence (and later Arthur's) as a pointless cruelty if he eventually pays his debt. The narrative points the way toward seeing the existing social system and its methods of criminal justice as corrupt beyond repair. It is no wonder that George Bernard Shaw accused the novel of being "a more seditious book than *Das Kapital*" (Price 1967: 1).[19] That Arthur upholds the equity of charging a prisoner money even after many years served indicates that his morality is shaped by rigid law and upholds conventional practice, while Amy is willing to think about a more ideal world. As the novel works hard to caricature, criticize, and inveigh against all sorts of social pretension, it appears that Amy's wistful regret marks her as a singular individual, not only in being more innocent than others, but as one who is capable of recognizing the falseness of society without making that into an obsession. Although Arthur recoils at Amy's idea of her father's paying twice as characterizing corruption, the narrator suggests that Arthur is already corrupted by socially conventional principles of gentility; perhaps his moral development owes too much to his mother's rigid religious principles. Readers who regard Amy as a figure of superhuman goodness, someone who inspires Clennam and Pancks to take on the Dorrit cause and Mr. Meagles to help release Arthur, might be more sympathetic to her point that demanding sentence and payment requires too much of Dorrit.

Like Amy, readers evaluate the appropriate relations of actions and consequences. Facing a plethora of characters identified by their weird tics, odd looks, and/or selfish attitudes, the reader inevitably classifies them according to similarities and differences and weaves assumptions about them into a narrative, much as their fellow characters do. Arthur's interest in figuring out who Little Dorrit is and what sin his mother might have committed against the long incarcerated William Dorrit has its counterpart in the reader's interest in figuring out what the escaped wife murderer Rigaud might be up to in befriending the Gowans (Book II, Chapter 1). The novel's depiction of social pretensions and hypocrisies and the inclusion of many twins, doubles, and shadows are

---

19 Quoting George Bernard Shaw, Foreword to a limited edition of *Great Expectations* (Edinburgh, 1937); reprinted in 'The Novel Library' (London, 1947).

hints that readers might productively classify characters within a moral hierarchy depending on the moral failings and corrupt associations of the purported elite. Sometimes references to moral failures such as tendencies to vapidity and violence connect literal twins such as the Meagles girls or the Flintwich men. Other doubles link characters according to their similar social roles (Amy and Arthur as moral centers, Tattycoram and Miss Wade as resentful women, Mrs. Merdle and Mrs. Gowan as socially prominent women seeking advantage). Certain characters stalk others; for instance, to close in on Mrs. Clennam, Rigaud shadows Arthur.[20]

Dickens's Criticism of Social Bonds

Discontinuities in characterizations are also critical in developing an understanding of how concerns about social propriety can trump moral actions. Brian Rosenberg argues that the enigmatic, fragmented presentations of characters suggest the instability and murkiness of the fictional world: "[T]he process of characterization in Dickens is one in which the novelist attempts to understand an unstable internal life through unreliable external signs and to convey his understanding through an imperfect medium" (Rosenberg 1996). Individual characters provide source material for developing the novel's identifiable, related themes of imprisonment, selfish obsessions, and social conventions depending on hypocritical proprieties rather than morality. Dickens establishes a chain of characters, linking them to reveal the haphazard arrangement of society, the precariousness of family and social relationships, and the likelihood of transgression. Plots developing suspicions about past behavior and criticisms of present actions emerge out of how/when/why these odd characters meet each other.

The themes of imprisonment, innocence, and propriety, which suggest that no one can be completely free of transgression in a corrupt society, also connect characters who never or scarcely meet in the narrative. Physical constraints and psychological attitudes are imprisoning for both Mrs. Clennam and the "Bohemians," those residents of Hampton Court (Dickens 1975: 360) whose pretensions toward aristocracy make possible their makeshift arrangements in a state-supported residence. As already noted, various other domestic situations hold individuals, including the economically, socially, or emotionally limited households (respectively the Plornishes and the Tite Barnacles, the Meagles, the Merdles, and the Sparkles). A number of discarded lovers are sentenced to lives deprived of romance (Flora Finching, Miss Rugg, John Chivery), and some married couples appear indissolubly glued to one another despite their different outlooks (the Merdles, the Gowans, the Sparkles), confirming that mental constructions limiting one's outlook or prospects can be as daunting as physical confinement.

---

20 Developing Miller's claim that "'shadow' is the 'most frequently recurring' of certain key words in *Little Dorrit*," Showalter (1979) connects various characters. See also Miller (1958: 230, 229).

Establishing a tone of bitter humor, Dickens describes class protocols reigning at all levels of society as harmful in that they hold innocence captive. Money and marriage mix inappropriately, thereby enabling abusive relationships. The Dorrits' predilection for trumpeting their supposed noble background and the Merdles' ostentatious grandeur share the same root. Mrs. Gowan's snobbish attempt to prevent her impoverished cad of a son from marrying sweet Pet Meagles mistakenly characterizes the girl's family as social upstarts, rather than as genuinely loving parents who regret their daughter's unfortunate choice of an arrogant suitor.

The marriage prison that Pet Meagles enters serves to warn the reader of the constraining aspects of romantic passion. While in some respects *Little Dorrit* can be described as a romance in that the two most moral and sympathetic characters Arthur and Amy marry and their marriage ends the tale, the novel more frequently intimates those high costs of the marriage market that make it resemble the Merdle stock market. Male privilege and financial power make it difficult for women to benefit from marriage, according to the numerous instances described in the book. Mismatched romances result in comedy and near tragedy for many women: Miss Ruggs, the successful plaintiff in a breach of promise suit; Flora Finching, Arthur's former sweetheart: and the always hopeful Mrs. General are all caricatures of female desire engaged in battle with male social authority to end their attenuated states as single women. Miss Wade's unfortunate romantic history includes a broken engagement and an ill-fated liaison with the same Henry Gowan who takes up with the wealthier Pet. Flora's legacy from her deceased husband Mr. Finching, Mr. F's Aunt, provides another sign that a system mixing marriage and money spits out eccentric women who are unable to accommodate normal interactions. Mr. F's Aunt sputters what some have regarded as inane nonsense and others regard as prescient social criticism, albeit issued in bursts of inappropriate comments on others' conversations. Social courtesies mean nothing to this old woman nor to Mrs. Clennam, whose marriage ended unhappily because it was arranged for economic and religious reasons rather than love. *Little Dorrit* represents marriage as a punishment for some and a withheld reward for others, indicating that women are always vulnerable and often abused by what is mistakenly assumed to be a sentimental institution rather than another social mechanism controlling individual desire.

Other social conventions and pretensions ensnare but fail to support individuals or families. Amy Dorrit's virtues remain invisible to her family (with the exception of her mentally confused uncle), despite her constant efforts to supply them with money, to find them jobs, and to furnish her father's meager household in the Marshalsea. William Dorrit presumes on his overweening sense of gentility to encourage his patriarchal persona as the Father of the Marshalsea, but he is, as many have noted, a poor father to Amy. He refuses to acknowledge her labors because to do so would put him to shame him as a gentleman. Instead, he lectures his younger daughter within prison and without on her duty to her family. The narrator's comparison of Amy to the Roman daughter who breast-fed her incarcerated father to keep him alive (273) accompanies William Dorrit's suggestion that Amy might respond affectionately to the turnkey John Chivery's courtship as a means of enhancing the quality of her father's life in prison. This suggestion falls hard on Amy, who understands, but never accustoms herself to her father's expectation of his daughter's uncomplaining sacrifice of everything, even her moral integrity, for his benefit. She consequently wonders if she has ever "seen" her father since all she has known is a man exploiting her to uphold his pride (276). Dorrit's behavior marks him as immature and selfish, while Amy's is stoic. She refuses to defend herself when her father or her sister berate her for wearing shabby clothes, helping paupers (421), and gently criticizes their morally dubious behavior.

After William Dorrit leaves the Marshalsea and becomes a wealthy gentleman, he resents Amy's unwillingness to play her assigned role as a socialite, and the tables turn. At this point, Amy's innocence becomes a lightning rod for criticisms that imprison her in others' expectations. Fanny, Tip, and the father are eager to forget that they ever resided in prison, while Amy cannot separate her new identity from her old one as the child of the Marshalsea. She is more constrained out of prison than she was as a resident, for she now has an overseer imposed on her in Mrs. General and more vociferous critics, as her father and sister lecture her about what their station requires. Mrs. General's advice to work at maintaining a surface rather than expressing any true feelings confuses Amy (530), and she is dumbfounded by her sister Fanny's determination to marry the deficient Sparkler because it would annoy his mother (Mrs. Merdle).

Amy's innocence resists general corruption, as she refuses to be mired down by others' moral failings. As Alison Booth argues in comparing Amy to Dorothea Brooke, Dickens and George Eliot reconfigure innocence as power: "[S]uch perdurable virtue, weighing rather heavily on the heroines expected to uphold it is ultimately no mere amenity of the parlor. Its diffusive influence could redeem the world from a deadly round of experience" (Booth 1986: 201). Edwin Barrett considers the novel's presentation of a diseased society with Merdle as a source of illness and Clennam as someone infected with the age's malady, while Amy is "the agent of that composed spiritual health" who exemplifies "the healing power of taking up the Duty which lies the nearest" (1970: 214, 213). No one thinks more highly of Amy than Arthur, Pancks, and Meagles, whose assistance in effecting respectively the release of her father and the release of Arthur from the Marshalsea makes her happiness possible. It is critical that Amy gains power in renunciation; as Hilary Schor notes of the novel, it "seems to argue that in a world without separate female property, sacrifice is common sense" (1999: 145). Amy's unwillingness to accept her family's claims regarding morality and appropriate behavior and her renunciation of conventions exemplify her innocence, while social proprieties, nonetheless, make it possible for her to be scapegoated.

The force of social approbation described in the novel serves as a means of surveillance, control, and punishment. Even when this force is recognized, it is not well understood by the characters or well represented by the narrator, for it is insidious in its capacities. As noted already, Arthur's love for Amy does not prevent him from seeing her as somewhat tainted by her wish for forgiveness for rather than payment from her father. Other characters tied to Amy and Arthur also represent the sufferings of innocence. The irrepressible Mr. Meagles, who, like Amy, is represented as loving his family too much, reveals a vulnerability to social conventions and courtesies, even those he recognizes as superfluous. His irritation with the Circumlocution Office does not prevent him from appreciating the Barnacles attending Pet's marriage dinner: "It's very gratifying [...]. Such high company" (459). The Meagles' fortunes, like those of Amy and Arthur, also improve: Mr. and Mrs. Meagle welcome back Tattycoram into their household and are relieved to see Pet and her child without her husband, a solution encouraged by the overbearing, condescending Henry, who prefers to take the Meagles' money without speaking with them.

Although Mr. Meagles has limitations, notably his inability to understand why Tattycoram might feel exploited and his tendency to behave as a boorish English tourist when abroad, he appreciates and articulates Amy Dorrit's virtues in pointing her out as a exemplar to his ward:

> If she had constantly thought of herself, and settled with herself that everybody visited this place upon her, turned it against her, and cast it at her, she would have led an irritable and probably a useless existence. Yet I have heard tell, Tattycoram, that her young life has been one of active resignation, goodness, and noble service. (881)

Mr. Meagles explains that he has always seen "duty" in Amy's eyes, echoing her uncle Frederick's praise of the girl to Clennam (134: "She does her duty."). Countering Amy's father's and sister's criticisms, Meagles's explanation credits her for rising above the circumstances of her birth in prison without criticizing her father. Like Arthur, he recognizes that Amy's innocence is based on many invisible labors rather than being an inherent quality of her character. To protect her as well as her lover, Mr. Meagles then takes off on a trip to France to bring back Doyce to help clear Clennam.

Concluding Thoughts

Like duty, innocence is questioned in a novel assuming most people combine good and bad qualities and suggesting generosity such as the Meagles' indulgence of Pet and forgiveness such as Amy's for her father can be viewed as tainted or transgressive.[21] Similarly, Amy's sympathy toward her family and Doyce's forgiveness of Arthur's poor management of their partnership funds are critical elements of their characters. Yet Amy and Doyce are largely unappreciated by others. Doyce finds life abroad more congenial to his inventive activities, while Amy is often abused by those who ought to thank her. Their treatment indicates that while sentimental logic recommends such selflessness, it is too rare to make much of an overall difference. Perhaps if everyone were to forgive people and renounce money as easily as Amy Dorrit and Daniel Doyce do, then the current general economy of crime and punishment would fall apart, for the hierarchy that depends on family connections, money, and manners cannot withstand a climate of generosity, helpfulness, and innovation.

---

21 For a study of the transformative powers of innocence, see Rogers (1972).

Near the end of the novel, as the convoluted plot unravels, readers observe that Amy has another defender in Mrs. Clennam. Assailed by the blackmailer Rigaud who insists he will proclaim her shameful secret, Mrs. Clennam admits to him, along with Flintwich and Affery, that after she learned of the illegitimate relationship between her husband and the singer, she forced Arthur's mother to cede him to her. Mrs. Clennam indicates she wanted to save the boy from the parents' shame and punish them at the same time. Arthur's mother lost the opportunity to raise her child and spent the rest of life as a lunatic mourning that loss; the singer was further defrauded of a bequest from Arthur's great uncle that was intended to ameliorate her predicament. By hiding proof of that bequest from a series of its intended legatees (Arthur's birth mother, her protector Frederick Dorrit, and his niece Amy), Mrs. Clennam refuses to forgive or ignore what she represents as injustices committed against her. In addition to being angry with her husband and his lover, she resents that Amy's uncle Frederick Dorrit trained the singer and supplied the meeting place for Arthur's parents.

Until Rigaud threatens to reveal her theft of the bequest, Mrs. Clennam hid the information that part of Gilbert Clennam's fortune was designated for Frederick Dorrit's youngest niece, Amy. Mrs. Clennam's explanation to Rigaud characterizes her actions as necessary, because to allow the bequest would be "a rewarding of sin; the wrong result of a delusion" (849). Her account of sin and money also pits love and art against religious duty. Her life has been devoted to a project that harms in seeking to benefit: she nearly destroys any chance of happiness for Arthur while aiming to save his soul. After Mrs. Clennam runs to find Amy at the Marshalsea, the old woman finally tells the girl the truth, calling her "innocent" and asking her to keep the truth from Arthur. According to her character, Amy protects Mrs. Clennam and Arthur by keeping the secret and abjuring the money.

Because many novel readers are more sympathetic to romantic passion than religious piety, Mrs. Clennam's punishing of sin appears worse than the secret relationship between Arthur's father and mother. One of Dickens's philanthropies involved supporting charitable homes for prostitutes that would help these women find marriages in Australia and South Africa.[22] Seen in the context of such progressive views of female sexuality, Arthur's birth mother was a victim of the rabidly religious Mrs. Clennam. In this way, Dickens's narrative connects the family plot to the sociopolitical critique in the novel in arguing against pious propriety and seemingly upstanding families, for appearances belie both the corrupting force of Mrs. Clennam's vindictive jealousy and its outcomes of repression and fear.

Arthur's birth mother's relationship with his father initiated a chain of events that could not be stopped until the secret marriage and Arthur's birth could be understood as innocent rather than guilty. Dickens's novel turns out to be a long plea of innocence for an offstage character – Arthur's mother, who only appears in the text as an imagined apparition frightening Affery and as a memory of Mrs. Clennam – whose love motivates the jealous hatred of a more powerful rival. That Amy finally receives

22 Dickens's work in the late 1840s on behalf of Urania Cottage, a home for former prostitutes, is noted in Kaplan (1988: 228-29).

the legacy long-denied Arthur's mother only to sacrifice a claim on it for the love of Arthur demonstrates the critical link between the child born in prison and the mother in the asylum who is deprived of her child. The outcomes for these two women designate them as innocent convicts, despite their different temperaments and appearances. Arthur's mother bends first to Clennam and then his wife, while Amy appears childlike and acts motherly with a quiet strength. Both women sacrifice their claims, to child and to money, for the sake of Arthur, and both women are subject to incarcerations that indict social conventions as heartless.

Little Dorrit offers an enigmatic ending of romantic lovers casting off an inheritance while continuing the burden of caring for others, as the younger generation (Amy and Arthur) pays for the actions of the older (Arthur's parents). There has been some social progress in that Amy's love improves her life and the lives of others who accept her influence, while Arthur's mother never had a chance to combat the deadly forces of social respectability that doomed her liaison and took away her child. Yet Amy continues to pay for crimes she did not commit; her story, like that of Arthur's mother, proposes that existing social values are hypocritical and cruel and that the criminal justice system, which causes needless suffering for those who do not deserve to be punished, ought to be reformed.

Works Cited

Barrett, Edwin (1970) "*Little Dorrit* and the Disease of Modern Life." *Nineteenth-Century Fiction* 25.2: 199-215.

Bell, Vereen (1965) "Mrs. General as Victorian England." *Nineteenth-Century Fiction* 20.2: 177-84.

Booth, Alison (1986) "Little Dorrit and Dorothea Brooke: Interpreting the Heroines of History." *Nineteenth-Century Literature* 41.2: 190-216.

Briggs, C. F. (1845) "The Innocent Convict." *United States Magazine and Democratic Review* 17.85: 17-23.

Carlisle, Janice (1975) "*Little Dorrit*: Necessary Fictions." *Studies in the Novel* 195-214.

Chevalier, Louis (1973) *Laboring Classes and Dangerous Classes*. Trans. Frank Jellinek. New York: Howard Fertig.

Clayton, Jay (1991) "Dickens and the Genealogy of Postmodernism." *Nineteenth-Century Literature*. 46.2: 181-95.

Colatrella, Carol (2002) "Summary Judgment in *Billy Budd*." *Literature and Moral Reform: Melville and the Discipline of Reading*. Gainesville, FL: Univ. Press of Florida. 227-245.

Collins, Philip (1962) *Dickens and Crime*. Bloomington, IN: Indiana Univ. Press, 1962.

The Compact Edition of the Oxford English Dictionary. Oxford: Oxford Univ. Press, 1971.

Dickens, Charles (1975) *Little Dorrit* [1855-57]. Ed. John Holloway. Harmondsworth: Penguin.

Easson, Angus (1974) "Marshalsea Prisoners: Mr. Dorrit and Mr. Hemens." *Dickens Studies Annual*: 77-86.

Gold, Joseph (1972) *Charles Dickens: Radical Moralist*. Minneapolis, MN: Univ. of Minnesota Press.

Hennelly, Mark (1997) "The Games of the Prison Children." *Nineteenth-Century Contexts* 20.2: 187-213.

Hobsbaum, Philip (1973) *A Reader's Guide to Charles Dickens*. New York: Farrar, Straus and Giroux.

Kaplan, Fred (1988) *Dickens*. New York: Avon.

Miller, J. Hillis (1958) *Charles Dickens: The World of His Novels*. Cambridge, MA: Harvard Univ. Press.

Phelan, James (1989) *Reading People, Reading Plots: Character, Progression, and the Interpretation of Narrative*. Chicago, IL: Univ. of Chicago Press.

Philpotts, Trey (1991) "The Real Marshalsea." *The Dickensian* 87: 130-45.

Price, Martin (1967) "Introduction." *Dickens: A Collection of Critical Essays*. Ed. Martin Price. Englewood Cliffs, NJ: Prentice-Hall. 1-15.

Rainsford, Dominic (1995) "Flatness and Ethical Responsibility in *Little Dorrit*." *Victorian Newsletter* 88: 11-17.

Rotkin, Charlotte (1989) *Deception in Dickens' Little Dorrit*. Frankfurt/Main: Peter Lang.

Reed, John R. (1998) *Dickens and Thackeray: Punishment and Forgiveness*. Athens, OH: Ohio Univ. Press.

Reynolds, David (1989) *Beneath the American Renaissance: The Subversive Imagination in the Age of Emerson and Melville*. Cambridge, MA: Harvard Univ. Press.

Rimmon-Kenan, Shlomith (1983) "Text: Characterization." *Narrative Fiction: Contemporary Poetics*. London: Routledge. 59-70.

Rogers, Philip (1972) "Mr. Pickwick's Innocence." *Nineteenth-Century Fiction* 27.1: 21-37.

Rosenberg, Brian (1996) *Little Dorrit's Shadows: Character and Contradiction in Dickens*. Columbia, MI: Univ. of Missouri Press.

Schor, Hilary M. (1999) *Dickens and the Daughter of the House*. Cambridge: Cambridge Univ. Press.

Sen, Sambudha (1998) "Bleak House and Little Dorrit: The Radical Heritage." *ELH* 65 (4): 945-970.

Showalter, Elaine (1979) "Guilt, Authority, and the Shadows of Little Dorrit." *Nineteenth-Century Fiction* 34.1: 20-40.

Sipe, Samuel (1975) "The Intentional World of Dickens' Fiction." *Nineteenth-Century Fiction* 30.1: 1-19.

Smith, Jonathan (2000) "Darwin's Barnacles, Dickens' *Little Dorrit*, and the Social Uses of Victorian Seaside Studies." *LIT* 10: 327-47.

Trilling, Lionel (1967) *"Little Dorrit."* *Dickens: A Collection of Critical Essays*. Ed. Martin Price. Englewood Cliffs, NJ: Prentice-Hall. 147-57.

Wilde, Alan (1964) "Mr. F's Aunt and the Analogical Structure of Little Dorrit." *Nineteenth-Century Fiction* 19.1: 33-44.

Young, Arlene (1999) *Culture, Class, and Gender in the Victorian Novel: Gentlemen, Gents and Working Women*. Basingstoke: Palgrave Macmillan.

Prison, Passion, and the Female Gaze: Twentieth-Century Representations of Nineteenth-Century Panopticons

Heidi Slettedahl Macpherson

Twentieth-century women writers engage in metaphorical rewritings of the panopticon, inserting explicit and implicit references to it within many of their novels on women and the law. Designed by Jeremy Bentham as an "inspection-house" and made famous by Michel Foucault's incisive reading of it, the panopticon is a place to set aside and observe the criminal, the damaged, or the subject who needs to be contained. Its central watchtower overlooking a circular arrangement of back-lit chambers, or cells, ensures that the prisoner believes herself to be threatened with observation at all times. The (apparently constant) gaze here becomes linked to punishment, with the observed prisoner always at risk of being caught breaking the rules. The result is an internalization of the law, of propriety, and a "new mode of obtaining power of mind over mind, in a quantity hitherto without example" (Bentham 1787: 2). Foucault (1975/1991) analyzes how the gaze becomes internalized, and feminist critics such as Sandra Lee Bartky (1988) have added a corrective to his work, by exploring the implications of gender in relation to the power structures of the panopticon.

Such is the power of this image that women writers of the twentieth century utilize its imposing structure in their own explorations of women, power, and the law. Thus we have Angela Carter exploring the labyrinths of power and the gaze in her fantastic novel, *Nights at the Circus* (1984/1994), Margaret Atwood examining the role of the gazed upon within and outside prison walls in *Alias Grace* (1996), and, perhaps most overtly, Sarah Waters investigating the "queer" effects of the panopticon on inmates and visitors alike in her novel *Affinity* (1999/2000). What these writers do, however, is subvert the hierarchical notion of the prisoners as powerless, the authorities as powerful; the women inmates in the texts above turn from gaze to touch, find the power in being gazed upon, or harness the illusion of control for their own purposes. Moreover, in explicitly or implicitly seeking "improper" relationships, these fictional prisoners step outside their prisons and wrest control from those who seek to contain them.

While the purpose of the panopticon, as Foucault reminds us, is "to see constantly and recognize immediately" (1991: 200), in these fictional texts about the nineteenth century, gaze, sight and recognition are far from equivalent. Indeed, it is in their very mapping of misrecognitions that they exert their force. Carter's female murderesses reject the part offered to them of penitent sinners and refuse to express repentance, even though they know such a stance will keep them in thrall to a governess's pitiless gaze. Alternatively, Grace Marks willingly (and wilfully?) plays the part of madwoman, murderess, and wrongfully accused. Finally, Selina Dawes, the "wrongfully" imprisoned spiritualist in *Affinity*, uses shadows and illusion – the central mechanisms of the panopticon – in order to control Margaret, her link to the outside world. In each of these texts, the female gaze constructs the love object; in *Alias Grace*, it even incorporates it, as Grace Marks "becomes" Mary Whitney, her friend and spectral conspirator.

The gaze has long been a subject of feminist analysis, with Laura Mulvey's article "Visual Pleasure and Narrative Cinema" (1975) kick-starting the exploration of how the male gaze is normalized in film. Scopophilia, or pleasure in looking, is clearly gendered. As Bartky acknowledges, "Under male scrutiny, women will avert their eyes or cast them downward; the female gaze is trained to abandon its claim to the sovereign status of seer" (1988: 67). Bartky further argues that "a panoptical male connoisseur resides within the consciousness of most women: they stand perpetually before his gaze and under his judgment. Woman lives her body as seen by another, by an anonymous patriarchal Other" (1988: 72). It is this patriarchal Other who is the implicit subject of each of the novels I analyze here, as the women who are being watched, themselves take control, subverting the underlying principles of the panopticon for their own ends. This essay explores *Nights at the Circus*, *Alias Grace* and *Affinity* as texts which utilize and subvert the power of the panopticon, inserting instead a feminine gaze that allows for illusion, performance, and subversive control.

Nights at the Circus: A Women's Panopticon?

Joanne Gass (1994) argues that Angela Carter's *Nights at the Circus* is "a novel about the ways in which the dominant, frequently male-centered discourses of power marginalize those whom society defines as freaks (...in particular, women) so that they may be contained and controlled because they are all possible sources of the chaotic disruption of established power" (Gass 1994: 71). In all aspects, then, and in all arenas where Carter's women perform (the circus of the title, the brothel, the freak show, and, in particular, the prison), power is central to the narrative. As is typical for Carter, though, such power is asserted only to be subverted. This is particularly apparent in her structuring of the prison as a panopticon. In contrast to *Alias Grace* and *Affinity*, the prison in *Nights at the Circus* serves as little more than an aside in the central, fantastic tale of Fevvers, Carter's peripatetic, winged woman. Indeed, the idea of a prison as an "aside" – a place to set aside and forget, as it were – makes the panoptical images particularly intriguing. Carter spends a mere two chapters exploring the panopticon before she allows her female prisoners the freedom to vanish from the prison and the text. What she does in this space, however, remains central to a feminist reading of punishment and release.

The Countess P., aware of her own guilt in relation to the poisoning of her husband, sets up a "private asylum for female criminals" (Carter 1994: 210).[1] The narrator cautions, "Do not run away with the idea it was a sense of sisterhood that moved her" (210). Indeed, in each of these texts, the concept of sisterhood is undermined, even as female relationships become central to the narratives, through design or desire. The Countess P. believes herself to be "a kind of conduit for the means of the repentance of the other murderesses" (210). Unpunished herself, she remains thus unforgiven, and can only approximate her own penitence through building a penitentiary for others:

> It was a *panopticon* she forced them to build, a hollow circle of cells shaped like a doughnut, the inward-facing wall of which was composed of grids of steel and, in the middle of the roofed, central courtyard, there was a round room surrounded by windows. In that room she'd sit all day and stare and stare and stare at her murderesses and they, in turn, sat all day and stared at her. (ibid.)

Carter's explicit awareness of Foucault's reading of the panopticon becomes clear in the way that she appropriates his language to describe it. Carter notes: "During the hours of darkness, the cells were lit up like so many small theatres in which each actor sat by herself in the trap of her visibility" (211), words which are more than reminiscent of Foucault's description: "They are like so many cages, so many small theatres, in which each actor is alone. [...] Visibility is a trap" (Foucault 1991: 200).

Carter's foray into the world of the panopticon starts with a factual, dry tone, indicating the power of the prison, while occasionally letting in a ray of humor, noting, for example: "There are many reasons, most of them good ones, why a woman should want to murder her husband" (210). The dry third-person narrative is disrupted by these insertions, as well as a later, second-person insertion: "[...] you were never alone, here, where her gaze was continually upon you, and yet you were always alone" (213). This change to second person voice implicates the reader, forcing us to join with the inmates in our visible solitude. At the same time, it provokes the question: are the inmates still imprisoned when we ourselves aren't looking? The convention of referring to textual events in the present tense suggests they are; the inmates are always stared at and staring back, always in the moment of being watched. That the past tense does not apply to discussions of textual events suggests no end to their imprisonment, as they are imprisoned afresh each time a new reader glances at the page. Thus we become both prisoners (addressed and included in "you") and prison wardens of a different kind in reading about these events.

Carter's postmodern and playful disruption of a stable position – you, I, they – is also in evidence in the way that she takes Foucault's reading one step further, acknowledging the manner in which the gazer becomes imprisoned within this dynamic as well. The narrator is aware of the Countess's own entrapment: "the price she paid for her hypothetical proxy repentance was her own incarceration, trapped as securely in her watchtower by the exercise of her power as its objects were in their

1 Future references to this edition will be given in the text.

cells" (214). Moreover, the Countess remains blind to this fact (despite her constant gaze), while the prisoners themselves acquire power through this knowledge. Furthermore, they realize, if she does not, that they will never be freed from this prison, despite her claim that she will release the truly penitent. Victims of male abuse, these women seek not humility but justice, and find it through a disruption of the patterns of behavior governing wardens and inmates.

Thus Olga Alexandrovna leads an "army of lovers" when she finally dares first to touch, and then to gaze upon her female warden, breaking the power of isolation and containment. Here, the prisoner breaks with what Bartky calls "the economy of touching" (1988: 67). Bartky argues that who touches whom, how often, and where, is influenced by hierarchical organizations of power. Thus, the powerless (in Bartky's example, women) suffer inappropriate touch (a grope, a slap) in ways that men do not, and men are licensed to touch women in a variety of ways. In Carter's novel, this power is reversed; it is the prisoner who touches first, who breaks the boundary between them. Once touch is established – as loving, as desirable – then gaze follows, at first surreptitiously, then more boldly.

Emboldened by mutual desire, the women in the prison begin longing, loving relationships hinted at through "notes, drawings, caresses, glances" (217) until they overthrow the central power of the Countess and effect their own release and freedom. Appropriately, "[t]hey left the countess secured in her observatory with nothing to observe any longer but the spectre of her own crime, which came in at once through the open gate to haunt her as she continued to turn round and round in her chair" (218). If sisterhood, in its idealized representation, suggests a loving relationship and a lack of violence, and aggression, it does not preclude, it seems, the meting out of justice.

Carter's exploration of the panopticon reveals the way in which the authoritative gaze inscribed by the panopticon is subverted, once the gazed upon understand the mutually-imprisoning aspect of this look. Moreover, her novel explores how these imprisoned and "docile" bodies assert themselves as uncontainable when their pleasures are released from normative control.

Kingston Penitentiary, *Alias Grace* and the Object of a Panoptical Gaze

In Atwood's *Alias Grace*, imprisonment lasts much longer, and takes more than one form, thus a longer discussion of this text is called for, beginning with the historical actualities of the prisoner and the prison to which Atwood refers. Atwood's Grace Marks is sent to the insane asylum, the prison, and, on separate but connected occasions, private homes in order to "play out" her penitence. The historical Marks was imprisoned for over twenty-eight years for her part in the murder of her employer, Thomas Kinnear. Kinnear's housekeeper-mistress, Nancy Montgomery, was also murdered, but neither Marks nor her co-accused, James McDermott, was ever convicted of this offence. Grace Marks was confined primarily in Kingston Penitentiary, Ontario, and finally pardoned in 1872, after which she disappeared from public record. The day before her release, like all convicts on their discharge from the Penitentiary, she was asked a series of "Liberation" questions, which were recorded in the Liberation Question Book.[2] Such questions concerned the conditions at the prison, the length of incarceration of the inmate, and the authorities' fears of a conspiracy; thus they move from enquiring about the prisoner's experiences, to any knowledge she might have about what others were plotting against the prison administration. Grace's answers are almost always single words – yes, or no – and reveal no further information than is strictly required. In this way, the historical Grace Marks is much like Atwood's construction of her: a withholding witness who refuses at some level to tell her own story. Indeed, there are enough versions around without her own contribution to create a multiple reading of her guilt or innocence.

Kingston Penitentiary, perhaps because of its unique history as the first federal prison in the Canadian criminal justice system, has seen its share of literary representations. In the same year that *Alias Grace* was published, Merilyn Simonds's *The Convict Lover* (1996) appeared. Subtitled "A True Story," it includes photographs of the prison and its prisoners as proof of the story's truth. Like Atwood, Simonds constructs the story from fragments that are lodged in Queen's University Archives in Kingston, Ontario; she also acknowledges the many memoirs and other texts written about Kingston Penitentiary, including Roger Caron's well-known *Go Boy* (1978). Kingston Penitentiary is thus symbolically important as a site of incarceration for Ontario and beyond. *The Convict Lover* explores what it meant to be labeled a prisoner, and how that label followed the prisoner wherever he went. As Simonds notes, "According to the [Penitentiary] Act, wherever a convict set foot was penitentiary land, and so the boundaries of Portsmouth village flexed as the prison work gangs passed" (1996: 29). That there is no escape from this label accords with contemporary investigations of the panopticon, a prison structure meant to enact the threat of constant surveillance while inhibiting the prisoner's ability to see (Foucault 1991: 200). Kingston Penitentiary was at least partly based on the ideal panopticon first described by Jeremy Bentham in his letters of 1787.

Kingston Penitentiary, the site of historical confinement and literary release, was built to be one of the largest public buildings in Upper Canada, and was erected for five main reasons: "the death penalty was not being executed for crimes less than murder, fines were unjust, local gaols were bad because they lumped young offenders with seasoned criminals, corporal punishment was improper and degrading, and banishment was unenforceable and often no punishment at all" (Taylor 1988: 224). The presence of a British garrison as well as large quantities of stone ensured that Kingston was an ideal site for this new prison. This admixture of moral and material reasons ironically highlights the mixed messages implied by the Canadian prison reform that Kingston Penitentiary represents.

In the article "The Kingston, Ontario Penitentiary and Moral Architecture," C. J. Taylor outlines the factors that contributed to the development of the Kingston Penitentiary. As Taylor notes, its walls "would allow the keeper to observe the prisoners through apertures even when they were in their cells but would prevent the prisoners from knowing whether or not they were being watched, giving the impression of continuous surveillance" (Taylor 1988: 229). In Bentham's proposed

2 Queen's University Archives MF 2342, Book 11, May 2, 1871-May 3, 1873.

panopticon, the purpose of this disjuncture between seeing and being seen is clear. It is through being constantly visible that the inmate is controlled:

> [...] the more constantly the persons to be inspected are under the eyes of the persons who should inspect them, the more perfectly will the purpose X of the establishment have been attained. Ideal perfection, if that were the object, would require that each person should actually be in that predicament, during every instant of time. This being impossible, the next thing to be wished for is, that, at every instant, seeing reason to believe as much, and not being able to satisfy himself to the contrary, he should *conceive* himself to be so. (Bentham 1787: Letter 1, p. 4)

Moreover, "[lateral] invisibility is a guarantee of order" (Foucault 1991: 200); that is, the inability to see one's fellow inmates prevented conspiracies, prison outbreaks, and organized unrest (though it did not, clearly, prevent the *fear* of these events from authorities, as evidenced by the liberation book questions).

Foucault argues that the panoptical mechanism is fundamentally about power:

> Hence the major effect of the Panopticon: to induce in the inmate a state of conscious and permanent visibility that assures the automatic functioning of power. So to arrange things that the surveillance is permanent in its effects, even if it is discontinuous in its action: that the perfection of power should tend to render its actual exercise unnecessary; that this architectural apparatus should be a machine for creating and sustaining a power relation independent of the person who exercises it; in short, that the inmates should be caught up in a power situation of which they are themselves the bearers. (1991: 201)

This is "moral" architecture at its height, a model prison that ensures solitary confinement, social control, and moral reform. Taylor's reading of the purpose of this type of architecture is clear, and related to Foucault's reading: "It was the architecture that should constrain and organize the inmate rather than the guard. In this way the penitentiary system would seem to embody an abstract moral principle which the inmate was supposed to adhere to when he was released" (Taylor 1988: 242). Thus, the penitentiary's role extended beyond "dealing with transgression of the law"; indeed, it became much more about "a projection of the world as it should be. The penitentiary represented a community, although an artificial one, where the old values of obedience by the lower orders to a higher power were implicit" (Taylor 1988: 241). The relevance of this for Atwood's text is clear: Grace is a servant who, whatever her active or passive role in the murder of her employer was, overstepped the mark of her social class – and she was an immigrant as well; this, if nothing else, appeared to deserve punishment.

If North American prison reformers, including the Boston Prison Discipline Society who were influential in the building of Kingston Penitentiary, were responding to real concerns about prisoner behavior, they were also, according to Taylor, responding to manufactured concerns about the rise in immigration and urbanization as threats to civilized society (1988: 237). Moral architecture, as Foucault reports, "arrests or regulates movements; it clears up confusion; it dissipates compact groupings of individuals wandering about the country in unpredictable ways; it establishes calculated distributions" (1991: 219): *it keeps people in their place*. As

Foucault makes clear, "one of the primary objects of discipline is to fix: it is an anti-nomadic technique" (Foucault 1991: 218). Such a recognition is important both for considering the Penitentiary Act that stated that the penitentiary is wherever the prisoner is, as well as for the way in which the immigrant – and social inferior – Grace Marks is treated.

She was a "celebrated murderess" who was often paraded in front of tourists (Susanna Moodie famously being one of them), and the story of her role in the murders of Thomas Kinnear and Nancy Montgomery is unclear. An immigrant and a servant, she had no real access to power – except, perhaps, sexual power – and much media speculation existed about her relationships both with Kinnear and with James McDermott, the man who was hanged for Kinnear's murder. Grace Marks was young, in some reports attractive. Her gender and youth spared her from the noose but not from public vilification. Indeed, the fact that she was wearing the murdered woman's clothes when she was caught became a sign, at least for some, of her clear guilt.

Atwood uses these details in her fictional recounting of Grace's life. In Atwood's version, Grace is allowed limited freedom on occasions and becomes a domestic helper to the prison governor's wife, acting both as servant and as spectacle for the women who gather in this private yet public home to get illicit thrills from their proximity to female violence. Confined by their respectability, the governor's wife, her companions, and her daughters live vicarious violence through a crime scrapbook that mimics contemporary interest in true crime narratives. Anita Biressi argues that an "emphasis upon secret and occluded knowledge stems from an extreme transgression of acceptable limits, a crossing of boundaries that seems to command a search 'into the mind of the murderer'" (Biressi 2001: 167). When Grace describes the scrapbook, however, her voice is subtly ironic:

> The Governor's wife cuts these crimes out of the newspapers and pastes them in; she will even write away for old newspapers with crimes that were done before her time. It is her collection, she is a lady and they are all collecting things these days, and so she must collect something, and she does this instead of pulling up ferns or pressing flowers, and in any case she likes to horrify her acquaintances. (Atwood 1996: 26)[3]

Grace also notes that what the women are most interested in are hints of sexuality: "They don't care if I killed anyone, I could have cut dozens of throats, it's only what they admire in a soldier, they'd scarcely blink. No: was I really a paramour, is their chief concern, and they don't even know themselves whether they want the answer to be no or yes" (26). Atwood utilizes a gothic framework in order to obscure her heroine's ultimate innocence or guilt. The gothic framework becomes even more explicit in Waters's *Affinity*, but in *Alias Grace*, it serves to introduce multiple and fantastic readings of pre-trial events. Norman Holland and Leona Sherman identify the gothic framework as one which includes the image of "woman-plus-habitation and the plot of mysterious sexual and supernatural threats in an atmosphere of [...] mysteries" (1988: 215). Indeed, Atwood's utilization of ghosts, entrapping homes, and caddish

---

3 Future references to this edition will be given in the text.

men, with the female body as prison works within most of the definitions of the gothic that critics offer. Susanne Becker argues that the female gothic

> [...] plays an important role throughout the almost two centuries of modern female culture: there has been a vigorous exchange of allusions and re-visions, and even of provocations and answers, a dynamic – and self-conscious – writing and rewriting of feminine texts haunting one another: around the interrogative texture of romantic love and female desire, of gender construction between *le propre* and the monstrous-feminine, of the (contextualising) dynamics of domestic horror. (Becker 1999: 68)

Romantic love, female desire, and domestic horror become entwined in illicit ways in the text, as servant and master transgress class boundaries, and as Grace herself "becomes" the object of her own (unacknowledged) love interest, Mary Whitney. Grace is presumed innocent or guilty by various observers, but never herself explains fully her own reading of the events. Peter Hutchings argues that "[l]ike the vampires with whom they came to be associated, women are not reflected in murder's mirror" (2001: 55). Hutchings's metaphors work well in relation to Atwood's *Alias Grace*. The novel provides us with several images of Grace in a mirror, the most important of which has Grace looking in a mirror and contemplating her own multiple descriptions:

> I think of all the things that have been written about me – that I am an inhuman female demon, that I am an innocent victim of a blackguard forced against my will and in danger of my own life, that I was too ignorant to know how to act and that to hang me would be judicial murder, that I am fond of animals, that I am very handsome with a brilliant complexion, that I have blue eyes, that I have green eyes, that I have auburn and also brown hair, that I am tall and also not above the average height, that I am well and decently dressed, that I robbed a dead woman to appear so, that I am brisk and smart about my work, that I am of a sullen disposition with a quarrelsome temper, that I have the appearance of a person rather above my humble station, that I am a good girl with a pliable nature and no harm is told of me, that I am cunning and devious, that I am soft in the head and little better than an idiot. And I wonder, how can I be all of these different things at once? (23)

This long list, quoted in full to represent the many versions of events and varying personal attributes that Atwood incorporates here, also, I think, provides a postmodern contemplation of the fluidity of identity as process, not product. Moreover, it may also covertly say something about how a lawyer constructs a case: using what is *useful* (not what is relevant or even necessarily truthful) and discarding anything that doesn't fit the "story." Grace claims, after all, that it was her lawyer's decision for her to appear stupid; it "fit" his case. Grace, reflected in many mirrors here, somehow continues to elude description; the many versions proffered of her give us less to go on, not more. Hutchings argues that the working-class female criminal was considered "feeble-minded," the middle class woman "mad" (2001: 66); despite her clearly-determinable class status, however, Grace takes up both positions. She is feeble-minded at her trial, a factor that may have spared her life when her accomplice – or dupe, or abusive captor – was hanged; she is mad at points in the narrative, too, shipped to the nearby asylum for periods of time. It is the "mad" Grace Marks that Susanna Moodie writes about in *Life in the Clearings* (a source that Atwood was later to discredit as sensationalist and inaccurate).

Instead of providing us with "her" story, the fictional Grace records her refusal to be subject to the usual "female story," a story that has entrapped all the women she knew. The results of romantic love are disgrace, betrayal, and abandonment; this message is reinforced not only in her own family circumstances, but by her fellow servant and friend, Mary Whitney, whose liaison with the master's son leads to betrayal, botched abortion, and subsequent death. They are all, as Grace notes, "the same story" (165).

Story itself comes to define the novel, as Grace's position alters depending on who is gazing upon her. As Dr. Simon Jordan, the man who is given the task of psychoanalyzing her for the purpose of recovering her memory, notes of her fate, "But what does an example do, afterwards? thought Simon. Her story is over. The main story, that is; the thing that has defined her. How is she supposed to fill in the rest of the time?" (91). Moreover, the narrator comments after one of their sessions together: "They've been talking together all afternoon as if in a parlor; and now he is free as air and may do whatever he likes, while she must be bolted and barred. Caged in a dreary prison. Deliberately dreary, for if a prison were not dreary, where would be the punishment?" (186).

The punishment enacted upon the women in *Nights at the Circus* – to be permanently visible – is circumvented in many respects by Grace. She records that the height of windows in her prison prevents any sight – either in or out: "They do not want you looking out, they do not want you thinking the word *out*, they do not want you looking at the horizon and thinking you might one day drop below it yourself, like the sail of a ship departing or a horse and rider vanishing down a far hillside" (237, italics in the original). It is when Grace is *outside* the prison walls, working for the governor's wife and thus subject to the female gaze, that she undermines the notion of being watched:

> There is a good deal that can be seen slantwise, especially by the ladies, who do not wish to be caught staring. They can also see through veils, and window curtains, and over the tops of fans; and it is a good thing they can see in this way, or they would never see much of anything. But those of us who do not have to be bothered with all the veils and fans manage to see a good deal more. (229)

In this text, Grace wrests control from her superiors by gazing herself, and by controlling the way in which she is gazed upon. Grace thus incorporates a jumble of contradictory roles: she is the "perfect" lady, serving food for the prison governor's wife, sewing intricate patterns, maintaining chastity, and generally conforming to expected feminine behavior; she is also a violent prisoner who may or may not have invited sexual congress with a variety of men. The "truth" depends on whichever story is being told. As Judith Knelman notes, Atwood "constructs Grace through a chain of texts – contextualizes their meaning – so that they represent more than the historical events that they were constructed to mark: the crime, the arrests, the inquest, the trial, the confessions, the execution [of her accomplice]" (1999: 683). These representations are decidedly plural, as Atwood keeps a variety of possible storylines afloat: Grace is possessed; Grace is mad; Grace is psychically disturbed; Grace is cunning; Grace is guilty. Each reading is given support in the novel; no reading is fully discounted as false. Each reading acts as a legal text, either conforming to or contradicting a lawyer's construction of innocence or guilt. Cristie March calls *Alias Grace* "an authorial mosaic" because it contains so many voices and elements. She argues that

> [t]his multitude of voices invites a reading through Bakhtin's theory of heteroglossia, the overlapping layers of language that at once connect and isolate character/author, reader/author, character/character, and that allow an exploration of the means by which characters understand and misunderstand one another in their attempts to establish meaningfully verbal communications. (1997: 66)

Verbal communications are both excessive in the text – Grace's interlocutor silently accuses her of fabricating her many memories – and secreted;[4] meaning is not readily supplied but frequently needs to be inferred, as with the hints of lesbian desire that the text both uncovers, and covers over. Grace loves her servant friend Mary so much that she appears to *become* her in a spooky, séance-invoked explanation of the murders, and she perhaps covets more than Nancy Montgomery's clothes, though supposed jealousy motives are (at least overtly) framed within assumed heterosexuality. The lesbian as ghostly spectacle (the unspeakable) and the female criminal as aberrant are clearly being connected here, and both "need" regulation. Indeed, as Peter Hutchings argues: "the nineteenth century subject is *haunted* by crime, by its signs and stories and the shapes of institutions designed for its regulation" (2001: 1, my italics). Thus is it very much in keeping with the notion of the aberrant female and the panopticon prison that Grace Marks may fabricate a story of ghostly possession; it is also in keeping with this story that she *appears* to offer an explanation that allows her to keep her innocence while permitting behavior and speech that are in themselves "unacceptable." If she is not responsible for the crimes committed while the spirit of Mary takes possession of her body, then she cannot be held responsible for the vulgar voice that describes such actions. Given the novel's focus on psychoanalysis, it is also possible that this story is one of multiple personalities, a diagnosis still under much debate in medical communities today. Either explanatory framework leaves Grace "innocent," a victim of spiritual or mental displacement.

Simon Jordan's reaction to the séance that invokes a contested confession is one of confusion, not least because the event is meant to be a scientific exploration of hypnosis, not the spectacle it becomes: "He was expecting a series of monosyllables, mere yes's and no's dragged out of her, out of lethargy and stupor; a series of completed and somnolent responses to his own firm demands. [...] This voice cannot be Grace's; yet in that case, whose voice is it?" (400). In the trial, Grace's voice is co-

4 In another context, Mary Lydon discusses the double meaning of the word "secreted": "its capacity to produce and conceal at the same time" (1988: 139). Both meanings of the word are implied here.

opted by her lawyer to tell a story of imbecility; under hypnosis, her voice conforms neither to the historical monosyllabic Marks, nor to the story of her innocence; this "other" voice may represent a slanted truth that no one present seems able to credit. Indeed, when asked to record his findings, Simon Jordan realizes that "[t]he safest thing would be to write nothing at all [...] the fact is that he can't state anything with certainty and still tell the truth, because the truth eludes him. Or rather it's Grace herself who eludes him. She glides ahead of him, just out of his grasp, turning her head to see if he's still following" (407).

This final rendering of Grace is not accidental in its ghostly metaphor. Hutchings argues that "[t]he criminal is, thus, not some shadowy counterpart of the law-abiding citizen but *as spectre* the very form of law and the shape it seeks to control, a specter jointly produced through the discourses of law, literature, psychiatry, aesthetics and criminology" (Hutchings 2001: 2, italics in original). As specter, Grace is the object of discourse as well as the object of the gaze: Dr. Jordan wants to capture the truth of her, to get her to speak; the governor's wife wants her to be a containable spectacle; and others want to know once and for all whether she is innocent or guilty, states of being that the courts suggest are mutually incompatible. However, Grace Marks has successfully eluded all such containers. She may be visible in her panopticon, and she may carry the penitentiary wherever she walks outside its walls, according to the Penitentiary Act, but in her refusal to speak except as Other than herself, *and* in her refusal to be penitent (just as the prisoners of *Nights of the Circus* refuse to be so), she unravels the power of panoptical structures, both real and metaphoric.

Luce Irigaray offers a reading of woman that fits with the multiple, elusive readings of Grace Marks, and the failures to contain her:

> Thus the 'object' is not as massive, as resistant, as one might wish to believe. And her possession by a 'subject,' a subject's desire to appropriate her, is yet another of his vertiginous failures. For where he projects a something to absorb, to take, to see, to possess [...] as well as a path of ground to stand upon, a mirror to catch his reflection, he is already faced by another specularization. Whose twisted character is her inability to say what she represents. (Irigaray 2003: 120)

Innocence or guilt is unassignable to Grace Marks; they are lost in history and remain unclear even then, despite a verdict of guilty. In the historical records, Grace provides monosyllabic answers to the Liberty Questions and departs for New York. In Atwood's version, Grace coincidentally ends up marrying a childhood friend, the boy who helped convict her, and he seeks her penance in oddly sexual ways. Thus Atwood provides a nineteenth-century closure to her text – the fallen woman raised, and married – but she hints at further degradation to come. Sarah Waters's *Affinity*, by contrast, chooses the "other" nineteenth-century closure for a wayward heroine: death.

Affinity: The Panopticon as Queer Geometry

Affinity is a lesbian gothic novel about a nineteenth-century "Lady Visitor" to the prison, named Margaret Prior, and her relationship with the seemingly wrongly accused spiritualist, Selina Dawes, whom she helps to escape from prison. Taking its place within the framework of lesbian gothic, *Affinity* offers an unreliable but somehow sympathetic narrator; a series of fantastical, spooky events; and a desire that cannot be readily acknowledged. The novel describes a model panopticon, Millbank Prison, which was originally designed by Jeremy Bentham and is now palimpsestically the site of Tate Britain. Its "queer geometry" (Waters 2000: 235),[5] recorded but only faultily understood by the narrator, is clear to the twenty-first century reader familiar both with Bentham's panopticon and Foucault's reading of it. Here, again, the gaze is feminized, as matron watches the women inmates, as Margaret's mother's gaze extends into the prison through Margaret's own awareness of propriety, and as Margaret first watches and then transgresses the space of the prisoners themselves; in this context, "queerness" takes on a more significant meaning, and double discourses become the norm. Indeed, language is as important as vision in the novel. The repeated references to the "queerness" of Selina's crimes, and/or of Millbank, or Margaret's passion for it, indicate a self-conscious reference to the lesbian desires of the text. A second, deliberately repeated word is "unnatural"; though not repeated as frequently as "queer," its connotations also remind one of nineteenth-century medical associations of lesbianism with illness or monstrosity.

Paraphrasing Freud, Paulina Palmer argues that "the power that Gothic fantasy reveals to disturb and frighten the reader stems from its ability to articulate emotions and anxieties related to 'the return of the repressed'" (Palmer 1999: 10). What is repressed, for Margaret, is any sense of lesbian desire. Indeed, near the beginning of the text she appears positively homophobic when she congratulates herself on having circumvented communication between two prisoners: "I followed, though uneasily – for I have heard them talk of 'pals' before, and have used the word myself, but it disturbed me to find that the term had *that* particular meaning and I hadn't known it. Nor, somehow, do I care to think that I had almost played the medium, innocently, for Jarvis' dark passion [...]" (67). This early passage highlights the ways in which Waters cleverly blends all of the aspects of her tightly woven text: Margaret is a typical naïve heroine, willingly expressing received societal values, while concealing – even from the reader at this point – her own passion. Moreover, the use of the word "medium" is deliberate, clearly conjuring the spiritualist for us.

When Margaret first enters the prison, her skirts get "caught upon some jutting iron or brick" (8). This telling detail, which marks clothes as significant in the narrative of women's (imprisoned) lives, is the first of many references to appearance, and it is linked to the female gaze: "it is in lifting my eyes from my sweeping hem that I first see the pentagons of Millbank [...] and the suddenness of that gaze, makes them seem terrible" (8). Despite this sight, Margaret Prior, a laudanum addict and bereaved spinster who is mourning the death of her scholar-father, becomes a Lady Visitor for Millbank Prison with the hope that her behavior will act as a model for the prisoners. Like the Countess P., however, Margaret nurses crimes of her own: addiction, a suicide attempt, and a "dark passion" for another woman, her (now) sister-in-law, Helen. The Gothic Romance focuses on issues of sexual or social transgression

5 Future references to this edition will be given in the text.

(Palmer 1999: 3) and depends upon a sense of enclosure – where better, then, to set a gothic text than in a model prison, with the protagonist a mere visitor? A second narrative entwines with Margaret's while also preceding it chronologically by a year. Selina Dawes, a spiritualist, recounts her life prior to imprisonment. Her diary entries are cruder and less accomplished than Margaret's, but the reader is given no reason to disbelieve them. Indeed, so well does Waters limn Selina's character that on a first reading, we are subject to the uncanniness of this spooky, sexy novel.

Palmer reminds us that "[h]aunting and spectral visitation, whether associated with an individual or a place, are among the most common signifiers of the uncanny in Gothic fiction" (Palmer 1999: 59). Waters's novel relies on uncanniness to seduce the reader, making the prison's "queer geometry" central to this mood. What is also clear is Foucault's underlying reading of the panopticon. Selina bitterly acknowledges that "'[a]ll the world may look at me, it is part of my punishment'" (47). Thus again we have a reminder of the major effect of the panopticon, which is "to induce in the inmate a state of conscious and permanent visibility that assures the automatic functioning of power" (Foucault 1991: 201). Moreover, "the perfection of power should tend to render its actual exercise unnecessary [...] the inmates should be caught up in a power situation of which they are themselves the bearers" (Foucault 1991: 201). In *Affinity*, Margaret acts as a bearer of power in two ways: as observer of the inmates, and as her own observer, aware of her position as a lady. Margaret is complicit in her own subjugation, always aware of propriety (even when, under the influence of her medication, she transgresses that space).

Indeed, despite the fact that Selina is the prisoner and Margaret a mere visitor, Margaret is the one who becomes locked within the panoptical moment. She thinks of the one of the wardens, "*You are as snared by Millbank as they are*" (244, italics in original), without recognizing that these words also encode her own ensnarement. While Selina, as prisoner, appears subject to the machinery of the panopticon, she in fact manages to circumvent it, creating illusions of ghostly contacts that heighten the sense of gothic power. Palmer argues that "[w]hereas Gothic narrative explores the disintegration of the self into double or multiple facets, queer theory foregrounds the multiple sexualities and roles that the subject produces and enacts" (1999: 8). Selina is a mistress of disguise, assuming the stance of the wronged innocent in order to entice Margaret into helping to free her. So desperate is Margaret for love that she refuses to acknowledge any artifice: "[Selina] has a way about her – I have noticed it, before today – a way of shifting mood, of changing tone, and pose. She does it very subtly – not as an actress might, with a gesture that must be seen across a dark and crowded theatre [...]" (86). Margaret rejects the link between Selina and an actress, as well she might, for to acknowledge Selina's acting ability would be to acknowledge that she herself is taken in. Moreover, historically, of course, there has been a perceived link between actresses and prostitution, and Margaret must also negate any sense that there is a sexual transaction taking place between them – even when she persuades Selina to strip for her in a scene that, upon re-reading, becomes a clear exercise of power.

The first reading of this scene is one of consensual pleasure: on her last visit to Millbank before the planned escape, Margaret visits Selina at bedtime, and it seems natural for Margaret to wish to watch Selina undress. Margaret exclaims, "'How beautiful you are!'" (310), and Selina's surprise and denial are responses any lover might make. Selina's shivering and reticence appear to be the results of a cold prison and a modest nature. Once the reader knows the truth of Selina's relationship to Margaret – rather than being in love with her, she is in fact duping her – the passage takes on a different meaning:

> [Selina] let the dress fall from her, and removed the under-skirt and the prison boots and then, after another hesitation, the bonnet, until she stood, shivering slightly, in her woollen stockings and her petticoat. She held herself stiffly, and kept her face turned from me – as if it hurt to have me gaze at her, yet she would suffer the pain of it, for my sake. (309)

Selina is an actress, the prison her theater, and Margaret as audience is duly taken in. She reads the scene as she wants to read it, not as it actually appears. She gazes upon a mere illusion, one designed to suggest that it is Margaret who is the powerful, rather than the other way around. In this, Margaret resembles the Countess P., whose desires for repentance become her own imprisonment.

Critics have noted the way in which lesbian desire has been decorporealized and made spectral (Palmer 1999: 4), as if the actual bodily connections that lesbianism connotes cannot be accommodated. In a lesbian gothic text, a ghost may act as a way of "negating physical intimacy between women" (Palmer 1999: 60). Indeed, I think that Waters, aware of the many and varied ways in which lesbianism has remained hidden, deliberately replicates this concealment with Margaret's only half-acknowledged desire and her references to hauntings. As the narrator suggests, "Perhaps, however, it is the same with spinsters as with ghosts; and one has to be of their ranks in order to see them at all" (58). For spinster, read lesbian, and one can see what tricks Waters is herself playing here.

Waters also plays with Selina's lesbian impulses, multiply covering over the real object of desire; her "love" for Margaret is a displaced, manufactured love that hides her passion for a woman named Ruth Vigers. At the same time, Ruth Vigers is herself doubly hidden. She is Ruth to Selina, and first introduced to us as a maid; she is Vigers to Margaret, also a maid, but there is no initial reason to connect the "two" women – Ruth and Vigers – in the text; it is only at the end that it becomes clear that Vigers acts as a conduit – or medium – of Selina's seemingly supernatural messages to Margaret. Finally, Ruth acts as an accomplice in Selina's séances, dressing up as the supposedly heterosexual ghostly "control," Peter Quick. Trickery and artifice signify such occurrences; thus it is doubly appropriate that Peter Quick, who jealously guards Selina's reputation and virtue, should himself be conjured as a lustful, heterosexual male who takes liberties with the young women at the séances. The word "control" is significant, for clearly Ruth does control Selina. Indeed, Ruth Vigers's essential voicelessness (throughout, the reader has seen her primarily as a background figure and a servant) is undercut by allowing her the last line of the novel, which claims Selina for her own: "'Remember [...] whose girl you are'" (352).

At the end of the novel, Margaret is betrayed, Selina and Ruth disappear like the ghosts they have been connected to, and Margaret chooses death above a return to her stifling, spinster life. The panopticon is breached: the physical prisoner has slipped away, and the gaze has shifted. As Margaret herself realizes, "But, then, that passion was always theirs. Every time I stood in Selina's cell, feeling my flesh yearn towards hers, there might as well have been Vigers at the gate, looking on, stealing Selina's gaze from me to her" (341-42). It is Margaret, finally, who, denied Selina's loving gaze, is trapped within the gaze of propriety. Despite her class status – or perhaps because of it – she is the victim of a metaphorical panopticon, watched for failure: by her family, by the prison wardens, and by herself. In the end, then, it is not surprising that she chooses to hide away – chooses, in some ways, to inhabit a dungeon, which Foucault argues is the reverse of a panopticon, its functions "to enclose, to deprive of light and to hide" (Foucault 1991: 200). The novel ends with Margaret ensconced in her home, hiding from the law in the form of a neighborhood policeman, and planning her own death. Waters's use of the panopticon as a real structure and a metaphorical enclosure is thus cleverly upturned, with the position of the prisoner finally assigned to the one who, had she not been a lady, would herself have been at Millbank, too. Margaret Prior's initial crime is attempted suicide; by the end of the novel, she has succeeded, and learned the lesson an inmate taught her:

> "You think of your crimes – you don't think, 'If I had not done that, I wouldn't be here,' you think, 'If I had only done that *better*... '" (108, ellipses and italics in original).

Conclusion

Marie Fox notes that "narratives in both law and literature utilize punishment to effect a closure" (1996: 148), yet these women's stories exist beyond the ending, or rather, provide a series of alternative endings that do not come together into a coherent whole: Carters's murderesses disappear, Grace Marks slides from history, and Selina Dawes is spirited away. The three texts that I have analyzed, *Nights at the Circus*, *Alias Grace*, and *Affinity*, are linked through their incorporation of the panoptic gaze, as well as the recognition of its ultimate failure to contain these female criminals. If the panopticon is more overtly referenced in the first and last texts, it is also in operation in Atwood's novel, with the recognition that Kingston Penitentiary was, like the fictional Countess P.'s prison and Millbank Prison, based upon Bentham's plans. Moreover, each of these texts foregrounds the gaze as a powerful medium of control, referencing back to Foucault's reading of the panopticon. What each of these texts also does, however, is ensure that the prisoners exert control through the gaze, by reflecting back or reflecting upon whose who think that they hold the power. The panoptical power of the prisons is thus reversed, with the prison-keepers subject to incarceration or control. The Countess P., Dr. Simon Jordan, and Margaret, and the Millbank prison wardens are thus connected through the ways in which their inspection of the prisoners results in a misrecognition of their own positions.

In this way, Carter, Atwood, and Waters engage with debates about power, illusion, and subversive control. Moreover, they explore the ways in which gender itself is implicated in these texts, as the female body comes under surveillance both by men and by women. More often than not, the gaze is feminized – though not necessarily with any kind of overarching "sisterhood" being trumpeted as the end result. Indeed, only in Carter's novel is the covert lesbian desire of the text eventually acknowledged freely. For the others, such "dark passion" takes its place as the historically hidden but more than potentially subversive element that disrupts Foucault's sense of the panopticon. Visibility may be a trap, with Foucault's prisoner remaining "the object of information, never the subject in communication" (Foucault 1991: 200), but Carter, Atwood, and Waters suggest that such a reading is only partial, as their prisoners communicate beyond – and outside – the walls that enclose them, registering desire, betrayal, and refusal to conform. As Bartky argues, "Foucault seems sometimes on the verge of depriving us of a vocabulary in which to conceptualize the nature and meaning of those periodic refusals of control that, just as much as the imposition of control, mark the course of human history" (1988: 82). If Foucault is silent on these matters, feminist writers are not, and in their explorations of women and the law, they indeed write beyond the ending of women's imprisonment, and see beyond the panoptical gaze that initially appeared inescapable.

Works Cited

Atwood, Margaret (1996) *Alias Grace*. London: Bloomsbury.

Bartky, Sandra Lee (1988) "Foucault, Femininity, and the Modernization of Patriarchal Power." In: Diamond and Quinby: 61-86.

Becker, Susanne (1999) *Gothic Forms of Feminine Fictions*. Manchester: Manchester Univ. Press.

Bentham, Jeremy (1787) *Panopticon, or The Inspection House*. 6 August 2003. <www.cartome.org/panopticon2.htm>.

Biressi, Anita (2001) *Crime, Fear and the Law in True Crime Stories*. Houndmills: Palgrave.

Caron, Roger (1978). *Go Boy*. Toronto: Methuen.

Carter, Angela (1994 [1984]) *Nights at the Circus*. London: Vintage.

Diamond, Irene and Lee Quinby ed. (1988) *Feminism and Foucault: Reflections on Resistance*. Boston, MA: Northeastern Univ. Press.

Foucault, Michel (1991 [1975]) "Panopticism." *Discipline and Punish: The Birth of the Prison*. Trans. Alan Sheridan. London: Penguin. 195-228.

Fox, Marie (1996) "Crime and Punishment: Representations of Female Killers in Law and Literature." *Tall Stories? Reading Law and Literature*. Ed. John Morison and Christine Bell. Aldershot: Dartmouth. 145-78.

Gass, Joanne M. (1994) "Panopticism in *Nights at the Circus*." *The Review of Contemporary Fiction* 14.3: 71-6.

Holland, Norman N. and Leona F. Sherman (1988 [1986]) "Gothic Possibilities." *Gender and Reading: Essays on Readers, Texts, and Contexts*. Eds. Elizabeth A. Flynn and Patrocinio Schweickart. Baltimore,. MD: Johns Hopkins Univ. Press.

Hutchings, Peter J. (2001) *The Criminal Spectre in Law, Literature and Aesthetics: Incriminating Subjects*. London: Routledge.

Irigaray, Luce (2003) "Any Theory of the 'Subject' Has Always been Appropriated by the 'Masculine.'" *The Feminism and Visual Culture Reader*. Ed. Amelia Jones. London: Routledge. 119-28.

Knelman, Judith (1999) "Can We Believe what the Newspapers tell Us? Missing Links in *Alias Grace*." *UTQ: A Canadian Journal of the Humanities* 68.2: 677-86.

Lydon, Mary (1988) "Foucault and Feminism: A Romance of Many Dimensions." In: Diamond and Quinby: 135-47.

March, Cristie. (1997) "Crimson Silks and New Potatoes: The Heteroglossic Power of the Object in Atwood's *Alias Grace*." *Studies in Canadian Literature* 22.2: 66-82.

Mulvey, Laura (1975) "Visual Pleasure and Narrative Cinema." *Screen* 16.3.

Palmer, Paulina (1999) *Lesbian Gothic*. London: Cassell.

Queen's University Archives 599, MF POS 599 and MF 2342

Simonds, Merilyn (1996) *The Convict Lover: A True Story*. Toronto: Macfarlane Walter and Ross.

Taylor, C. J. (1988) "The Kingston, Ontario Penitentiary and Moral Architecture." *Lawful Authority: Readings on the History of Criminal Justice in Canada*. Ed. R. C. Macleod. Toronto: Copp Clark Pitman. 223-45.

Waters, Sarah (2000 [1999]) *Affinity*. London: Virago.

Percival Everett's *Glyph*: Prisons of the Body Physical, Political, and Academic

Jacqueline Berben-Masi

Introduction

Percival Everett is both an accomplished painter and the successful author of fourteen publications to date. These span different genres in a broad range that includes children's literature, comic book, detective story, science fiction, allegory, and, in the case of *Glyph*, postmodernist parody. It is in this last category that Everett's genius emerges most clearly. In *Glyph*, Everett uses a gamut of allusions and puns that run from the highbrow to the lowbrow, while at the same time engaging in an effective protest that surpasses straightforward exposition. My goal is to introduce Everett's novel *Glyph*, first published in 1999, to a broader audience and to discuss it as a humorous critique of the institutionalized discrimination of African-American men in American society and in its penal system. By juxtaposing *Glyph* with passages from, or references to, John Edgar Wideman's *Brothers and Keepers* (1984), I intend to demonstrate how *Glyph* explores images of imprisonment, inscribes itself within the tradition of black protest literature, and subverts readers' expectations of racial identity and criminal behavior. This paper will explore the multiple ways in which baby Ralph, the protagonist of the novel, is imprisoned, and how these forms of incarceration relate to the manner in which black men are systematically discriminated against and victimized in American society.

After situating *Glyph* in the genre of protest literature, I will proceed to demonstrate how the novel's unique narrative structure, practice of mimicry, appropriation of deconstructionism, rewriting of the slave narrative, and use of organizational subheadings, academic footnotes, and technical vocabulary, all contribute to the text as an "act" or a performance rather than as "analysis" of the black man's plight. Moreover, I will argue that the novel's structure as a series of "cells" makes it resemble a prison, indeed a panopticon where, from a single vantage point, all the cells can be surveyed. Related to this cellular structure is the question of language, which, as I will demonstrate, can be utilized as either a form of imprisonment or of liberation.

Glyph is a wildly imaginative and humorous novel, a multi-layered text that deftly blends classic African-American lexical virtuoso performance and childish pranks, suspense tale and socio-literary criticism. One possible interpretation of the novel reposes upon the topos of the world as prison. According to this reading, mainstream society, i.e. the rich, powerful adults who write the rules that govern us, puts the minority protagonist, a physically helpless baby, through a cycle of perpetual experiments and sequestrations. Indeed, even we readers become collaborators and therefore jailers of a sort. Although we may style ourselves as intellectuals, in the mirror Everett holds up to us, we are confronted with our own racist reflections through our perceptions of a situation which is not immediately color-coded. Doubtlessly, our own racial background tints our apprehension of the characters and events Everett creates. Much as the O. J. Simpson trial divided America during the last decade and the new documentary film on the 1998 lynching of James Byrd, Jr. in Jasper, Texas, led to controversy between its black and white filmmakers, *Glyph*, too, will evoke varied reactions. This diversity would not perturb the author.

Synopsis

For those unfamiliar with the novel, I start with a brief plot summary. The text is a first-person narrative written by Ralph, the child who refuses to speak, son of a college professor of English and an artist. Ralph turns out to be a super genius unlike any the world has known. The reader must suspend disbelief regarding an infant born with the innate ability to read and write at a post-doctoral level and equally at home with the "hard" or exact, the social, and the human sciences. But as in the case of Jesus Christ or Superman, those talents do not dispense baby Ralph from having to endure normal growth cycles and progressively learn the elementary lessons of day-to-day living, including the discovery of the wonders of his own body and its functions. Much of the humor in the book arises from the conflict in development between the mind and the body, for instance when the protagonist attributes his urge for self-exploration to "some holandric gene" (1999: 14). This is probably an Everett neologism; on the analogy with "holarctic," "holandric" probably denotes "all men." Again, Everett is underlining the universality of baby Ralph's somatic experience and his intellectual range while at the same time underlining that an adult male dwells beneath the guise of his small body, in the soul of this child.

Ralph's unique gifts quickly provoke desires of possession and control from the scientific community to the military complex. His humanity is totally disregarded as his adversaries try to find out what makes him tick and how they can harness his abilities to their own vested interests. Through typical African-American subterfuge, the baby eventually outwits his enemies and manages to organize for himself a semi-normal life while awaiting maturity and the ideal moment to cash in on his potential.

What does this plot signify? Baby Ralph experiences captivity in four guises. He is

1. a subject of experimentation by social and medical scientists, who submit him to test after test, putting his credibility as well as his skills on trial and caging him like a chimp, regarding him as a lost link, or a quirky advanced stage of development in the evolutionary process;

2. a "prisoner for his own safety" in a true adult jail, again subject of tests and interrogations, labeled "Defense Stealth Operative" or human "camera" in the US army for the multifarious "Uncle Ned." The latter's true identity is Uncle Sam, playing on the dual value of the paternalistic "Uncle" used for old, submissive Negro slaves as in the popular American song sung in all grammar schools. He is also known as Colonel Bill, highlighting the military connection. The other half of this demonic duo is Nurse Nanna, partly a nurturing nipple of the plastic variety. She is also partly a sorcerer's apprentice as she reverently obeys all commands issued by her military boss, including stifling the subject permanently to prevent his falling into enemy hands;
3. a surrogate child for the Catholic Latino couple, who in contradistinction to the stereotype are sterile. They are his penultimate abductors, and would-be self-serving saviors, but are nonetheless keepers;
4. an intended victim of a pedophilic priest as the child is held captive in the cleric's bedroom.

Whether subject of psychological experimentation destined ultimately for dissection, spy for the military against the industrial complex, love object of frustrated parental instincts or sexual prey, Ralph is never allowed to be just Ralph, never permitted to live out his own personal destiny. Others consistently assign him a meaning, or recast him in a mode that flatters their own fantasies. In the course of these episodes, little Ralph composes his terse *bildungsroman* from ages 0 to 4 years, inviting us to ponder several hypotheses, all ostensibly of equal import to the pseudo-autobiography:

1. Meaning is a relative value, more or less valid in the culture that produces it. (I.e., if there is a fourth dimension of global cultural values, they are extremely reductive.)
2. American society is fundamentally racist and exclusionist. This society includes the reader of the present work as well as the highest echelons of society. Every interaction that takes place in the mainstream culture is a reciprocal test or trial by the adversaries.
3. The unrecognized potential of minorities – and all "prisoners are a unique minority; they exist in a political, ethical limbo vis-à-vis free-world people in our society" (Wideman 1984: 188) – will remain "imprisoned" until we as a society have matured from our intellectual and cultural infancy to a state of knowledge, tolerance, and indeed, recognition for the truths we overlook. Release for these prisoners can only occur when we are ready to assume our responsibilities.
4. Any deviance from perceived "norms" is worthy of punishment. The sentence varies from incarceration to dissection (consider the sequence title "Incision").

5. Mother-wit and trickery remain the only viable weapons of the vulnerable against the powerful.

The list could continue, but these five concepts cover the basics. The question henceforth turns on how the author incorporates these hypotheses into the structure of the novel and then mirrors them in a manner that explores the topic of literary and literal prisons.

The case study before us is that "enunciated" by the hypothetical, autobiographical narrator, Ralph, a name in which the combination of the phonemes /l/ and /f/ coincide with those of the title, *Glyph.* (Not to ignore the existence of a periodical called *Glyph: Textual Studies* published in the late 1970's and whose first two editions carried a dialogue between Jacques Derrida and John Searle.) Ralph/*Glyph* is synonymous with writing. The hero has chosen not to speak, although he is not "dumb." He does not "tell" his story, but orchestrates its written composition, which he embeds with forceful allusions. This novel is like a Rosetta stone, with multi-referential clues to help decipher the conundrums of the text.

Glyph as Prison Literature

Glyph is admittedly a far cry from books like Richard Wright's *Native Son* (1940), Lloyd Brown's *Iron City* (1952), Eldridge Cleaver's *Soul on Ice* (1968), or John Edgar Wideman's *Brothers and Keepers* (1984), indeed, a myriad of other titles by African or African-American writers whose works feature a more realistic setting and less fanciful exploration of the ramifications of trials and incarceration. *Glyph*'s allegory of American society relies upon those earlier works as a palimpsest to drive home similar messages while it extends the lessons it draws from them to all aspects of life. Nor do his proposals ignore the Quaker reformers' notion of prison as a time out from normal life, a hiatus to put the soul into contact with the inmate's conscience to induce purification and rehabilitation. In addition, prison as a form of punishment that works by denying freedom of movement and action certainly gets more than lip service in *Glyph.* At the same time, by choosing his black hero to be a little boy, Everett reminds us of American society's long denial of responsible adult status to dark men in mixed-race societies, be they colonialized from without, within, or both. The parallel with John Edgar Wideman's book-length essay *Brothers and Keepers* is unmistakable: in prison, everything is done to reduce the incarcerated to "an image of dependency and helplessness, [...]. Grown men treated like children by other grown men" (1984: 80).

There is a striking intertextuality between Wideman and Everett on many levels. Like real-life prisoner Robert Wideman in Wideman's text about his brother, the little child Ralph is perceived as a creature to be broken and dominated; he is an object subject to the whims of his keepers; there are shows of force and constant reminders of absolute power, even that over life and death (cp. Wideman 1984: 80-84). "The events, the atmosphere of the summer had brought home to Robby the futility of resistance. Power was absurdly apportioned all on one side. To pretend you could control your own destiny was a joke" (1984: 84). Ralph's various kidnappers differ little from

Robby Wideman's guards who are "militant," "gung-ho," "young Turks." Violence is but a breath away; this is a "crusade," a "war [...] waged [...] against men who were already certified casualties, prisoners of war" (1984: 80-81). (In Ralph's case, it is the war of intelligence versus mediocrity.) Consequently, the jailed must be more on his guard than his jailers, who scrutinize his every move. The same is true for baby Ralph, whose acts of resistance are, like Robby Wideman's, necessarily "natural" and disguised. It is interesting to note that Robby's survival in "the hole" partly depends on his reading poetry aloud to himself and his fellow inmates. Reading, as demonstrated below, also is Ralph's salvation, although, paradoxically, it at the same time serves as the hard labor imposed upon him by some of his jailers.

Unlike Everett, whose narrative "voice" addresses us in the first person in *Glyph*, Wideman channels Robby's experience alternatively through a third-person narrative, focalized partly through Robby's eyes, and through a peripheral first-person narrative by the autobiographical author, John Edgar Wideman. When Wideman changes to first-person, his rendition of his brother's voice is filtered through his own, thus adapting a fictional technique to a non-fictional mode. This results in heightening the impact on the reader who thus experiences the tale with greater immediacy. Wideman uses a fictional technique to make his non-fiction more real, more personal, whereas Everett exploits the improbably personal to bend the real world to his creative needs. Despite such disparities, *Brothers and Keepers* serves as a precursor for Everett's novel. Robby Wideman still awaits parole in his Pennsylvanian prison; *Glyph* ends with an adult mind still imprisoned in a child's body; the hero has attained philosophical patience and serenity while awaiting physical maturity and potential release.

By now, it should be obvious that there is meticulous method behind the apparent madness of the plot. This is no "*voyage autour de ma chambre*" itinerary, nor an armchair adventurer's flirtation with an elite criminal element. Although comically presented, the kidnappings, trials and incarcerations occur on the literal as well as metaphorical and metaphysical levels. Being caged is not his first humiliation, it is an essential component of the prison routine. "Caging" serves as a metaphor for imprisonments of various kinds. His later stay in the real "slammer" is a full-blown life behind bars, complete with a turn in solitary confinement. Ralph's carceral experience displays striking similarities with that of Robby Wideman. Traumatized by the atmosphere at the Pennsylvania carceral facility where Robby Wideman is being held, John Wideman relates a dream to his brother during one of their prison visits:

> I am a man, myself but not myself. The man wakes up and can't see the stars. The smell of death surrounds him. Fifteen hundred other men sleep in the honeycomb of steel that is his home forever. The fitful stirrings, clattering bars, groaning, the sudden outcries of fear, rage, madness, and God knows what else are finally over at this hour of the night or morning as he lies in his cell listening to other men sleep. The monotonous sawing sound reminds him of the funny papers, the little cloud containing saw and log drawn above a character's head so you can see the sound of sleeping. Only the man doesn't see logs floating above the prisoners' heads. As he listens and shuts his eyes and gets as close to praying as he ever does anymore, praying for sleep, for blessed oblivion, the cartoon he imagines behind his closed eyes is himself sawing away the

> parts of his own body. Doggedly, without passion or haste, drawing a dull saw up and back, up and back through his limbs. Slices drop away on the concrete floor. The man is cutting himself to pieces, there is less of him every time he saws through a section. He is lopping off his own flesh and blood but works methodically, concentrating on the up-and-back motion of the saw. When there's nothing left, he'll be finished. He seems almost bored, almost asleep, ready to snore like the saw's snoring as it chews through his body. (1984: 193-94)

John's surrealistic nightmare allegorizes the prison experience and the price it exacts upon the prisoner's body. It also recalls the exemplary punishment of Erisychthon in Ovid's tale.[1] (For his mockery and disrespect of the gods Erisychthon was condemned by Ceres to having an insatiable appetite. This culminated in his eating his own limbs and body to assuage his unbearable hunger.) The prison experience described in Wideman's dream both creates and denies the prisoner's hunger for freedom, sunlight, companionship, and education. Prison slowly and methodically destroys him. In *Glyph*, the destructive element consists of Ralph's steady prison reading diet of technical manuals, with no novels or poetry allowed for spiritual escape. Ralph is condemned to live off the special gift of his mind, to consume his talents while sharing the fate of the convicts who surround him.

Spaces of Confinement

The realization and discovery of Ralph's unique gifts filters first from his parents upward to the level of the mad, behavioral scientists, and from there up to the national defense level. Spatial organization in the novel gradually shifts from one form of prison to another. First, there is the baby's body, then his crib and playpen, next the monkey cage where he is kept by experimental child psychologist, Dr. Steimmel, and ultimately an actual adult carceral facility, where his fellow inmates wonder "what the kid is in for." Although the other prisoners do not compare him to "fresh meat" as they do Albert French's ten-year-old murderer on death row in his novel, *Billy* (1993), Ralph is a tender morsel in that tough atmosphere. That is, until "the kid" makes a daring prison escape, aided and abetted by a Chicano guard, named Mauricio la Puente ('the bridge'), and his wife, Rosenda Paz ('peace'). Mauricio's name and role are not free of irony. Although a "bridge" to the "peace" outside, Mauricio has internalized his keeper's role in the prison. As a guard, he always wants to be in charge of any situation that may arise and adopts dubious practices to deal with them. His "freeing" of Ralph turns out to be yet another confinement for the boy, as the prisoner does not leave his custody. Mauricio continues to do his job, to play out the role that has become psychologically ingrained. Again, as Wideman points out in *Brothers and Keepers*, apostrophizing those who hold the keys and the key role:

> The moral and ethical principles that bind society don't count inside prison. You, the custodians, formulate whatever rules, whatever system you require to keep the prisoners in captivity. You

---

1 Ovid, *Metamorphoses* 9, 725-884.

> must stand between them and us. You are not a connection between the free world and the prison world but a chasm, a wall, a two-sided, unbreakable mirror. (1984: 189)

Wideman overtly denies the "connection" between the two worlds, whereas Everett ironizes this similarity. Thus Mauricio perpetuates Ralph's existence as a prisoner, tantalizingly donning the image of a savior while continuing morally to keep his warder's uniform. Ultimately Ralph's prison break-out with the help of the la Puentes leads to illusory sanctuary in a Spanish mission church (shades of Bartolomé de Las Casas, who first proposed substituting African blacks for the indigenous Indians suffering from colonial enslavement), and finally, television transmission, "captured" on the small screen. This final "take" on the prisoner leads to his ultimate "liberation" into "Mo's" (for "Mom's") arms, a close call as all the bad guys start closing in on him. Ralph needs to be eliminated from circulation for daring to be born brilliant and black. Had the recognition-craving doctors, the national security specialists, or the "apostolic Roman-collar clan" had their way with him, Ralph would have been been "in for" maximum punishment, or for soul-destructive exorcism at the hands of a Joycean triumvirate, Fathers O'Blige, O'Boie, and O'Meye, led by the satanic Father Chacòn. Need we recall that sodomizing youthful inmates is part and parcel of the real prison experience?

None of this is lost on baby Ralph. Indeed, once "back on the outside," the tiny hero contemplates the evolution of his situation and realizes the ironic truth of his unaltered status:

> If language was my prison house, then writing was the wall over which I climbed for escape. But climbing the wall either way meant, finally, the same thing, and so language was the prison and the escape and therefore no prison at all, any more than freedom is confinement simply because it precludes one from being confined. Indeed, my much regarded and remarkable relationship and facility with language had caused my incarceration, but it had also freed me, though *I was still confined in the car of my new adults. I was still a prisoner to my size and to my inability to fend for myself.* I was called a genius, but I was not. A genius, as far as I was concerned, was someone who could drive a car. (1999: 145-46; my emphasis)

His new adults are captors, guards who define the rules and perpetuate the relative positions of the roles played by custodian and prisoner. Driving the car means making decisions, controlling destiny, something which the baby's superior talents cannot enable him to do due to his size. Of course, it is also a marvelous joke, a commonplace of childhood fantasies.

"If language was my prison house, then writing was the wall over which I climbed for escape. But climbing the wall either way meant, finally, the same thing, and so language was the prison and the escape [...]." How is Ralph to ignore the direct comparison between prison walls and reading? In this context, an intertextual reference to the life of Malcolm X and his discovery of freedom through literacy gained in prison is unmistakable. Everett thus confronts the centuries-old tradition of the black slave narrative wherein reading, and especially writing, were the keys that opened the doors to the prison of servitude (Gates 1989: xxxii). At the same time,

Everett also seems to be toying with the black aesthetic: the plea for blacks "to speak for themselves," as Pauline E. Hopkins put it, is negated, as language paradoxically entails both release and captivity (Andrews et al. 1997: 366-67). Language as prison rejoins the implicit theme of the structure of the novel, a point to which we now turn.

Signifiers, Structure, and Style

From the first chapter of the novel with its prefatory label of "Deconstruction Paper" with the second word crossed out, under erasure (the title of Everett's most recent novel) *Glyph* promises an act or performance rather than an analysis. This act represents a parody of the often misunderstood and misapplied French critical theories that were *à la mode* when the scholar Everett came of age. Indeed, the text's amalgamation of quotes, pseudo-dialogs between living and dead public figures and authors (who are refreshingly not all white and male), long intellectual digressions, and flights of poetry look rather like a cut-and-paste job at first glance. They appear to be at best peripherally connected with one another. Upon closer inspection, these allusions and footnotes enrich the text and constitute a repertoire of theme and variations, a wink of complicity directed at the academic reader. Some of the leitmotifs border on the scatological, such as the reference to an article actually published in the *American Journal of Human Genetics,* with a slight change in the credits: one author's name is misprinted (or "edited") to be slightly more suggestive. The research trio "Stern, Centerwall, and Starker" is cited as the writers of "New Data on the Problem of Y-Linkage of Hairy Pinnae" footnoting Ralph's first venture into masturbation and his father's angry disapproval of it (see my note on the "holandric gene" above). The real scholarly essay deals with men who have hairy ears, and the writers' names are Curt Stern, W. R. Centerwall, and S. S. Sarkar (1964: 455-56). This is a survey on the existing scholarship of "penetrating paper[s]" "on pedigree," on "Y-chromosome penetrance" or the "probability" of human males with congenitally hirsute ears (alliteration and double-entendre in the original text). Traditionally, the threat against practicing masturbation is that it will make hair grow on one's palms, but why not the ears as well, given how many elderly gentlemen have fuzzy aural apertures? Moreover, masturbation, as Wideman points out, is a ritual, part and parcel of the prisoner's daily, or rather nightly, regime (1984: 84). Everett echoes James Joyce and his peculiar mixture of low-level jokes and high-level artistry. The protagonist must retain the attributes of childhood, adolescence, and adulthood.

As we have just seen, Everett's ludic tendencies prevent his dwelling on the lugubrious side, no matter how pessimistic his outlook may be. Instead, he composes an encyclopedia with multilingual headings in no particular alphabetical order, although there is a theoretical consistency in the scheme. The same headings recur throughout the eight chapters. They pun on familiar academic and non-academic terms, collocations, and icons of popular culture. For instance, the chapter titles "A Plot with a View," "The Straight and Narrative," and "Lost in Place" play on the following items: E. M. Forster's novel *A Room with a View*, the cliché "the straight and narrow [path]" to salvation or a prisoner's parole on good behavior, the popular, long-running television series *Lost in Space* respectively. In *Lost in Space* the scientific member of the crew served as the butt of repeated jokes, and was clearly 'out of place.' Each heading is prefaced by a linguistic or semiotic model that loosely corresponds to the organization of the chapter, each is lettered rather than numbered from A to H, as in "Hyoid Bone" (see below). For baby Ralph is on a quest for meaning, which, like Ralph himself, often "goes missing." This connection between getting lost physically and lost meaning is established in the text by means of a a footnote musing on the putative media headlines, "Missing Meaning Turns Up Found" or "Meaning Found to Be Missing" (1999: 178). As in an earlier work by Everett, *Zulus* (1990), whose chapters run from A to Z with a rigorously alliterative abstract of each division, *Glyph* contains internal sequences that reflect key motifs to cue the reader in, provided he or she invests the effort to make the connections. For example, each chapter begins with a section labeled "*différance*." The word comes straight from the terminology of Jacques Derrida, author of *Grammatology,* i.e., the science that determines how one form relates to others and permits the articulation of signs among themselves within a given abstract graphic or phonic order, or between two orders of expression: "*parole*" or "utterance" and "writing" (Rey-Debove 1979: 48-49). An exception to this chapter-initial section title is made in the last chapter, where we read "difference." The narrator-prisoner has been "freed" from the shackles of other people's ambitions or pretentiousness; he has graduated from the semiotics of *différance* to the meaningfulness of difference. In large part, Everett's *Glyph* deploys deconstructivist schemata, beginning notably with the creation of a *commedia dell'arte* caricature of Roland Barthes. The author of *S/Z* is depicted as the American stereotype of the self-infatuated French intellectual, who is forever after other men's women (18-21). Barthes, who visits with Ralph's father Douglas – who is in turn presented as his equally ridiculous, if less successful and famous counterpart – is not the only icon up for smashing. Like Tweedledum and Tweedledee from Lewis Carroll, who also played with language and logic to explore the world of Sense, Barthes is virtually twinned to that other *monstre sacré* of French literary criticism, Derrida. The two make successful fictional creations. In addition, the letter that the fictive Derrida sends to Douglas is disdainful of the American scholar, indeed of the entire American academic community, and concludes with a banal and casual American expression, "Have to run now," which detaches itself from the style of the body of the text he has supposedly produced (1999: 129). As the nadir of humiliation, father Douglas is most often referred to as 'Inflato' because of his flabby cheeks that are a sheer temptation for the child to pinch. In a similar vein, we witness the antics surrounding the word "table" that Ralph's parents mouth exaggeratedly in an attempt to get their baby to imitate in speech; it is beyond their ken that their son has already made the leap from the signified and its signifier to the higher level concept of "tableness" (1999: 5-6). This is "food for thought" for overachieving parents, whose efforts often miss the mark and yet another trial for the brilliant child "prisoner," who struggles to give satisfaction, but cannot fathom the low level of expectations.

Let us continue our examination of the structural divisions of *Glyph.* Other recurring subheadings besides "*Différance*" include the following titles:

1. "pharmakon" for sections that seem to provide a "chemical" analysis of the ingredients of the story;
2. "unties of simulacrum" for sequences that further the estrangement and separation between the characters;
3. "supplement" for sections which seem to indicate physical and intellectual nourishment;
4. "bedeuten," the German verb 'to signify,' which alludes both to Saussurian and black English subtexts;
5. "Mary Mallon," a.k.a. "Typhoid Mary," who in American chronicles was an inadvertent criminal who killed the families she worked for as a cook by spreading typhus. This subheading is used for passages where Ralph is being "held" by Dr. Steimmel or Nurse Nanna;
6. "ennuyeux," the French for 'boring,' punctuated with a series of five lines of vocabulary, all beginning with A, then later B, then C, etc. The first in this series deals with 'Inflato's frustrated attempts to publish a paper on "Alterity." His subject provides a delicious ironic stab at Ralph's father, given his inability to accept his son's difference-*différance*. For the purpose of illustration, here is a quote from Ralph's commentary on his father's endeavors:

> Aliquid stat pro aliquo
> Alterity
> Aufhebung
> Atopos
> A (1999: 12)

A bit of explanation might be useful. "*Aliquid,*" roughly translated, yields "something stands for something else," but in semiotic terms, it refers to the "no-person" or the one who is being spoken about but who does not act.[2] "*Alterity*" plays with a favorite theme of the 1980's and could be contrasted with

> "altarity" or "[re]think[ing] the difference and otherness that lie beyond absolute knowledge. The 'unheard-of' thought of *altarity* provides the framework within which I cast my analysis. 'Altarity' is a slippery word whose meaning can be neither stated clearly nor fixed firmly. Although never completely decidable, the field of the word 'altarity' can be approached through the network of its associations: altar, alter, alternate, alternative, alternation, alterity." (Taylor 1987: xxvii-xxviii)

All of the above suit the instance. As for "Aufhebung," it translates as "abolition" in the legal sense in English. "Atopos" is none other than the opposite of a topos or commonplace, a no-place. Of course, this might also be Ralph's own primer, another parody on boredom or on the boring manner in which such books are written, i.e., "A

2 As developed by Göran Sonesson in his paper, "El lugar del rito en la semiotica des espectaculo." 22 October 2003 <http://w1.461.telia.com/~u46103777/Textos/hcas/H29/Sonesson.html>.

is for aardvark, B is for bison, etc." But boredom, as Jan Alber's study illustrates ("Bodies Behind Bars"), is the typical fare of the prison routine. Robby Wideman highlights the underlying paradox: "You got time but you can't do nothing with it. [...] you'd think you could take care of business, but ain't hardly no business gets taken care of in the joint. Cause it ain't really your time" (1984: 230). Baby Ralph's longing for Mo' shows that loneliness is linked to boredom. Again, in Robby Wideman's analysis, "Maybe it got something to do with being lonely. Being so fucked up inside you never feel like doing nothing. Being lonely's one the worst things about the joint. Probably *the* worst" (1984: 230). The paradoxical solution is to be alone, to get away from the craziness, to create one's own space, something Ralph also seeks during his time in confinement, and finally achieves (see below).

Returning to the analysis of the structural pattern of *Glyph* begun above, two sexually suggestive subheadings break the rhythm in the first chapter: "libidinal economy" and "*peccatum originale.*" This motif continues, ranging from innocence to infidelity in "*ens realissimum.*" Other sequences include the obvious, like "seme," "bridge," or "incision," as well as the obtuse like "ephexis" from either *éphexis*, "pretended reason," or *ephexēs*, adj., "one after the other, and so forth," and "exousai," which might be a consistent misprint for *exousía*, "power, knowledge." The German word *Vexierbild*, "picture puzzle," confronts the reader with Lacan's mirror mocked, given that the child has no problems with his own double. But prison is like a funhouse mirror that distorts reality; as we have seen, it is Wideman's "unbreakable two-sided mirror," a wall of deception. Everett gives no clues as to which interpretation he prefers: the reading belongs to the reader.

Within this paradigm, the "compleat" reader, at ease in letters and numbers, may quickly come to grips with an unusual formula: $(x)\ (Cx \rightarrow \sim Vx)\ \&\ (x)\ [(Cx \vdash Px) \rightarrow \sim Vx]$ (59). For the common mortal, text literacy here requires some knowledge of symbolic logic to penetrate the arcane and arrive at the proper reconstruction of the "rebus" of symbols used. But not too much knowledge; this could lead to false analogies. Let us assume that Cx is a propositional function containing the variable x. The possible values of x comprise the domain of discourse. By itself, C(x) is not a statement or a proposition since its truth or falsity depends on the value assigned to x. Thus, a statement in logic might be, "For every x, C(x) implies NOT V(x)," while another statement might be: "There exists an x in the domain for which C(x) implies NOT V(x)." The result seems to be a tautology, i.e., a compound statement that is always true, no matter what truth values are assigned to the components. Here, interpretations are almost limitless, given the multiple themes of the novel. Interestingly enough, the sentence that precedes the first appearance of the formula could be so represented: "No Children are Volunteers. Therefore, no children being tested by Psychologists are volunteers" (1999: 32). That Ralph is not a volunteer is what he repeats at the other locations in the text where he uses that notation. It reappears in each case when he is subjected to some psychological "interrogation." Whenever he cooperates, he is as a child not truly capable of giving real consent. Any contracts he thus tacitly signs are only binding for the adult party and should be rescindable at choice. But they are not. Hence, he is a victim of all systems, including the one that relies upon trials and prisons to arrive at its ends.

Both the line and the formula also serve as a reminder of Ludwig Wittgenstein's *Tractatus Logico-Philosophicus*, the opening lines of which are the first words read to baby Ralph by Mo after she has grasped his extraordinary abilities: "One: The world is all that is the case. One-point-one: The world is the totality of facts, not of things." A footnote proclaims these words to be "complete nonsense" but dear to their author, for:

> He loved the words, the pregnancy of them, how they swelled with meaning and at once fell stillborn from the page. I mention this to underscore that the reading was in no way speaking. Reading, amplified, is no crime, though it is unnecessary, not a luxury, just something that is not bad. (1999: 9)

Notice once again the preoccupation with the ethics of common, daily activity: speech, but not reading, falls under the Seven Capital Sins (luxury). Indeed, it verges on a criminal pursuit. Ralph is not guilty. Wittgenstein's influence does not stop here, however. Ralph follows a similar pattern under "Are Meanings in the Head? (Ralph's Theory of Fictive Space)." Like the Austrian-English philosopher, whose entire *Tractatus* is made up of numbered propositions and comments, Ralph provides "an appendix within the text for the purpose of serving the last sentence" (1999: 194). In contrast to Wittgenstein, baby Ralph uses letters instead of numbers for each of his propositions. *Glyph*'s intertextuality blurs the lines between plot and metatext, making it "too clever a work by far," as Salman Rushdie once confided to his colleague Jacqueline Bardolph about his own novel, *Grimus*. Perhaps the fictive space could be prisoner Ralph's escape valve, the only space where he can be alone and face the boredom and loneliness described above?

Language as Prison

Viewed as a set, *Glyph*'s theoretical models and recurring sequences resemble the cells of a prison. "Pigeonholes" or subjectively imposed categories are used to imprison language and text. Chapter by chapter, the cells can be revisited by the reader. From Ralph's unifying perspective, a central vision of the whole is maintained, both a panopticon and a *Weltanschauung*. The irony is that he has constructed a metatextual prison of his own: the jailed becomes a type of jailer himself ruling over the social, the literary, the linguistic and the penal aspects of the book. "A sign is a sign," a prison is a prison. This is no single-dimensional work: each aspect depends on the others for its significance and message. Cells meant to lock in meaning are nonetheless interpermeable: nuances from one subheading affect our apprehension of another. Internal communication between the cells cannot, indeed, must not be impeded. These artificial devices invented to isolate individuals or ideas within a community of people or of sense serve a limited purpose because it is only as an ensemble that they can function effectively. If, as Lovelace wrote in "To Althea, from Prison": "Stone Walls do not a Prison make," then it must be the combination of the physical and the metaphysical, the container and the contained, that is required to construct a successful container for men and for meaning.

Eventual escape from overt imprisonment requires a subversion of the power hierarchy. Similarly, a baby, physically limited by his infant body, learns to partially control his immediate situation. Having played detective to discover his whereabouts, earth-mother Eve as the empowered woman comes to save Ralph. Nonetheless, evading the scores of pursuers who are all out to recapture their unique specimen requires self-sacrifice. Not only must both mother and child assume false identities, but they must cloak the baby's gifts in pseudo-"normality," and live out their lives as marginalized figures with no hope of being "rehabilitated" as full-fledged members of society. They are condemned to preserve the lie/truth of the role reserved to bright African Americans in a culture which is still grappling with their existence. Like the first black "Mongoloid" child who was studied, Ralph as a black baby genius is a discomforting anomaly to social Darwinism. His existence is one that undermines long-revered theories of racial hierarchy and atavism important to the history of social deviance and criminality. The belief that ontogeny recapitulates phylogeny, though never without its critics, long enjoyed broad influence and continues to exercise its hold among certain revisionists. The generally received idea was that the Negroid race was at the bottom of the hierarchy, Mongolians at a more advanced evolutionary level than blacks, and of course, Europeans were at the apex of human perfection (Wolpe 1998: unpaginated). Establishing a link between the evolutionary level of the races and behavioral expectations for the same was the facile next step, as is illustrated by Cesare Lombroso's famous *The Criminal Man* (1876). In brief, Lombroso held that a direct correlation existed between race and criminal deviance: the lower his or her ranking in the racial hierarchy was, the dimmer his or her intelligence and the greater his or her likelihood of becoming a criminal (Wolpe 1998: unpaginated). Miscegenation was long held to be criminal because it allegedly undermined this "natural order."

That such notions beg to be challenged provides perhaps a partial explanation for the extreme complexity of Everett's vocabulary and structure. Compare, too, Inflato's early convictions about his son's being "mildly retarded." We never do learn whether the narrator's father is black, white, Native American, Asian, Latino, etc., only that Ralph is a black child. This point is made poignantly when the narrator apostrophises the reader, and wonders whether the latter has assigned him a color or not. Under the subheading, "Supernumber" 2, the secret is let out of the bag, for it is time to give the police a description of the kidnapped child:

> Have you to this point assumed that I am white? In my reading, I discovered that if a character was black, then he at some point was required to comb his Afro hairdo, speak on the street using an obvious, ethnically identifiable idiom, live in a certain part of a town, or be called a nigger by someone. [...] But you, dear reader, no doubt, whether you share my pigmentation or cultural origins, probably assumed that I was white. (1999: 54).

Score one point for the narrator, who has carefully avoided giving any clues to his reader until now. Only now can the reader consider how this withholding of information about the protagonist's race undercuts our expectations of protest literature even as it reinforces the message.

But let us return yet once more to the question of structure in *Glyph*. The sequences or "cells of story" that subdivide each chapter do not disappear in the final chapter, which relates the hero's "liberation" from his various forms of captivity. Titles that recur in the concluding chapter include "subjective-collective" in which mother and son are reunited and escape together; "vita nova" or the pair's compromise to avoid further harassment, he simulating normalcy while she, bereft of her artistic inspiration, is reduced to holding a simple job at a drugstore, a fate brightened only by her exchanges with her son. *Vexierbild*, "picture puzzle," the final subsection, brings us full circle from the novel's opening sarcastic image of baby Ralph embarking upon his picaresque tour through the models of Jacques Derrida and Roland Barthes to those of Ferdinand de Saussure, Charles Morris, Algiras Greimas, and Louis Hjelmslev, to reunion with his mother:

> In spite of my reunion with my mother, I learned that nothing comes full circle, but stretches out like a line, extending infinitely toward some ideal terminal point that is necessarily only a point, just like I am only a point on the line. But am I insignificant? No. The point is whole, the point is complete, but the line ... the line is everything.
>
> The *line* is everything. (207-8)

Now the "initiated" Ralph can see life and its meaning as a prosaic straight line, a sign equal to a sign (1999: 203). Which is exactly how the novel ends: "The point is whole, the point is complete, but the line ... the line is everything. The *line* is everything" (207-8). (Compare with Wittgenstein.) "Line" is another word with multiple denotations, connotations, associations, and collocations. Indeed, the line is essential not only to the story, to words spoken or written, to truth or falsehood, but to longevity, to suspect identification, to jokes, to links, to painterly expression, to the shape of the concept of time, and it is also the prisoner's nemesis.

Ralph's personal nemesis, speech, is assigned to the realm of violence. At the risk of "over-reading" his first poem, which leaves his parents stunned and in total disbelief, one discovers a reference to rape under slavery which led to "miscegenation":

> *The Hyoid Bone*
>
> *Brace the words,*
> *the delicate instrument,*
> *the tongue for sweet kissing,*
> *upsilon.*
>
> *Arch of bone,*
> *greater cornu, reaching,*
> *reaching, stretching*
> *above the lesser.*

Fracture this bone,
by the violence,
feel the sick
pain of swallowing.

Fracture the bone,
compromise the support,
feel the true anguish
of speech. (17-18; italics Everett's)

The contrast between the gentleness one expects from a Chaucerian or Shakespearean "sweet kiss" in the first stanza and the poem's sadistic, shocking conclusion conveys the notion that speech is torn from the throat. Speech is an unnatural and unpleasant reaction to forces that escape the subject's control and destroy it. Like prison guards. The syllabic count for each stanza is nearly identical, varying between 19 and 16, in decreasing numbers. The stanzas are not formal, three-line, seventeen-syllable haiku, but rather a four-line approximation. Similarly, the stress patterns are fairly regular, if not consistently iambic, anapestic, or dactylic. Other Ralph poems, devoted to various parts of the body, are written in free verse like the above; they continue the notion of deconstruction, a tearing apart limb from limb.

Let this one example suffice to illustrate the style and complexity of what the baby can compose. Once again, the term "free verse" is a misnomer here in that the poem's recurring rhythm patterns and frames force our attention to a certain distribution and deprive the reader of the choice of imposing intonational meter. "Freedom" – even of verse – is an illusion, a compromise between two opposite poles. And just what is the "hyoid bone"? It is none other than "A U-shaped bone between the mandible and the larynx at the base of the tongue" (*American Heritage Dictionary* 1969: 647). "U-shaped" as in "upsilon." "Cornu" as in "A protuberance of bone resembling a horn" (*American Heritage Dictionary* 1969: 297). In sum, the "hyoid bone" is an analytic, descriptive, and rhythmic exposition spiced up by the violence that is also kith and kin to the prison experience Ralph is about to encounter.

Finis

Modernism and authors as complex as himself such as John Wideman and T. S. Eliot have served as prime models for Percival Everett. Nonetheless, his theoretical paradigms come from post-modernist rather than Modernist sources. The autobiographical mode is "in," and literary archetypes run the gamut from the confessional mode to the apologetic one. With generic roots in the slave narrative, a plethora of other models comes to mind to pay homage to, and to "signify upon," in the African-American sense of mocking or undercutting (Andrews et al. 1997: 665-66). As a closing example, the image of pancakes sizzling in butter from the now banned children's story of "Little Black Sambo" becomes a recurring nightmare for baby Ralph.[3] No direct reference is made to the classic book, but the allusion is as unmistakable as the socio-legal intertext, a cultural wink to the initiated. As in the entire novel, *Glyph.* For how much longer will black brothers have nightmares of "getting fried" in "Old Sparky" while they wait on death row in myriad prisons around the USA? *Glyph* leaves the reader with a substantial agenda to consider. At the risk of overplaying the "black card," I read in *Glyph* an allegory of, and an indictment of, prison sentences that are the daily lot of many an African American today, disproportionately so to their percentage of the population. The situation has been chronic since the earliest days of US penal history, as John Edgar Wideman notes in *Brothers and Keepers* (1984: 41-42). With his natural sense of irony and wit, Everett communicates a similar message indirectly, gently, surgically, lancing the social abscess.

Works Cited

American Heritage Dictionary (1969) Boston, MA: Houghton Mifflin.

Andrews, William L., Frances Smith Foster, and Trudier Harris (1997) *The Oxford Companion to African American Literature.* Oxford: Oxford University Press.

Brown, Lloyd L. (1952) *Iron City: A Novel.* New York: Masses & Mainstream.

Cleaver, Eldridge (1968) *Soul on Ice.* With an introduction by Maxwell Geismar. New York: MacGraw-Hill.

Everett, Percival (1999) *Glyph.* St. Paul, MN: Graywolf Press.

Everett, Percival (1990) *Zulus.* Sag Harbor, NY: The Permanent Press.

French, Albert (1993) *Billy.* New York: Penguin.

Gates, Henry Louis, Jr. (1989) *Figures in Black: Words, Signs, and the "Racial" Self.* London: Oxford Univ. Press.

Ovid (1977) *P. Ovidii Nasonis Metamorphoses.* Ed. William S. Anderson. Leipzig: Teubner.

Rushdie, Salman. (1989) Personal communication to Jacqueline Bardolph.

3 "I was constantly afraid that some adult would fry me in a skillet. Frying is very much like hunting. The unsuspecting prey is startled by the sudden heat of attack and as I saw myself as likely prey, tender, helpless, small enough to carry back to the cave, I feared for my life. My only bad dream was discovering myself in a cast-iron pan, sitting in sizzling butter" (1999: 31). That whites and blacks interpret the story differently has a great deal to do with the perspective of the reader: most white readers fail to see discrimination in the tale, perceiving only the black child protagonist eating the pancakes made out of tiger butter, in a reversal that figures the boy as the intended prey of the tigers; blacks, by contrast, apparently see themselves as the prey of voracious white hunters. Innocence, like beauty, lies in the eye of the beholder.

Rey-Debove, Josette (1979) *Lexique sémiotique.* Paris: Presses Univérsitaires de France.

Sonesson, Göran in his paper (n. date) "El lugar del rito en la semiotica des espectaculo." 22 October 2003. <http://w1.461.telia.com/~u46103777/Textos/hcas /H29/Sonesson.html>.

Stern, Curt, W. R. Centerwall, and S. S. Sarkar (1964) "New Data on the Problem of Y-Linkage of Hairy Pinnae." *The American Journal of Human Genetics* 16.4: 455-71.

Taylor, Marc C. (1987) *Altarity.* Chicago, IL: Univ. of Chicago Press.

Wright, Richard (1940) *Native Son.* With an Introduction: "How Bigger was born." New York: Harper.

Wideman, John Edgar (1984) *Brothers and Keepers.* New York: Holt, Rinehart and Winston.

Wolpe, Paul Root (1998) "Explaining Social Deviance." Course No. 675. Chantilly, VA: The Teaching Company. Audio-cassette series.

Bodies Behind Bars: The Disciplining of the Prisoner's Body in British and American Prison Movies

Jan Alber

1. Introduction

Since the 1920s, at least 600 British and American prison movies have been produced.[1] However, surprisingly little has been written about these films, and little attempt has been made to define the prison movie (Nellis 1988: 2). This paper constitutes a first step into a larger investigation of British and American prison films. More precisely, I will provide a close reading of the disciplining of the prisoner's body in the audiovisual medium film (Chatman 1990: 135).[2] In what follows I will first

---

1 This figure is based on Querry (1973), Hale (1982), Nellis (1982), Nellis (1988), Crowther (1989), Parish (1991), Wilson (1993), Hardy (1997), Armstrong/Armstrong (2001), Bammann (2001), Becker (2001) as well as my own research at the *British Film Institute* (bfi) in London, for the funding of which I wish to thank the German Academic Exchange Program (DAAD) and the Wissenschaftliche Gesellschaft in Freiburg e.V.

2 I am primarily interested in the question of how the *experience* of imprisonment is represented in prison movies and less in metaphorical forms of imprisonment. Nevertheless, I would like to stress that metaphorical readings of the prisons in certain films are of course possible. Cinematic metaphors involve *interplicitness*, i.e. the mutual influence of disparate ideas or contexts upon one another (Whittock 1990: 27). The stronger denotation, the one more fully present in the film, will normally identify the *source domain*; the weaker denotation will be that of the *target domain* (Lakoff/Turner 1989). For example, one might argue that the state penitentiary in *The Shawshank Redemption* (dir. Frank Darabond, 1994) evokes associations with a womb and a tomb. The newcomer's entry ends in complete darkness so that we might get a sense that he is being swallowed by the building. On the one hand, the inward movement into prison, i.e. a great 'container,' may be seen as an entry into the mother's womb, which implies the possibility of being reborn; on the other hand, since prisoners are withdrawn from life in the outside world, one might correlate incarceration with death and see the inward movement into prison as an entry into a dark tomb. For the inmate 'Fat Ass' (Frank Medrano), who is beaten to death by Captain Hadley (Clancy Brown), the prison immediately becomes a tomb. For Andy Dufresne (Tim Robbins), on the other hand, the prison becomes a womb from which he is (spiritually) reborn. Andy's spiritual rebirth is conveyed by means of visual tropes. First, Andy's escape through a tight sewage pipe suggests some kind of birth or rebirth. Second, the film's context, i.e. Andy's inflicting poetic justice on crooks like Warden Norton (Bob Gunton) and Captain Hadley allows us to see rain washing down on Andy at the end of his 'rebirth' as a process of spiritual cleansing.

show that in a variety of ways, the prisoner's body plays a crucial role with regard to the experience of actual imprisonment (i.e. in real prisons). In this respect, Michel Foucault's interest in the inmate's corporeality, which he deals with in *Discipline and Punish* (1975/1979), serves as the starting point of my analysis. Second, I wish to illustrate the various cinematic techniques of rendering the power which the disciplinary space of the prison exercises over the human body. Finally, I will compare the actual experience of imprisonment to its representation in British and American prison films.

The relationship between fictional prison films and the 'reality' of penal practice is here analyzed within the framework of Stephen Greenblatt's New Historicism. Greenblatt postulates some sort of "exchange" or "negotiation" between fiction on the one hand and 'reality' on the other (1988: 1-20). For him, these two poles are located within a process of dialectical mediation. I argue that prison films tend to have a uniquely intimate relationship with their subject matter. On the one hand, they draw extensively on real events and use real prison locations (Nellis 1982: 5). That is to say, they are based on the reality of penal practices which they take up and transform; and it is only occasionally that such films exploit abuses in the penal system for the titillation of moviegoers. On the other hand, for good or ill, prison movies influence the cognitive categories of their recipients and thus, the popular understanding of the closed prison institution, often making it hard to separate fiction from reality (Alber 2003).

In the first part of this paper, I will illustrate Foucault's claim that the disciplinary techniques in prisons focus on the prisoner's body although the prison was initially designed with the aim of rehabilitation. According to Foucault, a punishment like imprisonment "has never functioned without a certain additional element of punishment that certainly concerns the body itself: rationing of food, sexual deprivation, corporal punishment, solitary confinement" (1979: 15-16). Historically speaking, disciplinary methods "made possible the meticulous control of the body, which assured the constant subjection of its forces and imposed upon them a relation of docility-utility" (ibid.: 137). In part 2, I will argue that prison movies are typical narratives in the sense of Monika Fludernik's new narratological paradigm. Fludernik downgrades events from the central role that they usually hold in definitions of narrative, and redefines narrativity[3] in terms of experientiality, i.e. "the quasi-mimetic evocation of 'real-life experience'" (1996: 12). Since nothing really happens in prison films in terms of event sequences, I will argue that the narrativity of such films is not constituted by plot. Rather, the genre's narrativity correlates with *human experientiality*, i.e. the prisoners' suffering and his feelings of pain, fear or agony, which are mediated through consciousness. More precisely, we as viewers establish experientiality and narrativize prison films, i.e. read such movies *as narratives*, by applying Fludernik's 'natural' VIEWING frame, the 'real-world' schema of perception. In the third part of this paper, I will analyze the ways in which Foucault's claim that

3 Narrativity is the intrinsic quality that makes a narrative a narrative and distinguishes narrative discourse from other discourse types. Gerald Prince calls this quality "narrativehood" (1995: 80).

the prison belongs to "a political technology of the body" (Foucault 1979: 30) is reflected in British and American prison movies. In *Discipline and Punish*, Foucault concentrates on the role of the inmate's corporality with regard to disciplinary techniques. As far as outbreaks of physical violence and rape in prison are concerned, I will go beyond Foucault's arguments. Foucault posits that uncontrolled violence between guards and inmates is counterproductive from the perspective of efficient punishment (Foucault 1979: 104ff.),[4] while inmate-on-inmate violence and rape are undesigned forms of violence. Regardless of whether such types of violence are counterproductive forms of quasi-official punishment inflicted by sadistic guards or whether they are entirely undesigned outbreaks between inmates, I will argue that they still constitute an important aspect of the bodily experience of imprisonment in Britain and America. This threat is then represented in prison films.

In this paper, I argue that within both real and cinematic prison systems, one can differentiate between *four types of the awareness of one's body*, namely first, that of the guards or the 'other' prisoners (Morris 1995: 253); second, that of 'normal' inmates who are allowed to have contact with others; third, that of convicts who are sentenced to solitary confinement in open, i.e. barred cells; and, finally, that of inmates who have to spend time in 'the hole,' i.e. the dark prison-within-the-prison. There is a gradual increase of the awareness of one's body along this scale from the first to the fourth level. In the 'hole,' the awareness of one's bodied physicality is most powerful because this experience involves a complete lack of sensory stimulation (no light, no sound, no communication, no clothes, no decent food) and frequently results in a dramatic loss of orientation. In the 'hole,' prisoners are made most acutely aware of what their bodies need, namely sensory stimulation, i.e. the possibility to move one's body and to deal with a variety of sensory stimuli. Additionally, I will show that this scale implies an increase of narrativity from the first to the fourth level within the framework of Fludernik's 'natural' narratology (1996).

2. Michel Foucault and the Prisoner's Body

In *Discipline and Punish*, Foucault argues that the prison was born at the end of he eighteenth century when rehabilitation and reform became the major objectives of penal practice. He also points out that the prisoner's body plays an important role with regard to the disciplinary techniques in prison because behavioral disciplining inevitably involves controlling the body. In 1975, Foucault said in an interview: "First

4 For Foucault, the birth of the prison does not betoken the advent of humanism but a more efficient form of punishment (1979: 80). He links the penitentiary to the deliberate creation of a group of delinquents and the accumulation of knowledge about these delinquents so that societies can be controlled more efficiently: "The circuit of delinquency would seem to be not the sub-product of a prison which, while punishing, does not succeed in correcting; it is rather the direct effect of a penalty which, in order to control illegal practices, seems to invest certain of them in a mechanism of 'punishment-reproduction,' of which imprisonment is one of the main parts" (1979: 278).

of all one must set aside the widely held thesis that power, in our bourgeois, capitalist societies has denied the reality of the body in favour of the soul, consciousness, ideality. In fact nothing is more material, physical, corporal than the exercise of power" (1980: 57-58). This is most certainly true of the exercise of power in the penitentiary. Before the 'birth of the prison' at the end of the eighteenth century, vengeance was directly wreaked on the criminal's body. However, in the course of the nineteenth century, the body of the criminal did not disappear. Rather, it *re*appeared in slightly altered form within the space frame of the prison.

> At the point that marks the disappearance of the branded, dismembered, burnt, annihilated body of the tortured criminal, there appeared the body of the prisoner, duplicated by the individuality of the 'delinquent', by the little soul of the criminal, which the very apparatus of punishment fabricated as a point of application of the power to punish and as the object of what is still called today penitentiary science. (Foucault 1979: 255)

The prisoner's physical body[5] provides the *interface* between the disciplinary techniques of the prison institution and the inmate's soul or conscience. Foucault sees any appearance of the body in social relations as "already marked: the body is the playing field of power" (Kuppers 2001: 47). For him, the body is bound into a system (the soul) which creates subjectivity and is thus itself a factor in the exercise of power over the body. "The soul is the effect and instrument of a political anatomy; the soul is the prison of the body" (Foucault 1979: 30). Furthermore, Foucault argues that the bodies in prison are 'fabricated' bodies. This is true in at least two respects. On the one hand, the body is constructed *from the outside* by prison officers who have to interpret the inmate's bodily movements in order to acquire knowledge about these bodies. On the basis of this (necessarily *external*) knowledge, the prison seeks to exercise power over the body in order to transform it (Armstrong 1994: 21). On the other hand, since the communicating of bodily experiences always involves theoretical conceptualizations, the body is also fabricated by the inmate *from the inside*. In the words of Peter Brooks, "our bodies are with us, though we have always had trouble saying exactly how. We are, in various conceptions or metaphors, in our body, or having a body, or at one with our body, or alienated from it" (1993: 1). From an 'outside' perspective, the disciplining of the body in prison is only possible if the inmate's body is properly confined in order to allow its surveillance and inspection. Mary Ann Frese Witt speaks of "the sequestration of the human body in a cell within a self-contained community shut away from the normal activities of life" (1985: 1). Second, since the guards are not in a position to *look into* the minds of the inmates, they are restricted to observing the prisoners' behavior, i.e. their bodily movements. According to Foucault, the 'total education' in prison has a set agenda with the purpose

5 For Plato, the body represents 'mere matter' ready to be transformed by the active mind. According to René Descartes, only consciousness is evident to itself; the body is still 'mere matter' experienced through the mind. On the other hand, thinkers like Benedict Spinoza think of consciousness as embodied. From this perspective, we only know ourselves through our bodies; there is no other viewpoint from which to cogitate about our condition (Kuppers 2001: 46).

of 'docilisation,' which, via the interface of the body, aims at the prisoner's mind or consciousness. The disciplinary apparatus of the prison tries to 'mould' individuals in specific ways in order to make them 'conform' socially. In this context, Foucault speaks of a kind of "dressage," which can only be measured by supervising "gestures and habits," i.e. the inmate's body (Foucault 1988: 105):

> What developed, then, was a whole technique of human dressage by location, confinement, surveillance, the perpetual supervision of behaviour and tasks, in short, a whole technique of 'management' of which the prison was merely one manifestation or its transportation into the penal domain. (ibid.)

In prison, bodies are inspected and analyzed with the purpose of effecting a passive and malleable body, but at the same time establishing those bodies as individual and discrete (Armstrong 1994: 21). That is to say that the prison creates the subjectivity of its inmates. The disciplining within the prison produces subjected and practised bodies, 'docile' bodies; at the same time, the disciplinary space produces the individuality of these bodies, or, more precisely, "the everyday individuality of everybody" (Foucault 1979: 191). In short, subjection produces subjectivity. From the perspective of an 'insider' or inmate, the experience of imprisonment creates a higher awareness of one's bodily functions. Penal institutions initiate a heightened sense of corporeality within the prison subject. Since the prison machine employs disciplinary measures involving deprivations of all sorts (sensory deprivation, sexual deprivation, etc.), the inmate is made acutely aware of the inescapability of the body and its needs (Fludernik 1999: 64). Prison routine also corresponds to deprivation because it involves a lack of free movement as well as a lack of free disposal of time.

3. What is a Prison Film?

I characterize prison films in their purest form as fictional films (rather than documentaries – even though the overlap can be considerable) which are set mainly in a penal institution for men, women or adolescents, and which take the *experience of imprisonment and its consequences* as a primary theme. This definition allows me to include both 'escaped prisoner' movies and 'released prisoner' movies.[6] On the other hand, films set in mental institutions and prisoner of war camps are excluded here because they would make my analysis unnecessarily complex. In contrast to Nellis (1988: 2), my definition of prison movies concentrates on the *experience* of imprisonment. Prison films are typical narratives in the sense of Monika Fludernik's 'natural' narratology (1996). In contrast to traditional plot-oriented approaches to narrative, Fludernik defines narrativity on the basis of experientiality. "Experientiality,

---

6 For instance, the film *Death and the Maiden* (dir. Roman Polanski, 1994) is not set in prison. Nevertheless, the movie is about prison experience in so far as the central protagonist Paulina (Sigourney Weaver) tries to come to terms with her past imprisonment in an unspecified South American country.

as everything else in narrative, reflects a cognitive schema of embodiedness that relates to human existence and human concerns" (1996: 13). Embodiedness (or embodiment) refers to one's bodily existence, to one's physical being in the world, and "evokes all the parameters of a real-life schema of existence which always has to be situated in a specific time and space frame" (ibid.: 30). In other words, embodiment correlates with the specificity of a protagonist's whereabouts, including his actions in a plot sequence.

In typical prison movies such as *Birdman of Alcatraz* (dir. John Frankenheimer, 1962) and *Escape from Alcatraz* (dir. Don Siegel, 1979), nothing really happens in terms of plot development. This obviously reflects the dull and unyielding routine of prison life (Morris 1995: 227). More precisely, prison films tend to marginalize plot and instead focus on the crucial position of the prison subject as the victim of penal practices. The majority of prison movies centrally engage with the *experience* of imprisonment and with how prisoners cope with the resulting identity crisis. Thus, the prison experience and its consequences are the topics of such narratives.

Most film theorists have traditionally made (a series of) action(s), the prime constituent of narrativity (Bordwell 1985: 53; Branigan 1992: 36; Fleishman 1992: 5; Lothe 2000: 3). If one follows the definition of narrative in terms of plot, one has to exclude prison films from the potential realm of narrativity because they do not concentrate on plot. However, this is of course counter-intuitive, because we as viewers of prison films get the sense that we are watching a narrative. Hence, I would like to follow Fludernik's proposals (1996: 352ff.) and redefine the narrativity of such films in terms of mediated experientiality. For Fludernik, "the emotional involvement" with an experience and "its evaluation provide cognitive anchor points for the constitution of narrativity" (1996: 13). For me, the core of the narrativity of prison movies lies in the mediation of the inmates' experience of imprisonment. In the medium film, the prisoners' suffering can be mediated through 'indirect' visualizations like facial expressions or submissive bodily positions; and on the auditory level, the inmates' pain or fear can be conveyed through screams of horror. According to Laura Mulvey, "the conventions of mainstream cinema focus on the *human form*. Scale, space, stories are all *anthropomorphic*. [...] Curiosity and the wish to look intermingle with a fascination with likeness and recognition: *the human face, the human body, the relationship between the human form and its surroundings, the visible presence of the person in the world*" (2000: 178; my emphasis). Additionally, I would argue that cinema audiences establish experientiality, i.e. narrativize films, mostly by applying Fludernik's 'natural' VIEWING script, which correlates with 'real-world' activities like watching and observing (1996: 43). In the process of narrativization, viewers engage in viewing films as manifesting experientiality, and construct them in terms of their alignment with experiential cognitive parameters: "we integrate the cinematic conventions of changes of angle and proportion with the schemata we possess for recognizing objects in the real world as we identify what we are viewing" (Whittock 1990: 23). That is to say that cinema audiences (re-)cognize disruptions of time and space, which have to do with the use of camera angles, camera movements and cuts, on the basis of assimilated categories of human knowledge and experience. Viewers interpret films by imposing cognitive schemata on them just as people have to interpret 'real-life' experiences in terms of available frames (Fludernik 1996: 12).

Moreover, I would like to note that in contrast to film theorists like Seymour Chatman (1990: 126-34) or Anke-Marie Lohmeier (1996: 31-32), I reject the thesis that a film's narrativity correlates with the existence of a cinematic narrator. Since for certain film theorists, there cannot be a narrative without a narrator, "the organizational and sending agency" (Chatman 1990: 127) behind the camera movements has to function as 'cinematic narrator.' Theorists like Chatman assert that there is a narrator in all narratives (Fludernik 1993: 738). The concept of the 'cinematic narrator' is of course a metaphorical extension of narration to non-verbal types of presentation. In the history of film theory, this metaphor has been given a wide variety of names.[7] Most film critics are aware of the fact that the 'cinematic' or 'film narrator' is not a human being (Chatman 1990: 134; Lothe 2000: 30). Thus, in contrast to David Bordwell, I would not criticize the anthropomorphization of the camera movements.[8] Rather, I question the *essentialization* of a narrator figure which *presents us with* what we see on the screen. David A. Black correctly points out that in contrast to the narrator of a novel or a short story, who can (at least theoretically) say 'I' at any given point in time, the so-called 'cinematic narrator' can never point to an 'I' in command of the narrative (2001: 301). What we are observing in film theorists needing a narrator for films is an illicit transfer of 'real-world' frames of storytelling onto the (much more complex) communicational process of cinematic narration. Like ordinary viewers, film critics seem to import a scenario of 'somebody must present us with this story' into the theoretical plane of narrative theory. By contrast, I would argue that with regard to film, we are not confronted with a communicational basic frame. Obviously, in the course of a film, narrative instances occur such as voice-over narrators, captions, intertitles, and narrators on the screen who address the audience or other characters (Fleishman 1992: 21). However, such narrative instances are invariably swallowed up in the overall narrative discourse of the film, which they do *not* produce (Bordwell 1985: 61; Branigan 1992: 108-10). Even though narrative instances may appear on several different narrative levels within a film, most parts of a film are *not* mediated by a narrator. Voice-over narrators or narrators on the screen

---

7 Sarah Kozloff uses the term "image-maker" in order to refer to "the narrating agent of all films" (1988: 44). Similarly, Jerrold Levinson speaks of "the presenter in a film" in terms of a "*perceptual enabler*" (1996: 252), Jakob Lothe suggests to use the term "film narrator" for "the superordinate 'instance' that presents all the means of communication that film has at its disposal" (2001: 30), and Manfred Jahn's uses the term *filmic compositional device* (FCD) to denote "the theoretical agency behind a film's organization and arrangement" (2002: F 4.1). Other terms for this narrative function include *camera* (Pudovkin), *grand imagier* (Metz), *fundamental narrator* (Gaudreault) and *external or cinematic narrator* (Burgoyne) (Griem/Voigts-Virchow 2002: 162).

8 In narrative theory of the twentieth century, there has been a gradual development from the anthropomorphization of narrator figures to the radical criticism of using any anthropomorphic schemata. According to Bordwell, "in watching films, we are seldom aware of being told something by an entity resembling a human being" (1985: 62).

hardly present us with the images we see on the screen; and with regard to film images, there are no clear markers to warrant the existence of a 'perceptual enabler.' For me, a film is a narrative (based on the mediation of experientiality) without a narrator. Films are not presented by a 'cinematic narrator.' Rather, they are mimetically performed[9] and cinema audiences narrativize them by means of the 'natural' VIEWING frame, the 'real world' schema of perception.

To summarize, the narrativity of prison films is neither constituted by plot nor by the ghostly figure of the 'cinematic narrator.' Instead, the narrativity of such movies reposes solely on the mediation of the prison experience, which correlates with pain, fear and agony. Films in general partake of the same stock of cognitive parameters and depend on the same receptional frames as do written narratives. However, they require a different analytic toolbox. According to Manfred Jahn, "a film is a multimedial narrative form based on a physical record of sounds and moving pictures" (2002: F 1.2). Therefore, with regard to film analysis, it is of primary importance to distinguish between the *auditory channel* (i.e. the use of sounds, voices and music) and the *visual channel* (i.e. actors, props, colors, *mise-en-scène*, camera movements, camera angles and cuts) (Chatman 1990: 135; Griem/Voigts-Virchow 2002: 164-67). In what follows I shall investigate Foucault's claim that the prisoner's body plays an important role in disciplining within the prison system. I will proceed along the scale that I have outlined above and I will concentrate on the question of how the heightened awareness of bodily functions is conveyed by the medium film.

4. Disciplining the Prisoner's Body in British and American Movies

4.1. *Level 1*: The Guards

Bruce Crowther is certainly right in pointing out that "prison guards rarely have a movie angled from their side" (1989: 9). Indeed, most prison films concentrate on the situation of the inmates and their experience of imprisonment.[10] However, even though

---

9 Avrom Fleishman argues that "cinema is a mimetic art" (1992: 19), thus referring to Plato's cardinal distinction between *mimesis* ('showing') and *diegesis* ('telling') (Plato 1987: Book III 392c-95). 'Telling' refers to a narrative mode of presentation that is mediated by a narrator figure, while 'showing' refers to a narrative mode of presentation, with regard to which there is little or no narratorial mediation or presence (Rimmon-Kenan 2002: 107).

10 In fact, there are only two exceptions. *The Quare Fellow* (dir. Arthur Dreifuss, 1962) focuses on Crimmin, a young prison officer (Patrick McGoohan) who at first approves of the penal system. When he later learns that men can be imprisoned for stealing firewood and hanged for killing the seducers of their wives, he begins to question his position. Similarly, *The Green Mile* (dir. Frank Darabont, 1999) is presented from the perspective of the guard Paul Edgecomb (Tom Hanks), who works on death row and is responsible for executions on the electric chair. One might add the two films *Prison Warden* (dir. Seymour Friedman, 1949) and *Brubaker* (dir. Stuart Rosenberg, 1980) which both depict the warden's point of view.

only two films in my corpus[11] concentrate on the role of the guards properly, almost every prison movie comments on the situation of the 'other prisoners.' In order to understand the interaction between cons and screws, one has to take a closer look at the guards' work. They belong to both the world outside and the world inside the prison. In *Scum* (dir. Alan Clarke, 1979) Archer (Mick Ford), the inmate of an English borstal, talks to the prison officer Mr. Duke (Bill Dean), and points out that after all the years he worked in borstals, Mr. Duke is still "just a basic officer." He asks him: "Who pays for that daily humiliation?" When Duke becomes aggressive, Archer says "I was only concerned with men being stripped off their dignity, cons and screws. We aren't much different in here you know." Similarly, in *Now Barabbas was a Robber ...* (dir. Gordon Parry, 1949), the visitor Kitty (Beatrice Campbell) says "It's a lovely day, isn't it?," to which the prison officer Mr Jackson (William Hartnell) replies "I wouldn't know. I haven't been out. All the days are the same in here." Also, when Sean Nokes (Kevin Bacon) and the other three sadistic prison officers of the Wilkinson Home for Boys are introduced by the voice-over narrator in *Sleepers*, the camera moves in circles around a table at which the four guards play cards. That is to say, we are confronted with a circular dolly move (Turner 1996: 37). This camera movement is again employed later on, when Shakes (Joe Perrino) and his three teenage friends sit at a table and discuss whether they should tell anyone about the sexual abuse they had to endure in the detention center. Here, an inherent common feature of guards and inmates is stressed by the way the two groups are presented cinematically (Whittock 1990: 51). The dialogs and camera movements referred to above suggest that the situation of guards and the situation of inmates hardly differ. As we can see in prison films, both groups have to wear uniforms, which correlates with a certain loss of individuality, and both groups spend a considerable time inside prisons. Most importantly, both are subject to the unforgiving and relentless routine of prison life. However, presumably guards *decide* to work in prison, and they can leave the institution at the end of their shift. Nevertheless, it is true that "during their working shifts, day and night," the guards too "are within the security perimeter of the prison, subjected to a routine reflecting that of the prisoners" (Morris 1995: 253). This lack of sensory stimulation on the part of the guards implies a heightened awareness of their bodies in comparison to the situation of citizens outside. Combined with their control over the prisoners, this sensory deprivation may partly explain the psychology of bullying, sadistic prison guards which frequently occur in prison movies (Crowther 1989: 8). Their boredom and the power they wield can occasionally drive prison officers to indulge in the subjecting of prisoners to degrading physical abuse. For instance, in *Sleepers*, the guard Sean Nokes and his gang repeatedly torture and rape Shakes and his friends. In a segment filmed in such a way as to highlight the descent into the darkest spheres of the human psyche, the camera slowly moves down the dark exterior of the reform school and into its lowest point, the basement (Wlodarz 2001: 70). We are then presented with a chilling long march to an underground 'torture room'

11 In this paper, I refer to thirty British and American prison movies, which were produced between the 1930s and the year 2000.

where the guards will sodomize the boys. Interestingly, once the abuse begins, the camera pulls away from showing anything explicitly and rushes backwards out of the tunnel. This camera movement may be seen as a visual correlative of anal sex which the boys have to endure in the 'torture room' (Felperin 1997: 46).[12]

Foucault refers to prison guards in terms of "supervisors" who are "perpetually supervised" and points out that although the "pyramidal organization" of the "hierarchized surveillance [...] gives it a 'head,' it is the apparatus as a whole that produces 'power' and distributes individuals in this permanent and continuous field" (1979: 177). The Stanford Prison Experiment which was carried out in 1971 by Philip G. Zimbardo illustrates how quickly the dull routine of prison life may turn mentally healthy individuals into brutal guards. The psychologist Zimbardo randomly assigned "mature, emotionally stable" young male volunteers to the roles of prisoners and prison officers. "The project was to last two weeks, but in only six days, he found that abuse had reached such proportions that it was necessary to stop the experiment" (Silberman 1995: 21). Some guards treated prisoners as "despicable animals," taking pleasure in cruelty, while prisoners were "dehumanized" (Zimbardo 1982: 196). Zimbardo (1999) even claims that no correlation exists between personality and sadistic behavior within the prison. Prison films illustrate that like the inmates, the guards are exposed to the spatial and monotonous limitations of the prison; together with their almost unlimited power over the inmates, this exposure appears to sometimes turn ordinary men into sadistic warders.

4.2. *Level 2*: The 'Normal' Inmates

The prisoner's transformation from outsider to insider is of primary importance with regard to bodily experience and the creation of 'docile' bodies. For instance, when Andy Dufresne (Tim Robbins) arrives at the Shawshank State Prison in *The Shawshank Redemption*, his body is hosed down with cold water and covered with delousing powder. He is then given his prison uniform and a bible and has to walk naked to his cell.[13] In the course of this dehumanizing process Andy becomes convict # 37927. Similarly, when Alex (Malcolm McDowell) is sent to H.M. Prison Parkmoor in *A Clockwork Orange* (dir. Stanley Kubrick, 1971), he has to hand over his clothes

12 Other examples of sadistic guards are Kramer (Crahan Denton) in *Birdman of Alcatraz*, Hamidou (Paul Smith), the big and brutish chief guard in *Midnight Express* (dir. Alan Parker, 1978) and Captain Hadley (Clancy Brown) in *The Shawshank Redemption* (dir. Frank Darabont, 1994).

13 Throughout the film, the prison in *The Shawshank Redemption* is associated with a womb and a tomb. The voice-over narrator Red (Morgan Freeman) compares the new fish to new-born babies: "They march you in *naked as the day you were born, skin burning and half blind* [my emphasis] [...]." For the inmate 'Fat Ass' (Frank Medrano), who is beaten to death by Captain Hadley, the prison immediately becomes a tomb. For Andy, on the other hand, the prison becomes a womb from which he is reborn. In the course of his escape, Andy has to inch his way through a sewage pipe. He emerges from the pipe in the middle of a rain shower, strips off his shirts and extends his arms up from his half-naked body to the sky, while the showery rain washes down on him. These images suggest some kind of birth or rebirth.

to a prison officer who places them in a box. At the same time, the Chief Guard interviews Alex about his bodily disposition, which places the new inmate in a field of surveillance and situates him in a network of written documentation. In the following scene, he has to stand naked before the Chief Guard who inspects Alex's ass with a torch before the new inmate is given his uniform. Alex thus becomes convict # 6655321. In *Caged* (dir. John Cromwell, 1949), the facial expressions of the new inmate Marie Allen (Eleanor Parker) tell us that she feels humiliated by the impersonal examination in the infirmary. A prison nurse looks into every available orifice with a querulous "I said open wide," which is of course reminiscent of male-dominated sexual intercourse or perhaps even rape. Later on, when they take photographs of her, we see a close-up of her face together with her number: she is now convict # 93850. Apart from the prison uniform, the shaved head represents the most striking visual difference between an insider and an outsider. The cutting of the hair is illustrated in films like *Papillon* (dir. Franklin Schaffner, 1973), *Nineteen Eighty-Four* (dir. Michael Radford, 1984) and *Caged* by means of close-ups of Henri Charrière's (Steve McQueen's), Winston Smith's (Richard Burton's) and Marie's faces. Such close-ups are a "principal method by which the filmmaker can achieve empathy for characters" (Beaver 1994: 69).

Even though a film "cannot convey a character's thoughts, feelings, plans, and so forth in the way fictional literature can" (Lothe 2000: 86), movies offer a number of interesting alternative (cinematic) means of rendering the transformation from outsider to insider. In a sense, we as viewers can observe or witness the slipping away of the newcomers' identities. In the course of the induction process, the new fish are stripped; their bodies are washed, searched, examined, shaved, photographed and, finally, pushed into uniforms.[14] The entry of new inmates is particularly apt for an audiovisual representation: naked bodies march through confined spaces; clanking doors are opened and closed;[15] guards shout at the disoriented newcomers; rude doctors inspect the bodies of the new fish. Additionally, such film images highlight the power the prison institution exercises over the inmates' bodies. In the words of Foucault, the human body enters "a machinery of power that explores it, breaks it down and rearranges it" (1979: 138). In the course of the induction process, prisoners become the objects of individual descriptions and biographical accounts. They are turned into numbers, files and statistics: "The examination surrounded by all its documentary evidence makes each individual a 'case': a case which [...] constitutes an object for a branch of knowledge and a hold for a branch of power" (ibid.: 191).

Once inside the prison machine with its impenetrable rules, the prisoners' bodies come under near-continuous observation. Most British and American prison films

---

14 In *Living Inside Prison Walls* (1998), Victoria R. DeRosia claims that prison films "distort the true nature of life behind bars." Therefore, she presents "a general but *truer* portrayal of prison life" (1998: 17; my emphasis). However, I do not see any difference between the induction process as she describes it (1998: 17-18) and what is usually depicted in prison movies.

15 This is frequently done in a very noisy manner (Becker 2001: 52) in order to heighten the newcomers' shock about being in prison.

present us with close-ups of iron bars which, since they allow prison officers to permanently observe the inmates, correspond to the complete denial of privacy. Historically speaking, the iron cage, which constitutes a "cruel refinement of the Benthamite panoptic surveillance model" (Fludernik 1999: 56), was institutionalized in American state and federal prisons of the twentieth century (Rotman 1995). Even though cages never became a routine manner of confinement in Great Britain and most cells in British prisons of the twentieth century have a metal door with an aperture or peep-hole (Fitzgerald/Sim 1982: 54), images of bars are used in British films because they emphasize the prisoners' enforced confinement and their barred access to the world. When a prisoner is shown physically subordinate to a guard, bars usually dominate the screen, often in silhouette, i.e. in a design of fierce abstraction (Sheehan 1991: 30). Close-ups of bars are used to isolate them "from the surrounding environment for emphasis" (Blandford et al. 2001: 48-49). In other words, they stress the fact that the inmates are caged and available to the permanent gaze of the warders. Many examples of scenes in which bars dominate the screen can be found in *Now Barabbas was a Robber…*, *Yield to the Night* (dir. J. Lee-Thompson, 1956), *Escape from Alcatraz* and *Down by Law* (dir. Jim Jarmusch, 1986). In *You Only Live Once* (dir. Fritz Lang, 1937), *Brubaker* (dir. Stuart Rosenberg, 1980) and *The Chamber* (dir. James Foley, 1996) the near-continuous surveillance of the inmates' bodies is alluded to by means of watchtowers that are filmed from below. Similarly, in *Caged* and *Cool Hand Luke* (dir. Stuart Rosenberg, 1967), guards are filmed from a position below eye level. For instance, in *Caged*, the inmates have to line up next to their beds before they go to sleep. In the course of this procedure, they have to say their second name first, then their first name.[16] In order to check that every prisoner is there, the sadistic matron Evelyn Harper (Hope Emerson) slowly walks through the dormitory. During such moments, she is filmed from below. Furthermore, in *Cool Hand Luke*, Carr, the supervisor of the inmates in Luke's dormitory (Clifton James), is filmed from a position below eye level during his machine-like instructions. Such low-angle shots in which the camera is positioned "below the object(s) being photographed or below eye level," tend to "convey connotations of power, strength and control" (Blandford et al. 2001: 139). Furthermore, films like *White Heat* (dir. Raoul Walsh, 1949) and *Last Dance* (dir. Bruce Beresford, 1996) present shots in which the camera is positioned behind guards who look down at the inmates while they eat, work or walk around the prison yard. Similarly, at the beginning of *The Shawshank Redemption*, when the new inmates arrive at the Shawshank State Prison, we are confronted with a shot of two guards with guns on a bridge that is connected to a watchtower. In the course of this sequence, the camera moves to a position between the two prison officers looking down at the inmates watching the arrival of the newcomers. Such high-angle shots can be said to stress the permanent surveillance of the inmates from the perspective of the warders. Furthermore, since the guards are physically higher in comparison to the prisoners, these shots additionally emphasize the prison hierarchy.

16 This is another allusion to the inmates' transformed identities.

For Foucault, "the exercise of discipline presupposes a mechanism that coerces by means of observation" (1979: 170). In prison films, low-angle and high-angle shots in a way convey two sides of the same coin, namely the inmates' feeling of being permanently watched and the dominance of the prison machine. In other words, such shots comment on hierarchical observation. They convey the fact that the inmates are exposed to the classificatory eyes of their masters, who control their bodies and impose "upon them a relation of docility-utility" (ibid.: 137). Interestingly, we as viewers usually find ourselves in a position which is reminiscent of the position of the guards who *watch* and interpret the inmates' bodies in prison but are not in a position to gain direct access to their minds. For example, in *The Loneliness of the Long-Distance Runner* (dir. Tony Richardson, 1964) Colin Smith (Tom Courtenay), an inmate of a borstal and an impressive long-distance runner, is supposed to win a cup in a running contest. Throughout the film, we do not learn anything about Colin's intentions of not getting the cup. We do not find out that Colin will lose until the end of the race itself, when he deliberately pauses near the finish in a final statement of contempt against authority: Colin arrives at the finishing line far in front of the other competitors and deliberately stops short of the tape (Crowther 1989: 34). Similarly, in the course of *The Shawshank Redemption*, we do not learn anything about Andy's escape plans before we see his escape on the screen. That is to say, the prisoner's body plays an important role in both real prisons and prison films because guards and viewers have to rely upon bodily signs or movements to gain knowledge about inmates.

The prisoner's body is of course also affected by the physical violence between keepers and their charges as well as inmate-on-inmate violence (Cooke et al. 1990: 42). Generally speaking, violence in prison films is not aestheticized.[17] Rather, its representation creates empathy with the victim. For instance, in *I Am a Fugitive From a Chain Gang!* (dir. Mervyn LeRoy, 1932), inmates are whipped for no reason at all. Russell Campbell describes such a scene as follows: "the shadow of the strap moves up and down the wall, as the crash of leather and [...] *excruciating yells of pain are heard*" (1971: 18; my emphasis). Similarly, at the beginning of *The Shawshank Redemption*, Captain Hadley (Clancy Brown) beats the prisoner "Fat Ass" (Frank Medrano) to death because he was crying in his cell. The sequence is played out in the darkness and silence of the Shawshank State Prison. The only sound we can hear apart from the noise of the fight is the murmuring of the other inmates in their cells. In the course of the sequence, their voices gradually fade away, which mirrors the gradual fading away of the prisoner's life force. When "Fat Ass" lies immobile on the cold floor, a state of total silence is achieved. The whole beating is presented by means of a long shot, which, in combination with the dark setting, reduces the protagonists to

---

17 The most important cinematic techniques that became the normative means of aestheticizing violence in the late 1960s were multicamera filming, slow motion, montage editing (i.e. building a sequence out of many very short shots) and the excessive use of non-diegetic music (i.e. music that does *not* come from a source located in the current scene) (Prince 2000: 10).

indistinct shadows. With regard to this sequence, "the point of view of the violence is external" and creates "empathy for the victim" (Bailey 2000: 82).

I shall now turn to cinematic representations of inmate-on-inmate violence. According to Zimbardo, the greatest threat to any prisoner's life comes from fellow prisoners. Due to the tense atmosphere in prison, the inmates' tempers can flare quite easily. For instance, in *Escape from Alcatraz* two fights between the newcomer Frank Morris (Clint Eastwood) and the muscular inmate Wolf (Bruce M. Fischer) occur. The first tussle takes place in the shower room, where Wolf leeringly announces that he is looking for a "new punk." However, his sexual suggestion results "in his having his mouth washed out with soap" (Combs 1980: 117). Later on, Wolf attempts a knifing in the prison yard. This time, the guards step in and send both of them to the 'hole' (Sheehan 1991: 30). The situation between the inmates of the English borstal in *Scum* can best be captured in terms of Thomas Hobbes's *bellum omnium contra omnes*: everyone fights everyone else. The major conflict takes place between Carlin on the one hand, and Banks (John Blundell), Richards (Phil Daniels) and Eckersley (Ray Burdis) on the other. In the most famous scene of the film, the camera follows Carlin down the stairs into the snooker room of the borstal where he puts two snooker balls into a sock. He then walks into an adjacent room and smashes Richards in the face. Having felled one rival, Carlin walks back upstairs, finds Banks in the bathroom and bangs his head against the sink.

As I have already said, for Foucault, inmate-on-inmate violence constitutes an undesigned form of prison violence, while uncontrolled outbreaks of violence between guards and inmates are counterproductive forms of official punishment. Nonetheless, he stresses that "corporal punishment" has always been an integral part of the prison system (1979: 16). This is definitely true from a historical perspective. Violent outbreaks between guards and prisoners have always constituted an important aspect of the experience of imprisonment in both Britain (House of Commons 1987; Prison Reform Trust 1990; Scraton et al. 1991: 61ff., 132ff.) and America (Braswell et al. 1994; Silberman 1995: 19-23). Moreover, in real prisons, violence between convicts occurs more frequently than violence between prisoners and prison officers (Silberman 1995: 15-19; O'Donnell/Edgar 1999). However, this type of violence tends to be underrepresented in prison movies. I would argue that this lack of prisoner-on-prisoner violence has to be attributed to the general perspective of the prison film. Since prison movies tend to sympathize with prisoners (Hardy 1997: 269) and concentrate on the unjust treatment they are given behind prison walls, inmate-on-inmate violence is not represented as frequently as it actually occurs. Additionally, I would argue that both types of violent outbreaks (i.e. between prison officers and convicts as well as between inmates) are partly caused by the monotony, that is by the endless repetitions and the deadening sameness of prison routine, which leads to a heightened awareness of one's bodily functions and consequently to frustration.

One major deprivational technique of the prison involves sexual deprivation. Even though most inmates are not homosexual, isolating men from women usually increases the incidence of homosexual behavior among inmates. Homoerotic practices can be romantic as in the movie *Midnight Express*, in which the heterosexual prisoner Bill

Hayes (Brad Davis) sleeps with Erich (Norbert Weisser). Similarly, in *Kiss of the Spiderwoman* (dir. Hector Babenco, 1985), the heterosexual inmate Valentin Arregui (Raul Julia) eventually agrees to sleep with the homosexual prisoner Erich Luis Molina (William Hurt). However, homoerotic practices in prison are usually based on violence and rape. Interestingly, sexual deprivation is not the only cause of homosexual rapes. Instead, in the prison context, where hierarchies play a crucial role, rape is also an expression of power (Mariner 2001: 96; Pinar 2001: 1013). It is also worth noting that most of the 'homosexual' rapists actually view themselves as heterosexuals. In order to preserve a heterosexual identity while engaging in homosexual behavior, the aggressors feminize their victims, placing men who play 'female' roles in 'submissive' positions (Mariner 2001: 70). "From this perspective the crucial point is not that they are having sex with a man; instead it is that they are the aggressor, as opposed to the victim – the person doing the penetration as opposed to the one being penetrated" (ibid.). For example, Andy is frequently raped by the 'sisters' in *The Shawshank Redemption* while Red explicitly states that the 'sisters' are not homosexual. He argues that "they'd have to be human first." We are also presented with 'homosexual' rapes in other prison movies. For example, in *Brubaker*, an old prisoner sodomizes a younger one, and no one intervenes. In the borstal in *Scum*, three older inmates gang-rape the young and introspective inmate Davis (Julian Firth) on a table in a greenhouse. While raping him, they punch him in the belly. Throughout the rape, we hear Davis's screams while viewing close-ups of his distorted face. Mr Sands, the senior officer of the borstal (John Judd), watches the whole rape without interfering. Later on in the film, Davis commits suicide because he cannot cope with this appalling situation. Interestingly, both the victims and the rapists in the films mentioned above match the typical description of the members of these group as they are put forward by criminologists. According to Joanne Mariner, rape victims in real prison are typically young, small in size, physically weak or unaggressive; sometimes they possess 'feminine' characteristics such as long hair or a high voice. Typical perpetrators on the other hand are usually stronger than their victims, more assertive, physically aggressive, and more at home in the prison environment (2001: 63).

As I have shown, in contrast to guards who are subject only to the monotony of prison life, 'normal' inmates additionally have to undergo the dehumanizing induction process, in the course of which their bodies are examined, washed and shaved. Moreover, once they are caged, their bodies come under constant surveillance. Additionally, they suffer from sexual deprivation and they face the danger of being beaten up or raped by guards or other inmates. Therefore, in comparison to the guards, the situation of the 'normal' inmates, who are allowed to have contact with one another, leads to a heightened awareness of their bodies.

4.3. *Level 3*: Solitary Confinement

Some convicts, like Stroud in *Birdman of Alcatraz*, are sentenced to solitary confinement, which involves even less sensory stimulation in comparison to the 'normal' inmates. At the beginning of the film, i.e. in 1959, Thomas Gaddis, the author of the novel *Birdman of Alcatraz* (1989/1955) (Edmond O'Brien), tells us that Stroud "spent most of his life behind bars including 43 years in solitary confinement. He has never used a telephone or driven an automobile. The last time he broke bread with another man was in 1916 [...]." Later on in the film, Edmond O'Brien's voice-over narration informs us that

> [...] being in solitary is like being on rails. A man pushes your food through the door. You eat alone. Once a week you get a shower. You walk in the bullpen. Once a month an inmate comes and cuts your hair. You read. You pace your cell. Once a week you get clean laundry. You pace your cell. The routine's always the same. [...] You sit and listen to your heartbeat and you hear your life ticking away. The thing that swells in your head until you lose your mind is you know absolutely for sure what's coming next.

O'Brien's voice-over is combined with close-ups of parts of Stroud's body, which may be interpreted as an allusion to the inmate's identity crisis. One may feel that Stroud is in a way falling apart. In this sequence, Stroud's body is represented as a series of fragmented parts that in themselves seem to have no identity or essential being. Indeed, the lack of sensory stimulation in solitary confinement drives many inmates crazy. Additionally, it makes every type of distraction interesting. In Stroud's case sparrows provide distraction. One might argue that the only thing that stops him from going insane is his birds and the construction of cages within cages.[18] Other convicts like Jimmy Boyle (David Hayman) in *A Sense of Freedom* (dir. John Mackenzie, 1981) end up in solitary confinement because of their misbehavior in prison. After an extremely violent fight with the screws, Boyle gets four months solitary in a white cell. First, we see the bored Boyle pacing his cell. Then, he hears the guards beating up another prisoner and hits his foot against the door of his cell. He wants them to fight him. Since pain at least involves a proof that one is still alive, he prefers being beaten up to the deadening monotony of solitary confinement. During the night, Boyle repeats the word "time" again and again. Boyle's talking to himself indicates that he is on the verge of madness. Later on, Boyle plans to commit suicide with a razor blade. However, since he does not wish to do the officers a favor, he decides not to kill himself: "Oh, fuck that. They'd love it. They'd think they'd beat me."

Solitary confinement[19] involves a more intense awareness of corporality in comparison to the guards and the 'normal' inmates. With regard to solitary confinement, the inmate is made aware of bodily needs like physical movement, sexuality, seeing and hearing. However, prisoners in solitary lack almost all of these

---

18 The actual prisoner Stroud became one of the leading ornithologists at the time. Since Stroud's birds had been taken away from him at the prison at Leavenworth before he was transferred to Alcatraz in 1942, he should actually be called 'Birdman of Leavenworth' rather than 'Birdman of Alcatraz' (Crowther 1989: 57; Hardy 1997: 270).

19 In the nineteenth century, the Quaker designers of the Pennsylvania (or 'separate') system believed that solitary confinement would be "beneficial to convicted criminals" because "they would be led to meditate upon 'the error of their ways,' with the result that they would refrain from further lawbreaking upon release" (Gibbons 1996: 351-52).

types of sensory stimulation. The fulfillment of the prisoner's bodily needs is deliberately postponed or denied with the result that the tyranny of the body becomes overwhelming (Fludernik 1999: 64). Additionally, prisoners in solitary confinement are not allowed to have newspapers, radios and conversations with others, and frequently (as in the case of Boyle) they are not even allowed to have a pen and paper. Nothing happens at all in solitary. The withdrawal of almost all sensory stimuli is certainly one of the major reasons why inmates in solitary confinement are driven to insanity (Gibbons 1996: 352). With regard to the films mentioned above, both Stroud and Boyle can be said to be about to go 'stir crazy.' For me, it is very obvious that in solitary confinement there remains "a trace of 'torture' in the modern mechanisms of criminal justice" (Foucault 1979: 16). This type of torture is still increased by the darkness of 'the hole,' which is an even more dramatic type of solitary confinement.

4.4. *Level 4*: The 'Hole'

The 'hole' is a dark and unventilated cell where inmates are deprived of decent food, exercise and all human contact (Rotman 1995: 184). In prison films, this form of solitary confinement in darkness is often used as a punishment for misbehaved convicts. Usually, there are no mattresses, washbasins or toilets in the 'hole.' Hence, having to spend time in this prison-within-the-prison involves a complete lack of sensory stimulation (not even light) and often results in a dramatic loss of orientation. In prison films the 'hole' is usually filmed from above. Additionally, convicts frequently have to share their small cells with rats, which carry negative connotations because of their association with dirt. For instance, both Shakes's 'hole' in *Sleepers* and Henri Young's (Kevin Bacon's) 'hole' in *Murder in the First* (dir. Marc Rocco, 1995) are filmed from above. This cinematic technique highlights the claustrophobic design of these tiny cells. Such 'overhead' or 'high-angle shots' tend "to increase the [...] importance of space around a character [...]" (Beaver 1994: 178) and are "often used to imply fate or entrapment" (Blandford et al. 2001: 171).

The sequence in the 'hole' in *Sleepers* is highly interesting from a narratological perspective because we are confronted with a rather confused visual representation (ICJDKEFLGMHNOAPBQ) of three temporal levels, namely (1) the 'now' of the younger Shakes who has to spend time in the 'hole,' (2) the touch football game in the Wilkinson Home for Boys and (3) Shakes's 'lost' childhood.[20] The *actual* chronological order would conform to the following formalization: AB (= childhood) – CDEFGH (= football game) – IJKLMNOPQ (= time in the 'hole').[21] In the film, we are first presented with a slow-motion shot[22] of the guard Nokes throwing the badly wounded

20 We are confronted with an additional fourth temporal level, namely the 'now' of the older Shakes (Jason Patric), the voice-over narrator, who relates his story in the past tense.

21 There is of course a large temporal gap between the time of B, which is part of Shakes's childhood, and the time of C, the beginning of the touch football game in the reform school.

22 "The usual method of achieving slow motion is through the technique of overcranking, or photographing more than 24 frames per second and then projecting the images at sound speed

Shakes into the 'hole' of the reformatory and closing the door, which is followed by a shot of the inmate inspecting his cell (I). The sequence in 'the hole' is intercut with black-and-white shots of the rather violent touch football game against the guards. These flashbacks or enacted mindscreens[23] (Fleishman 1992: 27) are supposed to represent the younger Shakes's memory. After the two shots referred to above, the black-and-white memory sequence sets in and we see the boys deciding that the black inmate Rizzo (Eugene Byrd) is the toughest touch football player (C). This is followed by another shot of Shakes (at a later stage) in his dark cell (J). Then, in the course of the flashback, we see Michael (Brad Renfro) persuading Rizzo to play the touch football game against the guards (D), which is followed by a close-up of Shakes's wounded face in the 'hole' (K). The flashback continues with Michael trying to persuade Rizzo (E), and the game begins (F). Then, we are presented with yet another shot of Shakes in his cell (L). This is followed by the sequence in which the boys win the game and they all begin to chant Rizzo's name (G). Shakes in the 'hole' whispers Rizzo's name, too (M). Then, in the course of the flashback sequence, Michael approaches Nokes and says "Hey Nokes! Good game!" (H). This is followed by a longer sequence of Shakes lying in foetal position on the cell's wet floor together with a rat (N). Since the cell does not even have a pail in the floor to relieve himself, much less a toilet or a washbasin, we can conclude that, the prisoner is lying in his own excrement. Then, once again, we see the inmate sitting in the dark cell (O). At this point, the narrative discourse goes even further back in the prisoner's memory when a projected image of his 'lost' childhood (Shakes and his friends cavorting in a gushing stream of water from an open fire hydrant) (A) is reflected onto actor Joe Perrino's hand (Turner 1996: 40-42).[24] This is then followed by another shot of Shakes in 'the hole' (P), a full-screen rendering of the projected sequence from his childhood (B), and

---

(24 fps)" (Beaver 1994: 313). Michael Ballhaus, the cinematographer of *Sleepers*, reports that this shot was filmed "at 120 fps" (Turner 1996: 42). According to Blandford et al., "slow motion inevitably has the effect of [...] highlighting a piece of action" (2001: 217).

23 An enacted mindscreen is "a dramatic rendering of narration that has itself been dramatized" (Fleishman 1992: 15). That is to say that the younger Shakes, the mindscreen narrator or character-narrator, is seen engaged in a dramatic situation, the touch football game. In this case, the older Shakes, the voice-over narrator, comments upon the images we see on the screen.

24 These narrative jumps are of course not accomplished by a ghostly 'cinematic narrator,' who is somehow in command of the narrative (Black 2001: 301). Rather, I would argue that we as viewers recuperate the sequence in the 'hole' by means of Fludernik's VIEWING frame and the ACTION schema (1996: 43-44), which allows us to reconstruct the actual chronology. As far as the black-and-white sequences are concerned, the younger Shakes becomes a narrative instance, a character-narrator, because – for a short time – we move into his mind and witness his memories as enacted mindscreens (Fleishman 1992: 27). Such character-narrators usually only occur as one part of the narrative discourse which they obviously do not produce. Additionally, I would argue that the projected image, which we can later on see on Shakes's hand even though it is part of the inmate's memory, can be attributed to the prisoner's deranged mind. After having spent a considerable time in the 'hole,' Shakes is not in a position to differentiate between reality and illusion any longer. Viewers can attribute this disruption to an experience of liminality, i.e. account for it by means of the EXPERIENCING frame (Fludernik 1996: 44).

a final shot of Shakes in the 'hole' (Q). Referring to the touch football game, the older Shakes (Jason Patric) states in his voice-over that

> [...] for once we had a victory. But it didn't last. It couldn't last. And *all I wanted to do was die*. I was not alone in the 'hole.' I knew my friends were down in the depths with me. Each in his own cell, each in his own *pain, suffering* his own *demons*. Rizzo was there, too. *I had lost any sense of time*. [My emphasis.]

For me, the confused representation of the actual chronology of 'events' in combination with the *voice-over* section is a brilliant cinematic representation of the younger Shakes's identity crisis, i.e. his feelings of disorientation, terror, fear and his wish to die. These emotions are additionally conveyed by images of the shivering Shakes in the 'hole.'

The movie *Murder in the First*, in which Henri Young has to spend three years naked in a damp and dark cell because he tried to escape from Alcatraz, illustrates how the ravages of the 'hole' and the lack of human contact can turn a relatively harmless criminal into a murderer. At the beginning of the film, a guard throws water from a bucket down at the inmate who lies naked on the floor of his claustrophobic cell. Viewing a close-up of Young's distorted face, we hear him scream in pain. Later on, the Associate Warden Glenn (Gary Oldman), who occasionally chains the inmate and beats him up, opens the small hole of the iron door of Young's cell and says "hello." Suffering from a complete lack of sensory stimulation, Young quickly says "hello" three times to signal that he is willing to communicate. Later on, when his (disgusting-looking) food is pushed into the cell, he says "hello" again. However, there is no answer. Then, in a very touching scene, he sees a small spider, imitates its shape with his left hand and, in order to have contact with this small animal, places a bit of his 'food' in front of it. Once the now deranged Young is released from the 'hole,' he kills his fellow inmate Rufus McCain with a spoon.

The ravages of the 'hole' are the most extreme and dramatic form of torture in the penitentiary. The deprivational techniques which focus on the curtailing of inmates' rights (in terms of having their needs and desires met) are here taken to an extreme. Prisoners have to remain in darkness all the time and hence they are not even in a position to distinguish between day and night. The 'hole' operates by means of strategic physical deprivation (lack of bedding, lack of heating, unpalatable food in insufficient quantity). Deprivation is further exacerbated by the deliberate infliction of physical discomfort (no bed or chair) and the refusal to supply even minimal 'tools' of civilization (no washbasin, no toothbrush, no comb, no sanitary towels). Even the most basic bodily needs (like having to go to the toilet) are curtailed in the 'hole.' Frequently, inmates have to sleep lying in their own excrement. As a result, the prisoner's suffering is intensified in comparison to the other three levels by making him or her most acutely aware of the body and its needs. The knowledge that one's bodily needs and desires will remain unfulfilled make the awareness of the ineluctability or inescapability of one's bodied physicality unbearable (Fludernik 1999: 64). Therefore, inmates in the 'hole' experience an increased sense of their bodies in comparison to the guards, the 'normal' inmates and the prisoners in solitary confinement. One might even argue that since the confined space frame and darkness of the 'hole' are reminiscent of a tomb, inmates in the 'hole' are forced to exist in a limbo world somewhere between life and death.

5. Consequences and Conclusions

As I have shown, Foucault's arguments in *Discipline and Punish* provide an interesting starting point for my own analysis of British and American prison films. Such movies illustrate the fact that the disciplining in the prison system is based on deprivational techniques which make inmates acutely aware of their bodily needs. Prison films present us with "the whole technology of power over the body" that prisons gather together in their enclosed architecture (Foucault 1979: 30-31). In this paper, I have amplified on Foucault's interest in the prisoner's corporality by distinguishing between four more or less dramatic types of the awareness of one's body, within the disciplinary space of the prison. Moreover, in contrast to Foucault, I have explicitly dealt with the prison officers' sense of corporality.[25] The whole prison population (guards and inmates) is subject to the boredom of the unyielding prison routine, i.e. the fact that nothing really happens behind prison walls. Interestingly, in a diary written for the historian Norval Morris, Simon "Sam" Gutierrez, an actual inmate of Stateville Prison, Illinois, states that "*the major problem is monotony. It is the dull sameness of prison life, its idleness and boredom, that grinds me down*" (qtd in Morris 1995: 228). Even though we as outsiders may feel that this is a relatively harmless form of sensory deprivation, it involves an increased sense of one's body in comparison to 'normal' life and partially explains outbreaks of violence between prisoners as well as the recurring sadistic behavior of prison guards. In comparison to the guards on *level 1*, 'normal' inmates on *level 2* are additionally exposed to the dehumanizing induction process and, once inside the prison, the penetrating gaze of the warders. What is more, they suffer from sexual deprivation, which increases the incidence of homosexual behavior, and they are also in permanent danger of being beaten up or raped. In 1996, an inmate of an American prison sent the following letter to Human Rights Watch:

> When I first came to prison, I had no idea what to expect. Certainly none of this. I'm a tall white male, who unfortunately has a small amount of feminine characteristics. And very shy. These characteristics have got me raped so many times I have no more feelings physically. I have been raped by up to 5 black men and two white men at a time. I've had knifes [sic] at my head and throat. I had fought and been beat [sic] so hard that I didn't ever think I'd see straight again. One time when I refused to enter a cell, I was brutally attacked by staff and taken to segregation

---

25 At this point, it is perhaps worth noting that Foucault does mention the guards. However, he does not elaborate on his argument (1979: 176-77). Additionally, one can criticize Foucault for not distinguishing between male and female senses of one's corporality. The prison experience is arguably different for women. For instance, in contrast to male inmates, female prisoners like Marie Allen in *Caged* may sometimes be forced to give birth in prison.

> though I had only wanted to prevent the same and worse by not locking up with my cell mate [...]. (Mariner 2001: xv)[26]

As far as solitary confinement (*level 3*) is concerned, the prisoners are in complete mental and physical isolation, which entails another increase of sensory deprivation and hence a heightened sense of one's body. One can of course argue that the bodily experience of being beaten up or raped involves a higher awareness of one's corporality than the sensory deprivation with which solitary confinement correlates. However, on the one hand, I would agree with the narrator of the short novel "Rita Hayworth and Shawshank Redemption" (1995/1982), who points out that "[...] as you go down into progressive darkness towards terrible, it gets harder and harder to make subdivisions" (1995: 70); on the other hand, I would like to stress that in the nineteenth century, the extreme conditions of solitary confinement at Pittsburgh Penitentiary and the Philadelphia prison drove many prisoners to insanity (Gibbons 1996: 352), which was most probably caused by the complete lack of sensory stimuli. Many inmates in solitary actually went and perhaps still go 'stir crazy.' A report by a former inmate of Ohio State Penitentiary who was placed in solitary confinement for an inhumane length of time confirms this:

> I was recently released from solitary confinement after being held therein for thirty-seven months. The silence system was imposed on me and if I even whispered to the man in the next cell resulted in being beaten by the guards, sprayed with chemical mace, black jaked, stomped, and thrown into a strip cell naked to sleep on a concrete floor without bedding, covering, washbasin, or even a toilet ... I know that thieves must be punished, and I don't justify stealing even though I am a thief myself. But now I don't think I will be a thief when I am released. No, I am not rehabilitated either. It is just that I no longer think of becoming wealthy or stealing. I now only think of killing – killing those who have beaten me and treated me as if I were a dog. (qtd in Zimbardo 1999)

The ex-prisoner here alludes to an even more dramatic form of punishment in a "strip cell." As I have shown, in such strip cells, 'pits' or 'holes' (*level 4*) the torture of the inmate's body by means of deprivational techniques reaches its climax. The lack of any type of visual stimulation and intellectual communication in combination with the lack of clothing, proper food, mattresses, toilets and washbasins make the awareness of one's body most powerful in 'the hole.' The acute awareness of their bodies in the darkness of these small cells frequently drives inmates to the verge of madness or even makes murderers out of relatively harmless criminals.[27]

---

26 The results of the report *No Escape - Male Rape in U.S. Prisons* (2001) are shocking. Male prisoner-on-prisoner sexual abuse is no aberrational occurrence. Rather, it is a deeply-rooted, systemic problem. A report about sexual misconduct in US women's prisons is also available (Human Rights Watch 1996).

27 The film *Murder in the First* is based on actual events and the final script is based on "painstaking research" (Fisher 1995: 37). David A. Ward at least implicitly verifies the story about Young by pointing out that James A. Johnston, the first warden of Alcatraz, "allowed for the confinement of particularly troublesome inmates in several cells located under the floor of

My four-level model applies first and foremost to prison films. The focus on what prisoners and guards lack in prison might help to explain the sadistic behavior of prison officers, violent outbreaks in prison as well as the question of why inmates in solitary confinement are sometimes driven to insanity. In other words, my four-level model, which is based on the awareness of one's body, can shed a light on what happens to protagonists in prison from a psychological point of view. The model additionally provides an interesting perspective on the 'mind-body' problem, i.e. on the question of whether both physical and mental states exist, and whether they interact or whether they are otherwise related. My investigation of guards and inmates in the liminal site of the prison suggests a very close link between the mind and the body which may be described in terms of 'dualist interactionism.' In other words, in prison, it is almost impossible to clearly separate psychological and corporal forces. Rather, they have to be conceptualized in terms of dialectical mediation.

As far as today's real prisons are concerned, it is perhaps worth noting that the 'hole' is not used any longer. Nevertheless, this type of punishment was used in both American (Orland 1975: 71-74; Ward 1994: 85)[28] and British prisons (Fitzgerald/Sims 1982: 109). Furthermore, the danger of being beaten up or raped still constitutes and important aspect of the experience of imprisonment in both Britain and America. That is to say, my four-level model also applies to the *historical* development of imprisonment in the two countries, and might help to explain the inner states and motivations of people in prison. Yet, I do not wish to suggest that prison films always present us with 'realistic' pictures of the situation behind bars or that authenticity is the ultimate criterion for a 'good' prison movie (Querry 1973: 197). Prison films transform and alter the reality of penal practices; sometimes for the sake of dramatic impact. For instance, prison movies usually concentrate on violence between guards and inmates, whereas in real prisons, inmate-on-inmate violence occurs much more frequently. Furthermore, homosexual rapes are often depicted in British prison movies. However, few facts are available about actual rapes in British prisons.[29] Also, notably, whereas a large percentage of inmates in US prisons are African American or Hispanic (Morris 1995: 240), in American prison movies the majority of inmates is still white.

At this point, I wish to note that Fludernik's 'natural' narratology accounts for our reactions as viewers of prison films. To begin with, her redefinition of narrativity in

---

the main cell-house – the so-called dungeon. Here inmates were locked up in alcoves behind a barred grille with only a pail for bodily functions. In some cases inmates were handcuffed to the grille door so that they had to remain standing during the workday hours" (Ward 1994: 85). Interestingly, Warden Johnston himself says about these dungeons that in "the few instances when" he "did use them," the men had to be chained "to keep them from breaking out and running amuck" (1949: 253).

28 In most American prisons, solitary confinement is still used as a form of punishment. In 1997 about 13,000 inmates had to serve time in solitary (Amnesty International 1998: 122). Interestingly, in some American prisons, even solitary confinement in darkness is still used as a form of punishment (Human Rights Watch 1991: 45; Conrad 1989: 284; DeRosia 1998: 22).

29 For example, a fairly recent British study of inmate victimization by Ian O'Donnell and Kimmett Edgar (1998) makes no reference to the issue at all.

terms of experientiality helps to explain why, despite the genre's typical lack of plot, we still feel that something is narrated when we watch a prison movie. Second, Fludernik's 'natural' narratology offers an explanation for the question of why we usually feel that narratives about inmates in the 'hole' are the most powerful and the most touching narratives despite the definite lack of event sequences. In British and American prison films, the highest level of experientiality is reached in representations of inmates in the 'hole.' Additionally, the highest level of narrativity occurs in these plotless depictions of the claustrophobic dark prison-within-the-prison. It is no coincidence that Bruce Crowther argues that the progressively deadening effect of Henri Charrière's lengthy spells – first two, then another five years in the 'hole' – in *Papillon* "wreak almost as much damage on the audience as they do on the hapless convict." Crowther goes on to speculate that "audiences stumbling out of movie theatres after this particular movie-going experience were probably as relieved as if they'd just completed hard time themselves" (1989: 46-47). The levels of both the awareness of one's corporality and narrativity reach their peak in the 'hole.' Fludernik argues that the specific aesthetic effect of narrative need not rely on the teleology of plot but can be produced also by the mimetically motivated evocation of human consciousness and its (sometimes chaotic) experience of being in the world (1996: 30). In depictions of the prison subject in the tomb-like 'hole,' plot elements do not occur. Rather, the viewer is confronted with a highly dramatic and chaotic type of the experience of being in the world. Since we as viewers become most emotionally involved in depictions of inmates suffering in 'the hole,' we establish a maximum of human experientiality and hence narrativity in the viewing process. For example, when Henri Charrière is sent to the 'hole' in *Papillon*, he refuses to admit that his friend Dega (Dustin Hoffman) has been smuggling him supplementary rations of food. The prisoner is then restricted to half-rations and locked in full darkness (Parish 1991: 319). Charrière begins to eat insects and to lose his teeth. When the disinterested warden (William Smithers) announces that "he's dying," we are confronted with a shot of the inmate's face, which is full of agony and despair. In such moments, viewers maximally empathize with the suffering of a protagonist.

As I have shown, in prison films, the inmates' interior states are usually alluded to by 'indirect' visualizations like facial expressions or bodily positions on the one hand, and screams of horror on the other. With regard to such images and sounds, cinema audiences mostly establish human experientiality by means of the VIEWING schema (Fludernik 1996: 43). Since concepts like the cinematic narrator or the *filmic compositional device* (FCD) have no heuristic value for the close reading of a film or the constitution of narrativity by the viewer, I suggest to eliminate them (cp. Griem/Voigts-Virchow 2002: 163).

Finally, I want to comment on the question of why it is important to deal with prison narratives, i.e. films, novels and autobiographies. In an article about contemporary prisons in the US, the historian Norval Morris argues that "it is not easy to portray life in prison; *bland description would miss the inner reality*." Therefore, he uses "the *literary device* of a diary in one day and one night in the life of a typical prisoner in a typical prison adjacent to a typical industrial city" (1995: 227-28; my emphasis). I would like to follow this argument and point out that prison films (as well as prison novels and prison autobiographies) fill a very important gap. Since they centrally engage with the *experience* of imprisonment and the *feelings* and *emotions* involved in penal practices, they force us as readers and viewers to reconstruct these feelings in the reading or viewing process. Hence, in contrast to a mere description of prisons, prison narratives contribute to a more profound understanding of the prison system and the interactions behind prison walls.

5. Works Cited

5.1. Films (in chronological order)

I Am a Fugitive from a Chain Gang. Dir. Mervyn LeRoy. Warner Bros., 1932.
You Only Live Once. Dir. Fritz Lang. United Artists, 1937.
Caged. Dir. John Cromwell. Warner Bros., 1949.
Now Barabbas was a Robber... Dir. Gordon Parry. Teddington Studios/Warner Bros., 1949.
Prison Warden. Dir. Seymour Friedman. Columbia, 1949.
White Heat. Dir. Raoul Walsh. Warner Bros., 1949.
Yield to the Night (US: *Blonde Sinner*). Dir. J. Lee-Thompson. ABP, 1956.
Birdman of Alcatraz. Dir. John Frankenheimer. United Artists, 1962.
The Quare Fellow. Dir. Arthur Dreifuss. British Lion/Bryanston, 1962.
The Loneliness of the Long-Distance Runner. Dir. Tony Richardson. British Lion/Bryanston, 1964.
Cool Hand Luke. Dir. Stuart Rosenberg. Warner Bros.-Seven Arts, 1967.
A Clockwork Orange. Dir. Stanley Kubrick. Warner Bros., 1971.
Papillon. Dir. Franklin J. Schaffner. Columbia Pictures, 1973.
Midnight Express. Dir. Alan Parker. Columbia, 1978.
Escape from Alcatraz. Dir. Don Siegel. Paramount, 1979.
Scum. Dir. Alan Clarke. Berwyn Street Films, 1979.
Brubaker. Dir. Stuart Rosenberg. Twentieth-Century-Fox, 1980.
A Sense of Freedom. Dir. John Mackenzie. Scottish TV, 1981.
Nineteen Eighty-Four. Dir. Michael Radford. Umbrella/Virgin/TCF, 1984.
Kiss of the Spiderwoman. Dir. Hector Babenco. HB Filmes/Island Available/Palace, 1985.
Down by Law. Dir. Jim Jarmusch. Island, 1986.
Death and the Maiden. Dir. Roman Polanski. Capitol Films, 1994.
The Shawshank Redemption. Dir. Frank Darabont. Castle Rock Entertainment, 1994.
Murder in the First. Dir. Marc Rocco. Le Studio Canal +, 1995.
The Chamber. Dir. James Foley. Universal Pictures, 1996.

Last Dance. Dir. Bruce Beresford. Touchstone Pictures, 1996.
Sleepers. Dir. Barry Levinson. Propaganda Films/Baltimore Pictures, 1996.
The Green Mile. Dir. Frank Darabont. Universal, 1999.

5.2. Secondary Works

Alber, Jan (2003) "Das Gefängnis im Hollywoodfilm: Strafvollzug zwischen Fiktion und Realität." *Zeitschrift für Strafvollzug und Straffälligenhilfe* 1: 31-40.

Amnesty International (1998) *USA: Hüter der Menschenrechte?* Bonn: Amnesty International.

Armstrong, David (1994) "Bodies of Knowledge/Knowledge of Bodies." *Reassessing Foucault: Power, Medicine and the Body*. Ed. Colin Jones and Roy Porter. London and New York: Routledge. 17-27.

Armstrong, Richard B., and Mary Willems Armstrong, ed., (2001) *Encyclopedia of Film Themes, Settings and Series*. Jefferson, NC and London: McFarland.

Bailey, John, ASC (2000) "Bang Bang Bang, Ad Nauseam [1994]." *Screening Violence*. Ed. Stephen Prince. London: The Athlone Press. 79-85.

Bammann, Kai (2001) "Orte der Bestrafung: Wo Hollywood seine Verbrecher hinschickt und warum dies weit weniger Science-fiction ist, als es auf den ersten Blick scheint." *Zeitschrift für Strafvollzug und Straffälligenhilfe* 4: 233-38.

Beaver, Frank E. (1994) *Dictionary of Film Terms: The Aesthetic Companion to Film*. New York: Twayne Publishers.

Becker, Jörg (2001) "Gefängnisbilder: Die Entlassung - Der Besuch." *Filmgeschichte* 15: 51-56.

Bentham, Jeremy (1995) *The Panopticon Writings*. Ed. with Introduction by Miran Bozovic. London and New York: Verso.

Black, David A. (2001) "Narrative." *Critical Dictionary of Film and Television Theory*. Ed. Roberta E. Pearson and Philip Simpson. London and New York: Routledge. 300-3.

Blandford, Steven, Barry Keith Grant, and Jim Hillier (2001) *The Film Studies Dictionary*. London: Arnold.

Bordwell, David (1985) *Narration in the Fiction Film*. London: Routledge.

Branigan, Edward (1992) *Narrative Comprehension and Film*. London and New York: Routledge.

Braswell, Michael C., Reid H. Montgomery, and Lucien X. Lombardo (1994) *Prison Violence in America*. Second Edition. Cincinnati, OH: Anderson.

Brooks, Peter (1993) *Body Work: Objects of Desire in Modern Narrative*. Cambridge, MA: Harvard Univ. Press.

Campbell, Russell (1971) "I Am a Fugitive from a Chain Gang." *The Velvet Light Trap Review of Cinema* 1: 17-20.

Chatman, Seymour (1990) *Coming to Terms: The Rhetoric of Narrative in Fiction and Film*. Ithaca, NY and London: Cornell Univ. Press.

Combs, Richard (1980) "Less is More: Don Siegel From the Block to the Rock." *Sight and Sound* 49.2: 117-21.

Conrad, John P. (1989) "The Researcher's Work is Never Done." *The American Prison: Issues in Research and Policy*. Ed. Lynne Goodstein and Doris Layton MacKenzie. New York and London: Plenum Press. 273-286.

Cooke, David J., Pamela J. Baldwin, and Jacqueline Howison (1990) *Psychology in Prisons*. London and New York: Routledge.

Crowther, Bruce (1989) *Captured on Film: The Prison Movie*. London: Batsford.

DeRosia, Victoria R. !998) *Living Inside Prison Walls: Adjustment Behavior*. Westport, CT and London: Praeger.

Felperin, Leslie (1997) "Sleepers." *Sight and Sound* 7.1: 45-46.

Fisher, Bob (1995) "*Murder in the First* Probes Humanity's Dark Side: Cinematographer Fred Murphy and Director Marc Rocco Measure Man's Inhumanity to Man." *American Cinematographer* 76.5: 36-44.

Fitzgerald, Mike, and Joe Sim (1982) *British Prisons*. Second Edition. Oxford: Basil Blackwell.

Fleishman, Avrom (1992) *Narrated Films: Storytelling Situations in Cinema History*. Baltimore, MD and London: The Johns Hopkins Univ. Press.

Fludernik, Monika (1993) "Narratology in Context." *Poetics Today* 14.4: 729-61.

Fludernik, Monika (1996) *Towards a 'Natural' Narratology*. London and New York: Routledge.

Fludernik, Monika (1999) "Carceral Topography: Spatiality and Liminality in the Literary Prison." *Textual Practice* 13.1: 43-77.

Foucault, Michel (1979) *Discipline and Punish: The Birth of the Prison* [1975]. Trans. Alan Sheridan. New York: Vintage Books.

Foucault, Michel (1980) *Power/Knowledge: Selected Interviews and Other Writings 1972-1977*. Ed. Colin Gordon. New York et al.: Prentice Hall.

Foucault, Michel (1988) *Politics, Philosophy, Culture: Interviews and Other Writings 1977-1984*. Ed. Lawrence D. Kritzman. Trans. Alan Sheridan. New York and London: Routledge.

Frese Witt, Mary Ann (1985) *Existential Prisons: Captivity in Mid-Twentieth Century French Literature*. Durham, NC: Duke Univ. Press.

Gaddis, Thomas E. (1989) *Birdman of Alcatraz: The Story of Robert Stroud* [1955]. With an Epilogue by Phyllis E. Gaddis. San Francisco: Comstock Editions.

Gibbons, Don C. (1996) "Pennsylvania System." *Encyclopedia of American Prisons*. Ed. Marilyn D. McShane and Frank R. Williams III. London and New York: Garland Publishing. 351-53.

Greenblatt, Stephen (1988) *Shakespearean Negotiations: The Circulation of Social Energy in Renaissance England*. Oxford: Clarendon Press.

Griem, Julika, and Eckart Voigts-Virchow (2002) "Filmnarratologie: Grundlagen, Tendenzen und Beispielanalysen." *Erzähltheorie transgenerisch, intermedial, interdisziplinär*. Ed. Ansgar Nünning and Vera Nünning. Trier: Wissenschaftlicher Verlag Trier. 155-83.

Hale, Christopher (1982) "Punishment and the Visible." *The Prison Movie*. Ed. Mike Nellis and Christopher Hale. London: Radical Alternatives to Prison. 50-64.

Hardy, Phil, ed., (1997) *The BFI Companion to Crime*. Foreworded by Richard Attenborough. London: Cassell.

House of Commons (1987) *Report of an Enquiry by Her Majesty's Chief Inspector of Prisons for England and Wales into the Disturbances in Prison Service Establishments in England Between 29 April-2 May 1986*. London: Her Majesty's Stationery Office.

Human Rights Watch (1991) *Prison Conditions in the United States*. A Human Rights Watch Report. New York et al.: Human Rights Watch.

Human Rights Watch (1996) *All Too Familiar: Sexual Abuse of Women in U.S. State Prisons*. A Human Rights Watch Report. New York et al.: Human Rights Watch.

Jahn, Manfred (2002) "A Guide to Narratological Film Analysis." 21 October 2003. <www.uni-koeln.de/~ame02/pppf.htm>.

Johnston, James A. (1949) *Alcatraz Island Prison*. New York and London: Charles Scribner's Sons.

King, Stephen (1995) "Rita Hayworth and Shawshank Redemption [1982]." *Different Seasons*. Ed. Stephen King. New York: Warner Books. 9-113.

Kozloff, Sarah (1988) *Invisible Storytellers: Voive-Over Narration in American Fiction Film*. Berkeley, CA: Univ. of California Press.

Kuppers, Petra (2001) "Body." *Critical Dictionary of Film and Television Theory*. Ed. Roberta E. Pearson and Philip Simpson. London and New York: Routledge. 45-50.

Lakoff, George, and Mark Turner (1989) *More than Cool Reason: A Field Guide to Poetic Metaphor*. Chicago, IL: Univ. of Chicago Press.

Levinsohn, Jerrold (1996) "Film Music and Narrative Agency." *Post-Theory. Reconstructing Film Studies*. Ed. David Bordwell and Noël Carroll. Madison, WI: Univ. of Wisconsin Press. 248-82.

Lohmeier, Anke-Marie (1996) *Hermeneutische Theorie des Films*. Tübingen: Niemeyer.

Lothe, Jakob (2000) *Narrative in Fiction and Film: An Introduction*. Oxford: Oxford Univ. Press.

Mariner, Joanne (2001) *No Escape: Male Rape in U.S. Prisons*. New York: Human Rights Watch.

McConville, Seán (1995) "The Victorian Prison. England, 1865-1965." *The Oxford History of the Prison: The Practice of Punishment in Western Society*. Ed. Norval Morris and David J.Rothman. New York and Oxford: Oxford Univ. Press. 131-67.

Morris, Norval (1995) "The Contemporary Prison. 1965-Present." *The Oxford History of the Prison: The Practice of Punishment in Western Society*. Ed. Norval Morris and David J.Rothman. New York and Oxford: Oxford Univ. Press. 227-59.

Mulvey, Laura (2000) "Visual Pleasure and Narrative Cinema [1975]." *The Narrative Reader*. Ed. Martin McQuillan. London and New York: Routledge. 177-81.

Nellis, Mike (1982) "Notes on the American Prison Film." *The Prison Movie*. Ed. Mike Nellis and Christopher Hale. London: Radical Alternatives to Prison. 5-49.

Nellis, Mike (1988) "British Prison Movies. The Case of 'Now Barabbas'." *The Howard Journal* 27.1: 2-31.

O'Donnell, Ian, and Kimmett Edgar (1998) *Bullying in Prisons*. Oxford: Centre for Criminological Research, Univ. of Oxford.

O'Donnell (1999) "Fear in Prison." *Prison Journal* 79: 90-99.

Orland, Leonard (1975) *Prisons: Houses of Darkness*. New York and London: The Free Press.

Parish, James R. (1991) *Prison Pictures from Hollywood: Plots, Critiques, Casts and Credits for 293 Theatrical and Made-for Television Releases*. Jefferson, NC: McFarland.

Pinar, William F. (2001) *The Gender of Racial Politics and Violence in America. Lynching, Prison Rape, and the Crisis of Masculinity*. New York et al.: Peter Lang.

Plato (1987) *The Republic*. Trans. Desmond Lee. London: Penguin.

Prince, Gerald (1995) "On Narratology: Criteria, Corpus, Context." *Narrative* 3.1: 73-84.

Prince, Stephen (2000) "Graphic Violence in the Cinema: Origins, Aesthetic Design, and Social Effects." *Screening Violence*. Ed. Stephen Prince. London: The Athlone Press. 1-44.

Prison Reform Trust (1990) *Submission to Phase 2 of the Woolf Inquiry into Prison Disturbances*. London: Prison Reform Trust.

Querry, Ronald B. (1973) "Prison Movies: An Annotated Filmography 1921-Present." *The Journal of Popular Film* 2: 181-97.

Rimmon-Kenan, Shlomith (2002) *Narrative Fiction: Contemporary Poetics* [1983]. London and New York: Routledge.

Rothman, David J. (1995) "Perfecting the Prison. United States, 1789-1865." *The Oxford History of the Prison: The Practice of Punishment in Western Society*. Ed. Norval Morris and David J.Rothman. New York and Oxford: Oxford Univ. Press. 111-29.

Rotman, Edgardo (1995) "The Failure of Reform. United States, 1865-1965." *The Oxford History of the Prison: The Practice of Punishment in Western Society*. Ed. Norval Morris and David J.Rothman. New York and Oxford: Oxford Univ. Press. 169-97.

Scraton, Phil, Joe Sim, and Paula Skidmore, ed., (1991) *Prisons Under Protest*. Milton Keynes, Philadelphia: Open Univ. Press.

Sheehan, Henry (1991) "Escape from Alcatraz." *Sight and Sound* 1.2: 28-30.

Silberman, Matthew (1995) *A World of Violence: Corrections in America*. Belmont, CA: Wadsworth.

Turner, George (1996) "Revenge Served Cold." *American Cinematographer* 77.10: 34-42.

Ward, David A. (1994) "Alcatraz and Marion: Confinement in Super Maximum Custody." *Escaping Prison Myths: Selected Topics in the History of Federal Corrections*. Ed. John W. Roberts. Washington, D.C.: The American Univ. Press. 81-93.

Ward, David A. (1996) "Architecture." *Encyclopedia of American Prisons*. Ed. Marilyn D. McShane and Frank R. Williams III. London and New York: Garland Publishing, Inc. 34-39.

Whittock, Trevor (1990) *Metaphor and Film*. Cambridge: Cambridge Univ. Press.

Wlodarz, Joe (2001) "Rape Fantasies: Hollywood and Homophobia." *Masculinity. Bodies, Movies, Culture*. New York and London: Routledge. 67-80.

Zimbardo, Philip G. (1982) "The Prison Game." *Legal Process and Corrections*. Ed. N. Johnston and L. D. Savitz. New York: Wiley. 195-98.

Zimbardo, Philip G. (1999) "The Stanford Prison Experiment: A Simulation Study of the Psychology of Imprisonment Conducted at Stanford University." 21 October 2003. <www.prisonexp.org>.

Caliban Revisited: Robben Island in the Autobiographical Record

Monika Fludernik

Robben Island moved into the realm of colonial history when Europeans first rounded the Cape and needed to acquire water supply and food. They landed on Robben Island because the mainland was considered too dangerous on account of the native tribes. Since the early colonial period, the island was used intermittently as a place of exile for political prisoners, other especially dangerous criminals, lunatics, and even lepers. In particular, after the banishment of a number of Xhosa chiefs to Robben Island in the nineteenth century (see Deacon 1997: 33-56) the Island continued to serve as a detention camp for leaders of the native resistance. Following the Sharpeville massacre of 1960 and particularly in the wake of the Rivonia trials (1963-64), Robben Island acceded to the position of eminence that it still holds in the native imagination. On the one hand, the "Island" became a symbol of the worst excesses of the apartheid state and, on the other, during the 70's and 80's was considered a beacon of hope for the country's anti-apartheid movements. As Deacon puts it,

> Regarded as Hell, Purgatory or rural Eden by various groups at various times, Robben Island has always been a powerful element within the symbolic geography of the Cape. [...] The representation of Robben Island as the 'hell hole' of Table Bay, South Africa's Alcatraz, an impregnable place of banishment for those who have opposed the status quo, has long been dominant. But within the South African discourse of liberation, Robben Island has also come to symbolise 'the indestructability of the spirit of resistance against colonialism, injustice and oppression.' The strong political symbolism of the Island has encouraged the historical emphasis that prevails today on the role of the Island as a prison. Both for the state and for its opponents the Island's symbolic value in this regard has at times outstripped its practical value as a place where the leaders of oppositional forces have been separated from their followers. (1997: 5)

This ambiguity of Robben Island as a "hell-hole" (Dlamini 1984) and a "university" of the native elite is reflected in most autobiographical accounts of the island experience. The former political prisoners tell shocking narratives of the treatment they underwent; at the same time they celebrate the pervasive solidarity displayed among comrades and glory in the small victories gained in their battles of resistance against the authorities. As an icon of apartheid cruelty and a site of political struggle, the

Island additionally acquired a symbolic status in the South African colonial imaginary and in the narratives of anti-colonialism.[1]

Because Robben Island prison is situated on an island, with its liminal status and administrative independence, the situation has additionally encouraged comparisons with the myth of Prospero and Caliban. It is indeed noticeable that two of the most influential South African intertextual sources relate to islands: *The Tempest* and *Robinson Crusoe*. Both works are tales of colonial appropriation and foreground a civilizing mission to subdue the supposedly barbarian natives. However, where these literary models attempt the establishment of a utopia on foreign shores, the site of Robben Island prison has been conceived as a dystopia from the start, as a place that is meant to house the rejects of society, to discipline them into mute submission, and to freeze them into political ineffectivity. Except during the very early days of colonial expansion, the Island therefore had a decidedly negative image, even though it was sometimes used as a safari spot for shooting quail or as a health recreation area. Unlike the South Sea island of fantasy that provided the prototype for Defoe's Caribbean location, or the Mediterranean island that constituted an exotic venue for Prospero's magic arts, Robben Island has acquired its grip on the literary and historical imagination as an outpost of progress, a liminal site of disciplinary rigor and exposure that functions both as the epitome of South African society and as its antithesis.

This essay will argue that Robben Island prison memoirs uncover the colonial subtext of the apartheid state by revealing the prison regime on the Island to be equivalent to a type of modern-day slavery. Since the prisoners were all non-whites, the inhuman treatment of them as de facto slaves invokes the colonial framework of American slavery. Secondly, by applying the Caliban metaphor in reference to the convicts, the essay attempts to draw some parallels between Caliban's linguistic resistance to Prospero's teachings and the various forms of resistance deployed by prisoners on the island. This includes discussing the relationship between warders and convicts in terms of the Prospero-Caliban schema. There will be some focus on the solidarity displayed among the prisoners as one of the major strategies of resistance to the dehumanizing treatment.

Section 1 of this paper will briefly characterize the typical features of the Robben Island memoir. In section 2, I will outline recurrent themes and images and point out in what way they differ from more typical prison memoirs. Section 3 will turn to the issue of slavery and to the colonial subtext of the memoirs, and section 4 is dedicated to the politics of resistance on Robben Island.

---

1 What Deacon calls the "symbolic geography" of the Cape can be rewritten into the colonial or racial imaginary of South Africa. I appropriate the now current term to signify the structure of symbolizations associated with South Africa and Robben Island in the colonial and anti-colonial projections on the place. The term itself of course derives from Lacan but has been adopted by postcolonial criticism to signal the imaginary nature of colonial views of the native other. See Linda Nochlin's "imaginary orient" and Vijay Mishra's "diasporic imaginary" (Nochlin 1989, Mishra 1996).

1. How to Write the Hell-Hole

In a superb essay in *Kunapipi*, J. U. Jacobs (1991) outlines the typical features of the South African prison autobiography. Jacobs points out that the titles of such memoirs frequently identify the writers with their administrative identification, i.e. their number, thus signalling the convicts' dehumanization even on the title page of texts published after their release. By contrast, the books' dedications tend to highlight the ex-prisoners' humanity by affirming their solidarity with suffering compatriots and particularly with those comrades still inside.[2] Jacobs goes on to enumerate a series of recurring phrases that are thematized in most texts:

> Thirdly, the actual narrative of the detention or prison process has identifiable contours: an autobiographical introduction; an account of arrest and pre-trial detention; the individual response to solitary confinement; the various methods of interrogation and degrees of torture; the ritual pattern of the security trial with its statements extracted often under duress; witnesses under police control and proceedings in courts often closed to the public; the sentence; induction into prison life; the routine humiliations of prison and the strategies of adjustment and survival that evolve; descriptions of superintendents and warders, prison doctors, psychiatrists and ministers of religion; the enforced and frequently tense fellowship of convicts and political prisoners; the various systems of support and antagonism among prisoners; the compulsion to develop channels of communication and cultivate human contacts; the solidarity with condemned prisoners; the knowledge of how people behave in the face of execution; all the habits of body and mind that define a prisoner until the day of his release. (1991: 116-17)

Jacobs correctly notes that this catalogue is a near-universal one, at least for the writings of political prisoners in authoritarian regimes.

Jacobs then goes on to emphasize two aspects of South African prison memoirs which she sees as "providing valuable access to these books as literary constructs." The two aspects are very different. The first concerns the body searches and literal stripping of prisoners and the harrowing psychological experience of this process. The stripping feels like the equivalent of solitary confinement (Makhoere) and induces a trauma of maximal exposure and complete control by the warders over the imprisoned subject:

> You are stripped bare of everything you can call your own, constantly stripped bare of anything you make your own; you are stripped bare in an endless process of peeling off your protective covering and leaving you naked. So they can watch you ... and watch. (Lewin 1981: 41; qtd Jacobs 1991: 117)

This trauma of being constantly available to the intrusive gaze of the warders is a recurrent feature in all prison literature, but it is exacerbated by the bareness of

---

2 See, for instance, Jeremy Cronin's moving poem "4 times 12": "I lie in bed/ picturing myself/ stepping out/ in a new set of clothes/ with a brown paper packet/ – letters/ seven years of letters/ under my arm/ – in 42 months time/ when some of those comrades/ [...] might/ STILL be inside" (Cronin 1987: 31-32).

maximum security environments and strip cells with which political prisoners have to contend:

> There is little to be seen; four grey walls, a grey floor, and the soles of the warders' boots on the catwalk overhead. (Cronin 1987: 33)[3]

Jacobs's second topic is interrogation under torture. In discussing this point – sadly a recurrent, almost constitutive feature of political imprisonment in South Africa during the apartheid years – Jacobs concentrates on the absurdities of the practice in which truth is being sought through the application of pain that always results in "nothing":

> Always they wanted the truth when I had no more truth to tell. I don't think they ever really understood that in fact there was nothing to give away. But they always tried to find it, this nothing. (Mashinini 1989: 75; qtd Jacobs 1991: 119)

Jacobs continues: "The truth insisted on in each of these interrogations emerges as the unequivocal ignorance of the victim" (120). Echoing Elaine Scarry's insights into the world-destroying functions of torture, Jacobs defines the story of South African prison memoirs as the account of "the destruction of [the prisoner's] own world and language by a whole range of physical and psychological stressors" (125). This destruction constitutes a further level of denudation and attempts to, almost literally, make the prisoner transparent to the interrogator's searching gaze.

Appropriately, South African prison memoirs typically conclude with the glorious moment of liberation. This occasion is used to address the comrades outside, to mark solidarity with former fellow prisoners, and to alert the democratic West to the fate of those still caught in the clutches of South African prison authorities. The Island acquires a symbolic status as an ordeal which freedom fighters have to pass through. In Zwelonke's account the Island has turned into the ultimate test of the ANC [African National Congress] or PAC [Pan-African Congress] member, a kind of martyrdom that will yield personal and collective glory to the resistance movement:

> We could not contain our excitement, mostly arising from the fact that we were at last at Makana Island. We so much loathed being in the mainland prisons, and dreaded being at the Island. But since we were already convicted, and nothing could alter that fact, let us proceed to the place of the martyrs. Our anxiety to be there removed any apprehension about this devil Island. (Zwelonke 1973: 13)

The hell-hole is a place cherished in the symbolic landscape of resistance to apartheid. Its contradictory meanings are underlined by its proximity to the Cape, its closeness to the beauty and normality of South African life across the bay:

3 The reference is to Pretoria Central's maximum security unit.

> Robben Island is eleven kilometres off Cape Town. The road to the quarry where prisoners perform slave labor lies along the sea; they see it and smell it. Just over there is the city of Cape Town, glaring at them with its tall skycrapers and shining lights. Table Mountain looms above, a white mist and clouds. This is a scene of great beauty; looking out at it, Moses Dlamini is standing in hell: he is a political prisoner on Robben Island, betrayed by an informer to Special Branch, the political police. "A cold wind blows and the waves plash over the seashore. The ride is rising and five kilometers away, two passenger liners ply slowly toward Cape Town Harbour. They carry many tourists from the Western countries who are going to tour 'sunny South Africa' ... these tourists will return back to their countries, some with disgust but others with pleasant memories," Dlamini says, watching the other world go by. (Millett 1994: 130)

This contrast between paradise and hell, between normality and human rights abuses is a spurious one – after all, South African Society is based on the system whose outpost of iniquity lies on Robben Island.

2. How to Survive in Hell: A Catalogue of Sufferings

Besides the various stages on the journey from freedom to incarceration and back to the outside world that the writers of Robben Island prison memoirs have to pass through, a number of typical themes are regularly articulated in the texts. These include a list of the most harrowing standard routines of humiliation and abuse on the Island as well as numerous instances and symbolic tokens of prisoners' solidarity. A recurrent topic is the antagonism between different groups of prisoners. On the one hand, the political prisoners during the early 60's (Deacon 1997: 98) were being harassed by the 'Big Five' gang, a group of criminals who operated with the encouragement of the warders and served as overseers. (The pattern corresponded closely to what went on in Nazi concentration camps.[4]) Secondly, extensive antagonism developed between the PAC members and the ANC prisoners who started to populate Robben Island during a second wave of arrests, eventually outnumbering PAC members.[5] The ANC convicts were eventually displaced by large numbers of prisoners belonging to the Black Consciousness movement who arrived at Robben Island after the Soweto uprising of 1976 (Naidoo/Sachs 1982: 267). Whereas, in the first instance, matters of revolutionary doctrine and the practical tactics of resistance on Robben Island were at issue and sometimes led to one party boycotting hunger strikes by the other, in the second instance a generational conflict as much as a political one opened up between the old inmates and a new generation of black activists.

The list of typical experiences and recurrent topics in the memoirs is decisively different from standard prison autobiographies, even South African ones. The nature of imprisonment on Robben Island corresponded to the pattern of concentration

---

4 Compare also Millett (1994: 131-32).

5 The antagonism can be analysed by comparing Naidoo's and Dlamini's accounts. Both are very biased (Dlamini is a PAC representative, Naidoo belongs to the ANC), and their versions of the Island experience at times differ drastically.

camps, Soviet gulags or American boot camps. The subhuman standards of incarceration on the island have been documented in great detail in memoirs as well as in the reports by the Red Cross which started to visit prisoners in the mid-70's.[6] The prevalent images of standard prison literature very rarely dominate in Robben Island memoirs. Thus, the claustrophobic fear of enclosure, of sensory deprivation, of complete loneliness and the unendurable monotony and boredom of solitary confinement are broached only rarely in Robben Island memoirs, and usually refer to the prisoners' detention experience before shipment to Robben Island. These topics are, however, strikingly present in the poetry of Dennis Brutus and Jeremy Cronin as well as the memoirs of Lewin and Breytenbach and refer to periods of incarceration in Pretoria Central or other continental maximum security units. Traditional prison literature additionally tends to dwell on the depressing greyness of walls, the uniformity of prison architecture, the clanging of keys and shuttings of gates and doors as well as the consolations of windows, brief glimpses of the sky, of a blade of grass or a flower or tree on the concrete yard. These motifs recur in fictional accounts of imprisonment as well as in autobiographical material and are clearly based on basic prison conditions which have developed into literary topoi (cp. Fludernik 1999).

By contrast, the topoi in Robben Island prison memoirs resemble those familiar from the holocaust and gulag literature. The most prevalent and lasting memory concerns the prisoners' togetherness in both a positive and a negative sense. Being herded into cells forty at a time, the prisoners have to contend with crowding, lack of privacy, competition for sleeping space, bad smells and insufficient sanitary arrangements (e.g. Zwelonke 1973: 72) as well as abuse from other prisoners including homosexual rape (Dlamini). On the positive side, comrades in arms keep together, protect themselves from other groups, support one another emotionally, and share food and warmth (for instance by sharing the insufficient number of blankets). The prisoners' solidarity additionally results in shrewd strategies of concealment and in survival tactics, the transmission of illegal information (e.g. newspaper extracts), and in common action (strikes, singing). The solidarity among comrades extends from saving new arrivals from being punished to acting in concert for their political aims – actions which tend to bring punishments on those who protest and participate in political activities.

> Before the advent of this type of prisoner, the warder was dealing with convicts: servile, ignorant, selling each other for favours, full of fear, every man for himself. Now they were confronted with united men, taking concerted actions like hungerstrikes, men who would never give witness against a brother who had committed any kind of offence in jail. (Zwelonke 1973: 68)

---

6 For visits by the Red Cross, see Deacon (1997: 106-7) and the moving account of this helpline in Dlamini and Naidoo/Sachs (1982: 162-64). See also Sedlak (1996, 1999).

The help received by newcomers was crucial to their survival. In the following passage Zwelonke describes how the help of his fellow convicts prevented him from losing three meals as a punishment for 'idleness' in the quarry:

> When lunch came, I had made a little heap of stones. I crushed again and again until I felt the muscles of my arm stretched taut to the point of snapping. Two hours after lunch the head-warder came on a round of inspection. He saw my little heap. The next moment his cane landed on my head. I jumped up. He ordered me to sit down and work. I sat and worked. My molehill of stones was dwarfed by the giant anthill of my neighbour. [...] To save me from mealstops, my neighbours gave me many of their crushed stones so that I had a larger heap. (Zwelonke 1973: 36)

Although some of these recurring motifs apply to the carceral experience of the big American correctional facilities, too – on account of the patterns of association practised there –, the extent of communal survival patterns in the Robben Island prison memoirs and the experience of solidarity are more pronounced and closer to the prison camp literature.

Inmates on Robben Island moreover repeatedly articulate their great admiration for their leaders incarcerated in the maximum security wing of the island and insist on the centrality of their political commitment. In fact, the psychological survival of prisoners often depended on their assumption of the role of a heroic martyr for the cause, and their adoration of Mandela or Sisulu clearly approached near-hagiographic proportions. Indeed, in the absence of religious sources of strength and hope, the political cause had to supply this ground of self-assurance and meaning. Political faith helped prisoners endure conditions of imprisonment that were egregiously inhumane and abusive. It fostered a spirit of camaraderie and mutual friendship, supplying badly needed support and care to comrades in circumstances where the authorities deprived inmates of the most basic decencies, medical attention or basic dietary requirements.

As a consequence of the excesses of violence and abuse encountered by prisoners and the support system instituted among politicals, several key features of the camp literature are also significantly inflected in Robben Island memoirs, although other accounts of political detention and imprisonment (e.g. El Sadaawi's work) display a similar focus. Thus, where much holocaust literature focuses on the individual inmate's excessive suffering, the Robben Island memoirs detail abuses at length but minimize the personal experience of pain, humiliation and fear. In fact, many of these texts are written as a record of communal suffering and addressed to comrades outside with the aim of serving as an encouragement to them. The authors want to appear strong in the cause, as models of endurance, and as examples of successful survival. The sufferings are harrowing enough to bear, but the emphasis of the authors is on 'overcoming.' The writers avoid hinting at their own physical and mental breakdown, modestly downplaying their own traumas. Instead they assume the role of witnesses and compassionately tell of the sufferings of others.

Because the PAC and the ANC activists were not religiously motivated, the issue of hope does not often come up.[7] Nevertheless, the utopia of a South Africa beyond apartheid presents itself frequently, and the discourse of endurance reaches quasi-religious proportions. Many of the writers did not emerge into a world of freedom and happiness when liberated from Robben Island but were greeted by a society still in the grip of the apartheid state and had to face years of banishment and exile. Most memoirs were published in the UK as documents delineating the excesses of the apartheid regime. The loyalty of those liberated is with comrades still inside with whom they shared ties often closer than those with family members. Just as early religious martyrs taught the doctrines of Christianity to other prisoners, South African political prisoners instructed each other and tried to impart political awareness to inmates who were not politicals. Raising the general level of literacy additionally helped to open strategies of contact with international organizations in order to draw attention to the human rights abuses prevalent on Robben Island.

> Robben Island was intended to be the place for the destruction of anti-apartheid militants, but instead has become a centre of resistance and the symbol of the indestructibility of the movement for the creation of a non-racial democratic South Africa. (Naidoo/Sachs 1982: 277)

3. Colonialism, Slavery and the Robben Island Experience

Robben Island not only became a symbol of political oppression and resistance – it also displayed colonial structures in particularly obvious ways. Thus, as I have argued elsewhere (Fludernik 2003b), the structures of South African apartheid society were reflected and condensed on Robben Island, emphasizing the oppression of a majority of Africans and Asians by a minority of white immigrants. This relationship was mirrored in the opposition of inmates to warders. Indeed, Robben Island prison became the only South African prison that had exclusively white prison personnel and only non-white inmates (Deacon 1997: 98), a situation that exacerbated abusive treatment and served to symbolize the basic power structure of South African society. The Island therefore represented both a utopian wish-fulfilment of white racists by instituting a place where blacks could be completely controlled and made to bow to the white man; conversely, the Island for non-white South Africans constituted the ultimate trauma of total colonial oppression. This symbolic significance comes out well in a scene in Dlamini's memoir:

> "He's cheeky baas," harps Meintjies pushing the man, "this is not South Africa; this is Robben Island. And this is White man's territory. C'mon." The man goes back with his load accompanied by Meintjies who keeps yelping at him. (Dlamini 1984: 30-31)

---

7 An exception to the rule is a passage in Zwelonke (1973: 115) which compares the suffering on Robben Island to that of Christ.

Conditions on the Island were drastic and much resembled concentration camp levels of physical abuse. Given the fact that the colonial legislation already allowed for the nearly complete subjection of the black population to forced labor and physical punishment (Marx 1998), extending original slavery into systems of near-slavery, what went on in Robben Island constituted an enhanced subjection to work and punishment in circumstances much resembling American chattel slavery. This parallel is underlined by the men's continual exposure to random abuse and harassment by the guards as much as by the conditions of imprisonment and labor themselves. Thus, the locking up of dozens of prisoners in one cell with insufficient sanitary arrangements and an insufficient number of blankets, the poor quality and quantity of food, the indiscriminate withholding of meal tickets (depriving prisoners of their three meals a day) and the refusal to provide proper medical treatment put the convicts into situations of crowding, neglect and abuse typical of slavery.[8]

Even more tellingly, conditions in the quarry were characterized by a complete disregard for prisoners' health[9] and consisted in forcing them to work beyond their physical capacities while keeping them under continuous duress. In addition prisoners were herded to and from the quarry (Dlamini 1984: 29), chained in pairs, with guards threatening them, hounding them with dogs and physically beating and abusing them. As Ogunyemi puts it:

> we sit on the concrete,
> stuff with our fingers
> the sugarless pap
> into our mouths.[10]
>
> As if such indignities and deprivations are not enough, the prisoners, these descendants of a race of slaves, are psychologically demoralized by being chained together in pairs. Brutus' choice of aspects of prison life to emphasize demonstrates his acute awareness of the humiliating experience that is prison life, its emasculation of the black South African in a hideous system that remains apparently unchanging. (Ogunyemi 1982: 68)

Quarry itself was difficult and dangerous slave labor, and it had to be performed under demeaning conditions that were deleterious to the prisoners' health. (Thus no proper clothing or shodding was supplied despite cold winds, nor did the men receive proper goggles to safeguard prisoners' eyesight.[11]) A particularly chilling epsiode recounted in a number of memoirs was the use of prisoners as human cattle forced to draw a big

---

8 See, for instance, Dlamini (1984: 39; 152).

9 Cp. Dlamini (75-76) on the medical treatment of prisoners, as well as Naidoo/Sachs (1982: 137).

10 Quoted from Brutus's "Letters to Martha" (1973: 52).

11 Compare: "The comrade from the Old Prison takes me to where he had been sitting and gives me his wire-mesh goggles to put over my eyes. I take the wire-mesh goggles which have one-eighth inch holes and put them over my eyes. With such big holes I wonder how are they going to protect my pupils from the sharp splinters of quarry stones that will shoot out like jets towards my face" (Dlamini 1984: 34), and the injury of a fellow prisoner (35). See also Naidoo/Sachs (1982: 137).

concrete roller, with a warder stationed on the machine whipping the human crew that was straining to move the machine along (Naidoo/Sachs 1982: 79-80).

Prisoners were also humiliated by being treated as boys dressed in shorts[12] who had to address warders as *baas* ('master'),[13] thereby resuscitating colonial patterns of patronizing condescension vs. obedience and deference. Unlike slaves, however, the Robben Island prisoners were not valued by their masters since the purpose of the forced labor project was less to produce a maximum of profit from the quarry than to treat convicts like slaves as a deliberate strategy of punishment and humiliation. This became particularly clear from the many episodes recounting irresponsible withholding of medical attention:

> We banged and shouted and cried to get the attention of the night warder. He appeared after a long, long time and then refused to open up. We explained that a prisoner had lost an eye in an accident and he eventually agreed to call higher authority, but Malambo was taken to the mainland only on the following day by which time the doctor told him that it was too late to do anything. (Naidoo/Sachs 1982: 89-90)

The rationale for these horrid conditions on Robben Island was provided by reference to the low living standards of the native population who were supposedly used to very basic needs in terms of the quality and quantity of food, sanitary arrangements and housing conditions. It was assumed, from a paternalistic standpoint, that Zulu prisoners would grow ill if they received too much meat and standard white fare since they were accustomed to substandard food in their homelands. In other words, the argument went that prisoners should be treated like animals since they supposedly lived like beasts in their natural habitat. That this sarcastic reasoning merely served as a cover for the deliberately demeaning treatment of prisoners can be gleaned from the fact that a large number of the prisoners were in fact well-educated men. Quite a few were even doctors or lawyers and teachers, who were hardly likely to have lived in the manner of savages before coming to the prison.

The stigma of slavery that adhered to the living conditions on Robben Island is also underlined by the practices of transport to the island and induction into the prison society. The regular routine of stripping and searching the inmates while terrorizing them with threats of physical abuse, and the use of flogging as punishment (besides food deprivation and solitary confinement) invoke well-known patterns of institutionalized slavery. More telling still were the conditions of transport to the island. More than one memoir discusses the fact that prisoners were shackled, herded into lorries, and driven across the country for hours without sanitary facilities, thus arriving at Robben Island in conditions very similar to those of slaves shipped to the New World.[14]

---

12 The introduction of long trousers was an improvement won by strikes.

13 See the account in Dlamini of prisoners being refused to go to the toilet for not saying "Baas" (1984: 34-35), quoted later in this article.

14 See especially the accounts by Naidoo/Sachs (1982: 58-59) and Shityuwete.

> As we went into the boat, we saw looming in the distance what was to be our home for a very long time. For me, with a six-year-sentence, it was to be my home for almost two-and-a-half years. For some of us it was going to be their home for life. With insults and shoving from the prison warders escorting us, there was not time to have a proper look at the island. A single sharp glance at the place assured me that it was full of trees. Manacled on our hands and legs in two, we were taken to the cabin and there made to lie down – flat on our backs despite the fact that there were seats nearby. We were one hundred in number, all of us dog-tired. My right ankle was still painful, suppurating with pus; the leg-irons had caused a wound. Many other comrades were complaining on the same problem. The ankle wounds of some comrades were already becoming septic. (Dlamini 1984: 15)

Practices of humiliation extended to the deliberate deprivations imposed on prisoners during detention and trial. The refusal to allow the prisoner to wash or change his clothes was employed as one of the many strategies of creating duress accompanying notabene physical torture (cp. Pheto). In Caribbean and American slavery the conditions of transport were dependent on contemporary levels of insanitation exacerbated by the needs of security, the drive for minimum costs and, one supposes, a view of the slaves as cattle rather than as human beings. By contrast, the very similar circumstances in South African prisoners' transports were obviously inflected by racist attitudes (regarding black prisoners as little better than 'animals' anyway). In addition these strategies displayed a deliberate policy of humiliation and abuse which was meant to signal to the prisoners that they were 'subhuman' and that South African society regarded them as so much 'filth.' In fact, the use of animal metaphors to refer to the prisoners was a common tactic of warder abuse. See, e.g., Dlamini (138), where the prisoners are being ordered about in the following terms: "'Dog, step' screamed Teeman. And we fell into step, left feet forward. | 'D-o-g-s, u-p,' he screamed again." Sadly, the prisoners themselves characterize one another as suffering animals, thereby suggesting that the dehumanizing treatment they have to undergo has even subjectively levelled them with beasts of burden:[15] "Doing any piece of manual labour at a human pace is good; but doing a mule's labour at a mule's pace is something else. The yells rained down harder: 'Come on, come on, black bastards ... do you think this is a picnic? Come on, kaffirs, come on, baboons ... push, push, push ...'" (Zwelonke 1973: 33).

In other words, the systematic human rights abuses on Robben Island were designed to teach political prisoners that they were nothing but slaves and that that was what they deserved. The system did not result in cruelty and neglect through inefficiency and institutional indifference but employed these effects deliberately as part of a racial and penal programme of degradation.

---

15 Compare, "I heard someone grunting like a hog and when I peeped, I saw him falling down on his buttocks, flat. There was a rain of blows on him, and in no time, he was up, his hands touching his toes again, feet astride" (Dlamini 1984: 19), and "Then their voices came out fearfully as though it was two beasts being slaughtered. My whole body shook as I trembled when I thought about what was happening to them. Other comrades woke up and sat up listening to the terrifying animal sounds that came from cell number three" (156).

4. Caliban's Tactics of Resistance

Caliban's much-noted observation that the acquisition of language has taught him how to curse traditionally stands for an indictment of the native: he abuses the gifts of civilization for his evil purposes. Postcolonial criticism, on the other hand, has insisted on Caliban's canny manipulation of the coloniser's discourse for his own purposes, particularly as a protest against oppression by the colonial master. The curse also epitomizes Caliban's victimization at the hands of Prospero since he can only curse him, but cannot gain his freedom. His gesture of token resistance allows him to vent his feelings but at the same time expresses the extent of his enslavement. He has acquired his master's words but cannot perform magic with them, turning them against Prospero's power over him.

Although prisoners on Robben Island were treated like slaves and symbolically continued a long South African tradition of the de facto enslavement of the native population, they were not exactly in the same situation as Caliban. Prisoners outnumbered guards on the island and had a community of mutual support. Their common (political) aims underscored their togetherness and provided an ideology of political resistance. Conversely, the place of Prospero as a single outcast on an island corresponds to a phalanx of warders and prison officials, with the 'real Prospero' acting behind the scenes from far-away Johannesburg or Pretoria. Ariel too, in this comparison, appears in the manifestation of black guards (who were only briefly on the island) and the 'Big Five' gang of criminals. These individuals were taken to be traitors to the cause of anti-apartheid. The experience of Robben Island was a *collective* experience, and one dealing with collective identities rather than individual choices and reactions. The relationship between Prospero, Caliban and Ariel, by contrast, becomes collective only in the postcolonial reading of *The Tempest*.

In Shakespeare's play, Caliban is a speechless beast who learns to speak through the 'good offices' of Prospero and Miranda (whatever his native language in which he communicated with his mother). On Robben Island, language becomes both a factor of prisoner solidarity (the native languages) and a means of colonial oppression (Afrikaans). Since there are many Calibans on Robben Island, they are able to communicate in their own languages among themselves but are forced to use the master's language when speaking to the guards. Even more infuriatingly, at visiting time many prisoners cannot speak to their relatives since only the four official languages (English, Afrikaans, Xhosa, Zulu) are allowed (for warders to be able to check on what is being said) and some mothers only speak Gujerati.[16] Such strategies reinforce the continual humiliation of prisoners and caused not only the prisoner himself but also his loved ones to be converted into speechless dumb animals, thus depriving them of their basic human rights.

---

16 See Dlamini, as well as Naidoo's account: "Those of us who could not speak English, Afrikaans, Xhosa or Zulu, the four permitted languages, were particularly hard hit – they struggled above the noise with their limited English, shouting to family members who frequently knew even less of English than themselves" (Naidoo/Sachs 1982: 115).

In contrast to the Shakespearian Caliban figure, the writers of the prison memoirs are indeed turning their knowledge of the English language to a very good use. If Caliban had penned an account of the indignities Prospero inflicted on him and described how he eventually evicted his oppressor from the island, such an epistle might have had some affinity with the texts under consideration. By not merely using the English language but additionally by demonstrating the ability to write it fluently, the earlier prisoners prove that they are equal in intellectual status to their former torturers and jailors. Indeed, the memoirs teem with sarcastic observations on the low level of education among white prison personnel, a feature absent from the prison autobiographies of white South Africans. The gradual conversion of Robben Island into a "university" not merely referred to the teaching of revolutionary theory by Mandela and others in the maximum security section (Mandela; Mbeki; Daniels); it also involved the teaching of literacy to illiterate comrades and the general prison population, and the successful completion of study courses including the acquisition of university degrees by the inmates.[17] (As an additional stab at the supposedly superior white race, many authors note with malicious relish that the guards who sat for the same exams frequently did not manage to pass them.) Unlike Caliban, whose ineffectual attempt at rebellion confines itself to merely symbolic retaliation by cursing,[18] Robben Island prisoners were thus able to compensate for their humiliations by turning the oppressor's language and culture to their own use and by proving to their readers (their comrades and the British public) that they were the very opposite of stupid, less-than-human creatures even though the South African regime treated them as such.

The most advanced strategy of putting the oppressor's language to good use naturally occurs in the teaching of revolutionary tactics and in the writing of political tracts (Mandela, Mbeki). Here resistance – otherwise limited to the occasional hunger strike and the support given to comrades – acquires practical importance in producing a new generation of revolutionaries who will return to the outside world as emissaries from Robben Island. (The leaders of ANC were life prisoners and therefore needed to train the political resistance from inside.) On Robben Island, Caliban was thus transformed into Gramsci.

---

17 See, for instance, Zwelonke: "My ambition on the Island was to study. So I was sent to cell C1, which was called the University of Makana. This cell was for those who had been granted permission to study. Many others wanted to go there. The craving for education was intense. In the other cells, learning – using the cement as paper – was undertaken by those who were semi-literate, and those who had left school at the elementary level. Those who were better educated helped those who were not. The aim was to wipe out illiteracy among us, und build a step to higher education. [...] but we paid for it in hungry stomachs. When we were having our concerts, an evening-duty guard would appear outside the window and shout: You're making too much noise there. Three meals off! And we would miss our three meals" (1973: 15).

18 I am of course excluding from consideration Caliban's naive attempt to overthrow Prospero, a course of action that, in the traditional colonial interpretation of the play, would tend to corroborate Caliban's moral and intellectual inferiority.

Resistance, even linguistic resistance, always has to be fought for and is often paid for with physical suffering. Just as seeking education was penalized with the loss of three meals a day (Zwelonke 1973: 15), the refusal to submit to the code of address instituted by the Afrikaans-speaking warders resulted in humiliation and suffering:

> Since morning all those who had wanted to go and pass urine or have bowel movements have been refused permission. They refused to say the password: 'baas'. A few old men had mentioned the password and had been allowed to go and relieve themselves. Oom Dellie and the other warders were uncompromising, "If you don't say 'baas' then you can't go relieve yourself". Oom Dellie had said, "otherwise you must sweat the urine out." And so we had worked with our bladders loaded to capacity. Some whose resistance was weak messed themselves up. What did it matter? After all, the trousers dried up quickly. It wasn't so easy to say 'baas'. (Dlamini 1984: 34)

> Comrade Baker Mogale sitting on my right is already in trouble. Nature calls. He stands up and walks heavily towards the warder called Fourie.
>
> "And now?" aks Fourie agressively in Afrikaans.
>
> "I'm asking for permission to go to the toilet sir," says Baker in English proudly.
>
> "Aha!" exclaims Fourie, "so you're an Englishman and you call me sir. Who's your sir?"
>
> "Well," says Baker, wire-mesh goggles still over his eyes, arms akimbo, "I didn't know that you do not want to be called sir. May I please go the toilet 'meener'?" (mister).
>
> "I'm not your 'sir' and I'm not your 'meneer'. I'm your baas. Understand." Baker is silent.
>
> "You must first say baas to me before I can consider whether to give you permission to go the toilet or not."
>
> "Going to the toilet is not a privilege," says Baker, "it is an act of nature. Surely you can't deny me that."
>
> "So you're a BA eh? I'll show you what we do to BA's here."
>
> "Being a BA has nothing to do with granting me permission to go and relieve myself."
>
> "Go and sit down and pound these rocks again," commands Fourie pushing Baker roughly away.
>
> "But surely you can't be so brutal," says Baker. Fourie continues to push him. Baker shakes his head, turns round and moves heavily to sit down. He begins pounding at the quarry stones again." (34-35)

The reference to Baker's educational achievements clearly serves as an additional point of attack; it is precisely because prisoners excel in courage, intelligence and solidarity that guards treat them as subhuman. Caliban's subversive use of education on Robben Island does not get him anywhere – the warders in the role of Prospero win by force of sheer physical brutality. There is, however, an interesting difference to Shakespeare's play. Dlamini, Zwelonke and the other ex-prisoners survive to write the tale of their subjection, and in these accounts 'Prospero,' i.e. the system that enslaved them, comes to look quite ridiculous. Caliban in *The Tempest* is refused this retrospective satisfaction – he never manages to acquire the audience's respect, nor does he ever have a chance to win against the magician Prospero, even when he joins forces with the underclasses against him. Unlike Caliban, the revolutionaries on Robben Island were actually successful rebels against the South African state. Since they were part of a movement motivated by solidarity and a clear vision of the future, they had managed to inflict serious damage on their enemy before their imprisonment.

Whereas Caliban's past remains vague and he only emerges into fictional existence as Prospero's helpmate and later slave, the imprisonment on Robben Island by the authors of the memoirs constitutes the endpoint of a successful career and a phase in their communal political struggle.

The comparison between Shakespeare's *Tempest* and South Africa's prison island is a flawed one. *The Tempest* deals with the beginnings of colonial conquest. Robben Island represents a phase in which Caliban has learned to rebel in successful ways and is suffering the retaliation of a Prospero who has decided to stay on the island for good. Despite the seeming defeat of the rebels, however, their ultimate victory over Caliban appears more and more clearly in these autobiographical texts. Because Prospero has resorted to inhuman cruelty, he will lose his kingdom in the end. The victory of moral stamina, intelligence, and endurance is imminent.

5. Concluding remarks

As I have tried to argue, Robben Island prison has acquired a symbolic place in the South African imaginary because it fruitfully brings together various aspects of colonial oppression. The Island serves as a microcosm of South African society but also as its antithesis (the "hell-hole" of the prisoners, and the desired utopia of complete racial subjugation for the ideologists of apartheid). Secondly, the island provides a collective myth for the African resistance, a myth that is enhanced by the Island's symbolic function as a 'university' of revolutionary thinking. Thirdly, the Island extends and openly implements the colonial legacy which moreover receives a peculiar racist inflection. Finally, from a literary perspective, the Island resuscitates one of the great scenarios of English literature, the story of Prospero's fated rule over Caliban on the island. The story epitomizes black victimization, but in the collective reality of a prison camp setting. Both the humor of Shakespeare's original and Caliban's defeat in the play become subjects of, and subject to, revolutionary rewriting.

In Shakespeare's text Caliban's enslavement, we remember, was the consequence of his supposed attempt to rape Miranda. (Rape fantasies of course also play a large role in apartheid discourse and apartheid legislation.) By claiming intellectual and civil equality with the white man, Robben Island prisoners again invoke that traumatic nightmare of (sexual) equality. Even more emphatically, the popularity of the motif of interracial love in South African literature[19] and the recurrence of the theme of 'passing' (both as a threat to racial purity and as a risky way to avoid racial discrimination[20]) demonstrate that this is the Achilles heel of the South African imaginary. The threat of miscegenation is repressed by the authorities in true Prospero-like fashion by trying to put Caliban in his place as the dumb animal, by treating the revolutionaries as slaves.

---

19 Compare, for instance, André Brink's *Looking on Darkness* and *An Instant in the Wind*, Nadine Gordimer's *A Sport of Nature*, or Nkosi's *Mating Birds*.

20 On 'passing' see Goetsch (1999).

In the reality of South Africa, Prospero is not rescued from the island or allowed a happy ending for his offspring. Robben Island's multifaceted symbolic meanings demonstrate that ultimately Caliban will overcome, and has symbolically already done so. It was the very excess of violence and inhumanity meted out to those fighting against apartheid that helped to bring about the demise of the system. Yet despite the happy ending (the abolition of apartheid) and the monument to the human spirit that Robben Island prisoners have erected in their memoirs, the story of Robben Island remains a blot on the South African landscape. Too much suffering had to be endured, too many families were ruined, too many hearts broken in the process of victory. Like Caliban, who has haunted the British literary imagination since the early days of empire, Robben Island accounts may well remain a touchstone of South African literature for decades to come and serve as a kind of conscience to future generations. The generosity, endurance and strength evinced by Robben Island prisoners provide an example of the human spirit at its most sublime, just as their treatment negatively reflects on the depths to which South African society sank in its attempt to preserve colonial injustice into the late twentieth century.

Works Cited

Memoirs and other Sources

Brink, André (1991 [1976]) *An Instant in the Wind*. London: Minerva.

Brink, André (1993 [1974]) *Looking on Darkness*. London: Minerva.

Brutus, Dennis (1973) *A Simple Lust: Collected Poems of South African Jail and Exile, including Letters to Martha*. London: Heinemann.

Cronin, Jeremy (1987 [1983]) *Inside*. London: Cape.

Daniels, Eddie (1998) *There & Back: Robben Island, 1964-1979*. Bellville, SA: Mayibuye Books.

Dlamini, Moses (1984) *Hell-Hole, Robben Island: Prisoner No. 872/63. Reminiscences of a Political Prisoner*. Nottingham: Spokesman.

Kathrada, Ahmed (1999) *Letters from Robben Island: A Selection of Ahmed Kathrada's Prison Correspondence, 1964-1989*. Ed. Robert D. Vassen. East Lansing, MI: Michigan State Univ. Press.

Lekota, Mosiuoa Patrick (Terror) (1999) *Prison Letters to a Daughter*. Bramley, SA: Taurus.

Lewin, Hugh (1981 [1974]). *Bandiet: Seven Years in a South African Prison*. London: Heinemann.

Mandela, Nelson (1973) *No Easy Walk to Freedom: Articles, Speeches and Trial Addresses*. With a new foreword by Ruth First. London: Heinemann.

Mashinini, Emma (1989) *Strikes Have Followed Me All My Life*. London: Women's Press.
Mbeki, Govan (1991) *Learning from Robben Island: The Prison Writings of Govan Mbeki*. London: James Currey.
Naidoo, Indres, and Albie Sachs (1982) *Prisoner 885/63. Island in Chains: Ten Years on Robben Island as Told by Indres Naidoo to Albie Sachs*. London: Penguin.
Nkosi, Lewis (1987 [1986]) *Mating Birds*. New York: Harper & Row.
Pheto, Molefe (1985 [1983]) *And Night Fell. Memoirs of a Political Prisoner in South Africa*. London: Heinemann.
El Saadawi, Nawal (1994 [1983]) *Memoirs from the Women's Prison*. Trans. Marilyn Booth. Berkeley, CA: Univ. of California Press.
Shityuwete, Helao (1990) *Never Follow the Wolf*. London: Kliptown Books.
Zwelonke, D. M. (1973) *Robben Island*. London : Heinemann.

Criticism

Deacon, Harriet, ed. (1997) *The Island. A History of Robben Island, 1488-1990*. Mayibuye History and Literature Series, 60. Cape Town, SA: David Philip Publishers.
Fludernik, Monika (1999) "Carceral Topography: Spatiality and Liminality in the Literary Prison." *Textual Practice* 13.1: 43-77.
Fludernik, Monika (2003a) "The Prison as World – The World as Prison: Theoretical and Historical Aspects of two Recurrent Topoi." *Symbolism* 3: 145-89.
Fludernik, Monika (2003b) "The Prison as Colonial Space." *Cycnos* 19.2: 175-90 (=Special Issue "Droit et littérature. Actes du Colloque Nice 28-29 Juin, 2001." Ed. Jacqueline Berben-Masi).
Fludernik, Monika (2004) "'Stone Walls Do (Not) a Prison Make': Rhetorical Strategies and Sentimentalism in the Representation of the Victorian Prison Experience." *Captivating Subjects: Writing Confinement, Citizenship and Nationhood in the Nineteenth Century*. Ed. Julia Wright and Jason Haslam. Toronto: Univ. of Toronto Press (in print).
Goetsch, Paul (1999) "Passing in South African Literature." *Intercultural Encounters – Studies in English Literatures. Essays Presented to Rüdiger Ahrens on the Occasion of his Sixtieth Birthday*. Ed. Heinz Antor and Kevin L. Cope. Heidelberg: Winter. 479-95.
Harper, Graeme, ed. (2001) *Colonial and Postcolonial Incarceration*. London: Continuum.
Jacobs, J. U. (1991) "Confession, Interrogation and Self-Incrimination in the New South African Prison Writing." *Kunapipi* 13: 115-27.
Jacobs, J. U. (1992) "Narrating the Island: Robben Island in South African Literature." *Current Writing. Text and Reception in Southern Africa* 4: 73-84.

Marx, Christoph (1998) *Im Zeichen des Ochsenwagens: Der radikale Afrikaaner-Nationalismus in Südafrika und die Geschichte der Ossewabrandwag.* Studien zur afrikanischen Geschichte, 22. Hamburg: Lit.

Marx, Christoph (2000) "Folter und Rassismus. Südafrika während der Apartheid." *Das Quälen des Körpers. Eine historische Anthropologie der Folter*. Ed. Peter Burschel, Götz Distelrath, and Sven Lembke. Cologne: Böhlau. 257-79.

Millett, Kate (1994) *The Politics of Cruelty. An Essay on the Literature of Political Imprisonment.* New York: Norton.

Mishra, Vijay (1996) "The Diasporic Imaginary: Theorizing the Indian Diaspora." *Textual Practice* 10: 421-47.

Nochlin, Linda (1989) "The Imaginary Orient." *The Politics of Vision. Essays on Nineteenth-Century Art and Society.* London: Thames and Hudson. 33-59.

Ogunyemi, Chikwenye Okonjo (1982) "The Song of the Caged Bird: Contemporary African Prison Poetry." *Ariel* 13.4: 65-84.

Scarry, Elaine (1985) *The Body in Pain. The Making and Unmaking of the World.* New York: Oxford Univ. Press.

Sedlak, Werner (1996) "Prison Memoirs by African Writers (Nyugi, Pheto, Soyninka). The cultural unity and complexity of resistance." *Fusion of Cultures?* Ed. P. Stummer and Christopher Balme. ASNEL Papers 2. Amsterdam: Rodopi. 183-92.

Sedlak, Wener (1999) "Ways of Appropriating Space in South African Prison Memoirs. From Ruth First to Nelson Mandela." *Borderlands: Negotioating Boundaries in Post-Colonial Writing.* Ed. Monika Reif-Hülser. ASNEL Papers 4. Amsterdam: Rodopi. 189-204.

Contributors

JAN ALBER studied English, Political Sciences and Philosophy at the Universities of Freiburg (Germany) and Reading (GB), and teaches English literature at the University of Freiburg. He is currently completing a Ph.D. thesis on the depiction of prisons from the Victorian novel to twentieth-century film. Publications: "The 'Moreness' or 'Lessness' of 'Natural' Narratology: Samuel Beckett's "Lessness" Reconsidered." *Style* 36.1 (2002): 54-75; "Das Gefängnis im Hollywoodfilm: Strafvollzug zwischen Fiktion und Realität." *Zeitschrift für Strafvollzug und Straffälligenhilfe* 52.1 (2003): 31-40; (co-edited with Monika Fludernik): *Moderne/Postmoderne* (Wissenschaftlicher Verlag Trier, 2003).

JACQUELINE BERBEN-MASI is Maître de Conférence in English at the University of Nice Law and Economics Faculty. Most recently, she edited the "Droit et littérature" or Law and Literature issue of *Cycnos* (Volume 19, n° 2, 2002). Her background is both in French and in American literature, and she has published in the two fields in France and the USA (*AFRAM*, *GRAAT*, *Cycnos*, *Dictionnaire universel des littératures, les Annales* of the universities of Nice and Aix-en Provence, *La Revue Française d'Etudes Américaines*, *Callaloo*, *Black American Literature Forum*, *Texas Studies in Language and Literature*, *Contemporary Literary Criticism*). Her work has primarily focused on John Edgar Wideman, but also on Toni Morrison, James Baldwin, Toni Cade Bambara, and Ishmael Reed as well as on studies of nineteenth-century French travel literature. An A. J. Greimas-inspired study on John Grisham's *A Time To Kill* presented to the Society for the Study of Narrative Literature in 1995 was her first venture into Law and Literature, which has become a favorite area of research. At press with the University of Tennessee is a chapter in a collection of essays on John Edgar Wideman, and in progress with the University François Rabelais de Tours is a piece on Percival Everett's early writing.

CAROL COLATRELLA is Associate Professor of Literature and Culture in the School of Literature, Communication, and Culture and co-director of the Center for the Study of Women, Science, and Technology at the Georgia Institute of Technology. She is the author of *Evolution, Sacrifice, and Narrative: Balzac, Zola, and Faulkner* (Garland, 1990) and *Literature and Moral Reform: Melville and the Discipline of Reading* (Univ. Press of Florida, 2002), and co-editor of *Cohesion and Dissent in America* (State Univ. of New York Press, 1994).

MONIKA FLUDERNIK is Professor of English literature at the University of Freiburg/Germany. She is the author of *The Fictions of Language and the Languages of Fiction* (Routledge, 1993), *Towards a 'Natural' Narratology* (Routledge, 1996), which was awarded the Perkins Prize by the Society for the Study of Narrative Literature (SSNL), and *Echoes and Mirrorings: Gabriel Josipovici's Creative Ouevre* (Peter Lang, 2000). She has edited a special issue on second-person fiction (*Style* 28.3, 1994), a special issue of *EJES* on "Language and Literature" (*EJES* 2.2, 1998), and (co-edited with Donald and Margaret Freeman) a special issue of *Poetics Today* 20.3 (1999) on "Metaphor and Beyond: New Cognitive Developments." Further publications include several collections of essays (*Hybridity and Postcolonialism: Twentieth-Century Indian Literature*, Stauffenburg, 1998; *Das 18. Jahrhundert* [co-edited with Ruth Nestvold], WVT, 1998; *Romantik* [co-edited with Vera Alexander], WVT, 2000; *Fin de siècle* [co-edited with Ariane Huml, WVT, 2001] *Moderne/Postmoderne* [co-edited with Jan Alber, WVT, 2003] and *Diaspora and Multiculturalism: Common Traditions and New Developments*, Rodopi, 2003). Work in progress includes a project on the development of narrative structure in English literature between 1250 and 1750. Forthcoming are articles on expatriate Indian literature in English, British aesthetics in the eighteenth century, and narratological questions.

BEATRIX HESSE obtained her Ph.D. from the University of Paderborn for a book on Shakespeare's comedies (*Shakespeares Komödien aus der Sicht der pragmatischen Kommunikationstheorie* [LIT, 1998]). She is currently teaching at Bamberg University and working on a book outlining the history and generic traits of the British crime play in the twentieth century. Additionally, she has published work on contemporary British drama, particularly on the works of Tom Stoppard, Shakespeare in performance, and on drama translation.

CHRISTOPH HOUSWITSCHKA is Professor of English literature at the Otto-Friedrich-University in Bamberg, Germany. He wrote his *Habilitation* on "The Legal Culture of the High Treason Trials of 1794 and the Literature of Democratization." He has published several articles on the radical culture of the 1790s, eighteenth-century literature (the socio-cultural meaning of ageing, the concept of change, incest), on contemporary English drama, Holocaust literature (e.g. Karen Gershon, Ronald Harwood's *Taking Sides*, Holocaust drama and theater), literature and science, and fifteenth-century literature (articles on Thomas Malory and Boethius in Late Medieval England). He is the author of *Politik und Liebe in der Literatur des englischen Spätmittelalters am Beispiel von Thomas Malorys "Morte Darthur"* [Politics and Love in Late-Medieval English Literature] (Peter Lang 1991). An anthology entitled *Freedom - Treason - Revolution: Uncollected Sources of the Political and Legal Culture of the London Treason Trials (1794)* is in press (Lang 2004). He has also co-edited with Uwe Böker *Literatur, Kriminalität und Rechtskultur im 17. und 18. Jahrhundert* [Literature, Crime and Legal Culture in the seventeenth and eighteenth Century] (Blaue Eule, 1996) and *Einführung in das Studium der Anglistik und Amerikanistik* [Introduction to the Study of English and American Literature and Culture] (Beck 2000).

ANNA-CHRISTINA GIOVANOPOULOS studied English Literature, Teaching German as a Foreign Language, and History at Bielefeld, Reading (U.K.), and Dresden. She received her Ph.D. from Dresden in 2000 with a dissertation on American Literature in the GDR. Between 2000 and 2002, she worked in a Collaborative Research Group, "Sonderforschungsbereich 537 - Institutionality and Historicity," at the Technical University Dresden. She now works in the English Department of TU Dresden.

MARTIN A. KAYMAN is Professor of English and Cultural Criticism and a member of the Centre for Critical and Cultural Theory at Cardiff University. Previous to his appointment to this post in 2000, he was Professor of Anglo-American Studies at the University of Coimbra, Portugal. From 1997 to 2003 he was editor of *The European English Messenger*, the newsletter of the European Society for the Study of English. He is the author of *The Modernism of Ezra Pound: The Science of Poetry* (Macmillan, 1986), *From Bow Street to Baker Street: Mystery, Detection and Narrative* (Macmillan, 1992), and of *Revolution and Counter-Revolution in Portugal* (Merlin Press, 1987). He has also published a number of articles on law and literature, including, most recently, "Law-and-Literature: Questions of Jurisdiction," *REAL Yearbook of Research in English and American Literature* 18, ed. Brook Thomas (Gunter Narr, 2002), 1-20. He also writes on the cultural politics of English. He is a Fellow of the English Association and of the Royal Society of Arts.

FRANK LAUTERBACH teaches English, Hispanic, and Comparative Literature at Georg-August-University Göttingen. His research focuses on prison writing, urban literature, nation-building in the Americas, and Chicano literature. He is the co-editor of *Abgrenzung – Eingrenzung: Komparatistische Studien zur Dialektik kultureller Identitätsbildung* (2004), and has published on post-independence US-American and Spanish American prose and poetry, nineteenth-century British travel writing, Victorian prison literature, as well as on Juan Boscán, Andrés Bello, and Raymond Williams.

THOMAS LEDERER studied Classical Philology, English and Historical Linguistics at the University of Salzburg, Austria, where he received his M.A. in 2001. He has worked on the dramatic traditions of the Salzburg Benedictine University of the seventeenth and eighteenth centuries and on controversial literature (hagiography and pamphlets) of the Renaissance and the Reformation. He co-published *Aristeion Carinthiae Claudiforum* (Kärntner Landesarchiv, 2002), a critical edition and commentary of an early sixteenth-century neo-Latin epic poem by an exiled Austrian Protestant, which features, among other things, a discussion of national and denominational belonging and exclusion. His doctoral dissertation, *Sacred Demonization*, which he is presently writing at the University of Freiburg, Germany is a study of mutual canonization and criminalization/demonization in hagiographic writings from the English Reformation and Counter-Reformation.

HEIDI SLETTEDAHL MACPHERSON is Reader in North American Literature at the University of Central Lancashire, England. She is the author of *Women's Movement: Escape as Transgression in North American Feminist Fiction* (Rodopi, 2000) and the co-editor of *Transatlantic Studies* (University Press of America, 2000) and *New Perspectives in Transatlantic Studies* (UPA, 2002). In addition, she has co-edited *British-American Relations Encyclopaedia* (ABC-Clio, forthcoming), and is on the board of directors of the Maastricht Center for Transatlantic Studies. She has published widely on contemporary women's literature and is currently at work on her second monograph, *Courting Failure: Women and the Law in 20th Century Literature.*

GRETA OLSON is a research fellow at Freiburg University. She was a Visiting Professor to the North American Studies Program at Bonn University and has also taught at the Universities of Basel, Freiburg, and Innsbruck. She is the author of *Reading Eating Disorders: Writings on Bulimia and Anorexia as Confessions of American Culture* (Lang, 2003) and has published work on narratology, the eighteenth-century English novel, images of the body as a monster in contemporary women's writing, and Martin Heidegger's ethics. Forthcoming in American Studies are essays on Alice Sebold, violent white men in post-war drama and film, and the obsession with the body in contemporary culture and theory. In English studies essays on Shakespeare's *Richard III*, criminal bodies in literature and penology, and depictions of women as fetishists are also forthcoming as is an essay on teaching gender studies through creative writing and drama. She is at work on her second book *Stigmatized Criminals from Shakespeare to Conrad: Animalistic Representations of Criminals in Literature and the Rise of Positivist Criminology.*

STU REES Esquire is, in addition to publishing law and lawyer cartoons ("Stu's Views"), an entertainment lawyer who represents mostly visual arts creators. To put it simply, Stu is the lawyer for cartoonists and the cartoonist for lawyers. It wasn't until early 2002 that he began cartooning in earnest. Stu graduated cum laude from Harvard Law School. Stu lives in San Diego with his lovely wife and cranky cat. The cartoons "Do you promise to tell the truth" and "Juvenile Crime" are printed in this volume with permission of CartoonStock Ltd of London.

HARRY E. SHAW is Professor of English at Cornell University, where he has served as Chair of the Department of English and is currently Senior Associate Dean of the College of Arts and Sciences. He is the author of *The Forms of Historical Fiction: Scott and his Successors* (Cornell Univ. Press, 1983) and *Narrating Reality: Austen, Scott, and Eliot* (Cornell Univ. Press, 1999), and the editor of *Critical Articles on Sir Walter Scott: The Waverley Novels* (G. K. Hall, 1996). Essays on Scott, J. L. Austin, and narrative theory have appeared in such journals as *JEGP*, *Diacritics*, *Narrative*, and *European Romantic Review*; an essay on the "narrative communications diagram" is forthcoming in the *Blackwell Companion to Narrative Theory.* He is presently at work on a book on the nineteenth-century British realist novel for a general audience, in collaboration with Alison Case.

www.ingramcontent.com/pod-product-compliance
Ingram Content Group UK Ltd.
Pitfield, Milton Keynes, MK11 3LW, UK
UKHW021843100926
8556IPUK00019B/1016

9 783631 524558